Charles
Duke of Orleans

Charles
Duke of Orleans

A LITERARY BIOGRAPHY

by Norma Lorre *Goodrich*

THE MACMILLAN COMPANY, NEW YORK

First Printing

The Macmillan Company, New York
Collier-Macmillan Canada, Ltd., Toronto, Ontario

Designed by Jack Meserole

Library of Congress catalog card number: 63-15681

Printed in the United States of America

Preface

I WISH TO ACKNOWLEDGE MY INDEBTEDNESS FIRST OF ALL TO MY friend and colleague Renée Spodheim, who suggested the idea of this book. I also wish to thank another friend and colleague, the artist Jorge Goya-Lukich, for his conversations concerning the medieval curriculum.

Deep gratitude is expressed to librarians of the Butler and Avery libraries of Columbia University, to those of the New York Public Library, to those of the Reading Room and Manuscript Collection of the National Library of France in Paris, to those at the Blois Castle Library, and finally to the Archivists at the Préfecture of the Loir-et-Cher. The Guides at Blois Castle showed me extraordinary courtesy and assistance, particularly Mr. Jacques Petit. I want also to thank all those people in England, including the Keeper of the Muniments and Library at Westminster Abbey, who so cordially came to my assistance.

I owe especial thanks to Professor Otis Fellows of Columbia University, whose recommendation made it possible for me to work at the National Library of France and to acquire a microfilm copy of the personal book of Duke Charles of Orléans.

Last of all, I express my gratitude to my fellow author, the gifted medievalist Miss Régine Pernoud of Paris, whose books and whose friendship are a source of joy and constant inspiration. Miss Pernoud, as a friend of the late Henri Matisse, informed me of that artist's love of the poetry of Duke Charles and of the anthology of favorite poems that Matisse made by hand.

The poems cited or translated in this volume are numbered according to the Champion work, as listed under Primary Sources. Certain poems of Charles of Orléans have been beautifully translated by Andrew Lang, Ezra Pound, and W. E. Henley.

NORMA LORRE GOODRICH

v

Contents

King Philippe VI
(1293-1350)

King Jean II
(1319-1364)

King Charles V   Louis, Duke of Anjou
(1337-1380)

King Charles VI   m. Isabeau de Bavière   Louis of France,   Duke I of Orléans
(1368-1422)   (1370-1407)

Louis	Louis	Jean m. Jacqueline	King Charles VII m. Marie	Marie
(1396-1400)	Duke of Guyenne (1396-1415)	(1398-1415 or 1417) of Hainault	(1403-1461) of Anjou	(took orders 1397)

King Louis XI.
(1423-1483)

King Charles VIII
(1470-1498)

VALOIS – ORLEANS,

King Charles V
(1337-1380)

Louis of France,   Duke I of Orléans   m.   Valentine, Visconti of Milan
(1370-1407)   (d. 1408)

Charles, Duke of Orléans   m.   Queen Isabelle
(1394-1465)   of England
(1389-1409)

Philip of Vertus
(1396-1420)

Joan of Orléans
(1409-1432)

Marguerite of Orléans

Duke Francis II of Brittany
(d. 1488)

John of Angoulême (ancestor of King Francis I of France) **
(1494-1547)

Jean, Count Dumois (Bastard of Orleans)
(1403-1467)

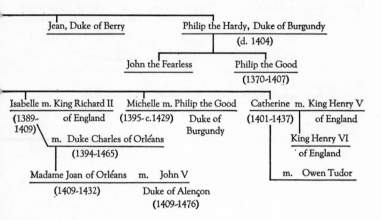

VALOIS – ANGOULÊME

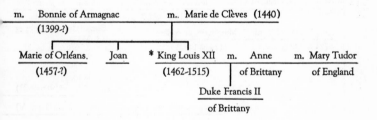

HOUSE OF PLANTAGENET

Edward III of Windsor m.
(1312-1377)

Edward, the Black m. Joan, the Fair	Lionel of Antwerp	John of Gaunt m. Constance
Prince of Wales	Maid of Kent	Duke of Clarence	(1340-1399) of Castile
(1330-1376)		Duke of Lancaster (1386)
		(1362)
		Duke of Aquitania (1389)

King Richard II m. Anne of Bohemia m. Isabelle of Valois
of Bordeaux. (1382) (1396)
(1367-c. 1399)

HOUSE OF LANCASTER

King Henry IV m.
(1367-1413)

King Henry V m. Catherine of Valois John, Duke of Bedford m. Anne m. Jacqueline
(1387-1422) (1389-1435) of of
King Henry VI m. Marguerite of Anjou Burgundy Luxemburg
(1421-1471) (1429-1482) (d. 1432)

HOUSE OF TUDOR (1485-1603)

Queen Catherine (Valois) (widow of King Henry V)
(1401-1437)

Edmund, Earl of Richmond m. Margaret Beaufort

King Henry VII m. Elizabeth Woodville
(1457-1509)

King Henry VIII Margaret Tudor m. King James IV of Scotland
(1491-1547)

L A N D

(ANGEVIN) (1154-1399)

Philippa of Hainault

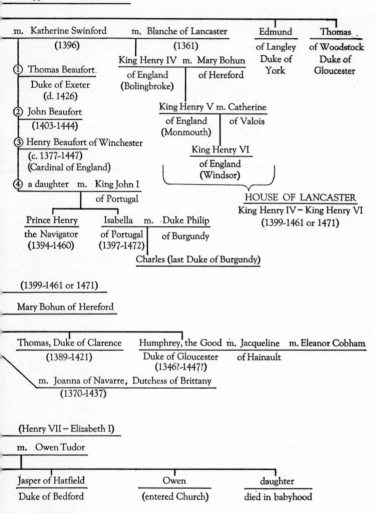

m. Katherine Swinford   m. Blanche of Lancaster   Edmund   Thomas
(1396)   (1361)   of Langley   of Woodstock
     King Henry IV m. Mary Bohun   Duke of   Duke of
① Thomas Beaufort.   of England   of Hereford   York   Gloucester
   Duke of Exeter   (Bolingbroke)
   (d. 1426)
② John Beaufort   King Henry V m. Catherine
   (1403-1444)   of England   of Valois
         (Monmouth)
③ Henry Beaufort of Winchester
   (c. 1377-1447)   King Henry VI
   (Cardinal of England)   of England
           (Windsor)
④ a daughter m. King John I
     of Portugal   HOUSE OF LANCASTER
           King Henry IV – King Henry VI
Prince Henry   Isabella m. Duke Philip   (1399-1461 or 1471)
the Navigator   of Portugal   of Burgundy
(1394-1460)   (1397-1472)
     Charles (last Duke of Burgundy)

(1399-1461 or 1471)

Mary Bohun of Hereford

Thomas, Duke of Clarence   Humphrey, the Good m. Jacqueline   m. Eleanor Cobham
(1389-1421)   Duke of Gloucester   of Hainault
         (1346?-1447?)
   m. Joanna of Navarre, Dutchess of Brittany
     (1370-1437)

(Henry VII – Elizabeth I)

m. Owen Tudor

Jasper of Hatfield   Owen   daughter
Duke of Bedford   (entered Church)   died in babyhood

   Mary of England   m.   King Louis XII of France
            (1462-1515)

Part One

FRANCE

I [*1394*] ROYAL INFANTS ARE NOT
born. They are ushered into the
world while thousands wait upon their first cry. At the birth of
certain princes the whole world stands still. Sometimes this pause
is justified.

When a royal infant is delivered, the swaddling blanket that re-
ceives him as he leaves his mother's body is a matter of national
concern. A five-page inventory of purchases made in anticipation
has been entered in the Royal Archives months in advance of the
royal event. It lists the finest linens, the downiest imported woolens,
and satins embroidered with pearls from the Orient.

A special chamber has been prepared for the lying-in ceremony.
In it has been placed upon a dais draped with cloth of gold a carved
bed with the appropriate number of steps leading up to it as befits
the couch of a princess. Its canopy and curtains are cut from dark
green velvet tasseled with gold. A carved buffet with a corresponding
number of shelves—just one less than for a reigning queen—stands
ready, laden with golden goblets, silver candlesticks, and candy bowls
for the ritual *dragées* that will be offered according to an etiquette
most rigorously observed over the centuries. Under the jealous eye
of the lady's maître d'hôtel, three hundred and fifty valets, hardly
daring to breathe, line the halls of the palace. One of them will
have the extraordinary honor of bringing ceremonial spiced cordial
up to the door of the chamber in the event of a successful delivery.

An Italian princess lies in labor, attended by the queen and
the noble ladies of the court, in great pain in a foreign land far from
Milan and from her father, who wept so hard to see her depart over
the mountains into the Kingdom of France that he could hardly
say a single farewell word.

In the private chapel of the Duchess Valentine, her confessor
has knelt for hours in prayer beside his sovereign lord, the Archbishop of Paris himself. In a separate wing of the palace the infant's

apartments are ready. A fire has been burning since morning in the marble fireplace of the bedchamber, a fireplace so large that tree trunks are required to fill it. Sitting in her cushioned chair, the wet nurse smiles and nods at the ornate cradle that has been carved and quilted for this child and no other. No doubt she wonders at the good fortune that could bring to lie upon her common breasts a dark-haired child of the House of Valois whom a quarter of a million citizens of Paris will acclaim if it survives the dangerous hours.

In their observatory the duke's personal astronomers prepare to draw up the official horoscope. It is a memorable day. A city holds its breath.

Inside the palace courtyard footmen stand ready to distribute bread, wine, and cases of golden coins to the throngs outside the main portal. Along the tower stairs the sentries who guard the king's treasure stand at attention under the severe eye of the captain of the watch. In the palace stables fast horses are already saddled and their riders booted and gloved. The hooded secretaries and their clerks have duly prepared alternate messages and are anxious for the signal that will cause one of them to be folded into the saddle pouch. What speed the horsemen will muster as they spur madly, any second now, through the Porte-Barbette, along the cobblestones of Vincennes, and southward on the way to Italy! If the princess lives, if her infant is born alive, if it draws its first breath and wails—and especially if it is a male child, a possible heir to the whole Kingdom of France—the bearer of such news will be so rewarded that he can retire for life, a famous and wealthy man.

High in the belfry of the Church of Saint-Paul the sexton waits with one hand on the bell rope. At a signal from below, the seventy-nine-pound clapper will peal the news across the first rooftops to the Convent of the Celestine monks, who out of love for His Highness will be the second to toll, and so on until the massive bells of Notre-Dame of Paris alert the suburbs outside the city walls. Bells will toll long into the November night, for the House of Valois has as yet no male heir, and the young King of France has been deathly ill for two years.

From the new fortress of the Bastille all the way to the river, the king's palace, called by his father the Hôtel Saint-Paul, lies sprawling. It extends along the Seine River the length of the Quai des Célestins up to the palace of the Archbishop of Sens. The former King Charles V, dead now for fourteen years, had noted with satisfaction that this palace was his personal property, and in no way the domain of the Crown. He had much preferred it to the Louvre. Even though it was not fortified as the Louvre was, the kings of France felt safer at Saint-Paul's. From there they had only a few feet to go and they could hasten out of the city, the walls of which bordered the palace on the east. Paris was not the safest corner of France for her kings. The Hôtel Saint-Paul was home to them. "There we have found love, pleasure, affection; there we have recovered and recuperated from several serious illnesses. We bought the Hôtel Saint-Paul with our own moneys," said King Charles V of France. Four royal children have already been born in one of the residences that make up this palace—the present King Charles VI; his brother, Louis of France; and the king's two infant daughters, the Princess Isabelle and her sister Marie.

Under the palace windows the twelve formal gardens lie bare of leaves. In freshly spaded plots the three hundred lily bulbs the king ordered have just been planted in front of his three hundred red or white rosebushes. Along the Rue de la Ceriseraie the thousand cherry trees shiver in the cold November air. Only the bay trees and the laurels show dark green as the pages run by with their lighted torches to feed the animals in the royal menagerie. The lions of Saint-Paul are famous throughout Europe, and are a thrilling sight for the visiting Emperor of Germany. Beside them are turtledoves in their cages, pure-blooded greyhounds in their kennels, salmon from the Loire River in their aquaria, nightingales whose song perhaps may charm the sick king from his melancholy, and a royal parrot that Louis of France has purchased for his diversion. There are wild boars from the forests, and—most carefully tended of all— the queen's birds, for Her Majesty never stirs from the palace unless accompanied by her massive golden birdcages.

In each antechamber the honored heralds sit through the long hours, fighting off lethargy, for their minds must at any instant commit to memory a royal proclamation. Inside his Grand Cabinet the expectant father sits, long-nosed and silent, reciting his prayers. His dearest friend and his three royal uncles wait beside him. He is Louis, the king's only brother.

Louis is named for France's most noble king—he who died in Africa during the Eighth Crusade and who became a saint not long afterward. Louis of France waits, more anguished than all the others, for news from his Duchess Valentine's bedchamber. He, more than all others present, has prepared for this day and prayed for it for the past five years. Louis of France, only brother of the king, has been for the past two years the virtual regent of the kingdom. It was Louis who at the age of ten proudly bore the great sword of Charlemagne down the aisle of Rheims Cathedral at the crowning of his brother, the twelve-year-old King Charles VI.

Between the ages of ten and twenty-four, Louis of France, one-time Count of Touraine, has not remained idle. His preparations for a son and heir have been carefully made and executed. If the child being born in the upstairs chamber is a son, he will one day proudly style himself Duke of Orléans, Duke of Périgord, Count of Valois, Beaumont, Dreux, Blois, Dunois, Soissons, Angoulême, Porcien, Montargis . . . Lord of Coucy, Château-Thierry, La Fère, Chauni, Provins, and in addition, Duke of Luxembourg and Count of Asti in Italy. He will claim descent from King Jean of France on both his father's and his mother's sides. Their marriage five years earlier has also established a solid claim, by uniting the Houses of Valois and Visconti . . . a *solid* claim to northern Italy.

The expectant father is himself accounted almost an "Italian" prince. He is held to be the most accomplished knight of France—first in battlefield and tournament after his sick brother, the king. More than that, he is a diplomat and a scholar before whom the most learned doctors of the university tremble. His knowledge of Latin and of theology, as well as the quickness of his wit and the fluency of his French, has already earned him an international reputation. He is a patron of the arts, generous to the point of lavishness to Christina of Pisa, the learned lady who has been his father's biographer. The most famous poets of the century, friends of the English Chaucer, are recipients of his gifts, for Louis of France is himself a poet upon occasion. The influential bourgeois chancellors and members of Parliament, men such as Montaigu and Juvénal des Ursins, look upon him with respect and admiration, if not with a kind of fatherly love. In politics Louis of France is a conservative, as the next in line to the throne and the virtual regent since his brother's illness should be. During the Babylonian captivity of the Papacy, Louis of France championed the Avignon Pope Benoît XIII against the University of Paris: "Doctors, return to your books. Leave statecraft to those who understand it."

Perhaps the masterstroke of his diplomatic career came when he won the Visconti heiress Valentine, the Duchess of Milan, who now lies in her state chamber laboring to bring him an heir. The lady is young and beautiful. She is the daughter of Gian Galeazzo

Visconti of Milan, an able and astute ruler who is negotiating at present for a dukedom. The lady is also educated in literature, music, and languages. The famous poet Petrarch once lived at her court. Her dowry was so munificent that it was the talk of the decade. With the Visconti gold alone, to say nothing of her lands and her jewels, Louis of France has purchased for himself and his heirs domains fit for a king. Three years before the birth of his heir, Louis of France became Louis I, Duke of Orléans.

For 200,000 gold francs and an annuity of 6,000 pounds Louis negotiated the acquisition of one of the most fertile, one of the richest areas of the kingdom, with a title that goes back through the Houses of Blois and Vermandois to the ancient Counts of Champagne. From the obese Guy II of Châtillon he has actually bought the County of Blois. It is Blois on the Loire River that will eventually be the chief seat of the Dukes of Orléans.

The first Count of Blois died in 834. In ancient metrical romances like *Le Roman du Rou,* old Count Thibault the Cheater had galloped through the oak forests near Blois Castle with a thunder of hooves that could still be heard on a dark night under the wet trees. Count Guy has the use of the lands and title during his lifetime, but despite his bravery in battle, he eats so voraciously that he has already been obliged to command the rear guard from his litter. Count Guy II of Châtillon is as big "as a barrel," while Louis of France, with his dark face and long nose, is a slender man who thinks long and plans carefully.

It is true, of course, and well known that the expectant father, with all his facile charm and brilliance, or perhaps because of it, is not entirely reliable. For one thing, he is addicted to reading romances. He is always willing to hire copyists, illuminators, and especially translators, whom he sets to work rendering into French his favorite stories, particularly those dealing with King Arthur, Lancelot, Gawain, and the Knights of the Round Table. This in itself perhaps cannot give his enemies much of an advantage. The fact that he has married an Italian lady can be used against him to greater detriment—not in the County of Blois, of course. There the inhabitants rang the bells and sang in the streets at the news that the chief Prince of France, and his lovely heiress with her millions, would soon replace the drunken and incapable House of Châtillon. The fact that Count Guy II later contested the sale price and sued for a revision of contract was unpleasant, but not particularly damaging.

When a handsome, cultivated, forceful, and glamorous prince of twenty-four accedes to the virtual regency of France, when through a brilliant marriage he rises to wealth and position that rival his uncles of Anjou, Berry and Burgundy, by whose hands the throne should be guided during a king's minority—then the enemies seek weapons. As Louis of France sits with his closest friend, waiting for the birth of his child, he has to count not only his blessings but also the dangers that surround him on all sides.

First of all, there are his three uncles, all brothers of his father, the late King Charles V. In theory (for the question of a regency during the minority of the kings has never been officially settled) all three have shared power since 1380. The Duke of Anjou promptly set out to conquer Naples, where he was promptly ruined, partly through his own lack of foresight and poor timing, and partly through the treachery of his messenger, Pierre de Craon. Then the full-scale invasion of England, the preparations for which almost prostrated the crown, was ruined by the Duke of Berry. He did, indeed, arrive at the rendezvous, but so late in the fall that winter was at hand. The 1,297 vessels assembled at Écluse never left port. Nor did the two subsequent flotillas in the year 1387.

The third uncle, Philip the Hardy, is a different kind of threat altogether. By his marriage he has acquired in the way of dowry the opulent counties of Burgundy, Artois, Flanders, Rhétel, and Nevers. He has managed to ward off the Dukes of Buckingham and Lancaster, who have threatened his domains from their dangerous proximity across the North Sea. He therefore possesses the industrial North with its prosperous spinning and weaving centers. His domains surround France from the Rhone River northward to the seaboard. He is Dean of Peers and twice a peer of France. The boy King Charles VI has handled him with care. After the suppression of insurrections in the important town of Ghent in 1382 Burgundy has been acknowledged "the most powerful Prince in Christendom."

More dangerous than all that, as far as Louis of France is concerned, however, is the fact that his uncle of Burgundy has a son named John. When this John becomes Duke of Burgundy, he will constitute a threat to the new Duke of Orléans. Far from jovial—on the contrary, thin, dark, ambitious, haughty—John is the heir to a duchy that far surpasses in power and resources the entire Kingdom of France. The only control in this event will be the oath of fealty the future Duke John will be obliged to swear as he kneels and places his joined hands between the hands of the ill King Charles VI. Such an oath is in principle binding. Only the Pope has the power to release a feudal lord from such a contract.

In the realm of foreign affairs the picture is somewhat brighter. If a sick King Charles VI rules in France—or rather, if Louis and the uncles rule for him—the situation in England is similar. There Richard Plantagenet, born at Bordeaux in France, has also survived a dangerous minority and is still under the more or less direct control of his three uncles, the Dukes of Lancaster, Gloucester, and York. The first of the three is a man to be reckoned with certainly, and Louis of France plans to keep him peaceful by personal contact. Lancaster and York met with the French only two years before and signed a truce in the war that has gone on now since 1337 or so, unless one accepts that England's claims to territory on the Continent are based upon the rights of the first Plantagenet King of England, William the Conqueror—in which case the war has smoldered for over four hundred years. As far as Louis of France can see, the situation was nicely reversed under his father King Charles V, who with the aid of the Breton Du Guesclin won back most of the territorial soil of France from the English invaders. France reached a nadir after two crushing defeats in the field at Crécy and Poitiers. The way to defeat the English, thinks Louis of France, is obviously not to meet them in pitched battle, but to beguile them singly at the conference table, where, deprived of their dangerous solidarity, they can be overawed by French opulence, grace of chivalry, and superior numbers.

English policy at the present time consists in forming alliances against the French Pope at Avignon, who is championed by Louis of France in particular and who is obeyed by Spain as well as by France's faithful friend and old ally, the Kingdom of Scotland. England, which supports Urban VI at Rome, has attracted into this strategy her somewhat ineffectual and most undependable allies east of the Rhine and in Italy. The uncle of Burgundy favors obeying both Popes; but, of course, he intends also to keep the English out of Flanders. The masterstroke, it seems to Louis of France, will be to entice King Richard II of England into a close personal alliance with himself. It will bear consideration, particularly since Richard's Queen Anne of Bohemia has just died childless. If Richard ever shows enough strength of character to escape from the turbulence of Gloucester or from the cold calculations of Lancaster, there may be a way to win him. After all, Richard was born in

France. He is by no means entirely English. And because he is weak, he is therefore to be led.

Louis of France was not so plunged in reflection that he did not hear the descending steps of the king's chamberlain, not so lost in thought that he did not grasp the news that was announced to him even though the bell in the lofty church tower above his head had already begun its solemn announcement. With great poise and deliberation he rose to his feet, feeling as he did so that he was paying his first respects to an infant of his blood, to a newborn child that came not naked into the world but garbed in the deference and love that was due his princely lineage. The Duchess of Orléans, Valentine Visconti of Milan, is safely delivered of a male child! Long live the House of Orléans-Valois! King Charles VI, Charles the Beloved, has a nephew. Long live the king!

As Louis of France passed down the long, vaulted corridors of the palace, followed closely by his dearest friend, John IV of Alençon, a faint smile came to his lips. The silent palace had sprung to life and light within that minute. As he passed before the oak table he could see that the monks of Saint-Denis, the official historians of the Crown, were already writing in their massive Chronicle the Latin sentences that would remain for posterity to read as a solemn statement of that hour: "Toward the middle of November was born in the king's palace of Saint-Paul a son named ———, to His Highness, the Duke of Orléans, and to the Lady Valentine Visconti of Milan."

By the time the cortège had fallen in behind him, in precedence according to rank, and by the time that Louis of France had reached his lady's state chamber, the infant had already been dressed and wrapped in his blanket encrusted with the three golden lilies of Orléans. Louis of France stopped only for a second to peer into his son's face. "It is a strong child," he was told.

The dark red skin, the abundant black hair, and the dark eyes he could see for himself. The newborn Count of Touraine, he thought, has a square, rather short body. His hands are remarkably small. Louis of France smiled to himself under his mask of ceremony. Very well. He would have another look at this child in seven years' time when the tutor was appointed. Once the baptismal ceremony was completed, the infant could be handed over to his nurse and to his noble governess. In seven years' time they would see what potential the future Duke of Orléans possessed. In the meantime he was a distinct achievement, a political weapon, a promise for future reference. None other than the king himself shall hold my son over the baptismal font, thought Louis of France.

King Charles the Beloved, crowned Charles VI at the age of twelve, had begun his career as King of France under the most auspicious circumstances. He was a handsome boy who had become a promising, affable, affectionate, and most handsome man. Although the narrow face and the long, pointed nose that protruded down over his upper lip marked him as a Valois, his hair and eyes were not dark like those of the Valois. In scholarship and learning he might never equal his father, King Charles V, who had been accounted, along with Edward III of England, one of the most highly educated kings ever to grace a throne. Charles VI excelled particularly in physical exercises, preferring to leave his father's magnificent library to his younger brother, Louis. As the years of his minority wore away, certain wise courtiers began to observe in this handsome king a passion for physical pleasures that amounted to a frenzy. He seemed never to tire of tournaments, festivals, long voyages through the kingdom, parades, and dances. He surpassed all the knights of the realm at jousting, tilting, horsemanship, darts, and all games. In battle he had on several occasions during the Flanders campaigns demonstrated a high degree of physical courage.

At the age of seventeen King Charles VI had suddenly determined to marry. He had fallen utterly in love with the miniature of a fourteen-year-old princess named Isabeau de Bavière, German on her father's side and Italian on her mother's. Nothing would do but Charles VI must marry her at once. The young lady was therefore escorted into the kingdom and wedded to the king in a double ceremony at the Cathedral of Amiens on July 18, 1385. She made her royal entrance into Paris during that summer, past fountains that flowed with wine and through streets festooned with garlands. Instead of decreasing, the revels and riotous celebrations at the court increased. Despite the births of her two daughters, Isabelle in 1389 and Marie in 1392, Queen Isabeau's pursuit of pleasure and luxuries became more frenzied with the years. Her apartments in the Hôtel Saint-Paul were decorated by the most famous artists of the century. No cost was spared. No whim went ungratified.

The queen's dressing chamber was a huge room that had eight

windows overlooking the rose gardens. Beside it was her bedroom, which had three windows. Her wardrobe was a room measuring thirty feet by four feet. There were her Grand Cabinet and her Small Cabinet with a gallery one hundred and twenty-five feet long that led into a formal audience chamber called Theseus' Room because a contemporary artist had painted on its walls murals representing the adventures of the Athenian hero. The queen had three separate chapels for her personal use, one near her chamber, one off the Theseus Room, and a third in the Church of Saint-Paul itself. She had access to this last chapel by a corridor, thirty feet by four feet, screened off on one side by a lattice so that the queen could remain unseen there while looking down into the churchyard to hear the sermons.

Her favorite chapel had green walls, a "gay green," that rose to the cross vaults, which were painted a "German azure." On the walls was represented a multifloral forest where children wandered, picking fruits, lilies, and pink plum blossoms. In the Saint-Paul Chapel were twelve famous statues, each four and one-half feet high, of the twelve Apostles. The stone had been beautifully painted by the noted artist François d'Orléans. The mantles of the Apostles were thick with gold. Each saint wore on his head a diadem a foot wide, decorated to match his robes—gold, red, green, and white. This chapel was also remarkable for its luxuriant carpet.

Since Queen Isabeau took great care of her widely heralded beauty, especial care had been taken in planning her bathroom. The floors had been paved with fine-grained quartz. The doors of "Irish" wood were inlaid and trellised. The knobs were gold-plated, as were the metal rings that were attached to them by means of copper nails— also gold-plated.

Water in the city had long been one of the principal problems. Even though the southern residences in the Hôtel Saint-Paul area stood along the Seine, the river was thick with refuse, particularly at low water. The palace was therefore supplied from the Fountain of the Lion, which had been constructed in the largest courtyard. Permission to pipe water to the neighboring Celestine monastery, even through a pipe the diameter of a pin, required complicated contractual agreements.

Queen Isabeau was not alone in her demand for luxuries. During the first years of her marriage her husband's worship of her had made them equally important to him. This tall queen, with her proud carriage, beautiful fair skin and eyes, and dark hair, was the maker of manners at her court. Her cosmetics came from the Orient. Her gowns were elaborate—low-necked, with sloping shoulders, tight sleeves, high waists—so cut that the abdomen and hips were rounded and emphasized. Soon after her arrival in Paris the palace masons were summoned and ordered to recut the doors of the palace. They were all too low for the queen. Her Majesty wore a cone-shaped cap that covered her hairline and fitted close around her face. The cone was well over a foot high, and draped with a fine, transparent white silk that floated behind her gracefully when she walked.

When Louis of France brought his Italian bride into the city for the first time, Charles VI decided to make a second entry for the queen. Therefore the two ladies rode through the gates at Saint-Denis and crossed the city from north to south. Each one, magnificently attired in silks and furs, rode on her own chariot, like a goddess of love. At each square or important crossroads pageants were played for their diversion. Acrobats, jesters, and musicians performed. Poetry composed in their honor was declaimed. Certain of the leading magistrates were shocked to behold naked nymphs parading for the royal inspection. As the queen's chariot arrived at Notre-Dame Bridge, two golden angels blowing trumpets descended tight-wires that stretched from the tops of the cathedral's towers to the banks of the Seine River. Counselors and members of Parliament were scandalized at the spectacle, but even more so when they learned that the young king had wandered through the throngs along the bridge disguised as a commoner, so that he could savor the whole effect of his queen's triumph. It was also whispered that an officer had reprimanded the king on this occasion for ungentlemanly behavior, not dreaming that he was scolding His Majesty. The wise shook their heads. They thanked the revolts and the revolutionaries that kept King Richard II so busy in Ireland. Until 1392 it was thought, even so, that the king would outgrow his youthful excesses.

During that summer Charles VI became justly outraged at the sovereign Duke of Brittany. This haughty lord was harboring an outlaw who had attacked and almost killed the king's constable in the very streets of the capital. King Charles VI assembled a large party of knights and set out for the frontiers of Brittany. As his party left the gates of Le Mans, they plunged into the vast forest that lay to the west of that city. It was August. The heat was intense, the forest paths dusty and dry, and the woods oppressive.

For hours the knights pressed forward in single file, the king first, followed by his squire, then Louis of France, then Burgundy and the other great lords behind him. The heavy horses plodded along under the tremendous weight of the knights in full coats of armor, for the king had insisted that they be prepared for emergencies at any moment. In addition to his armor plate, which covered him from neck to foot, the king also wore his battle helmet, with the visor closed, and over that a ceremonial cloak of heavy black velvet. The party rode on through the early afternoon hours, sweltering, and stunned by the heat.

Suddenly a wild, half-naked man darted out from the underbrush, grabbed the king's bridle, tugged on it until the war-horse halted, and then cried to the king; "Take care for your life! They are going to kill you!"

It all happened so fast that the squire who was plodding along behind the king, half asleep and dozing over the pommel of his saddle, lurched forward when his horse's head bunted into the king's horse. The impact caused the lance that the squire was holding to topple forward in such a way that no sooner had the wild man pronounced his terrifying words than the heavy metal tip of the lance struck the king's helmet a ringing blow on the right side of his head, just above the ear.

Before the party of knights were aware of what had occurred, and certainly before they could understand the two almost simultaneous events, the king had raised his battle sword, wheeled his massive Percheron, and charged furiously upon his brother, Louis of France! The latter had only time to swerve out of the king's furious charge. In a flash the king wheeled again and was thundering back across the sunlit path at the younger man. According to the Burgundian chroniclers, it was only the presence of mind of Philip the Hardy that saved the day. According to them, the Duke of Burgundy called out that the king was in a "furious delirium." It was he who also shouted to young Louis of France to ride out of the way into the trees.

The combined efforts of several skilled knights were required to head off the king, to disarm him, to pull him down from the foaming horse. It took several of them to unbuckle his armor and to tie him down hand and foot to the litter that was brought up from the rear. Once immobilized, the king lapsed into a catatonic state. He seemed not to recognize anyone. He lay this way, neither speaking nor moving, for several days in the city of Le Mans. All this time he was completely unresponsive. Then, perhaps with the coming of the fall rains and cooler days, he seemed much better. He was finally able to be transported to Paris.

Prayers for the king's recovery were sung in all churches of the realm. Processions were made to Saint-Denis and to Notre-Dame. Holy relics were taken from the treasuries. Weeping crowds waited outside the palace of Saint-Paul. All France understood that God chastened well him whom well He loved. The king had been severely tried. From that day forward King Charles VI was rechristened throughout the kingdom *Charles the Beloved*. This was the unfortunate uncle of the newborn prince—of the newborn son of Louis of France.

Despite a thorough investigation in Le Mans and a careful search through the forest that had earned its sinister reputation centuries earlier when Charlemagne's mother had been lost there for so many sad years, no trace was ever found of the wild man. No satisfactory explanation was ever advanced for his words that had so startled the young king. Certain historians believed that it must have been a crazed and desperate leper who had escaped from a neighboring leprosarium. In any event, the King of France returned to normal. After his illness he seemed to avoid being with his queen, however. More and more he sought the company of the Duchess Valentine. Her presence seemed to quiet his fears. Her gentleness seemed to soothe him.

At this time the regency had been granted to the Duke of Burgundy. The official reason advanced for bypassing the king's only brother, Louis, was the latter's extreme youth. Louis of France bided his time. He continued to acquire domains one by one; he listened attentively to Jean Juvénal and to his other sage advisers; he waited for an heir; and he began to cultivate the queen. From time to time he spared a few minutes to pass through the apartments of the oldest princess, Isabelle—a tall child like her mother—a very tall child for her age. Meanwhile, the king recovered and began to visit the queen's apartments at night. It was thought that the way to ward off a second attack of the paralyzing illness was to keep the king surrounded by gaiety, music, and lights. Ideas were not lacking. Louis of France and Queen Isabeau imagined more daring diversions.

About a year after the king's illness in the forest of Le Mans, an incident occurred at his court in Paris that cast the first serious aspersions on Louis of France. It was a drama of such nightmarish

proportions, so many hundreds of people were present and actually
witnessed it, that although several teams of learned investigators
were appointed the very next morning, no coherent and truthful
account or explanation was ever forthcoming. The lawyer Jean
Juvénal says that the testimonies of the eyewitnesses were so glaringly
contradictory that no one was ever able to sift their diverse asser-
tions. The conclusions of the courtiers, transmitted to all Paris
overnight, it seemed, were so damning that Louis of France must
have been able to estimate the venom of his enemies for the first
time. Without doubt he could have named them. Under his mask
of ceremony, as he bent over his newborn son, he must have seen
their eyes upon him. But Louis of France was twenty-four years
old. His whole life lay before him—and he had a son!

Two of the contemporary chroniclers laid no blame for this
awful scandal upon Louis of France. One was his own friend and
adviser, Jean Juvénal. The monks of Saint-Denis had heard the
damning slander, but they were unwilling to credit it entirely. As
honest historians, however, they did record it.

All are agreed that a masquerade ball was given somewhere
in one of the princely residences or hôtels within the unofficial palace
of Saint-Paul. Some explain that it was in celebration of someone's
second marriage and that the party was a kind of travesty of a
wedding reception since a widow could not receive the same kind
of homage as a virgin bride. In any event, the young king attended,
and in costume. He and four of his companions wore costumes that
made them look like furry animals. Against their bodies they wore
fitted cloth suits that had been covered with tar so that an even
coating of hairy fibers could be stuck to them. Then the furry
tufts had been touched with oil so that they shone. The five masqueraders were chained together with heavy lengths of chain. They
made their grand entrance into the torchlit hall, full to overflowing
with revelers dancing and moving about merrily under the lighted
torches. The Burgundian chroniclers record that Louis of France,
curious to learn the identity of the wild men, grabbed a torch,
rushed wildly up to them laughing and brandishing his torch—
and that he, Louis of France, set them on fire!

Within a split second the five tarred figures were sheathed in
flames, leaping and screaming in agony, while the lords and ladies
shrieked and fell back from their anguished gyrations. Two of the
men managed to break from their chains, run blindly out of the
hall, plunge into the cisterns in the courtyard, and thus save their

lives. A lady—it is uncertain who, since two afterward claimed that honor—had the presence of mind to pull off her velvet cloak and the skill and courage to wrap it about the central figure. The two other masqueraders were burned alive. The one saved by the cloak was the King of France!

Louis of France never dignified the slander that so viciously accused him of trying to assassinate his brother in this horrible way. Jean Juvénal says that the investigation proved nothing except that *a* spark from *a* torch—and there were hundreds in the hall—ignited one of the costumes. The terrible result of this evening's revelry was that the king relapsed into his comatose condition and that this recurrence was longer and more terrible than the first. The only person he recognized was his brother's young bride, Valentine Visconti. He would often lie and weep for hours on end until she entered his room. Day after day the Italian princess, during the long months of her pregnancy, sat stroking the king's forehead and singing to him.

When the day arrived for the baptism of Louis of France's son and heir, the pitiful king was persuaded to participate. He allowed himself to be dressed in his robes of state. Sad-eyed and pale, he took his place at the head of the solemn procession that comprised the six ecclesiastical and the six lay peers of his realm. There was barely standing room in the chapel of Saint-Paul's for the most eminent nobles of the realm. Those of lesser importance silently lined the various halls and courtyards of the palace. All the streets outside the palace walls were thronged with the poor, who waited confidently through the long hours, knowing that the first duty of a feudal noble was to show his generosity and that the fulfillment of this responsibility would include all those who came to pay homage to the future Duke of Orléans. Louis of France was known and admired for his munificence.

The royal child was held over the baptismal font by his uncle, King Charles VI, and baptized by the Archbishop of Paris. After the ceremony the monks of Saint-Denis were able to write his name on their vellum pages. The parents had chosen nobly. The future Duke of Orléans was named *Karolus* in honor of the uncle who held him, in honor of his illustrious grandfather King Charles V, and in memory of that greatest of Frankish kings, the Great Charles —Charlemagne. With such a heavy name was the son of Louis and Valentine endowed.

Thus he was officially entered—Karolus—Charles—in the Royal

Archives of the kingdom. From that moment he became an actor in the drama that is a man's life. Within a few feet of the infant Charles on his baptismal day were many of those people who would play major roles in his story. Along with the Princess Isabelle he was the first of the new generation. Philip the Hardy and his son John, the future Duke of Burgundy, were present. Count John of Alençon, friend to the death to the Crown of France, was present. Queen Isabeau of France attended in robes and furs so rich that even the rich gasped. Envoys and visiting dignitaries from the Papacy, from England, and from Milan witnessed the solemn sacrament.

Twenty-four knights adjourned immediately after the ceremony in the chapel to follow Louis of France into his Grand Cabinet. They had been privately convoked. Each one was able to prove his descent from at least four of the ancient noble lines of France. Each was wealthy. Each was of proved courage.

In a second and most impressive ritual the twenty-five nobles knelt and were invested in a private order of knighthood such as only a king or a prince was empowered to create. In honor of his son's baptism, Louis of France created the Order of the Golden Porcupine. The vows the twenty-four pledged to their founder were political as well as religious. The intention was to bind the twenty-five noblemen to each other and by a solemn religious ceremony to engage them to defend the House of Orléans and the newborn Prince Charles against all dangers and all adversaries. The order that Louis of France created upon this occasion was similar to the English Order of the Garter. The vows were binding for life. Regular chapter meetings would be held during which any member and any infringement could be publicly censured.

During their assemblies the member knights were to wear the vestments provided for them by their founder—a violet silken cassock that fell to the floor, covered by a mantle of azure velvet lined with crimson satin and over this the badge of their order—a collar of heavy gold chains that had been cunningly entwined and from which hung, just over the heart, the emblem of the Golden Porcupine. The little animal, finely wrought in gold, was raised upon a background of enamelwork representing a mound of grass strewn with bright flowers.

The significance of this particular mascot was not difficult to understand. The tiny animal was represented in side view, with its four paws on the ground. In other words, it was a terrestrial creature, and therefore to Louis's pleasure—for his own ambitions

17

were clearly terrestrial. Second, the porcupine was in France nocturnal in its habits, covering its doings under a mantle of darkness. Third, it possessed a most effective means of defense—quills that were easily twice as high as its body. Last of all, it was not an aggressor—a quiet, busy little animal unless molested. To the twenty-four initiates present at this solemn investiture, it undoubtedly became clearer and clearer, as the agenda of the first session was discussed, that Louis of France understood the dangers that threatened not only him but also his wife and his infant son. In the game he played the stakes were very high—the command, the welfare, and the security of the entire Kingdom of France. No less. The immediate purpose of the Order of the Golden Porcupine showed a father's love for his helpless infant.

This infant Charles, already a count, one day to be the master of a thousand cities and towns, nephew and grandson of a King of France, grandson also of the politically astute Visconti family, son equally of the facile and intelligent Louis as of the gentle Lady Valentine, was weighted from his birth with heavy responsibility. The lives of thousands would one day depend upon his power and upon his sense of justice. Without doubt his father hoped for a son who would spend his years in the consolidation of a dynastic purpose that would curb and limit the rising House of Burgundy. Within the next few years the infant's mother would have occasion to tell him in no uncertain terms what she expected of him. For the present he could be sent away from the turbulent, disease-ridden city. Within a short while he would be carried by his nurse and his governess, escorted through the streets of the capital in a sumptuous litter adorned with the golden lilies of Orléans, surrounded and guarded by his first company of those knights-at-arms who had solemnly sworn their readiness to die for him.

Cuddled in his nurse's lap the baby Count of Touraine would be transported to the safety of his father's heavily fortified castle at Château-Thierry. From there daily bulletins would reach Louis of France as he continued to plan, fully aware though he was that one son would not be sufficient to guarantee the security of his line.

Louis of France could not have known that one son would be more than sufficient, however, to ensure the eternal luster of his name—if that son was baptized Charles of Orléans.

II [*1394–1399*] SOON AFTER THE BIRTH of her son, the Duchess Valentine felt in her turn the growing malice of her husband's enemies. Prince Charles had hardly been safely tucked away at Château-Thierry when there was made against his mother the most dangerous of all accusations, a charge so serious that the whole might of her husband's feudal vassals, or even the power of their combined wealths, or the awe of their position would all be powerless to protect her in the event of a trial and conviction. Charges of grand larceny, of patricide, or even of treason after the fact need not entail such consequences as this accusation might cause to ensue. Valentine, Duchess of Orléans, was accused of sorcery! It was said that she was the source of the king's illness. It was also generally claimed that she had brought dark arts from Italy and that this explained the king's dependence on her. It was more than hinted that she had bewitched the king in order to gain the throne, if not for her husband, then for her infant son Charles.

The lady's father in Milan reacted energetically and immediately. He sent open letters to the French Court, angrily protesting any pretensions to the throne of France, categorically denying any collusion between his daughter and himself on any subject whatsoever. He also took the precaution of calling his daughter's accusers "false liars." He then proceeded to challenge them to a trial by arms. The Duke of Milan proposed to come to France and to meet in single combat any and all accusers. God would not fail to show which knight had the truth on his side!

In this critical situation Louis of France displayed a presence of mind and a sense of diplomacy that were probably more politic than the measures suggested by his father-in-law. The Lady Valentine left Paris and the court altogether, retired "in disgrace," far from the queen's jealousy, far from the king's demands, to her husband's castle at Château-Thierry. However lonely the lady may have been during the succeeding years—it is certain that she saw her husband, but perhaps not too frequently—she may have consoled herself by being able to devote most of her time to the infant Charles.

During the years following the birth of Charles of Orléans, there were many more royal births—children who were to play important roles within a very few years of their births; for child marriages were frequent among the rulers of kingdoms, and a boy came of age at fourteen. On January 12, 1395, a third daughter was born to the king and to Queen Isabeau—Michelle, who was affianced in the cradle to Philip, son of John, the future Duke of Burgundy. The following year a dauphin, or heir to the throne, was finally born. He was named Louis, Duke of Guyenne. This birth served to divert attention from the infant Charles. The same year Valentine Visconti of Orléans bore a second son, also named Philip, Count of Vertus. That same year a truce between France and England was signed with Richard II, who seemed to be a growing power in England and who appeared more and more friendly to overtures from Louis of Orléans.

News from England was regular and reliable. The French chronicler Froissart, who lived at the English Court, was a personal friend of Louis of France. He had at one moment, during the accusations against the Duchess Valentine, written in her defense. He was on more than one occasion the recipient of lavish gifts from the Duke of Orléans. Through Froissart, as through other notables, the French Court formed its own opinion of Richard and of his favorites: "His subjects were uneasy to perceive that from time to time Richard II claimed to himself a Power above the Laws. As he was very fond of Pomp and Magnificence, his expense far exceeded his Revenues, so that he was forced to make use of several illegal methods to supply his Occasions." The French learned with great amusement of the difficulties the English king encountered with the City of London, which had once bluntly refused him the loan of a thousand pounds sterling, which was "no great sum." In revenge the king seized upon a pretext to turn the lord mayor out of his office, revoke the city's charter, and remove the courts of law to the City of York. He then obliged the citizens of London to pay him ten thousand pounds for the return of their charter. Although Richard II was not "a Prince of the greatest abilities, he had a high opinion of his own Merit."

The French Court also noted with satisfaction that Richard relied on certain favorites who seemed indisposed to renewing the war with France. One courtier in particular had already played an important role as contact between the two kingdoms. This was a Michael de la Pole, whom Richard II had created Earl of Suffolk in 1385. He was actually the son of a merchant from Kingston-on-Hull who had lent money to Edward III and who had been therefore advanced to the degree of banneret in lieu of payment. King Edward used to call him his "beloved merchant." The son Michael de la Pole, three years after becoming an earl, had been convicted of using his office for his own enrichment, and had been banished along with the Earl of Oxford. Following a traditional policy, the French received all exiles from England and used them for political purposes. This Knight of the Garter Suffolk had descendants in England who would make their mettle known during the century, when the time was ripe for fighting. William de la Pole was two years younger than Charles of Orléans.

In 1395 Richard II made an open move for the friendship of France, an offer that Louis of France had doubtless anticipated. A party of twenty knights, forty squires, and five nobles headed by the Archbishop of Dublin arrived in Paris on important Crown business. Their purpose was to entreat a marriage between the King of England and the oldest royal princess the Lady Isabelle, who was not yet eight years old—but tall for her age. During the negotiations the princess received the ambassadors in person; for it was essential that they form their own opinions as to her traits of personality, as to her general culture and intelligence, and also as to her physical development and promise. The English lords saw a tall, dark child with the aristocratic, long nose of the French royal family. They were impressed with her dignity and charm, and even more with her prompt replies. The princess was asked if she would like to travel to England and live there for the rest of her life.

"Would I be a queen?" asked the Lady Isabelle. "Would you swear homage to me?" When the nobles replied that this would be so, the princess assured them that she would gladly consent. The English ambassadors were lavishly entertained at the Hôtel Saint-Paul. They were banqueted and feasted and so "cherished" that their royal master could not fail to be flattered. All the expenses they incurred for their voyage were, incidentally, most joyously defrayed by the French Court. By such a union the French hoped to win from the English what they had failed to wrest from them on the fields of battle, and also to ensure a permanent peace in the "hundred" years' war.

Richard II was beset with difficulties at home. He had recalled John of Gaunt, or Ghent, the Duke of Lancaster, from southern France, where the Gascons were again in open rebellion against an English rule. This duke had returned gladly, and promptly caused a scandal. After having ridden all night to Lincoln, he had shortly afterward—to the righteous indignation of the great ladies—married his mistress Katharine Swinford. This lady had been raised in his house, had attended his two duchesses, had been married and widowed. During her twenty or so years as mistress to the Duke of Lancaster she had borne him three sons. It was for love of them, said the duke, that he had finally married her. Those ladies of England who were descended from the great families assured each other that they would never set foot in a room where the former Katharine Swinford appeared. They held it a shame for such a person to have become the second personage in the realm and thereby preferred before them according to protocol. It was unthinkable to them that a person who had been the duke's concubine while his first two duchesses were alive, a concubine of ordinary birth and without fortune, should arrive so undeservedly to a position of great honor. Such a scandal subsided slowly despite the "honorable demeanor" of the new Duchess of Lancaster.

The French Court also noted that Richard II legitimized the children born prior to this marriage, two sons and a daughter. One of these sons, Henry Beaufort, was about eighteen years old at the time. It was argued that such a great lord as John of Gaunt should father many sons. It was also said that he loved Henry Beaufort as much as he did his legitimate son, Henry Bolingbroke. Henry Beaufort was being educated in the law, in preparation for a career in the Church. It was said that he was a tall, handsome, blue-eyed boy and a fairly apt student. In point of fact, he was more probably a superior student. Louis of France would have understood the need for many sons and also the need to train a promising young man in all the aspects of feudal law.

In the fall of 1396 the ambassadors from Richard II returned to France, where they contracted a solemn marriage by procuration between Princess Isabelle and their sovereign lord and where they also concluded a treaty or truce between the two nations for thirty years. The princess was called Queen of England from that day.

Her device of the white falcon was adopted by her new subjects, and her pennant was flown from her lodging along with that of King Richard, whose devices were a white hart kneeling and collared in gold, the sun in splendor, a pod of the broom (*planta genista* for Plantagenet), and branches of rosemary. The princess spent longer hours at her English lessons, which included now the names and genealogies of her nobles. She was advised, rehearsed, and beguiled with stories of England. Miniatures of King Richard no doubt pleased her, for her fair-haired husband had a gentle face— as the English now had a child queen, but a child that already promised the slender beauty that would one day endear her to people of both kingdoms; a beauty, in fact, that would make this princess immortal. It was a marriage arranged by Louis of France, and accepted proudly by those who completed its fastidious negotiations.

True, the question of the disparity of ages had arisen. Here was a King of England, already a widower, still without an heir at the age of twenty-nine, proposing to wed, and then actually wedding, a princess aged eight, who according to French records was not eight after all but seven, going on eight. Richard II's answer was that he had been widowed only a short time, that two years were hardly long enough to have recovered from his desperate grief at the loss of Queen Anne. It seemed to him that he should be allowed a proper period of mourning commensurate with the extent of his sorrow. He further replied that he was in perfectly good health and that he would be able to father many sons once the new Queen Isabelle had reached an age that allowed her to receive him. He added that he was truly delighted with the miniatures of the French princess and that he would enjoy watching her education and her development into womanhood.

Louis of France was hardly swayed by such specious arguments. A French priest in England wrote such lines about King Richard: "King Richard is of the common stature, his face fair and rosy, rather round than long, and sometimes flushed; abrupt and somewhat stammering in his speech, capricious in his manner, and too apt to prefer the recommendations of the young to the advice of the elder nobles. He is prodigal in his gifts, extravagantly splendid in his entertainments and dress, *timid as to war,* very passionate towards his domestics, haughty and much too devoted to voluptuousness. . . . So fond of late hours that he sometimes sits up all night drinking . . . Heavily taxing his people . . . He loves the clergy

. . . encourages architecture . . . built the church of Westminster almost entirely. . . ."

Louis of France had instigated and directed the parleys that led to this marriage contract. He wanted not only a truce but the return to France as a gift of territories still held by the English. It was not enough to establish his small, but already very tall, niece upon the throne of England. This in itself was no extraordinary achievement. Three preceding kings of England had married French princesses, but without doubt Richard II's marriage would be more fortunate.

Therefore, in the twentieth year of his reign, King Richard humbled himself to the extent of going in person to Calais on the Continent, where he was on English-held soil. He was accompanied by his uncles of Gloucester and Lancaster. There he was met by King Charles VI, accompanied by Louis of France and their uncles of Burgundy and Berry. Magnificent pavilions were set up for each king at that boundary line where their two dominions met, and at a distance from each other of seventy paces. Midway between the two was a third silken pavilion where their meetings would take place. As each king passed toward this conference tent, he walked between a double row of knights in armor, sword in hand, four hundred knights for each monarch. As an added precaution each ruler swore a solemn oath "to observe the sacred laws of amity one toward the other," promised to refrain from any recrimination, violence, arrogance, insult, or arrest during the time set for the conferences, a time that was extended to cover "eight days before, and seven days after." The French dukes escorted King Richard, while an equal number of English dukes attended King Charles. This was a Saturday, October 27, 1396.

On the following Monday the French king visited King Richard in the latter's pavilion. It was there that the two awaited the arrival of the Princess Isabelle, there that she and Richard met for the first time. King Charles took his daughter by the hand and led her to her husband. King Richard received her hand, leaned down and kissed Queen Isabelle. Then he thanked her father for so lovely a gift, "openly protesting that he did receive her, that by such affinity both the realms might continue in quietness." After this ceremony the bride was handed over to those English ladies attending the Duchesses of Lancaster and Gloucester, who would henceforth be responsible for the little girl's education and health.

In addition to a collection of crown jewels that would make

her almost as richly ornamented as Queen Isabeau, King Charles settled upon his daughter the fortified castle of Pembroke in Wales. One never knew, and a father could not take too many precautions. Wales was a land long hostile to England, a mountainous country the French had been supplying with leaders and arms all through the century. From Pembroke the Queen of England could, if an emergency ever arose, take ship for home. Meanwhile, twelve chariots full of ladies escorted the new queen to Calais, where she was wed in another ceremony, by the Archbishop of Canterbury himself, on or around Halloween Day.

After the ladies had departed, the two kings dined together, each one on his side of the pavilion, each served according to the customs and cuisine of his own land. Louis of France presented each dish to King Richard. The French chroniclers were very much impressed by this humility. They felt that no greater honor could possibly have been done the English. More rich gifts and jewels were exchanged—as if each ruler vied with the other in a display of wealth and generosity. The story told in England had it that King Richard II had spent the staggering, the almost unbelievable, sum of 300,000 marks for this jaunt to the Continent in which he gained a nubile bride and gave away hardly earned lands—the ports of Brest and Cherbourg!

It was on the following Thursday that King Charles VI and his brother Louis rode into Calais to bid their last farewell to Queen Isabelle of England. The young queen did not rise to the occasion. Instead she clung to her father at the last moment, and sobbed. It was finally necessary to tear her away by force. Among the French ladies who were to travel into England with her was her own servant, a Saracen maiden who had been brought from the Orient as a slave. This was Simonette, who appears never to have left her mistress's side and to have been a consolation and a companion as well as a maid.

The passage from Calais to Dover took only three hours. The Lord Mayor of London, all superb in scarlet robes, waited upon Their Majesties. On November 13th the young queen was conveyed to the Tower of London with all pomp and magnificence. The crowds were so large on London Bridge that several people were crushed to death, among them "two people of importance," says the English chronicler Holinshed. Queen Isabelle was crowned at Westminster on a Sunday morning, January 7th. All had taken place with the most auspicious success. New banners and ensigns

25

could be embroidered endlessly uniting on a background of gules with the three golden lions of England the three golden lilies of France on their field of sapphire. France and England were at peace. The oldest child in the new generation had been royally wed.

In accordance with his promise, King Richard withdrew his garrisons from the French port of Brest. During the peace negotiations his uncle of Gloucester, present under duress, had sulked and maintained the bare minimum of civility. When he saw the returning and unpaid English troops, he openly berated his nephew.

"Sir," said Gloucester to the king, "your grace ought to put your body in pain to win a stronghold or town by feats of war, yet you take it upon you to sell or deliver any town or stronghold gotten by the manhood and policy of your noble progenitors."

"Uncle, how say you that?" asked King Richard.

It was for those same words repeated that King Richard called upon his Uncle Gloucester one morning while the duke was still in bed. King Richard apologized to the duchess for getting her out of bed so early in the morning. They chatted pleasantly while the duke dressed. Gloucester was then arrested and put to death, although whether he was smothered by a feather tick or strangled with towels the contemporary chroniclers were never quite in agreement. At the succeeding session of Parliament the Archbishop of Canterbury lost his see and was condemned to perpetual banishment for complicity with Gloucester. At the same time the Earl of Arundel, who did not condescend to perjure himself in his own defense, was escorted to Tower Hill and beheaded. Soon afterward it was said that this earl's head had grown back on his body; but when King Richard, troubled with nightmares, sent certain of his courtiers at ten o'clock one night to dig up the grave and see if this was true, he found the story baseless.

When the Earl of Warwick was brought to trial, he acknowledged treason and threw himself upon the king's mercy, which neither Gloucester nor Arundel had done. King Richard therefore only banished him and his family to poverty on the Isle of Man. Many others were arrested and condemned. Still King Richard could not live in peace and find sufficient time to ride down the Thames often and play ball with his new queen in Windsor. Louis of France watched carefully and breathed easily to see the English so busy at home.

The next serious dissension in England came as the result of a quarrel begun by John of Gaunt's legitimate son Henry Bolingbroke.

This was Henry of Lancaster, who had recently returned to England from crusades in Lithuania and the Holy Land. His opponent was Thomas Mowbray, the Duke of Norfolk. Henry of Lancaster, Duke of Hereford, while riding along a road, became angry and called Mowbray a "traiter, false and disloyal to the Crown." The Duke of Norfolk in turn called Lancaster a "false and disloyal traiter and a liar." When King Richard interceded, requesting each nobleman to make peace, each one refused. At a second hearing, held six weeks later at Windsor Castle, both nobles still replied flatly, "No," to the king's urgent plea. Therefore a day was set for them to meet in single combat.

Lancaster arrived in the lists on a white charger canopied with green and blue velvet that had been embroidered with golden swans and antelopes. Norfolk was splendid on a crimson-caparisoned horse, his trappings rich with silver lions and silver mulberry trees. Louis of France has sent his special ambassador to witness this trial. Rather than allow the two dukes to fight to the death, however, Richard found it more profitable to halt the combat and confiscate their vast domains. He therefore banished Henry of Lancaster for ten years, giving him fifteen days in which to prepare his departure. Thomas Mowbray he banished in perpetuity. The latter died in Italy, grieving because his king had abandoned him. The former found a warm reception at the court of Charles VI in Paris. In fact, the French extended their hospitality so far as to offer this Duke of Lancaster as a wife the only daughter to the Duke of Berry! King Richard was informed of this barely in time to call his father-in-law to order and to forbid any such alliance.

Louis of France found the banished Duke of Lancaster very good company indeed. He was happy to entertain him in Paris, to provide him with all the comforts of a new home. He even allowed Henry of Lancaster to renew acquaintances with his old friends, such as the despoiled Archbishop of Canterbury! Even Charles VI felt that King Richard had treated this charming and gallant duke very badly.

While Richard II was desperately striving to keep the peace his marriage had arranged, and even more desperately to curb the aspirations of his great nobles and to rule his realm, an appalling catastrophe occurred in the Balkan Peninsula and shook every European king upon his throne. For the past hundred and fifty years the Ottoman Turks had been pouring from the Near East into Europe. Their progress had been steady and relentless, and their religious zeal a threat to Christianity. In 1365 they had captured Adrianople and were within striking distance of Constantinople, the ancient capital of the Eastern Roman Empire. When their fierce and skillful leader, Bajazet I, moved up the Danube into Bulgaria, the Emperor Sigismund of Hungary, seconded by the Pope, called all western Europe to his assistance. Priests, poets, and friars exhorted the great nobles to "cross themselves" and embark on this Crusade. Any reluctant knights were censured in the open chapter meetings of the various orders of chivalry. On bended knee Louis of France sought permission to lead the French knights into Hungary. This permission was refused on the grounds that he was too near the throne and that his son Charles of Orléans was too young.

Instead of allowing his brother to depart, King Charles VI granted this honorable and coveted post to John, Count of Nevers, who was three years younger than Louis and the heir of the Duke of Burgundy. Every noble house of France equipped its sons to ride with Count John—one hundred thousand of them altogether. At their head one thousand of the finest and bravest young nobles of France, escorted by their thousand squires, rode proudly on their throughbred palfreys. Boucicault, the Marshal of France, was among them—he who had fought so long and bravely in Italy. The Count d'Eu, the Count de la Marche, and the Lord of Coucy led three hundred lances, all knights of high heart and spirit, all eager for travel and adventure. After them, for miles across Europe, trundled their baggage train—their treasure, their jeweled helms and swords, their war-horses, their wine casks, their baskets of delicacies packed in their home castles, their silken gowns, their fur tippets, their velvet hoods, their satin tents, their cushions, their carpets. With them rode their favorite jesters, their musicians, their poets, their astrologers, their confessors, their physicians, and their chroniclers. Bajazet laughed to hear how confidently the French knights pressed forward, taking no precautions, stationing no sentinels, listening to no warnings, proud in the invincibility of their personal valor, straight into his trap. They died almost to the last man at a town on the Danube called Nikopol, a place in nothern Bulgaria.

Bajazet had those knights who remained after this swift carnage, those who could still walk, brought before him. John, Count of Nevers, had survived, along with Marshal Boucicault and a few others. Bajazet ordered their lives spared if Count John would humiliate himself before the Turk and beg for their skins. Count

John did not deign to reply. He was then obliged to watch his friends and relatives, all noble knights like himself, tortured to death before his very eyes. Count John endured this spectacle hour after hour without flinching. Nor would he plead for his own life. Bajazet finally wearied of the sport. Impressed by the stoicism of his antagonist, he granted Count John and Boucicault their lives on condition that the French could meet his terms of ransom, which he doubted.

It was on Christmas evening, while the court was assembled before beginning of Mass, that a haggard and desperate knight, the Sire of Helly, rode into the courtyard of the king's palace at Saint-Paul. Racked with grief and fatigue, he blurted out to the king how the French knights had died, many of them lingering deaths. That Christmas Day of 1396 was one the noble houses of France never forgot. One hundred thousand youngsters would never be heard of again—could not be found, could not even be given burial. Amid their tears, however, all paid tribute to Burgundy's son, John of Nevers. He was rechristened John the Fearless. What ordeals had this young man, just twenty-three years old, not survived! What brazen effrontery had he not shown in the teeth of the cruel Oriental khan! While all agreed that his ransom must be paid, no matter what it cost, no matter if every noble coffer in France was emptied of its gold, its rubies and its pearls, there were many who would henceforth shrink from looking Count John of Nevers in the eye. He would return. His knights were dead.

Louis of France forgot his quarrel with Burgundy long enough to exert himself on his cousin's behalf. Dispatches were sent posthaste to Gian Galeazzo Visconti, who took responsibility for the negotiations with Bajazet. It was said that Visconti was an ally of Bajazet, even that he had warned him of the arrival of the knights. However that may have been, the Duke of Visconti, and consequently his daughter Valentine, returned to favor. As a result of their efforts, John the Fearless returned to France along with Boucicaut. In fact, money and treasure poured in so abundantly that Philip the Hardy collected many times the sum required. No matter. He kept the difference.

As the last years of the fourteenth century drew to a close, there was an aura of foreboding in western Europe. In 1396 there was a terrible hurricane that toppled church belfries and flooded large areas on the Continent and in England. That was remembered as the year of the Great Wind.

In 1397 the King of France suffered a relapse of his malady so severe and so prolonged that people wondered what had caused it. He was removed to the fortified Louvre Castle, where he huddled in a filthy chamber, allowing no one to touch him for weeks on end. The queen no longer kept him near her at the Hôtel Saint-Paul, no longer visited his bed during the increasingly severe attacks now that the Duchess of Orléans was not able to calm him and persuade him to be bathed and dressed. Rather than approach him herself, for Queen Isabeau dreaded his hatred of her, she sent a girl from the commons who resembled her into his chamber at night. When the royal Princess Michelle was five years old, it was decided that she should take the veil and spend her lifetime praying for her father's recovery. King Charles VI also issued a proclamation entreating all witches and sorcerers who might wish him ill to cease torturing him. Quack doctors came from all over Europe, demanding all sorts of rare and costly ingredients for their cures. None seemed to help the poor king in the least. The quack doctors were in their turn tried and executed for witchcraft. This did not appear to relieve the king, either.

Games were sought, entertainers were sought, and applicants with ideas were all heard and examined. One diversion did interest the king, and it caught the fancy of the court as well. A game was invented that could be played with partners who used slender pieces of parchment that had been beautifully painted with the king's likeness and with the queen's. The sick king played this one game week in and year out. It brought him much pleasure. The game was called "playing cards."

Disasters, predictions of disaster, and premonitions of disaster spread through the kingdoms in 1399. Under the ordinary worries of everyday living was the certain knowledge that the Ottoman Turks, led by the competent Bajazet, were every season drawing closer and closer, moving their vast hordes up the Danube, more and more tightly encircling Constantinople.

The great nobles of England, remembering the recent treason trials, glanced anxiously over their shoulders. People wept and sighed for Henry of Lancaster, born at Bolingbroke. With him away in France, it seemed that their very shield and defender had been torn away from them. Down at Windsor Castle King Richard might well disport himself. The queen was only a child, and a French one at that.

Then suddenly, on a New Year's Day, a river not far from Bedford dropped out of sight into the ground, only to reappear as mysteriously three miles downstream. People knew this phenomenon had a meaning. A river does not disappear and then reappear for no reason at all. People remembered Henry of Lancaster, son of the great John of Gaunt. He, too, had disappeared from England. In Paris his old friend and accomplice the Archbishop of Canterbury paid a call on Henry Lancaster—a perfectly natural thing to do. Perhaps they discussed England. A perfectly natural thing to do. Perhaps they gave a feast in honor of the safe return of the somber John, heir of the Duke of Burgundy. Perhaps they smiled at the stupid prophecy the common people were repeating endlessly. In the Book of Merlin it said . . . in the Book of Merlin, the great bard of Wales in the bygone days, it was written . . . it was whispered from ear to ear the length of two kingdoms that it was already recorded down through the centuries in the Book of the Welsh magician Merlin, who had second sight and who could predict the future, that "in the year 1400 less one, at a triangular castle shall be betrayed a king after he shall have reigned powerfully twenty-two years!"

In 1399 there was a sudden recurrence of the plague. All western Europe was afflicted. People dropped black and swollen in the streets of the cities. Of a certainty God's wrath had fallen this time. Flint Castle was triangular. Richard II had reigned for twenty-two years! The day of judgment came in 1399. Like all great upheavals, it had been carefully caused and skillfully planned for a very long time. Like all great upheavals, it came as a complete surprise. Take down the pennants bearing the white falcon! Take down the broom and the rosemary! The last Plantaganet King of England has ceased to rule!

Everyone was to blame and no one was at fault. Louis of France, who could not believe his ears, who had to ask to have the message repeated, was blamed, and severely so. Who had welcomed this Henry of Lancaster, this Earl of Derby, this Duke of Hereford, this Duke of Lancaster, this King Henry IV of England, into Paris? Who else but Louis, Duke of Orléans? Who had given him permission to converse with the Archbishop of Canterbury, if not Louis of France? Who had acceded graciously to the pleasant request of Henry of Lancaster, who desired to pay a social visit in

31

Brittany? Who had let him slip through French fingers and land on the Yorkshire coast near his home castles of Knaresborough and Pontefract? Louis of France was blamed for Henry IV's "extraordinary leap to the throne."

The news from England was true. While King Richard was in Ireland, Henry of Lancaster had sailed from Brittany with the former Archbishop of Canterbury, Thomas Arundel, Lord Reginald Cobham, Sir Thomas Erpingham, and Robert Waterton, Esquire. It was also true that the Duke of Lancaster was so loved that no one would lift a finger to impede his passage. Meanwhile, King Richard, who had at least taken the precaution of having Lancaster's son Henry imprisoned in Ireland, was unable to return to England because of storms and rough seas that lasted for six weeks. Henry of Lancaster had not needed six weeks! When Richard did land in England, he appeared to have lost all initiative and all confidence. From Flint Castle he meekly allowed Henry of Lancaster to lead him to London, and so to his first prison in the Tower. Shortly afterward Richard renounced the Crown to the Duke of Lancaster after a rule of twenty-two years, three months, and eight days. From London he was conveyed to Leeds Castle in Kent and thence to Pontefract in Yorkshire. He was sentenced to life imprisonment.

These events had happened so fast that the French Court could hardly believe them either. They were for some time without any news at all of the Princess Isabelle. They were shocked to hear how Richard had been led through the streets of London on a "poor horse" while a boy who followed him dared point his finger and call out, "Behold King Richard, who has done so much good to the Kingdom of England!"

Cries from the Londoners had answered, "Now are we well revenged on the wicked bastard who has governed us so ill!"

Henry of Lancaster's letter to the citizens of London was accounted a masterstroke:

"I, Henry of Lancaster, Duke of Hereford and Earl of Derby, commend myself to all the people of London, high and low. My good friends, I send you my salutations, and I acquaint you that I have come over to take my rightful inheritance. I beg of you to let me know if you will be on my side, or not; and I care not which, for I have enough people to fight all the world for one day, thank God! But take in good part the present I send you."

On January 16, 1400, Henry IV sent a present to London—eight human heads with their quarters, and twelve living gentlemen who were his prisoners. The living were bound with whipcord and led along the streets by peasants. First in the procession of presents came the head of the Duke of Surrey. It had been affixed to the tallest pole. The presents were escorted by the "greater part of the trumpeters and minstrels of the country, and the men of London made great rejoicing."

The French Court was incensed against Henry IV himself, not only because of his boldness and violence but also because of his illegal pretensions to the throne. In the proclamation made on his coronation day, King Henry IV claimed the throne by right of conquest, by virtue of Richard's resignation of it to him, and because he was the next male heir. This third claim made very little sense because the Duke of York was actually nearer in blood than Henry IV, who was only nearest of kin. As Rymer says, Henry IV "should have stuck to the plea, the only one of any Colour," that he had been elected to the throne by vote of Parliament. Henry IV could also have claimed with veracity that it was the people of England themselves who had "advanced him to the Throne." Because of the reasons he chose to argue in his proclamation, Henry IV was to the French Court only a usurper. If his crown sat uneasily upon his head, then he had deserved it. What sat so uneasily might be made to topple altogether.

The principal concern in France was for the welfare of Queen Isabelle. Richard II had gone down to Windsor to say farewell to her before his Irish expedition. After his departure the young queen had been ill for two weeks. Upon the arrival and immediate success of the future Henry IV, the ten-year-old princess had been deprived of her French counselors and, in fact, of all her servants with the exception of the Saracen maiden Simonette and her personal confessor. Then she had been conveyed from her accustomed residence at Windsor Castle, taken to Wallingford, then to Reading, later to Leeds Castle in Kent, and finally to Havering-on-Bower, Essex. For several months the French ambassadors, dispatched with all speed from Paris while Louis of France fumed and stormed, were unable to find any trace at all of their young princess. Two legates, Jean de Hengest and Pierre Blanchet, both fell seriously ill on their arrival in England. Blanchet died from a strange malady, and Hengest vomited a light-colored blood. Hengest recovered and reported to Jean Juvénal in Paris that he had been poisoned by the English. It seems that Henry IV had his own plans for the former Queen Isabelle.

The period following the usurpation of Henry IV was a troubled one. Rebellions broke out among the nobles who found willing allies among the Welsh and the Scots. To complicate matters even more, there was no certainty as to the whereabouts or the existence even of Richard II. This did not change the determination of the French to recover their princess. The English had only one reason that might induce them to allow her departure—the fact that while she remained in England, devoted to her husband as she was, nobles would flock to her and foment insurrections. This was the case at Cirencester, where even the princess thought that the puppet they had dressed in royal garments was really King Richard. On the other hand, there were two excellent reasons for keeping her in England. One was her dowry, the crown jewels that her father had bestowed so lavishly upon her. The ambassadors from France specifically requested the return of "Queen Isabelle, virgin," and of her dowry. They had been provided with an itemized list. To strengthen the subsequent ambassadors' arguments and to reinforce their powers of persuasion, the French Court let it be known that they were preparing to invade England, if such action was necessary to recover the daughter of France. The second reason suggested to the ambassadors was one that horrified them. King Henry IV either insinuated or proposed that Queen Isabelle should remain in England and that she should marry his son!

It was Henry, Prince of Wales, who was offered as a prospective husband to Queen Isabelle. The lady is said to have refused in high dudgeon and to have added that King Richard was still alive. The French legates also spurned the offer, remarking caustically that it was not the custom in France for a lady to marry into a family that had deposed her husband, that had murdered her husband —or that intended to murder her husband.

While the ambassadors continued to plead and to threaten, the long series of rumors concerning Richard II's return to the throne began. They were to last well over ten years and to poison the reign of Henry IV. Some were hearsay; some were reputed to be prophecies from Merlin. The Welsh sang their sad ballad of "Sweet Richard." However, whether or not Richard II ever returned, the beautiful Isabelle must be brought home to France.

Louis of France spent many an anxious hour turning her future over in his mind. Where was he ever to find a husband handsome enough, sufficiently well born, of a suitable age, of high enough hopes, to spite Henry IV and make his profligate son feel deeply humiliated at his rejection? Where was he to find a husband who could match the excellent qualities of education, position, breeding, and beauty that were in this unfortunate princess? Perhaps the solution occurred to him at once. What Prince of France possessed such qualities? Certainly no young nobleman outside the House of Valois itself! Certainly not the drunken wastrel who would one day become Henry V. Heaven forbid!

There was only one prince who could match her. Louis of France rode home to Château-Thierry and studied his older son, Charles of Orléans.

III [*1400–1406*] IT HAS HAPPENED IN THE history of the world that certain children are never given time enough in which to grow slowly and naturally to manhood. Certain children seem to have been expected to play an adult role from early childhood. Such was the sad case of the Princess Isabelle, who had become Queen of England at the age of seven, who had been dethroned at the age of ten, married and perhaps widowed before she reached adolescence. The case of her male cousin, Prince Charles of Orléans, was a parallel one. Destined at birth for a position of absolute power over the lives of thousands of his future subjects; desperately needed by his father, who was fighting with every weapon in his power to ensure a succession to the duchy he had created; surrounded from his baptismal day by the House of Burgundy, which had no particular concern for the sanctity of the monarchy and certainly no love for the Valois king or his younger brother of Orléans; perhaps even fated one day to rule France and northern Italy, the child Charles was groomed for these responsibilities from the cradle.

This prince was educated under the careful supervision of his mother, attended by his nurse, and taught manners by his noble governess. From his first steps and his first words he was taught rigid obedience, service, and respect for women—three of the most essential precepts of chivalry. The theory was that a man could never command unless he had first been steeled to instant and unquestioning obedience. It also followed that his vassals could not serve him with fidelity to the death if he himself had not realized from infancy that his life as a knight would be measured by the way in which he fulfilled his vows of service. A knight swore to serve the weak against the strong, the poor against the rich, women because they could not defend themselves. The future knight, after his lonely vigil on his knees before the altar, swore service to his liege lord, service to the king, and absolute devotion to his God.

The early education of a prince was primarily designed to inculcate in him those attitudes and traits of character that would sustain him throughout life, that would make his word a bond upon which thousands could rely unswervingly, that would make his actions predictable in any given situation. Under the reign of his grandfather, Charles V, a book on the education of princes had been written by Vincent de Beauvais. It was a subject that concerned not only the parents but even the most distant vassals in their faraway provinces. Examples of a similar education were not lacking. In the Cabinet of King Charles VI's Hôtel Saint-Paul hung a portrait of the great King of England, Edward III, who might be taken as an almost perfect example of the efficacy of a medieval education.

"Edward III was wise and provident in Council; well-learned in the Laws, in History, in the Humanities, and in Divinity. He understood Latin, French, Spanish, Italian, and High and Low Dutch, besides his Native Language." King Charles V of France was a similar product. By the time of the education of Prince Charles, the idea was firmly established that learning should not be grafted upon a weak foundation. The belief was that if the child's character and his sense of morality were not well rooted first, the learning he might acquire would be not only superfluous but downright dangerous. As is usually the case, such strong beliefs came not from the nobility in general, but from the philosophical arguments of an intellectual giant.

The thinking in France for the past ten years or so had been greatly affected or largely shaped by the words of a gigantic man, who through his position and because of his charm and courage exerted a direct influence upon the court as well as upon intellectuals throughout the land. This was Jean Gerson. His career was an interesting one. He was born around 1363 in northern France—more properly, in the territories of the Duke of Burgundy. His original name, Jean Charlier, was amended to include in it the place of his birth, making him Jean Charlier de Gerson, and then was shortened again to Jean Gerson.

Jean Gerson had begun school with the other boys of his age at the church school of his native village. Although his parents were poor, there was in medieval France no problem about educating sons so long as they lived near enough to the church to attend classes. No fees were required. From the early school days of this particular boy the priests, who were also professional teachers, easily recognized the intellectual capacity of their student, and applied to the Duke of Burgundy for the requisite permission and funds to send him to Paris. Therefore, the youngster Jean Charlier from Gerson enrolled in courses at the most highly qualified school in the Western world, under teachers who were themselves the most learned and most accomplished that could be found. After seventeen years of continuous study at this university, Jean Gerson became a Doctor at the age of thirty.

During his last years he followed a program of graduate studies that had varied little down through the centuries. In the three-year period he took the step from B.A. to M.A., and then the final difficult program to the Doctoral Dissertation and defense.

Jean Gerson, the most brilliant Doctoral candidate at the finest school in the West, received a major appointment three years after graduation. In 1395 he became the official representative of the Pope at the University of Paris. He became its chancellor, and also the Dean of Notre-Dame Cathedral. From that day he was assured a large and varied audience. Not only did he often preach to the masses to fulfill the obligations of his post; he preached to them also out of love, for he was himself a man from a humble and impoverished family. One of his novel ideas, an idea that he put into practice with characteristic courage and straightforwardness, was to address his congregation not in Latin, as had been the custom, but in their own clumsy vernacular, French. This was not the easy task it might appear to be. The French language was not taught in any school. It had no system of grammar, no codification, and no dictionary. Wandering poets or scribes alone could give lessons in its composition. Therefore, the only proper way to learn it was to read its literature and listen to its speech in the streets. Jean Gerson was bursting with innovations. For example, he prevailed upon King Charles VI to make it henceforward mandatory for a criminal to be allowed a confessor and for that confessor to accompany him to the scaffold.

During the years before and after the turn of the century, Jean Gerson preached the state sermons at the Court of Charles VI. Aside from his books and treatises, he wrote and delivered sixty sermons. Those for the Court were generally given in Latin. He took his position as royal mentor seriously; and since he had the attention of the king, of Louis of France, and of Burgundy, Gerson was prompt in attempting to indoctrinate them with his political views. He could see, first and foremost, no reason for war between England and France. Many times he urged the king instead to give away his territories, to cut his realm in half, if need be, rather than bring down upon the heads of the poor—who already suffered from hard work and destitution—the awful miseries of fire, murder, and hatred. Gerson held the king and his nobles directly responsible before God for their greed, their belligerence, and their criminal ambitions. "Too lightly are we used to saying: 'He who has lands will have war!'" Gerson prayed for the sick king, and shamed the court into paying him every sign of homage they had pledged.

In addition to firm convictions against the immorality of war, Gerson also had original ideas on education, as the best student of the century might be expected to have. His essential thesis was this: Learning will not, and in fact cannot, take place where fear is present. The rod, according to Gerson, should not be spared, but utterly discarded. Learning should come from love, the love of the teacher for the child, the child's reciprocal love of the teacher, the child's trust in him, both of which alone could generate that love so ardently to be desired on both their parts—the love of learning for the sake of itself.

Many of Jean Gerson's ideas were applied in the educational program that Louis of France and the Duchess Valentine planned for their sons. They had both heard Jean Gerson say: "Let us not turn a deaf ear, but let us rather pray devoutly, saying: 'Come, Holy Ghost,' and also 'Oh Holy Ghost, sovereign master and physician of the soul, come, come, we entreat thee, come into the heart of thy subjects. Fill us with the light of thy grace. . . .'" Gerson would argue that young intellectuals might study the seven liberal arts at Paris, or ride down to the University of Orléans for their law, or

into Italy to study medicine with great teachers, but where would
they go to study that branch of learning that was above all others?
Where, indeed, were they to learn the rule of life? Men might
travel to the ends of Europe in search of learning. Of what use was
learning without morality? Gerson was fond of citing Saint Bernard:
"Many people know many things, but do not know themselves."
How can one know himself? "Do you not see that you can be
yourself and alone, even when among many, and that among many
how you are alone?" Saint Bernard had asked. Despite this emphasis
upon character, Jean Gerson recommended a life not of contemplation from the start, but rather a life of action in the world. He also
quoted that saint to whom he felt the closest, perhaps, Saint Bona-
venture, who said, "He who wishes to lead a life of contemplation
ought first to lead a life full of activity." Prince Charles of Orléans
was therefore prepared for a double career.

According to Jean Gerson's treatise on the education of a dauphin,
a young prince should spend his first years listening to certain
books that would be read aloud to him every day. Thus he would
learn thoroughly, while his mind was easily influenced, the Bible,
the stories of great kings and great Romans, and the Chronicles
of France. As the Bible says, Jean Gerson would wish the prince
to have a gentle heart so that he might be fit to judge his people,
so that he might learn to distinguish between good and evil. Twenty-
two titles of books are then listed, books that Jean Gerson felt
were essential for the young prince to study from the age of seven
or even before, if he had the capacity of the son of Louis of Orléans.
Among the authors of these books were Saint Augustine, Saint
Bernard, Saint Anslem, Aristotle, Valerius Maximus, Sallust, Ve-
getius, Boethius, Seneca, Suetonius, Livy, John of Holywood, and
Vincent de Beauvais. In his list Jean Gerson emphasized the Bible
and Bible commentaries, the Church Fathers, works of philosophy,
military strategy, Roman and French history, political science,
morality, and physics.

It was from such authors that Charles, the future Duke of Orléans, began to read. The Duchess Valentine very early had beautifully embossed and illuminated books made as gifts for her sons,
Charles and Philip. In addition to the books recommended by the
great Gerson, Charles had the priceless heirlooms in the library of
Louis of France, books that he had inherited from his father, the
erudite King Charles V. This collection boasted gold-illuminated
copies of writers whose principal aim was not morality. Prince

Charles as a young boy had access to the Grail stories, to Merlin, to King Arthur, to Lancelot, to the Life of Julius Caesar, to books on astrology and surgery, to a revision of Ovid—and Ovid-made-moral—and to another book that was to shape his private thoughts, his pattern of thinking by allegory—the celebrated *Romance of the Rose.*

Life in a medieval castle was not all study and lessons from the learned doctor who had been carefully chosen and appointed tutor to Prince Charles. Inside the castle walls was an entire world made up of the living, the statues of the illustrious dead, and the ghosts of robber barons and fabled Crusaders who had died in the Holy Land. Around the large, sunny courtyard were the four wings of the palace where each royal personage had his own chamber, his study, his balcony with intricate metal grilles, his audience hall, his wardrobe and bath closet, and his private chapel. At each corner of the castle were the guardrooms where the watch relieved one another with loud calls and shouted orders. Above there were the towers that wound upward and around their central cylinders to belfries overlooking the valleys, rivers, and thick woods of the fertile countryside. On sunny days there were endless games that children could play up and down the stairs to the towers, in and out the long stone halls, through the secret closets, and along the galleries. On rainy days the huge fireplaces crackled warmly, and the heavy tapestries of unicorns in flower gardens, of royal stag hunts, and of the heroes of Greece and Rome kept in the warmth. The young princes learned to play chess, a silent pleasure that was to amuse them throughout their lives.

History was around them. Great lords before their century had walked along the very halls, stepped with dignity down the oaken stairs into the assembly halls, feasted their friends, drunk deeply after their long boar hunts under the dripping beech trees, de-livered sentences of life and death, and taken solemn oaths to defend their kings. Under the smooth white stones of the chapels lay the ancestresses who had given them birth, and died. Upon these very altar stones had knelt some brave knight who had fallen under the Saracen scimitar and who had had only the time to re-quest that his heart be enclosed in a golden casket and sent home to his "lady" in distant France. On holy days the relics that Saint Louis and his knights had purchased in the East could be seen and reverenced.

For young boys it was a world of history and adventure, for they lived freely in the present while anchored securely to the past. Their lives were their own and not their own. When parties of knights rode across the drawbridge, the young princes were dressed in crimson and green silken gowns embroidered with the three lilies of Orléans. Then they slowly descended the sunlit white steps into the courtyard and spoke gentle words of greeting to accomplished men who knelt before them and kissed their outstretched right hands.

"Be welcome in our castle and at our board, dear cousins. Ask and it shall be yours." The first gesture of a noble prince is to show his generosity to those who serve him. When learned prelates called to pay their respects, Prince Charles was summoned and questioned about his studies. Hour after hour he learned to listen while points of law were discussed.

Prince Charles learned also how to receive gifts and how to acknowledge them. As Count of Touraine he accepted the offerings from the Loire Valley which one day he would rule, learned to appreciate the *rosé* wines and the salmon from this river, learned to know the special taste of its grapes and its own Brie cheeses. He learned also about building and architecture and masonry; for the medieval castle was not only a home but a fortress, designed to be opened quickly and shut tightly. He watched famous artists carving gargoyles from the solid blocks of stone and fitting them under the cornices. He watched the masons laying ceramic tiles under the galleries. He watched the painters at work on the chapel ceiling, painting Saint Gabriel and Saint Michael with the writhing dragon at his feet. Especially he absorbed the cult of the Virgin, who still interceded for man and ruled supreme behind the flashing rose windows of her chapel.

The princes studied music and wrote their own tunes to the rondels they were taught to compose. They listened in the evenings as their accomplished mother recited in her soft Italian accent the lines of the great poet Petrarch, whom she had known when she was a child across the plains of France, across the Alps, in Milan, where the Po passes on its way to the eastern sea. They heard her speak the verses of that other poet from northern Italy whose verses burned into the heart of Prince Charles—the sonorous words and music of Vergil. Whether or not the younger brother, Count Philip of Vertus, heard the somber or flashing words cannot be known, but it is certain that they sank deep into the private thoughts of the older son. Prince Charles heard them so well that they became a part of his own brain, as any other image once seen is graven forever upon the photographic plate of memory.

When the glamorous, the dashing, Louis of France dispatched his messengers to announce his arrival, the castle leaped to new life and gaiety. The gardeners culled their ripest fruits of the season from the espalier trees where they had sweetened safely against the yellow stone walls. The stewards selected their finest wines and tenderly laid them to cool. The cooks prepared their dainties— woodcock and pheasant, venison, trout from the rivers, pasties fit for a king. The stray dogs were kenneled and the sleek palfreys groomed until they glistened, and the silken pennants of Orléans were flown from the towers. The Lady Valentine spent longer hours with her maidens, for she loved her brilliant husband with a passion that burned and was not spent.

As her husband rode into the courtyard, the Lady Valentine sank to her knees. She waited with bowed head until he had leaped from his horse and raised her to her feet. Prince Charles, accustomed to waiting, stood gowned and rehearsed until his lord father summoned him to the august presence. Then the prince knelt also and awaited the blessing and the permission to approach and kiss his lord father's hand. At the age of ten Prince Charles showed the dignity of his rank and that command of his emotions so essential to the future leader of men. Louis of France, Duke of Orléans, did not see himself in his son, despite the dark hair worn to the shoulders, despite the crimson robe, despite the dark eyes. What he saw was a greater strength than his own, a calmer glance, more level eyes, a wider forehead, a gentleness, and, to his surprise, the language of the scholar.

Whether or not he could see this from their conversation, he heard it from the prince's tutor. Prince Charles had made astonishing progress for his age. His Latin was excellent. His knowledge of history was, if not profound, at least very wide. He excelled in grammar, composition, and rhetoric. He had not found his match in chess. His ear for music was good—better than necessary, in fact. He had translated the sentences of Cato. When Prince Charles was instructed to write a composition on Honor and to incorporate in it the wise sayings of Cato and also his catechism, the boy had amazed the tutor. No doubt he also amazed his lord father and his lady mother. Indeed, Louis of France may have received the news with mixed feelings. An appreciation for literature seemed a hereditary trait in the House of Valois; but he required from his

son other traits, far different interests. Louis of France required
from his son the fire and the valor of the warrior, the shrewdness
and the cunning of the politician, the suavity and the unctuousness
of the diplomat. Louis of France may well have frowned when the
tutor first presented him with several vellum pages representing
his son's first gift. Prince Charles, the future Duke of Orléans,
appeared to show promise, even at the age of ten, of becoming a
poet!

How many parents down through the ages have saved and
treasured their children's homework! How many parents have
swelled with pride as they read the halting efforts of their small
sons struggling to express their own or other's thoughts in words!
How many parents have made copies of their son's compositions,
carried them in their wallets, sent them to their uncles of Berry
and Anjou, read them to the king!

Thus, down the ages the homework assignment carefully penned
by Charles of Orléans when he was "only ten," his composition
on Honor, has been passed from hand to hand. How many hundreds
of other boys in 1406 wrote similar exercises can only be imagined.
The poem of Charles remains for posterity to scan with a smile.
His first childish poem remains, for he was the king's nephew:

THE BOOK AGAINST SIN

"Those who to honor aspire
Must the love of God acquire;
Without this intermediary
No good deed can ever be
Done by him who but man is,
If God's grace withholden is.
For our task the Trinity
And Virgin's humility
Do beseech to help us write,
Light our way and lead aright
So our book may useful be
And profit humanity.
Honoring God and serving true
He who writes this book for you
Takes as title to begin
This: *The Book Against Sin.*

"He who puffs himself with pride
Takes as pattern and as guide
The evil angel Lucifer,
(Devils in hell there ever were!)
He who in ugly vainglory
Sought for greater mastery
Than His who created earth,
Out of chaos gave us birth.
The lesson that God draws from this
Shows He bars from heaven's bliss
Him who puffed with pride will be;
God damns his soul eternally.
He who keeps pride secretly
Fosters sins unceasingly.
First are anger and envy,
Avarice and gluttony;
Horrid lust and laziness
Cause a boy to retrogress
To the nature of a beast,
Honorless, to say the least.

"Now have reached the boundary;
Let our book now ended be
That we, named Charles of Orléans, told
When we were just ten years old.
Much more wisdom is your due
Though of years we have too few
To a learned treatise write
Ponderous and erudite.
So pray God in Paradise
That our words assure the wise
And all those that hear us say:
We shall try to live today
So to glory we shall grow.
Now herewith lay down our pen
Praising God above. Amen."

At the age of ten Charles of Orléans had reached a crossroads.
From that day forward he would be two people in one—the public
and the private man. Faithful to the death to the responsibilities and
onerous duties as a feudal lord, he would travel down the roads of

the fifteenth century like a royal automaton that thinks, acts, responds, moves, and speaks as if all his actions had been determined long in advance, like the hour hand of the gigantic clock in the tower of the Hôtel Saint-Paul. Thousands would cheer his passage, would know him as a symbol of dignity and power. Stories of his chivalry would reach the ears of even the lowliest maidens of Lorraine. Thousands would feel secure and comfortable as this great personage lived out his life by the book, in the full light of public gaze.

Charles of Orléans tasted a double joy. With open eyes he willingly assumed the heavy garb of state, prepared to move step by step henceforth and word by measured word, according to protocol. This was his inherited role as the public man. But he tasted a second joy, a pleasure more heady, a power so sweet that it filled his heart and stung behind the level eyes of ceremony. He found a way to hold the whole world in his arms while appearing on the outside to be the solemn marionette specified by feudal etiquette. At the age of ten Charles of Orléans had felt with a gush of gratitude a better way to love the world, closely and secretly. He had also discovered the way to be himself and alone, even among many. He had felt the first quiver of the power hidden within himself. He had been born with the gift of poetry.

⚜   ⚜   ⚜

On August 7, 1401, the Princess Isabelle was conveyed to Calais on the Continent in a large two-masted sailing ship that dropped anchor only a few feet offshore. The princess was brought to land in a rowboat maneuvered by two English sailors. Her escort consisted of merely four ladies, one of whom was her maid Simonette, and with her a dwarf. Each lady-in-waiting wore a high headdress that looked like the folded wings of a white bird. At first sight the Princess Isabelle seemed fully grown—tall, slender, willowy. She wore a dark velvet gown with a long train that her ladies carried behind her. The hem of her gown was bordered with a wide band of ermine. A similar band formed a collar to her dress and met in a V over her chest. The princess was still too young to have a woman's figure. As she stepped from the rowboat, she pressed her left hand tightly over her stomach. In her right hand she held the dwarf's left hand. Her eyes were so downcast that they were almost closed, and her head was bowed forward. Her long, straight hair was combed simply away from her high forehead. It hugged her small head and fell perfectly thin and straight down her back. On her head she wore a circlet of gold with high gold and jeweled ornaments placed at intervals around it. She was a picture of sweetness and girlishness.

Stern-faced soldiers holding pikes were massed silently on either side of her passage. The knights who received her, however, knelt as she approached. She was escorted to the frontier outside the town where the French knights, ambassadors, artists, chroniclers, lords, and princes waited. An especially beautiful tent had been set up for her arrival. Carpets and flowers strewed her path on the French side and up to the English-held town. Louis of France was giving the English a lesson by inference: in France kings are not deposed, nor queens dethroned, nor a princess of the House of Valois treated with disrespect. The great nobles of France were waiting upon her arrival all the way to the gates of Paris. The princess walked step by step, sedately, with dropped eyes, up to the French tent. When she had safely negotiated all but the last few steps, she halted. Then, and only then, the Princess Isabelle covered her face with her thin hands and burst into tears.

At the gates of Paris she was met by the Dukes of Orléans, Berry, and Bourbon, drawn up in full regalia. Again the princess sobbed girlishly. The uncles escorted her through cheering crowds to the Church of Saint-Denis, patron saint of France, where a thanksgiving Mass was celebrated for her safe return. After this ceremony she was escorted home across Paris to the palace of her birth, the Hôtel Saint-Paul. She had no sooner seen its familiar Lion Fountain than she burst into tears again.

The princess brought no jewels other than her crown with her. The question of what had happened to her wedding treasure was endlessly disputed. The French were consoled that she had been returned safely and that she was still a virgin. After two years of negotiations that was triumph enough for everyone except Louis of France.

There was uncertainty in France, and even more in England, as to what had really happened to Richard II. Stories circulated widely. One was that he had been murdered in the underground room at Pontefract Castle by Sir Piers Exton, who had been more or less requested to kill him by Henry IV. This was the Froissart account. Others said that he had been starved to death by order of Henry IV. The Monk of Evesham believed that King Richard had starved himself and expired on St. Valentine's Day. Still other rumors had it that he had escaped to Stirling Castle in Scotland, or that he had gone insane, or that he was assembling an army in Scotland, or that he would come like the wrath of God, at any moment.

Louis of France decided to dispatch his own secret agents to find the truth of the matter. Among others, a private valet of King Charles VI, a Jehan Creton, was sent secretly into England and Scotland to see if he could find King Richard. Henry IV had "Richard's" body brought the length of England, displayed in the towns, and royally entombed in London. However, since the corpse had been covered with molten lead, except for the face, the French could not be absolutely sure that the Princess Isabelle was really a widow. They certainly were not ready to take Henry IV's word for it. Perhaps the uneasy king of England could be baited.

An event of major significance occurred in 1402 that allowed Louis of France to breathe more easily and to give Henry IV more of his attention. Very good news, indeed, came from the Near East. An Oriental khan from Samarkand, a warrior named Tamerlane, had stopped the Ottoman Turks. In fact, he had actually captured the dreaded Bajazet. Within a few months Tamerlane's ambassadors arrived bearing gifts to the Hôtel Saint-Paul. They were most courteously received. Constantinople was safe!

Freed from this worry, with Isabelle safe in Paris, Louis of France found time on October 14, 1403, to draft a letter he had no doubt been meditating for some time. Among other things he told Henry IV:

"As to the trespassing of your above-named Sovereign King Richard and my nephew, may God rest his soul, and whose soul is with God, and about whom you have re-written us that God knew by whom he was killed; God knows it very well, in this much of what you say I agree.

"It is common knowledge that you detained him in your prisons; it is certain that you moved with armed force towards him, in a certain castle where he was, coming from Ireland; there you went towards him, betraying his person; under the pretense of greeting him, betraying his nobles; under the guise of a benefactor, betraying his people; promising them franchises, blinding his clergy—for reasons that are obscure; taking his servants and doing them to death like a tyrant; always keeping in your hands or in the hands of your party the fate of the above-named personage.

"Where is King Richard's life? Where is his body? Is God the only one who knows this? Does the world not know it? Most certain, people know, for yours is the responsibility! If he is alive, then produce him! If he is dead, then he was done to death by you!

"According to your very words, you never thought that I (when once I swore an alliance with you) ever made an exception for your above-named lord, King Richard my nephew, and my most honored lady and niece, Madame the Queen of England; and do not think that I ever excepted them in general!

"Where are the allies of my most feared lord, Monseigneur the King of France, who were not excepted either? . . . How do you suppose that you can so blind the world? Do you think that you can deceive me? Do you believe that by your falsehood and by your malice you can manage to cause dissension between me and my dearly beloved Uncle of Burgundy,—all that too,—all by your allegations?

"Let it be sufficient unto you to have split asunder your own country; for beyond that, with the help of God before me, I shall see that you never cease to be a living wonder—so assure yourself by these words *that I now challenge you and call in question your honor.*"

When princes challenged one another, theirs was not a private affair. Their personal heralds, who enjoyed diplomatic immunity, delivered the challenge in full audience. In addition, open letters were sent to the Pope, to relatives, and to the crowned heads of neighboring states. King Henry IV did not accept the challenge. He preferred not to meet Louis of France in single combat, although the latter had offered to travel to England alone, if need be, in order to put his accusations to trial. King Henry IV replied that Louis of France had no right to challenge a king.

"By God's honor, by the honor of the Holy Virgin, and by Sir Saint George, you lie falsely when you say that we have no pity for our liege lord and Sovereign Lord," replied Henry IV.

In the meantime, at the French Court a second dauphin had been born, a thin, sickly child. The first dauphin, Louis, had died, and in 1401, the year of Isabelle's return, Queen Isabeau had given birth to another baby girl. This one was named Catherine. Her baptism was not celebrated lavishly, for King Charles VI was ill again, and the Princess Isabelle was the chief concern. In later years no one could imagine how Catherine had ever even learned to read and write. Perhaps she had spent part of her childhood in the convent of her sister Marie. Another princess born in such a busy time could really not be accounted of much importance. This event was overshadowed by other births of much greater interest.

Louis of France, aside from his very active political and diplomatic career, had also been rather much in the public eye for his private life. He attended Queen Isabeau so assiduously that there was a good deal of gossip, particularly with King Charles VI so often very ill. Once, in fact, Louis of France and Queen Isabeau, driving in a closed carriage through Paris, were almost killed when their horses bolted and ran out of control. Tongues wagged. Jean Juvénal says that his father spoke to Louis of France, who promised to be more cautious and more moderate. In fact, to show his good intentions, the regent decided to endow the chapel of the Celestine monks there in Paris. Always fond of building, like his uncle of Berry, Louis spared no cost to make this chapel a monument to his name. He ordered tombs to be carved there for himself and for the Lady Valentine. At about this time also, Maître d'Hôtel Montaigu gave Louis a house he and his wife owned in the area of the chapel. It was a little house safely near the city wall, in the Saint-Paul area, where the duke could have privacy. Queen Isabeau bought a house for herself in the same area, a simple hôtel where she could escape from court etiquette occasionally.

In 1403 Queen Isabeau bore another dauphin, the third. This child was not strong, no stronger perhaps than the two preceding sons. He was not fair like his father, but dark and long. He was baptized Charles.

That same year Louis of France was also blessed with another son, an illegitimate one this time. This birth caused a major scandal in Paris. "In plain sight and to the knowledge of everyone" the Duke of Orléans had kidnapped a noble lady named Mariette, had kept her with him until she had borne her child, and then had released her. Everyone knew the story of Louis of France and the Lady of Canny. After the birth of this son, the duke bundled up the infant and carried it openly to Château-Thierry. There he laid the healthy baby boy at his wife's feet and asked her what she wanted him to do with it. The Lady Valentine rose to the occasion nobly. On that day, as on all others, she merited her husband's confidence. She bent down and lifted the baby in her arms, kissed it, and declared that she would receive it and love it as much as her own sons. The Lady Valentine said, however, that she had one regret. She regretted only that she had not borne the child herself. The illegitimate baby, referred to throughout most of his life as the Bastard of Orléans, was baptized Ferdinand. In later years he was referred to as Jean.

Although the Lady Valentine later bore another son named John and a daughter named Marguerite, she seemed always to have an especial preference for the Bastard of Orléans. This child was very different from her own. While it is true that Jean studied well and was apt and quick in the classroom, he was perhaps even quicker outside it. He was a sturdy, rough little boy, very able to defend himself. No doubt because he was loved like one of the family, little Jean was always devoted to his older brother, Charles of Orléans.

Upon his return to Paris, Louis of France made his will. It is dated in that city, October 19, 1403:

> "*Item:* I wish and ordain that my body after my death be carried *all entire* to the Celestine Monks in Paris, and order . . . that I be buried in the chapel which I have built and founded, before the altar of the said chapel and that in whatsoever place that I may be outside Paris that they bring me here and that they bear me on a chariot draped with black cloth and over me the great white cross,—and if it is in Paris then [they are to bear me] without chariot."

The will filled hundreds of pages. The essential was that the lands and titles of Louis of France were to pass entire into the hands and discretion of his oldest son, Charles, and that the Lady Valentine was to have the guardianship of the children until Charles of Orléans had reached the age of fourteen. No mention was made of the bastard Jean. No mention was made of the Queen Isabeau. Louis of France was thirty-two years old.

The following year the Duke of Burgundy, aged seventy-two or seventy-three, died in Brussels. It was an event. It was also a major catastrophe. The long-dreaded day had finally arrived when the House of Orléans would enter the active stage of its struggle to survive and to protect the monarchy. John the Fearless, who had defied Bajazet and lived to boast of it, became Duke of Burgundy. The hour was critical. As Louis of France knew full well, his cousin John had no intention of sharing the regency. The Duke of

Burgundy planned to rule France first of all, and second to destroy all who stood in his way. Louis of France was almost ready. His will was made. The knights of the Golden Porcupine were faithful. In an emergency he could count on John of Alençon. His son Charles of Orléans would soon be married to the former Queen of England, but Prince Charles was still only a boy. Louis of France sat late into the night with his counselors. What he chiefly needed for the next few years was sure allies. He needed bold men who would swear to defend, not the House of Orléans, but the King of France himself.

Even a short study of the map of France sufficed to orient Louis of France and his counselors as to the strategy they should adopt. With John of Burgundy holding lands along the eastern boundaries of the kingdom, from Dijon all the way north and west to Brussels; with King Charles VI and his brother solidly entrenched in central France, from Paris south through the Duchy of Orléans, the vassals they must bind to them could come only from the turbulent South. Therefore, on November 17, 1403, Louis of France signed a treaty of mutual defense with the most feared and most valiant of the southerners, Count Bernard VII of Armagnac. In exchange for his pledge Louis granted his new ally an annual pension of 6,000 francs. Count Bernard was worth every franc of it. He was a formidable warrior.

The Count of Armagnac came from the Rouergue, an area between Languedoc and Guyenne, a territory that he had won back from John of Gaunt and his English forces. Armagnac was a county Bernard VII intended to expand. His home castle was a huge thirteenth century fortress at Gages. Count Bernard VII, descended from the Frankish King Clovis, ruled a territory that Julius Caesar had first conquered and mapped.

Encouraged by this unexpected alliance with the Crown, Count Bernard returned to Gascony, or Armagnac, where he promptly wiped out the younger branch of his family. He captured the rival Count of Pardiac, shut him up in a cistern on a diet of bread and water, thus giving him ten to twelve days in which to expire. Then Count Bernard pursued Pardiac's sons, who were persuaded to surrender and beg for clemency from him. The boys were brought before Count Bernard on Holy Thursday in 1404. Their uncle knelt before Armagnac and sued for their pardon.

Count Bernard, from his state seat in the Archbishop's Palace, replied in his Gascon dialect, "Uncle, you went to get them of your own free will, by which if they want to throw themselves upon our mercy, it amounts to the same thing."

"Sire," pleaded the uncle, "it is a plea for mercy to beg pardon thus."

"Asking for mercy is something else again," insisted Count Bernard.

"Very well," consented the uncle. "They beg for pardon and for mercy."

Count Bernard, who had already decided what he wanted to do anyway, had the two youngsters led away separately. The younger, taken to Rodelle Castle where his father had starved in the cistern, was so struck by its awful aspect that he begged to be untied and helped down from his horse. His guards refused. At that, the boy toppled forward in the saddle, stone dead. His older brother was escorted under heavy guard to Brousse Castle, where he was blinded the instant he entered its dungeon. A red-hot bowl was held before his eyes. Then he was enclosed in the underground chamber of the dungeon and deprived of aid or medical care. He languished a certain time and then died "burdened with misery," agree the horrified French chroniclers.

These swift murders left only the two daughters of the dead Count of Pardiac. They and their husbands brought suit against Count Bernard before King Charles VI. Count Bernard won, of course, but it was an interesting case and might have become very famous had it not been eclipsed by a much more important and sensational one. Nonetheless, Count Bernard VII is generally said to have brought the House of Orléans his violence, his military skill, his patriotism, and "the malediction of France." The court ladies in Paris noted that his second child was a daughter named Bonnie who had been born on February 17, 1400. Count Bernard's wife was a very fine and pious daughter of Berry.

While Louis of France was binding to him that unscrupulous "robber baron" who could at any moment most ruthlessly second his ambitions, he was also reputed to be hand in glove with the queen. At one point they had together managed a *coup d'état* by supposedly seizing the king's keys and carrying off the Royal Treasury. Duke John of Burgundy prepared for open war. Louis of France continued to dominate the court and to make his plans for a showdown. In particular, he spared no effort to curry favor with the Parisians by treating them to festivals, tournaments, and morality plays given in great splendor in the squares of the city. His political alliance with the queen was twisted by the Burgundians into another kind of alliance. It was whispered more and more loudly that he and Queen Isabeau were more than friends. When the queen became pregnant again, it was more than whispered.

By 1405 the situation was so serious that an Augustine monk, Jacques le Grand, dared preach openly to the court on the subject of adultery.

"Great Queen, I should like my duty to be in accord with the passion I have not to broach any subject here but that which is agreeable to you; but your salvation is dearer to me than your good graces: and even were I to fall into the misfortune of displeasing you, it is still impossible for me not to declaim against the sway which the goddess of languor and voluptuousness has established in your heart. She has, as her inseparable companions, high living and moral turpitude, which makes it so that day and night are spent in dissolute living. . . ."

One of the ladies attendant upon the queen interrupted: "We are astonished at your audacity."

Jacques le Grand continued, "And I—I am even more astonished that you have the temerity to deliver your bodies to such disorders as I shall reveal to the king whenever he shall be pleased to hear me."

Then a courtier warned the preacher, "If my words are believed by the king, you shall be punished for your insolence!"

"It is true that that would be easy," retorted the monk, "and if I am not mistaken, you are the most suitable messenger that one could select for the execution of so cowardly a resentment and so black a revenge."

Thus, from 1405, other scandals concerning Louis of France were well known. How much real truth there was to such allegations cannot be known, however. Counselors who were wise, moral, and experienced, men such as Montaigu and Jean Juvénal, drew closer to Louis of France. His allies, the old ones like John of Alençon, and the new ones like Bernard VII of Armagnac, did not flinch in their absolute loyalty. Perhaps they knew the truth. Perhaps they did not care. Perhaps they considered such a sermon only propaganda on the part of Burgundy, and servile copyings on the parts of his college of historians and diplomats. Sooner or later there would have to be a decision. France was not large enough for both Louis of France and John of Burgundy. When the final encounter was reached, it would be interesting to see whose part Jean Gerson would dignify with his approval, if either. Jean Gerson was a protégé of the Duke of Burgundy. What evidence would he give as to the guilt or innocence of Louis of France? What conclusion would he, the conscience of the century, have reached?

Meanwhile, the boy Charles of Orléans put aside his compositions on Honor. While his two brothers, his sister, and the bastard Jean watched gravely from the castle courtyard, Prince Charles, the oldest of the male heirs to the House of Valois, left his study in the sunny wing of the castle. With the right and duty of the oldest, he first donned the elaborate robes of state and, laying aside childish things, rode out into the world for the second impressive ceremony of his life. He prepared to wed his cousin Isabelle, the tall, thin child who had already lost a throne. The Pope had sent ambassadors bearing a dispensation, for the children were first cousins. In the event that the other sickly dauphins died before their insane father, Prince Charles would have a right to the throne that would through this marriage be doubly secure.

The wedding of Charles of Orléans and the Queen of England was held in the Cathedral of Senlis on June 29, 1406. It was a double ceremony, for a Dauphin Jean was wedded at the same time to a Jaqueline of Bavaria from the Duchy of Burgundy. Louis of France had consented to this compromise, knowing or surmising that this dauphin would not live long either—a guess that proved to have been correct.

It was a strange wedding ceremony for four children. It may be that Charles of Orléans never had another opportunity during his lifetime to speak of Jacoba of Bavaria, but he must often have remembered how she looked, a little girl dressed up for her marriage ceremony in the robes of an adult. This little princess was to have, during her short and turbulent career, the strange honor of once saving the Kingdom of France, quite unintentionally, however.

Jean Juvénal has described the ceremony at Senlis succinctly, and he was probably an eyewitness: "And wept hard the above-named Isabelle, which Lady was of fairly good age, as from about twelve to thirteen years, and Charles at the above-named time was only eleven years old. And were held the wedding celebrations at Senlis great and notable."

Charles of Orléans became the husband of a weeping bride. Throughout the kingdom people pitied the Princess Isabelle, assuming that the cause of her tears was her humiliation in being married to a count after having once been the Queen of England. The chroniclers give this as the reason. In any event, she wept as she stood beside her eleven-year-old husband. The Lady Isabelle could not have known that her boy husband possessed a certain secret treasury that, once unlocked, would quickly dry any girl's tears. All present at the ceremony noted the extraordinary beauty of the Princess Isabelle. Even a boy of eleven must have been proud.

Although the historians had no access to state secrets, they concluded from this marriage that Richard II of England was dead. No one of the princes present ever mentioned the subject to them, of course. Prince Charles of Orléans, for example, would witness in person most of the great events of the next decades. There would be no secret he would not know at first hand. As for the great happenings in which he personally did not participate, he would have immediate access to eyewitness reports, as well as to letters and archives that would subsequently be sedulously destroyed. However, Prince Charles had been well trained for his role as future Duke of Orléans. Never once would he let fall a word about the true fate of Richard II. Never once would he even refer to the second great mystery of the century—a mystery, in fact, that upon closer inspection over the ages becomes more unfathomable than the death of King Richard II.

I V [*1407–1411*]   THE PRINCESS ISABELLE could not have wept for a very long time. Instead of being surrounded by foreigners who disliked her, who murdered her King Richard, who whisked her away from castle to gloomy fortress, who tricked her into identifying some valet as the king, who used her as a pawn in their political advancement, who robbed her of her jewels—instead of all this, the princess lived safely in a beautiful castle surrounded by the rolling, emerald fields of central France. Not only were there sunshine and loveliness all about her. All about her breathed of love.

Her new mother was quite different from her real mother, Queen Isabeau. The Duchess Valentine was gentle and affectionate. She was more cultured and more intelligent than Queen Isabeau. She was also deeply in love with one of the handsomest men of the century, who by a stroke of great good fortune happened to be her own husband. She loved him so deeply that she had seen his philandering as a manifestation of his love for her. She had borne him four children who loved their father as she did. She was raising his illegitimate son, Jean, and creating between herself and this youngster a bond of love that would make all future historians pause and marvel. The Duchess Valentine was no ordinary woman, any more than her husband was a man of ordinary talents or average attractions.

For the first time in her life the Princess Isabelle could unbend, could relax, could sigh or smile when she felt like it, could bask in the circle of admiration that, although youthful, was nevertheless definitely masculine. Prince Charles was her lord and her servant who attended upon her every wish with bended knee. His little brothers, Count Philip, Count John, and the baby Jean formed her Court of Love. The little sister Marguerite, who the records show was especially petted and adored by her big brother Charles, no doubt followed in the wake. The Princess Isabelle had become a new sort of queen, the queen of hearts.

Prince Charles had begun to write verses in earnest. The Lady Isabelle was not seduced by the beauty of her new surroundings alone, not melted by the love of her new family alone, nor alone wooed by their eager acceptance of her. The Princess Isabelle was wooed with words. What lovely young lady of thirteen or fourteen could resist the dreamy verses of a boy who has it in his heart to become the greatest lyric poet of the Middle Ages? The words Prince Charles began to form into song for his lovely bride appear in writing—perhaps written years later—written neatly and carefully in his book, for poetry is also "emotion recollected in tranquillity." There they remain today, in the handwriting of their author, in Paris.

Prince Charles loved his mother, Valentine. Hardly a year went by from his childhood to the grave that he did not compose his Valentine Day's greeting to love, so tenderly, so gracefully, that what had been in antiquity a celebration of the re-greening of spring became a feast day in honor of love itself. It was the Princess Isabelle who awoke Charles of Orléans to the love of a boy for a girl, and also to the love of a man for the woman he has married. "With what good gifts is my beloved blessed," mused Prince Charles as he gazed at the slender girl, the smooth dark hair, the deep dark eyes, the white, white skin of the lady who would one day rule the Duchy of Orléans beside him. "True beauty, very rich in youthfulness," sang the words. "Fresh beauty, wholly new in gentleness." And her especial qualities: laughter, proud carriage, slim body, modestly lowered eyes, delight, nobility. "Gestures she does are done so graciously . . . whether she sings or dances blissfully. . . . Goodness and Honor, with them Gentleness . . . Fill her full heart. . . ." And the conclusion that all boys who are in love reach as soon as did Charles of Orléans: "And sure think I God sent her knowingly. . . . For such rich treasure has He utterly . . . Showered on her person so unsparingly. . . . With what good gifts is my beloved blessed!"

Prince Charles laid his best gifts at the feet of his beloved. Their first summer passed like a dream of sunlit patches under red and green apple trees. The harvest was garnered. The leaves turned yellow overhead and red along the vines. The grapes grew swollen and red and perfumed. The fall came in with a flash of red costumes and a blare of the hunting horn. Prince Charles and the Princess Isabelle lived on in a dream of love that brought tears to their eyes, blushes to their cheeks, smiles to their lips. Side by side they knelt each morning at the altar of the Lady Chapel and prayed. Side by side they rode their dappled palfreys down the country roads. Side by side they danced to the music of lute and viol, sat on velvet cushions before the crackling fireplaces, listened to the merry and the sad songs of their minstrels, read together the stories of Lancelot and Elaine, of Troilus and Cressida, and of Percival and the Holy Grail. The princess began to teach Charles English. She told him of Westminster Hall and the Tower of London. Together they read the new books of the English Chaucer. Their hands touched as they turned the pages. Their lips met. Prince Charles whispered the words of love to his beautiful wife. A year went by, and their bodies grew and bloomed and began to long for love too.

Whether it struck by day, or whether by night, the crash was the same. Imagine a blue sky split with thunder, streaked with the hideous, red, blinding, forked lightning! Imagine the halting words from the trembling, cracked, bleeding, parched lips of the messenger! And through the echoing castle halls the screams of the Duchess of Orléans, hands raised to her mouth, eyes wide with horror, fingers over her eyes, palms outward, shrieking with an agony that struck her like a hammer hitting her naked abdomen. "Louis! Louis!" And the death bell begins its solemn toll! *Dong! Dong!* every two seconds from castle to church to castle throughout Orléans, throughout France, to Milan, to Rome, to England. Louis of France has been murdered! The first prince of the blood has been chopped to pieces—he who wanted to be buried "all entire"—chopped to pieces with an ax until his lovely hands lie in the gutter and his brains streak out over the filthy, sewer-stained midnight streets of Paris. Dear God! What a way for a prince to die!

After the marriage of Prince Charles and the Princess Isabelle there had been a lull in the hostilities between Louis of France and John Duke of Burgundy. Each duke had departed pompously to lead an army, Burgundy against Calais and Louis against the English in Guyenne. Neither lord had succeeded. Both returned to Paris convinced that the evils of the English occupation had been caused, or at least were being prolonged, by the other. The old Duke of Berry attempted to reconcile them in some formal way that would be publicly witnessed and legally binding. Early in November of 1407 Queen Isabeau was confined to her hôtel in the Rue Vieille-du-Temple in Paris. At about the same time Louis of France was ill in his castle of Beauté. John of Burgundy, prompted by the uncle of Berry, paid Louis a visit and offered him his sincere wishes for a speedy recovery. On a Sunday, November 20th, the Duke of Berry persuaded both haughty lords to attend Mass with him at the Augustines in Paris. After the service he even managed to talk each one into humbling himself before the other. On that memorable Sunday Louis of France swore a solemn, binding oath never to break the peace with his cousin of Burgundy. He also vowed he would from that day forward feel and show only friendship toward Burgundy. Then John of Burgundy swore likewise. The uncle of Berry joined their hands and bore witness to their pledges.

On the following Tuesday both nephews dined at their relative's hôtel, where they performed the feudal ceremony of taking spices and wine together. Thus their pact was confirmed, and there was no more reason to fear an outbreak of civil war in the Kingdom of France. John of Burgundy invited his relative Louis of France to dine with him on the following Sunday. Louis of France thanked him kindly and accepted the invitation.

Meanwhile, the Queen Isabeau had been delivered of a stillborn child. She was said to be particularly grieved at the loss of this baby. Therefore, on Wednesday evening, the day after he had partaken of the spices and wine with his cousin of Burgundy, Louis of France left his own hôtel in the Saint-Paul area and went to spend the evening with the convalescent queen.

In his own household Louis of France employed two hundred forty servants, plus three jesters and a female fool. On this particular Wednesday he took as an escort only three valets who carried torches and two grooms who jogged along after him, both astraddle the same horse. Louis rode a palfrey. He had only a few streets to cross from his house of the Poterne Saint-Paul, close to the Barbette Gate, over to the queen's hôtel. He left orders at home that his personal retinue of men-at-arms were to fetch him at midnight. He jogged along the cobblestones in the cold November night. He was singing.

Louis of France and Queen Isabeau dined and spent the evening together. Around nine o'clock they were informed that a messenger had come from the king. The message was for Louis, the king's brother. The messenger was duly admitted. He was one of the king's bedchamber valets, a man named Courteheuse. Both Louis of France and the queen knew him, at least by sight. Courteheuse told them that the king requested his brother's attendance at once and that the business was urgent. Louis of France leaped to his feet. He did not even bother to buckle on his sword. He did not wait for his cloak or his hood. He went just as he was, in the long, silken cassock that he wore every evening. He called for his palfrey and was out the door before the grooms were on their horses.

The three valets grabbed for torches and set out alongside their lord. They were on foot. Louis caused them to run, for he was anxious. The king had said that the business was "serious and urgent." It was a dark night, that 23rd of November. Aside from the streaks of smoky light from the torches, there was not another glimmer in any of the streets. The sky was overcast. All the hôtels, or private residences, were bolted and barred for the night. The streets were deserted.

The main thoroughfare of that section of Paris is the Rue Saint-Antoine, which runs through the Hôtel Saint-Paul area on its way from the Bastille Fortress to the Louvre Fortress. The Rue Vieille-du-Temple began on the north side of the Rue Saint-Antoine, from which it curved off to the northeast until it came to the Barbette Gate and the wall that encircled Paris. As one went down the Rue Vieille-du-Temple, that is to say, northeastward, with the Rue Saint-Antoine and the Seine River behind, one passed the Church of the Blancs-Manteaux on the left, the Rue des Rosiers on the right, passed across the wide street of the Francs Bourgeois, and then came to the Rue Barbette, which was the next street to the right. Louis of France rode down the street called Vieille-du-Temple, in the direction of the Porte-Barbette. He was humming under his breath.

Suddenly, from the dark corner of a side street, about twenty armed men rushed at him. They lurched forward in the shadows cast by the three torches. Their swords clanged against stone in the still night. The horse that bore the two grooms sidestepped curiously, shied, then bolted and went galloping loudly away down the street. Louis of France halted his palfrey, peered through the darkness, made out the shape of his assailants, saw that they were masked, and took them for thieves.

"I am the Duke of Orléans," he called out to them.

"That's what we're looking for!" one of them replied.

Louis of France had barely time to realize that it was the leader of the group who had replied when an ax fell across the pommel of his saddle. It severed his right hand at the first stroke. Then the masked leader raised the ax again. The second time he struck the duke on the head. That blow toppled him from his palfrey. The third blow crushed his skull. His brains oozed out onto the damp cobblestones. As Louis of France fell to the ground, one of his pages dropped his torch and threw himself across his lord's body. The leader dispatched the page with one swing of the ax.

Then the assassins dragged the body of the mangled duke across to a stone marker at the intersection. They lighted a lantern and bent over to examine the corpse, to make a positive identification and assure themselves that Louis of France was really dead. The red glow of the lantern lighted the dark cloaks that covered their armor. Their leader wore a red riding hood that came down over his face. Even then, when he could see that the duke's brains trailed along the cobblestones where they had dragged him, the leader took a last precaution. Once more he raised his ax and brought it down upon the duke's head. Then he signaled to his men. The party fled as fast as they could go. Again the street was deserted.

At the moment of his death Louis of France did not cry out, did not call for assistance. He apparently realized the futility of such a cry. His little page, on the other hand, screamed as he lay sprawling over his master, waiting for the ax to fall and silence him. His wail aroused the neighborhood. Lights appeared in the nearby hôtels. Heads leaned out upper-story windows as the assailants ran up the street. Gates were unbarred. Servants started to run out into the Rue Vieille-du-Temple. It took them some time to find the duke's body, first because of the darkness, and second because the murderers had blocked off the access to it with wooden entanglements. Finally the Duke of Orléans was recognized by the three golden fleurs-de-lis on his crimson silk robe. Carefully his remains were laid on a sheet, along with his right hand and whatever else could be scooped up. Then he was deposited before the altar in the chapel of the Hôtel de Rieux.

Messengers were then dispatched to the king, to Queen Isabeau, and to his own home at the Poterne. Within minutes riders and a heavily armed escort spurred across the city and out its gates on the way to Château-Thierry.

King Charles was himself the night he heard the news of his brother's cruel murder. He was deeply afflicted, so broken by grief, in fact, that those near him expected a relapse at any second. As the terrible news spread through the city, worried lords and barons hurried to the king's side. Perhaps an attempt against his life would follow. Within the hour Queen Isabeau had herself transported safely, under heavy escort, to her husband's side. The Provost Marshal of Paris was ordered to close the city gates. He sent out patrols from the Bastille. Martial law prevailed that night. By daybreak the lords and barons had assembled at the nearby Church of the Blancs-Manteaux and at the hôtel of King René of Sicily. All hastened to protest their innocence and to insist that their residences be searched for any trace of the twenty men, especially of the man in the red riding hood whom the neighbors had glimpsed.

By the middle of the morning the mutilated body of Louis I, Duke of Orleans, had been laid in state at the Church of the Blancs-Manteaux, only a few blocks from the spot where he had been assassinated. The king and queen, attended by the peers of the realm, passed before his bier to pay their last respects. The old uncle of Berry was bowed in grief. He had raised Louis of France. So was the cousin, John Duke of Burgundy. No one could explain what had occurred. The provost marshal was dispatched first to find and question the Lord of Canny. It was supposed that he had finally taken a jealous husband's revenge for the kidnapping of his wife, Mariette. To everyone's surprise the Lord of Canny had a watertight alibi. He could not have assassinated the Duke of Orléans.

The barons, assembled in open session, were nonplussed. All they could think of to do was to authorize the provost to search for the murderers in the very hôtels of the mightiest peers of the realm. One by one, around the hall, each great duke gave his assent. Even the uncles of Berry and Bourbon acceded to this degradation. When it came to the turn of John Duke of Burgundy, that powerful lord hesitated. With all eyes upon him, he grew pale. Then he rose to his feet and asked to speak privately with the Duke of Berry.

"Blinded by evil passions," he muttered to the Duke of Berry, "I charged Raoul d'Octonville, the treasurer my cousin of Orléans caused to be impeached, to kill him." Then drawing himself up haughtily, John the Fearless withdrew from the council. The Duke of Berry announced that the mystery had been solved. The meeting was adjourned until the next morning. During the night the fearful took cover. Again riders were dispatched to head off young Charles of Orléans, who by that time was riding posthaste toward Paris—surely and obviously toward his death. With his usual gallantry John of Alençon ordered three hundred of his best knights with a company of archers to set out for the young Charles. They were told never to leave his side and also to stop him from entering the city. The Duke of Orléans was dead. The new Duke of Orléans was thirteen years old. He was in great danger of a similar or a worse death.

On the morning of the second day the council reconvened at the Hôtel de Nesle. They had hardly begun their session when to their amazement John Duke of Burgundy entered the room, accompanied by his vassal, the Count of Saint-Pol. He had regained his composure. He glanced unblushingly about the hall and proceeded to his usual seat at the king's right hand. Before he could take his place, however, the old Duke of Berry rose and commanded the Count of Saint-Pol to arrest Burgundy in the name of the king.

John the Fearless laughed in their faces. How could they think to arrest the most powerful baron in all Christendom? Turning on his heel, he strode from the hall, remounted, and rode back to his own hôtel. Minutes later he burst through its portals, followed by a party of Burgundian knights among whom were Octonville, the man in the red riding hood, and his twenty accomplices. At full speed their party galloped across Paris, followed not far behind by the Admiral of Brabant, the king's deputy, and 120 knights from the House of Orléans.

The Burgundians had the advantage of surprise. They were first through the northern gates of the city. Once out in the open country they halted to destroy a bridge on the main road to the North. This saved their necks. For thirty-five hours the pursuers followed as fast as they could, stopping only at post stations for fresh mounts. They halted only at the frontiers of Burgundy. Duke John slackened speed once he had set foot on home soil. It was eleven o'clock in the morning when he rode through the streets of his town of Bapaume. The clocks were just chiming the hour. He ordained that henceforward all the chimes in Burgundy should strike at eleven every day and that this peal should be called The Angelus of the Duke of Burgundy. Duke John assigned a stronghold to Octonville and his men. Then he rode jauntily home to Lille, very satisfied with himself. He would like to see the thirteen-year-old son of Louis try to stop him now—the thirteen-year-old who wrote poetry. He would really like to see that!

Prince Charles, soon to be emancipated as Duke Charles of Orléans, was, in fact, thirteen years old. That did not halt his advance toward Paris. Nor did the fear of his own assassination stop his progress. Within a few short days, while John of Burgundy hid in the North, the future Duke of Orléans made his first official entrance into Paris. It was a sensational one. The crowds gasped. The young son of Orléans was dressed in black from head to foot. He rode through the streets in stony silence, his strong jaw set. He made no bows and acknowledged no greeting. His head was bowed in grief. He rode his black horse at a walk. He had no guards with him.

At some distance behind the young Charles of Orléans came his party of men-at-arms. Behind them came an open litter draped in black on which was seated the Duchess Valentine, entirely swathed in black. On the sides of her chariot were written in large letters: "Nothing is more mine! No longer is anything mine!" Behind her came the new Duchess of Orléans, the Princess Isabelle, also swathed in black. This somber procession crossed the city in dead silence and entered the Hôtel Saint-Paul, where the three mourners prostrated themselves at the king's feet. Charles of Orléans then uttered one word: "Justice."

The king promised weakly to avenge the crime. He promised that there would be a trial. He claimed that there would be a thorough investigation. He said that Duke John would be summoned, would be requested to appear, would perhaps be asked . . . Duke Charles understood the situation. Probably the only way by which John the Fearless could ever be made answerable would be by force. However, force would be the last resort. What would Louis of France have done in a similar situation? First, he would have assured the safety of his family. Second, he would have looked to his allies. Third, he would have met with his lawyers. Therefore, Duke Charles of Orléans retired, no longer to Château-Thierry, but this time to the new Duchy of Orléans his father had so recently purchased. Charles of Orléans took his family southward to Blois Castle on the Loire. It was to Blois Castle on the Loire River that he summoned his vassals and his allies. At the age of thirteen, Charles of Orléans went home for the first time.

The ovation that the members of the family received as they rode into the Duchy of Orléans, the lands that Prince Charles would rule outright in a year or when the king emancipated him, was enough to warm their hearts. The young Charles realized, perhaps for the first time, the wisdom and the greatness of his father. He saw, perhaps for the first time, as he rode into the city of Blois, the staunch heart of France. As Duke of Orléans he would rule many castles and many cities, none of which would ever be a home in the true sense of the word. Blois Castle was home, a home on the Loire River prepared by Louis of France. There on the Loire, that silver river that cuts France in half, Charles of Orléans would make a stand that would strike respect, and then fear, into the enemies.

To Blois Castle the loyalists assembled—the uncles of Berry and Bourbon, the Count of Alençon, and Bernard VII of Armagnac. The lawyers came with their university-bred clerks, with their law-books and their precedents, with their vellum and their scribes and their coypists. At Blois Castle during the last months of 1407 and early into 1408, the nobles of Orléans and their counselors mapped out their strategy and drew up their briefs. They heard that Duke John had thrown himself upon the king's mercy. After consultation with his lawyers he had changed his plea from "blinded with evil passions" to "assassination justified in order to protect the state." It was a nice question. The lawyers shook their heads and rubbed their hands. It was in many respects the case of Brutus, Cassius, and Julius Caesar. The pleas would be heard in open court at the Louvre Fortress, before the king, in 1408. Doctor Jean Petit would address the court for Burgundy. He would be answered by Doctor Serisy for Orléans. All France would be present. The fifteenth century witnessed two great trials and a retrial. The first, hinging upon the issue of justifiable homicide, was heard in Paris in 1408.

On March 8, 1408, Doctor Jean Petit, Doctor of Theology of the University of Paris, harangued the court in a speech based upon the rules of oratory and rhetoric as established by Cicero and Quintillian. He asserted categorically, and made some attempt to prove, that Louis of France had been a tyrant, that John Duke of Burgundy had every right to rid the state of such a despot, that murder for the good of the kingdom is always justifiable—that it was not only justified in the present case but even praiseworthy—and finally that the Duke of Burgundy should be rewarded by the king for his action. His speech was recorded by Monstrelet, chronicler for the Duke of Burgundy.

The Duchess Valentine listened to this speech with a growing horror equaled only perhaps by that of Queen Isabeau. Charles of Orléans listened, too, although with the usual idealism and optimism of the young he could not believe his ears, could not understand the sympathetic nods of the listeners. Instead, his mind kept remembering his dear father. His thoughts flashed back to the description the learned biographer, Christina of Pisa, had written of Louis of Orléans in her book on the life of Charles V. The lady writer, imported from Italy, had written only incidentally about Louis of France. It seems that she had dedicated one of her books to that great prince, and then had waited upon him among the dozens of suitors in his outer office—a poor writer asking favors of the greatest prince of Europe. Contrary to her fears, Louis of France had been neither too proud nor too important to acknowledge her admiration. He had instructed one of his secretaries to ask the lady to step inside. He had looked up from the masses of papers on his desk, had taken the trouble to smile at her, had thanked her for the book, and had asked her to accept a purse from him. Then he had himself handed her the purse and had said good-bye. The lady writer, recently a widow and therefore obliged to support herself and her children by her books, had inserted in her biography that portrait of Charles V's son. What a kind, what a handsome, what a charming person, she had said! How humble are truly great men! Only the truly great have time for the small!

Doctor Serisy delivered an impassioned oration before the court. Despite his eloquence and his arguments, the case had been lost to fear before he began to orate. His speech was heard, however. It was not only heard: it was also entered in the Royal Archives. From somewhere would have to come another champion if Louis of France was ever to be avenged. His son had acted by the book. He had followed legal procedure. He had asked for retribution and for justice. The latter was a concept in which he firmly believed, as he would one day say and record for posterity. Whatever decision the court made as a result of this trial, however easily they condoned murder, it was obvious that they were only blackening their own names. If Burgundy was allowed to go scot-free, if he was not punished, then thinking people all over Europe—however much they might dread his power—would hold Burgundy in disrepute. Immediate humiliation would result to the House of Orléans, but it would not last. Therefore, by all standards of feudal law, the brief of Doctor Serisy was restrained and moderate. The House of Orléans sought only justice. Charles of Orléans did not believe in capital punishment.

The Duchess Valentine and her son Charles of Orléans lost their case before the court. Some sort of official pardon ceremony would be enacted, but it would be a mere formality. To the consternation of Queen Isabeau, to the despair of the Lady Valentine, John the Fearless was accorded formal letters of immunity.

Charles of Orléans had lost his first great political and personal contest. He did not, however, lose his allies. The uncles of Berry and Bourbon rallied to this great nephew who had conducted himself honorably and with great dignity. The chroniclers had only to look upon the face of the future Duke of Orléans to write as an afterthought on their vellum pages that John the Fearless had acquired the "undying hatred" of Charles of Orléans. His friends and counselors consoled each other with the hope that the youngster Charles had lost only the first round.

Meanwhile, the young Charles returned to Blois Castle with his mother. He returned this time to the loving arms of his young wife. Charles of Orléans had passed the threshold from boyhood to manhood. Those who knew him began to have an idea that when strength was required, this prince had only to dip into his reserves. If John the Fearless did not assassinate him soon, he would meet another kind of adversary than the Duke Louis whom he had disgraced and ambushed.

The Lady Valentine, abandoning herself to the violence and excesses of her grief, was one of the persons who misjudged Charles of Orléans. She found him not violent enough. No doubt acceeding to her reproaches and to the extent of her hatred, the boy began to exercise at arms day after day at Blois Castle. His mother was consumed with fury. Her grief did not lessen with the passing months. It increased. Her violence was fed by her mournful voice, her black garments, and her device, "Nothing is more mine. No longer is anything mine." In the months after the cruel reversal of the trial, she became ill. It was obvious from her behavior that she no longer wanted to live, that she had lost all reason to live in losing her husband and her pride. Summoning her sons to her deathbed, she obliged each one to swear before her that he would never rest until he had avenged the assassination of his father.

As she bade farewell to her sons, the Duchess Valentine drew the Bastard Jean of Orléans to her. "This son," she said, "is better endowed and more apt to avenge us than any of my other sons." Such dying words from a beloved mother would seem sufficient to plunge a son into despair. The Lady Valentine died in Blois Castle in the early days of December, only eight months after the trial. By her orders her heart was taken to Paris and placed in her husband's tomb. Her body was interred splendidly and elaborately by her son Charles in the Church of Saint-Laumer at Blois. From the castle walls her son could look down to this church with its gray spires that rise from the level of the Loire up to the foundations of the castle. He was now an orphan, and responsible for the welfare of a feudal house. He alone could protect the younger children until they were grown. Now that his marriage had been consummated, his position was unique. He was the prince who had stripped from the future Henry V that lady he had hoped to make a second time the Queen of England!

The solemn but mock ceremony of pardon took place in the Cathedral of Chartres on March 9, 1409. The king, the queen, the dauphin, and the rest of the royal family had arrived in Chartres toward the middle of February. The terms of the peace treaty between the Dukes of Burgundy and Orléans had been drawn up, approved, proclaimed, and memorized long before the date of the actual ceremony. Martial law prevailed. Each duke was allowed a certain escort, a certain number of weapons, a certain number of counselors and attendants. The straight roads into Chartres were heavy with rain and deeply marked with wheel tracks and horses' hooves. Along the roadside the daffodils bloomed like nodding yellow bells, and the woods were blue with grape hyacinth. The sky was overcast, but the wet west wind of spring blew the clouds along briskly so that the sun shone brightly at intervals. Notre-Dame de Chartres rose straight into the air from the flat plain—massive, slender-spired, elegant in color and line—with her Norman tower and her higher Gothic tower fingering the sky.

A wooden platform had been constructed from the central portal all the way to the main altar. There a throne had been raised with seats for the royal party. From their standing room on the stone floor the assembled spectators would neither see nor hear what transpired on the platform, no matter how hard they listened or craned their necks. They would not even see the king, but only the jeweled crucifix upon which the two dukes would be constrained to swear—or rather to perjure themselves.

The ceremony began at two hours before noon, while the sun was still behind the church, casting its rays through the stained glass of the ambulatory, throwing ruby splotches from the windows that depicted the life of Charlemagne and pale blue splotches and yellow splotches upon the stones of the floor. The whole cathedral was bathed in a vague bluish light that changed suddenly to long ruby and orange shafts when the cloud passed by.

Even at such a humiliating moment in his life, when he was about to betray his oath to his dying mother, Charles of Orléans, must have felt the thrilling beauty of Notre-Dame de Chartres. As he and his brother Count Philip passed down the central aisle, perhaps he glanced up to the western windows on his left side and saw the magnificent head of Christ upheld by the doves of the Holy Ghost—a tender Christ in green sleeves, brown toga, a bearded Christ with a brilliant sapphire halo behind his pale and downcast head.

In front of the king the Duke of Burgundy's lawyer droned the words that had been written long before and carefully memorized: "Most greatly feared and most sovereign lord, here is His Highness the Duke of Burgundy, your cousin, who presents himself before you like a faithful and humble subject . . . for the deed which was committed on the person of His Highness of Orléans, by his will and at his orders, for your own good and for the good of the kingdom, as he is here ready to declare if that is agreeable to you. He has learned that your displeasure has fallen upon him ... he is afflicted that this should be so. . . . He begs you to banish this displeasure from your heart. . . ."

Then from his mouth Burgundy to the king: "Sire, this I beg you."

After this, the queen, the dauphin plead with the king to forgive His Highness of Burgundy and to render unto him the favor and friendship his loyalty and obedience had always deserved. Their suit is granted. Then the Duke of Orléans is entreated to banish all animosity. Count Philip of Vertus is likewise entreated to banish all animosity.

Then from his mouth Burgundy to the Duke of Orléans and to his brother: "Yes, very dear cousins, this I beg you."

The king then says: "My very dear nephews, approve and sanction that which has been done. Accord unto him your full and entire pardon."

The young princes then answer one after the other: "My very dear lord, in accordance with your commands, I accept, I approve, and I sanction all that which has been done, and I pass over all things done by him."

Then all the princes of the blood royal promise and swear these things with their hands between the hands of the king, upon the cross of our Lord and upon the Holy Gospel.

The Burgundian chronicler Monstrelet says that the two princes of Orléans stood behind the king during the ceremony and that they wept. Other historians repeat this story and add that Charles of Orléans forgot his lines and had either to be prompted or urged to say them by the king himself. It is unlikely, however, that any chronciler witnessed the ceremony. The platform had been erected to ensure privacy for the great lords concerned. If Monstrelet heard that the princes of Orléans wept, then he must have heard it as common gossip in Burgundy.

An hour after this charade Duke John rode away to dine in a neighboring town. Many people rejoiced that the pardon had taken place so peacefully. Many believed that the ghost of Louis I was laid in peace. Others grumbled. There were, as always, a few who thought under their breaths that henceforth it would be perfectly acceptable throughout the Kingdom of France to go about killing and murdering princes of the blood, since Duke John had performed such a deed with perfect impunity and without reparation. Charles of Orléans rode home to Blois with his brother Philip. Neither one was in any way satisfied, nor were the members of their counsel.

As he rode through the spring fields of the Île-de-France on his way southward to the Loire Valley, Duke Charles was anxious. More than ever they needed the counsel of the Duchess Valentine. The Lady Isabelle had not been well for some time. Her confidante and personal maid Simonette, whom Duke Charles had loaded with presents, had intimated as much to him. A special bed had been prepared for the lady in the west wing of the palace at Blois where the afternoon sunlight would fall into her chamber on the second floor. A superb bedspread of taffeta woven with gold thread had been cut and stitched. In counsel it had been decided that Blois Castle would be the best residence for the princess. The air in that part of the Loire Valley is famous for its therapeutic effects. The lack of wind and the soft, almost southern sunlight create a soporific effect.

The Duchess Isabelle was carried into her special room, the one with the taffeta bedspread woven with gold, on the 12th of August, 1409. The beautiful bedspread had been embroidered with a silken picture of the Four Gospels. Ladies-in-waiting folded it back so that the duchess could be properly attended. The surgeons and midwives bustled to and fro while the fifteen-year-old prospective father knelt in prayer at the Lady Chapel just a few feet from her room. The news was not good. All day long on the 12th of August the slender princess lay in labor—and all that night, and all the morning of the 13th, while her husband still knelt in silent vigil in the church. Finally he received word that he could enter her room. Their child had been born. It was a little girl.

Duke Charles hurried to the room. The Duchess Isabelle lay looking at her newborn daughter. For a few minutes she lay still looking at her daughter. Then she closed her eyes, and died.

Her young husband's "grief was excessive." All France heard of it and pitied the two of them. They pitied the unfortunate princess who had been so celebrated, so beautiful, so beloved, and who had died before she was even twenty years old. Duke Charles asked the monks at the nearby abbatial Church of Saint-Laumer to celebrate her funeral. The monks replied that they felt unequal to a task requiring such pomp and honor but that they "would do the best they could."

A marble sarcophagus was carved to contain the princess's body. All around its lid was inscribed a verse written by her husband: "Here lies truly the treasure of all earthly goods." Bands of white linen and quicksilver were wrapped around her frail body. Her coffin was draped with sheets of sapphire, the color of loyalty, and embroidered with the golden lilies of Orléans. She was laid to rest not far from the Lady Valentine, just under the altar of the Virgin in the Church of Saint-Laumer.

Some time afterward Duke Charles ordered that all her beautiful dresses and robes of state should be delivered to Paris to the monks of Saint-Denis. They were to be cut up and reworked into garments for the monks and cloths for the high altar. Through all the perils and the many adventures of his life, Charles of Orléans was never to love again as he had loved this princess. He was never to forget her as long as he lived. His most beautiful verses, his most sincere, would always be in her honor:

"I held the last rites for my Lady in the minster of our love . . . and the Masses for her soul sung by Painful Thought. Countless candles of Pitiful Sighs were placed as a light for her. And I ordered that her tomb be carved from Regrets all filled with tears, and all around very richly had written: 'Here truly lies the treasure of all earthly goods.'

"Above her rests a slab made of gold and blue sapphires, for sapphire is called the gem of Loyalty, and gold is happiness. Well they belong to her, these two; for Happiness and Loyalty their portrait wished in her, the most highborn. God shaped her with his two hands and formed her marvelously: she was, to speak simply, the treasure of all earthly goods. . . .

"Yet, let us not speak. My heart faints when it hears the virtuous deeds of her who was blameless, as swear those men and women who knew her counsels. I think myself that God desired to draw her towards Him, to adorn his house in Paradise where dwell the saints. For she will be there a vision fair since she was commonly called by all of us 'The treasure of all earthly goods.'

"Of no avail are tears or complaints. We shall all die or soon or late. No man can keep for a very long time the treasure of all earthly goods."

The little maid born at Blois Castle on the 13th of August, 1409, was baptized Joan of Orléans.

Joan . . . and Orléans. A curious coincidence.

V [*1409–1415*] BY THE FALL OF 1409 John of Burgundy was Regent of France and the darling of the Parisians, whom he courted assiduously. The king, the queen, and the dauphin cowered before him and resided as much as possible outside the city gates.

In his Castle of Blois, Duke Charles of Orléans was hard at work from morning to night, day in and day out, learning to administer the affairs of his duchy. He was also still settling the estates of his parents. His duties left him little time for grief. His activities were in themselves a homage to the dead.

Not a franc could be advanced by his treasurers unless the duke's signature had been first affixed to the draft; not a creditor could be reimbursed without his knowledge and sanction. Unlike the former Duchess of Burgundy, who had defiantly performed the medieval bankruptcy ceremony by laying her belt and her keys upon her husband's coffin—thus escaping the mountainous bills and promises to pay that follow the death of a great lord—Charles of Orléans attended to each creditor and honored those debts of his father that appeared to be legitimate. His own picture of the kind of man Louis of France had been became clearer as the nature of his minor obligations was revealed.

A servant was reimbursed for alms money he had lent the dead duke. Minstrels who had come from distant Savoy to sing for him were paid and sent home. A chamberlain received a refund on six écus he had once advanced. Louis of France had given the six écus to two servants who had brought him a gift of dogs and birds. A bill for ten écus was paid to defray the expenses of a valet and his greyhound to and from Paris "so they might have a comfortable trip." One hundred francs went to Bonifaces de Mores for two horses he had furnished Louis; the horses were gifts to two of those young Crusaders who had died in the Hungary campaign. Twenty écus each went to two "translators of the Big Bible." One hundred écus were paid also as court costs to two counselors of the Paris Parliament, as well as to two doctors of theology, one of whom was the infamous Doctor Jean Petit. Still another one hundred francs went for another horse that Louis had bought for a friend. In order to meet all the demands upon him, Duke Charles was obliged to sell back "certain jewels" to a Paris merchant who "promised to pay for them within six months." He was also obliged to sell three "famous heirlooms" and to melt gold from some of the family jewels.

Aside from the debts, Duke Charles began to spend large sums to repair, fortify, and arm his various castles in Blois, Valois, Beaumont, and Champagne. One of his purchases included thirty cannons, 800 pounds of powder, 600 kegs of shot, 60 crossbows, and 60 cases of arrows for them (armed with their revolving metal heads), 100 lances, and 50 axes. Such preparations required long hours of hard work, the best antidote for grief.

Meanwhile, John the Fearless could not seem to forget Louis I. He was reported seething because he had been summoned to Chartres at all, resentful that he had acceded to the king's command to humiliate himself. It was also reported that he had sworn to be avenged against Montaigu, the king's maître d'hôtel, because the latter had, as his function required, made the arrangements for the pardon ceremony. Burgundy had not struck directly as yet; he was not yet able to ambush the new Duke of Orléans in Blois Castle.

While exercising his dictatorship in Paris, he could only roam about the periphery of the Orléans faction, sending some of his homeward-bound mercenaries to ravage the lands of the Duke of Bourbon, for example. In December his hirelings, growing bolder by the month, waylaid a messenger from Duke Charles and, despite the official business that should have protected the unfortunate sergeant, since he was the bearer of a letter to the king, they strung him up to an elm. Such successful affronts emboldened Burgundy. Finally he grew daring enough to have the king's trusted maître d'hôtel arrested and imprisoned on charges of having caused the king's madness and the schism in the Church, and of having misappropriated public funds. This last charge was a clear reference to Louis I, whose reputation Duke John had not finished belaboring.

The distinguished and affluent Montaigu, who had given the little house in the Saint-Paul area to Louis I, was put to torture. No intercession on his behalf was allowed by the Provost of Paris, who now revealed himself as a supporter of Burgundy. Despite his fifteen years of faithful if well-remunerated services, despite the fact that his son was married to the High Constable Albret's daughter, despite his two brothers (who were bishop and archbishop respectively), Montaigu was sentenced to death. His judges only ridiculed his lack of education, his puny stature, his gray beard, and his pronounced stammer. They reminded him that a member of the middle class has no business meddling in the affairs of great lords, particularly in those of Burgundy. What they also meant was that Montaigu had no business remaining faithful to Louis I and his son Charles.

One morning Montaigu was led through the streets of Paris toward Les Halles, escorted by troops and advertised with trumpets. However, the little man held his wooden cross staunchly. He met all taunts with a calm denial. On the scafford he retracted the admissions made under torture, proclaimed the innocence of Louis I, and then, to the consternation of the crowds who had gathered to cheer at his execution, the maître d'hôtel loosened his garments and showed the throngs how his lower abdomen had been ripped open by instruments of torture. Still denying his guilt, he kissed the cross devoutly and then held up his hands so the spectators could further see that his finger joints had been cruelly broken. He was then beheaded. His head was impaled on a lance to remain there as a reminder of his fate, and his body was left swinging on the gibbet. John the Fearless had scored another victory. After such a fate the other friends, possibly even the allies of Orléans, would want to abandon Duke Charles.

A few days later Montaigu's brother, the Archbishop of Sens, returned to Paris from Amiens, where he had been delegated to await ambassadors from England. He had not yet been informed of his brother's fate. Imagine his surprise then when he was met by one of Burgundy's officers empowered to arrest him also.

"You are not the bearer of an order signed in the king's hand," said the archbishop, smiling, "but anyway, in my function as the king's ambassador, I shall give you ample proof of my obedience." Thereupon he spurred his horse suddenly and managed to escape.

Although Burgundy's men searched for him for months, they never found him. In anger Burgundy confiscated his estates and presented them to one of his men. Unfortunately, however, the Burgundian never took possession of that property. One night it was burned to the ground by unknown hands. The other brother of Montaigu, the Bishop of Paris, escaped to the Italian frontier where Duke Charles held fiefs.

There was no government in Paris. The king made no attempt to avenge the death of Montaigu. For several more months, however, the Dukes of Berry, representing the Orléanists, still tried to mediate with Burgundy. It was suggested that the king abdicate in favor of the dauphin, the sickly Duke of Guyenne. The argument was that the English might refuse to extend their truce and that war between the two kingdoms might break out again at any moment. When no compromise had been reached by Easter of 1410, the Dukes of Berry and Bourbon, without delaying for farewells and without even requesting leave of the king, abruptly and secretly left Paris. Their destination was the Loire Valley. They had decided at long last that only force could prevail.

An alliance was made and formally adopted by Duke Charles of Orléans, along with the Dukes of Berry, Bourbon, and Brittany, and the Counts of Clermont, Alençon, and Armagnac. Their purpose was to work openly and henceforward in conjunction with one another to reform the abuses in the kingdom, since clearly the king had lost all power at the death of Louis I. Burgundy had given ample proof that he would not abide by the Treaty of Chartres. His tyranny had become open and outrageous. Since he had continually broken the peace, since he continued his career of slander and crime, they would ally to forestall his future plots. The allies voted to notify the king of their decision, to raise and equip an army at their own expense, and to march openly to Paris. The news of their decision was received with dismay throughout France. The English had not invaded. Why was such an army being levied? There could be only one reply: Civil war was at hand.

"Thus would I gladly have laid down my pen," writes the Monk of Saint-Denis, "if I had not taken as my guiding principle to transmit all events—happy and unhappy—that occurred during the reign of King Charles VI. But as I continued to record these events, I kept reminding myself of the words of the Gospel: 'All kingdoms divided among themselves shall be made desolate,' and

I cursed the blindness of French chivalry which, lost through its excesses of implacable hatred, was making plans to turn its arms against the breast of its own native land."

By the middle of July it was apparent to anyone who was at all informed that blood would soon flow freely over the soil of France. A strange and unnatural event had foretold it—even if the mustering of knights in Burgundy in the North and in Orléans in the South had not been ample enough proof. A strange, another unheard-of, occurrence had taken place in midair along the Meuse River. Flocks of storks, herons, and magpies had attacked another flock made up of rooks, crows, and jays. The screaming and croaking of these embattled birds had been awful to hear. The larger species had carried the day, but two wagons could have been filled with the bodies of the dead!

Both armies moved toward Paris and camped around the city, where Burgundy, always very popular with the Parisians, reigned supreme. While attempts at negotiation continued and the king feebly ordered peace, the troops of both factions looted and burned. No major action was undertaken for several reasons: the opposing forces seemed to be of equal strength; the Orléanists feared that they might be tricked into attacking the king, who had in a lucid moment threatened to march forth under the sacred banner of Saint Denis; and the fall had come early, bringing the west wind and chill rains. The Parliament marveled to think that the dukes and princes had found enough funds even in all France to maintain 200,000 men-at-arms for over five weeks. Finally a meager truce, a token cessation of hostilities for that winter, was drafted.

This truce was signed by the old Duke of Berry as representative of the Orléanist coalition. The intentions and purposes of Duke Charles were attested to, however, by his capture of a nobleman attached to Burgundy. Convinced that his captive had taken an active part in his father's murder, Duke Charles refused to yield his prisoner. His own determination to be revenged, truce or no truce, became open knowledge when all Paris learned that Duke Charles had refused to accede to the court's request and put his prisoner to torture several times. He released him, however, after repeated requests from Queen Isabeau and from the Duke of Berry, but only on condition that the said nobleman present himself at Paris *when the case of Louis of France's murder was re-examined!*

Thus people rethought the issues at stake and began to wonder if the young Duke of Orléans was not the true son of the violent Duchess Valentine, and the true instigator of the alliance after all, instead of the eloquent Duke of Berry. It still seemed unlikely that one so young could have acquired a real domination over proud nobles two and three times his age!

Early in 1410 the suspicions of the Parisians were confirmed. Toward the end of March a stunning bit of news was proclaimed. Duke Charles of Orléans announced his forthcoming marriage. In a private agreement that surprised many and appalled some, particularly the Burgundians, Duke Charles had contracted to marry the oldest daughter of Bernard VII, the Count of Armagnac. His choice could not have been more judicious if his real intent was a duel to the death with John the Fearless. If the latter had his royal cousin slaughtered in the dark streets of Paris, Bernard VII disposed of his relatives by dropping them into cisterns and blinding them with hot metals. Such an alliance could mean only that Duke Charles had wearied of negotiations, that he had allied himself and his brothers with the most radical and most blood-thirsty element of his faction. Again people began to retell the story of the Lady Valentine and the oath her sons had sworn at her deathbed. The ghost of Louis I was not yet appeased. It was also recalled that the present Duke Charles was half Italian. The "evil deeds" of the Viscontis were again remembered with awe.

The court buzzed with this news! Who was this daughter of Bernard VII? No one had seen her, or even heard of her, in fact. Who could replace the Princess Isabelle in the bed of the Duke Charles? News of the unknown young lady was forthcoming, for-tunately, from her home castle in Gages, not far from the Spanish frontier. Her name was Bonnie, like that of her mother, who had been a daughter of Berry and who therefore had hopefully taught her daughter to speak some French at least. Her name was Bonnie of Armagnac, and she was eleven years old. Like her mother and her murdering father, she also had a great reputation for piety. More than that was not known. It was learned, however, that this engagement had been solemnly ratified at Gien on the fol-lowing April 5th. Again people wondered what sort of duke this Charles had become.

By May of 1410 even the court was obliged to admit that the leadership of the Orléans party had passed from the hands of the Duke of Berry to those of Duke Charles of Orléans. In answer to a message from the king, Berry had formally deferred: "Go first find our beloved nephew the Duke of Orléans, inform him of the king's intentions, and come back and tell me what his dispositions will be!" Within a few days Duke Charles, now sixteen years of age, spoke for himself in open letters addressed to the king, the queen, the dauphin, and the University of Paris:

". . . After deliberation I will name for you and declare those in your service who are my enemies . . . those who are guilty of the cruel and enormous murder of my lord and father, your only brother. They are entirely in the favor of the Duke of Burgundy, who is chiefly responsible for the above-said murder, in that they are sworn servants, hirelings, or allies of the Duke. . . . I therefore beseech you most humbly that they be apprehended as your enemies and mine, that you boot out and separate from your side those accomplices and favorites of the above-named Duke of Burgundy, your enemy and mine, and that you convoke to your Council good and loyal servants and advisers, and such other men of good will as you will find plentifully throughout your kingdom."

The courtiers could not have failed to find his prose even better than that of his father. For a boy he expressed himself directly, to say the least:

"Once these things have been done, I shall make such a clear statement of my intentions to you that God, you, and the whole world will be satisfied with me. And for the love of God, most dreaded lord, do not fail me in this: for again and again, as I see it most clearly, my requests and petitions will every time be intercepted, all those that I couch in terms reasonable and just, and you will not be able to govern us. . . . And for these reasons, do not fail me now, Sire, for truly I crave from you only that which is just and reasonable, as it may appear to you and to every man.

"Most feared lord, may you be pleased to convey your good pleasure in this matter to us, and to command us to do your bidding which, God willing, we shall fulfill.

CHARLES DUKE OF ORLÉANS"

The only answer made to this letter was that the king came to his senses enough to order both dukes to lay down their arms. He sent John of Burgundy home to his own territories, forbade the citizens of Paris to bear arms, set extra sentinels in the streets, and closed the gates to the city. With Burgundy gone the courtiers breathed easily and considered the whole matter settled once for all. The Duke of Orléans was only wasting his words. He would never be revenged!

When the second letter arrived, however, they had to admit that this Duke Charles was persistent. He apparently had plenty of words to waste. He also apparently had not yet decided to take no for an answer.

"We, Charles Duke of Orléans and Valois, Count of Blois and Beaumont and Lord of Coucy, Philip of Vertus and John of Angoulême, your sons and nephews, have resolved to notify you, as follows:

"It is only too notorious that a certain John, who calls himself Duke of Burgundy, driven by a hidden and implacable hatred, by a detestable jealousy, by greed and the desire to dominate the kingdom alone, did cause our father treacherously to be assassinated in your good city of Paris, during the night of November 23, 1407. . . . A man would have to hunt in vain for examples of a more loathsome crime!

"Is there a man with heart so black that he would not shudder with horror to see the brother of the King wrapped about by a band of murderers, his brains oozing out upon the pavement, his hand and his arm mutilated, his body pierced through by a thousand deadly thrusts, . . . and then dragged in the mud? It is a spectacle that would fill the hearts of royal princes with pity, were it to be the body of the least of men. Then do they now see with no stirrings of pain that such a detestable murder remains unpunished? Once this crime committed, what did the murderer do? He put on the robes of mourning and, assuming the appearance of grief, along with the other princes he attended the funeral services of the man he had done to death. . . .

"You thought it your duty to go to Chartres . . . which treaty *we now declare null and void* for the reasons hereinafter stated:

"The above-named treaty is contrary to divine law. . . .

"This treaty contains a manifest error and an obvious contradiction. The above-said traitor pretends that he performed in this murder a good action for which he merits a reward. Then he adds that you granted him a pardon! As if a man needs a pardon when he performs a good deed!

"Nothing has as yet been done concerning the salvation of the soul of our father. Were you to ratify this treaty, your action would be contrary to all the principles of law, justice, and reason.

"We add that this infamous murderer has infringed upon the treaty directly and in divers manners. . . . He threw your maître d'hôtel into prison . . . and put him to torture with a cruelty unmatched even by infidels. . . . It is therefore evident that the above-named duke has never had any real intention of enacting what he swore at Chartres to enact.

"Our beloved mother on several occasions asked that justice for this detestable crime be done. That is why I, Charles of Orléans, have begged you to punish all those who dipped their hands into this homicide; I have labored for nearly four years in this attempt, without having as yet received any satisfaction.

"And as it is allowed us by law to obtain reparation under pain of exposing our own selves to infamy and to the charges of no longer being considered legitimate sons of the deceased, we beseech you to lend us your assistance . . . and to stretch over our heads the protection of your powerful arm.

"In witness of which I place my seal to these letters. Given at Jargeau-sur-Loire, the 14th day of July, the year of our Lord, 1411.
CHARLES DUKE OF ORLÉANS"

Even such a letter, ten or more pages long in its original form, failed to bring any satisfaction to its author. However, the terms of the letter amounted to a declaration of war. The young Duke Charles had clearly taken the bit between his teeth. Although courtiers could not in all fairness fail to agree with his claims, they could blame their failure to honor them by alleging his lack of good faith. One does not beseech the king with protestations of humility and affection while all this time continuing to fortify the chain of castles that stretch from just south of Paris the length of the Loire River until it passes into Brittany—especially when the sovereign Duke of Brittany is also your sworn ally. This letter also remained unanswered. In time even the most literary young duke would become bored with his own eloquence and consistently unavailing pleas. No one bears a grudge forever—particularly a youngster about to be married for the second time.

Furthermore, the young and so humble Duke of Orléans had taken a pleasure trip that summer. He deigned to honor barbaric Gascony with his elegant presence. As far as southern France was concerned, this was *the* event of the century. Several years before, it is true, they had been honored by a flying visit and tour made by Charles VI and his brother Louis when both were hardly more than boys. This time they were not only honored; they were overwhelmed! This time the Duke of Orléans was coming with a full retinue of attendant knights, minstrels, jesters, court fools, musicians, learned counselors, lawyers, scribes, and physicians. He was doing them the signal honor, the most appreciated honor, of making little Bonnie of Armagnac one of the first ladies of the land. If the Duchess of Orléans passed safely through puberty, she might become the mother of a king. Much more than that, the young Duke of Orléans was to them infinitely more than his father Louis I could ever have been. Duke Charles was the living embodiment of a southern ideal. He was a poet whose works had already proved that he had attained perfection in the school of courteous love.

It was troubadours from the South of France who in their own soft languages had imposed, three centuries before, the arts of courteous love. It was they who had put the rose in the cathedral walls, who had enthroned the Virgin, and who had raised women to supremacy in the medieval world. It was their impenetrable and precious verses that had formed from women's desires the code of chivalry that had softened the crudest manners, phrased the most beautiful oaths, curbed the most violent passions, and inspired the most deathless loves. It was the South that had produced France's noblest Queen, Blanche of Castille, that lady so perfect and so fine that she had raised her son to be Saint Louis. Over the centuries it was the southerners who had formulated the code of manners, the way of life that had sustained thousands of young Crusaders and furnished them with the fidelity and the courage to die in the sandstorms of Syria.

This Duke of Orléans was also the Lord of Coucy. No wonder he was a poet! All the South knew the verses of that other Lord of Coucy who centuries before had sent his heart home to his lady. Her jealous husband had stolen the heart, had served it up to the lady in a pudding—and the Lady of Faël had eaten the heart of her true love. Prince Charles of Orléans would not fail to bring them a poem, would not fail to rhyme it with the most skilled of the troubadours, would not fail to submit verses as veiled, as metaphysical, as secret, as complicated, as fresh as any they could compose in his honor. Of course, there would be jousts, there would be tilting and tournaments with stands for the ladies and satins for the horses and jeweled swords and golden swords flashing in the sun. No doubt there would be rich gifts for the bride, presents for the family, and casks of wine from Touraine and Champagne. But there would also be the contests of poetry, which to the southerners would stir echoes of the days when their great, early bards had changed the face of society. Even his enemies could afford to forget their wrath for a few days and admit that if Bernard VII of Armagnac was a beast of a man, he was a great captain and a splendid beast of a man. What a prize he had brought home to Gascony! All southern France swelled with pride and longed to be seen and to see the splendid, elegant, courtly, accomplished nephew of a king, this Duke Charles of Orléans-Valois.

During the summer of 1411 Duke Charles of Orléans and his company rode southward from Blois toward the Rouergue with its capital of Rodez and its old castle of Gages, just north of Toulouse. The southern chroniclers state that, in fact, all the nobility of the area turned out in splendor to do honor to him and themselves. Gages Castle was surrounded, up hill and down dale, with silken pavilions. The festivals lasted a week. Duke Charles met the pious maiden Bonnie and took her to wife, much to the great pride and delight of the House of Armagnac.

Perhaps the rugged Gascon captains whose very names and swaggering persons had struck terror into the otherwise dauntless John of Gaunt were present. In any case, for the coming struggle between Orléans and Burgundy, they would be very much present. Whether or not the northern chroniclers had heard of their resounding names by 1411, they would soon hear of their resounding feats of arms. Bernard VII was a man's man who attracted to him the swashbuckling Gascons whose names were Ramonet de la Guerre —La Hire, who was soon to learn not to curse in a lady's presence; Barbazan; and the dreaded Xaintrailles. It is no wonder that the pious Bonnie of Berry, and her daughter Bonnie of Armagnac— whom no chronicler has ever styled the Duchess of Orléans, probably because this marriage in Gages Castle was never consummated —spent their lives in one convent after another.

Now that Duke Charles had annexed Bernard VII of Armagnac and his horde of guerrillas, the question was, Who would lead whom? And further, What would he do with them? Would he be able to control them?

The third letter sent by Duke Charles was very much terser than the first two. It was also, unlike its predecessors, not directed to the king, nor to the queen, nor to the Dauphin of France. The third letter, its original at least, was dispatched in proper conformity with the medieval laws of challenge and warfare, directly to the man Duke Charles now felt was ready to attack at the head of his army. The third letter went to John the Fearless himself:

"Charles Duke of Orléans and of Valois, Count of Blois and of Beaumont, and Lord of Coucy,—Philip Count of Vertus,—and John Count of Angoulême,—to you, John, who call yourself Duke of Burgundy.

"In view of the hideous homicide which you committed like the traitor you are, by ambush and by the intermediary of infamous assassins, upon the person of our very dreaded lord and father, Louis Duke of Orléans, only brother to the King, your very dreaded sovereign and ours, notwithstanding your oaths, your alliances, and the brotherhood of arms which united you; in view of your treachery, your perfidy, and the other machinations which you sparked in a thousand manners against our above-said lord and also against our persons, we hereby notify you that as of this day forward we intend to do you injury with every ounce of our strength and in every way possible within our means; and we call to our assistance against your disloyalty as against your treacheries God himself and all men of good will within this world.

"In earnest of which I, Charles above-named, have affixed my seal to these letters, the 18th of July, 1411."

If the slightest trace of hesitancy remained in the seventeen-year-old Charles of Orléans as to his proper course of action, the answer to his challenge would have been sufficient to erase it. In a letter twice as long as the one sent him, Duke John said among other things: "We put to death this evil traitor, as he deserved, and in that we did a thing agreeable to God. . . . And since you and your brothers are following in the footsteps of your perfidious father, and want to come to the same end as him, we receive your letter of challenge with the keenest joy . . . and we shall finally manage to make you undergo the same chastisement which is due to traitors and to criminals like yourselves. In earnest of which we affix our seal in our city of Douay, the thirteenth of August, 1411."

During the month of July, soon after the reception of the challenge, John the Fearless had taken the one step that the allies of Orléans had not foreseen—nor had any other loyal Frenchman. He had opened negotiations with Henry IV of England, promising him his daughter as a bride for the once-disdained son, the future Henry V. Although the Princess Isabelle had left England many years before, the future Henry V had still not married. His drunkenness, his bawdy companions, and his turbulence were common knowledge. When Charles of Orléans wrote to Henry IV protesting such an alliance, the King of England replied that it was too late. It was openly announced at the court that Burgundy had yielded four ports in Flanders, including Dunkirk, to the English king in exchange for soldiers. It was also known that he had further promised Henry IV both Normandy and Aquitania! The latter province included the fiefs of Bernard VII of Armagnac.

The Duke of Orléans marched at the head of over twenty thousand knights to meet his enemy of Burgundy. He encountered resistance around Paris where the inhabitants did all in their power to hinder his passage, where they showered his army with projectiles from their walls. Instead of Orléanists they called the allies Armagnacs. The uniform of the allied forces was a white hood and a white band from shoulder to wrist on the left arm. The Burgundians wore blue hoods and the red cross of Saint Andrew. North of Senlis the Orléanists were unmercifully attacked along every road by armed bands and brigands, but they were still able to continue, thanks to the Gascon captains who, used to woody and hilly country, tracked down the enemy and killed them in the forests. After crossing the Oise River at Beaumont, Duke Charles halted to review his troops and assign commands. He then had "800 knights and squires, 1,200 armed men, without counting the archers and footsoldiers." So far, the captains under his command had promptly obeyed his orders. Duke Charles gave the advance contingent to Armagnac, the rear guard to his lifelong friend John of Alençon, and kept the center for himself.

After they had passed the bridge at Beaumont, their rear was surprised and their retreat cut off by a king's officer who happened also to be a celebrated knight. However, the young Duke of Orléans still seemed strongly favored by fortune. For no reason at all, apparently, the king's officer withdrew from the war two days later.

Toward the end of September the two armies finally encamped, facing each other and only a few miles apart, at Montdidier. For nine days they lay there, engaging in minor skirmishes, while the allies held councils and tried to adopt a plan of attack that the majority would approve. Duke Charles favored a full and frontal attack, while Bernard VII championed something more crafty and less spectacular, such as an ambush. Other, less impetuous, less young, knights shuddered at the thought that at any time—within a very few hours—the élite of France's knighthood would be strewn dead over the plain. What happened augured a kinder destiny. Suddenly the Burgundian army withdrew!

It was hard to believe. It seems that John the Fearless had lied to his Flemish contingents and informed them that the Orléanist vanguard was weak. Learning subsequently that it was composed of Gascons commanded by Bernard VII in person, the Flemish had deserted, alleging an expiration of enlistment. They were followed by the Picards, who had been unhappy about the situation from the beginning. At this point Duke Charles made a grave error. All are agreed that he should have followed Burgundy and cut him to pieces as he was slowed up at the crossing of the Somme River. Instead, Duke Charles returned to Paris. He thought the war was ended.

By the 3rd of October Burgundy had sent couriers to Paris who informed the citizens that the Orléanists planned to enter and to sack the city. A Burgundian army was stationed at Saint-Denis on the north of Paris and commanded by a personal friend of Burgundy. Mystified at the refusal of Saint-Denis to open its gates, Duke Charles, arriving there on the 4th, settled down to besiege this stronghold. Once he learned the reason for its defense, he and the lords of his army sent sealed letters to the king and to the Provost of Paris explaining that their only purpose was to avenge the murder of Louis I, which had become a national scandal, and to deliver the king and the royal family from their Burgundian dictator. The Orléanist heralds who bore these letters were reviled and threatened with decapitation if they returned to Paris.

At this news Duke Charles left part of his army encircling Saint-Denis, with orders to end the siege by constant batterings of its gates, by mining its walls, by diverting the course of its river so that the mills could no longer grind grain, and by making the besieged listen to reason. Then the duke rode away to attack Paris by way of Montmartre. The Parisians made no sign of coming out to fight. Finally, on October 11th, those inside Saint-Denis negotiated a treaty with the Orléanists. Putting their hands one after the other between the hands of Duke Charles, the lords inside Saint-Denis swore to depart for home without killing anyone or damaging any property en route. They also swore to remain neutral from that day until Christmas of 1411. The Burgundian troops withdrew in good order, and the Archbishop of Sens, who had not been lost after all, attended personally to the entrance of the Orléanists.

Meanwhile, the Parisians were furiously angry, fearing that Saint-Denis could no longer supply them with saltwater fish from Normandy, firewood, and other provisions. They began to panic when they learned that the Orléanists had also captured the bridge at Saint-Cloud. Three hundred Orléanists had, in fact, crossed the river on a rope, climbed up the bridge, and found the king's officer in bed with his wife. No harm was done, however, for the king's officer, like almost everyone else, had relatives in the Orléanist camp. He had not been taken prisoner. He had only been released from the Burgundians.

Meanwhile, Duke Charles organized his captains and led them in a splendid procession to worship in the Basilica of Saint-Denis, where the oriflamme, or sacred banner of France, was kept. He remained in prayer, fasting at the altar throughout that day, while further Masses were said for the repose of the Duchess Isabelle's soul. As a result of this act of devotion very wild rumors spread through Paris. It was alleged that the monks of Saint-Denis had besought Duke Charles to assume the Crown of France! It was said that they had begged him to take the holy oriflamme into his hands, and even that they had anointed him King of France and true successor of his namesake Charlemagne. In his history of the reign of Charles VI, the Monk of Saint-Denis denies these allegations. One thing, however, does appear certain. If Charles of Orléans had been other than the kind of man he was, he might in October of 1411 have become the King of France. Aside from Paris and the North, all France recognized in him their leader. In his army were the most powerful barons of the kingdom who so far had obeyed him like lambs—seasoned warriors like Bernard VII, Alençon, the High Constable d'Albret, and the Marshal Boucicault. This situation was too good to last, and Duke Charles would have been the last to usurp his sick uncle's throne.

As the stalemate enforced idleness, two contingents of the Orléanist forces grew ungovernable—the Bretons and the Gascons, both of whom, because of their language as well as their customs, were considered foreigners by the French. The Duke of Orléans tried to protect the neighboring peasants and townsfolk by having them wear white stripes down their left arms. None of his measures could stop either Breton or Gascon. During one raid the Duke of Berry's town residence was burned. This was a major catastrophe, for it housed the most valuable single art collection in all France.

The war took a decided turn for the worse when the allies allowed John the Fearless to enter Paris. Their money was running so low that despite their successful commencement, their situation would soon become intolerable. Therefore, after consultation they decided to adopt Bernard VII's suggestion to confiscate the queen's treasure in Saint-Denis and to leave their personal notes for payment in its place. Their punishment was prompt. By order of Burgundy the University of Paris excommunicated Charles Duke of Orléans and his confederates as being "criminals, insurgents, and enemies of the Crown." At the very hour when with tolling bells and extinguished candles Notre-Dame was hearing this sentence read, the Burgundians, aided by their English reinforcements, were fighting a major battle around the Saint-Cloud bridge. Both sides retired after a hand-to-hand combat that had lasted three hours. Each side claimed the victory. During that night, however, the Orléanists retired. An excommunication is a shame not to be lightly endured.

The war had definitely gone from bad to worse. During the long month of December the Orléanists lost one castle after another, especially the magnificent ones that Louis I had fortified in Champagne. When King Charles VI recovered slightly in January of 1412, he was easily persuaded by Burgundy to declare the Orléanists outlaws. That news was the cruelest of all. Later in the month Duke Charles was abandoned by Arthur of Richmond, the future Duke of Brittany. By Eastertime the king was sufficiently recovered to seize the oriflamme himself and set out on his own behalf against his uncle, the Duke of Berry. The royal troops pushed forward so speedily and so successfully that all seemed lost. Few knights in France would dare refuse to surrender their strongholds when summoned to do so by the king in person.

At that moment, when Duke Charles might reasonably have been expected to surrender to the king and meekly accept his "chastisement" at the hands of Burgundy, he had in fact seconded the suggestion that was to save his life. By means of two monks sent by Bernard VII from Saint-Denis into England, the Orléanists had acquired the favor and friendship of Henry IV's second son, John of Lancaster. This John was the distinguished prince who would be known later in the century as the Duke of Bedford. One English army was sent into Gascony, for Bernard VII—officially banished from France—had a private war of his own to fight at home. His lands had been declared forfeited. The king's commissioners had entered the Rouergue in April. Without waiting for reinforcements from England, Bernard VII had stormed back home, where he and his loyal Gascon captains had retaken one castle after another. He claimed boastfully that his officers, La Hire and Xaintrailles in particular, were only warming up for the real test of their merit. Not having second sight, Bernard VII could not have known how pregnant with truth his words really were.

By the 8th of June, despite English reinforcements and also because of them, the end of the civil war was more or less in sight. The king's army drew near the city of Bourges, where his uncle and the Orléanist princes had shut themselves. They could not fail to surrender eventually. However, the night the king arrived there was a frightful storm with driving rain and hail so heavy that it ripped through the royal tent. That was a presage difficult to interpret!

All that summer the king's army lay encamped around Bourges. Duke Charles of Orléans would not surrender. Aside from brief forays into the neighboring provinces, no major action was attempted by either side. It was rather a war of attrition in which each army lamented its own casualties as much as those of the "enemy." By September a strange illness broke out in the king's camp. His men were afflicted with tumors at the armpits, neck, and groin. The illness, blamed on putrescent cadavers, spread throughout the country. Using this contagion as a further means to persuade the Duke of Berry, the Peace of Bourges was effected. It was a treaty that returned to the *status quo* of Chartres. It was not negotiated by Charles of Orléans. This stubborn prince was later, however, obliged to ratify it. His position had become very embarrassing. The English army under another brother of the future Henry V, the Duke of Clarence, was so successful in Normandy that it would have to be stopped by a power greater than that of Duke Charles.

The Duke of Orléans finally ratified the Peace of Bourges, but not before he had let them all feel his reluctance. He arrived late at the ceremony of ratification, and to the unease of his friends and to the astonishment of his enemies Duke Charles arrived magnificently attired—more magnificently than the King of France himself —but robed from head to feet in unbroken black. The whole court was embarrassed in its turn. The duke was still in mourning for his father.

At Bourges the Dukes of Orléans and Burgundy were again

commanded to swear eternal friendship, complete pardon, and—what is more—they swore never again to ally themselves with England. Charles of Orléans was left exactly where he had begun five years before, except that he was personally obliged to defray the expenses of Lancaster's army—300,000 écus in gold. No longer having such a sum, he was obliged to deliver up his young brother, Count John of Angoulême, as a hostage to the English. Therefore his defeat was almost total, except for the fact that the king upon his return to Paris ordered that the body of the Maître d'Hôtel Montaigu be detached from the gibbet and buried and that his possessions be returned to his heirs. The year 1412 ended on one hopeful note. It was reported that King Henry IV of England was afflicted with leprosy. It was also believed that at his death civil war would break out in England.

After the so-called Peace of Bourges, Dukes Charles retired to Blois Castle, where he spent the early months of 1413 trying to recover those of his lands the new treaty supposedly guaranteed him. Burgundy meanwhile contrived to rule Paris, this time allying himself with mobs led by butchers, thugs, barbers, and surgeons who kept the royal family terrorized. The bands of terrorists and their followers even dared enter the Hôtel Saint-Paul, where, showing no respect for the monarchy, they harangued the dauphin on the subject of his late hours, his drinking, and his preoccupation with music lessons. Philip of Vertus, whom the dauphin had attached to his person, managed to escape and return to Blois. The dauphin then wrote to Charles of Orléans a letter in his own hand, asking to be rescued. During the heat of that summer, between eleven o'clock and midnight on the ninth of July, a mob actually forced its way into the ballroom where the dauphin was dancing. They openly berated him and told him that he was a disgrace to France. The Duke of Burgundy appeased his new henchmen, but only after blows had been exchanged. The dauphin was so humiliated and so angry that he became ill and even spat blood.

The only security that saved either the dauphin or the royal family from a total revolution fomented by Burgundy was the fact that the Orléans faction remained united, if not intact, just south of the city and that their ambassadors throughout that summer continually pleaded with the nobles inside the city, with the University of Paris, and with capable and moderate citizens everywhere to enact a just and lasting peace. These arguments stemmed the tide so successfully that by August 23, 1413, the Duke of Burgundy "voluntarily" withdrew from the city. A few days later the princes of the Orléans allies—Charles of Orléans, his brother Philip of Vertus, King René of Sicily, the Duke of Bourbon, and Count John of Alençon—entered in triumphal procession to the sound of trumpets. The dauphin on that solemn occasion displayed a particular affection to his cousin Charles of Orléans, whom he asked to put off his somber black as a favor to the court. Charles of Orléans acceded to this request and soon appeared in a sumptuous costume embroidered with 960 pearls that spelled the words on his sleeves, "Madame, I am more joyous." It has always been supposed that the word "Madame" meant that he had consummated his marriage with Bonnie of Armagnac.

The princes were thus reinstated in the king's favor, and peace was made, although Duke Charles apparently still had not forgiven the Duke of Brittany for his desertion of the Orléanists' cause. It was then the turn of Burgundy to remain in his own domains and to try by insinuating letters to reinstate himself in the king's good graces.

While the princes were in session to settle the civil war and to draft a peace acceptable to all, they also received the Duke of York, who came from England to treat of matters of great import. The French had been so busy ousting Burgundy that the death of Henry IV had passed almost unnoticed. With their own dissension well on the way to being settled, they could afford to remember that the new King Henry V was still without a queen. Fortunately, the King of France had one marriageable daughter left, Isabelle's youngest sister. This was the child Catherine who had learned to read in some unexplained manner. For years she had remained at the side of her insane father. Like him, she was often in rags while the mob ruled Paris, and often hungry, also. People whispered that once the king had roused from his melancholy enough to request food. His maidservant had burst into tears and confessed that there was no money for food. The king had then given her his golden goblet so that the maid could purchase something for him and for the dirty little princess by his side.

It was this neglected, almost forgotten, Princess Catherine who was hastily outfitted and suddenly raised to a position of honor now that the princes, her near relatives, had returned to Paris. Having failed in his attempts to marry Isabelle, Henry V was now requesting the hand of the Princess Catherine. Both the English ambassadors and the princes were very much surprised. Just like her oldest sister, the Princess Catherine had become a beauty. The day she made her appearance at court she was thirteen years old. She wore a dress made of a magnificent fabric, gold threads and silken threads woven together. She was adorned with jewels and escorted into the Green Room at Saint-Paul's by a bevy of young ladies.

Later in the year the last of the dauphins, a thin, nervous boy named Charles, was also affianced to Marie of Anjou, the sister of King René of Sicily. This young nobleman had been a staunch supporter of Charles of Orléans. It was a minor ceremony between two children. No one could imagine that this diffident, sallow youth would ever be needed, or that he would ever play an important role in affairs of the kingdom.

Charles of Orléans might never have won his full revenge against John the Fearless if the latter had not decided to make history repeat itself. Perhaps the king and the dauphin needed one more evidence of his perfidy. In any event, after proclaiming that he had come to deliver the king and the dauphin, who were being held prisoners by Charles of Orléans, John of Burgundy marched southward once more at the head of an army! He counted on an insurrection inside Paris. He was mistaken. The princes, ably seconded by Bernard VII, not only kept order in the city but also forced Burgundy to withdraw from Saint-Denis.

After this threat the king published, on February 13, 1413, a formal edict against Burgundy. In the very first sentence of this proclamation the king referred to the "damnable and cruel homicide committed and perpetrated . . . upon the person of our only brother, Louis Duke of Orléans." The letters also accused Burgundy of having wanted "to exterminate entirely our nephews," Charles of Orléans and his brothers. In addition, he had violated the Peace of Bourges by refusing to return castles to the Duke of Orléans. It was only owing to "the wisdom and the efforts" of Duke Charles and his allies that the king was now able "to govern freely for the interest of the realm." Burgundy was now going to be punished.

The next step in the revenge of Duke Charles concerned the University of Paris. By order of the king, those learned prelates and doctors reexamined the speech of Doctor Jean Petit in which he argued that homicide was justified. After deliberation the learned participants voted to condemn Burgundy's justification of his assassination on nine counts. A scaffold was erected before Notre-Dame Cathedral. There, before Duke Charles of Orléans, the court, the university, and the populace, a proclamation to this effect was read. Then the speech of Jean Petit was held up for all to see. As they watched, it was set on fire and burned before their eyes. Even so Duke Charles had not quite finished! During the seven years of his adolescence, through deaths of his beloved ones, through war, through defeat, through periods when all seemed irrevocably lost, this young man had persisted. He could be outwitted—he had been vanquished—but he still had persisted in his determination, as stubbornly through the bright days as through the many dark ones.

There was very little rest for Duke Charles the year that he was twenty. That year he became the most influential person in the Kingdom of France—a man of proved honor, a man whose principles had remained unshaken through defeat and civil war, a man who had matured in the midst of personal tragedy and humiliation. Even though he had regained the favor of the king and had led his friends and allies to victory, his position was not secure. For years John of Burgundy had planned to murder him. Nor was it at all certain that the king and the princes could force Burgundy to give up the towns he still held illegally in northern France and Champagne. Charles of Orléans patrolled the streets of Paris in person. He sat day in and day out at the King's Council. He listened, he debated, he proposed, and he continued to learn how to manipulate people. His every action was observed. His every word had to be constantly measured.

It was not often that he could ride down to Blois Castle, for the king was equipping an army to ride toward Flanders and force Burgundy to surrender the Crown's cities. In February of 1414 Duke Charles signed authorizations that would repair his castle at Pierrefonds, that would replace stones damaged by winter storms, that would lay in a store of cannons, powder, arms and food for twenty-five men-at-arms. He had also to replace the lead pipes that Burgundy's men had ripped from the castles they had occupied, and such fittings cost a small fortune. In July he settled his household accounts at Blois Castle. Among the fabrics bought for clothing there was brown wool from Monsterville for doublets and hoods. The sleeves of these garments were to be embroidered with jewels in a design of white flowers and silver chains. Other garments were to have an embroidered pattern of green leaves with pipings of silver. Scarlet woolens were ordered from Brussels for riding cloaks and hoods, and red woolens from Neufchastel, and white linens for "other things."

The bill for shoes alone was astonishing. In their castle at Blois it seems that the little sister Marguerite wore out four pairs of shoes per month. The records also show that Prince Charles's little daughter Joan was a busy toddler, for she also wore out four pairs of shoes per month. The jester needed three pairs, and Coquinette, the female fool, only one pair. The youngest brother, the Bastard Jean, used six pairs per month. As the duke had bestowed the County of Vertus in Champagne on his brother Philip and Angoulême in central France upon the unfortunate John, so he was to be equally generous to the Bastard of Orléans. Jean would one day receive the County of Dunois from his brother as an outright gift to himself and to his heirs in perpetuity. Between Duke Charles and his family there was only love—no selfishness, no quarrels over property, no quibbling over who would pay the bills. Like his father, Louis I, Duke Charles was openhanded. He had been raised according to the precepts of Jean Gerson. Those precepts had already borne fruit.

Of all the persons who required new clothes and new shoes in Blois Castle that year, the records signed for payment by Duke Charles show that he did the most walking. He required twelve pairs of felted shoes per month, one pair of German hose, and a pair of new riding boots of Cordovan leather with fold-over cuffs of scarlet felt.

One of his major preoccupations in 1414 was the ransoming of his brother John d'Angoulême from Thomas Duke of Clarence. "May God pardon him" for having taken Count John d'Angoulême into England, says the French chronicler. With many of his castles in ruins and his townsfolk despoiled, with the king relying on him to equip another army and pursue the war against Burgundy, where was Duke Charles to find a prince's ransom for his brother? There was only one fortunate aspect to this situation. Count John was not desperately unhappy in England. He was very well treated. He could still study, compose his Latin works, learn English, and read Chaucer from the copy he had ordered written for himself. He could also play chess. Count John was studious and literary-minded, as his brother Charles had been before he was immersed in campaigns and the business of ruling France. In temperament these two brothers were similar.

At the age of twenty Duke Charles must have been full-grown. No large portrait of him has come down the ages; and although many chroniclers described his splendid robes of ceremony, no one of them described his person. However, the number of shoes he wore out in a month bears witness to his sturdiness, as does the record of his months in the field sleeping in a tent, riding at the head of an army through all kinds of weather, living through the plague at Bourges, always present at the major events and at the council tables. Like almost all the Valois family, he was dark-haired. He was also of average height. In 1414 he wore his dark hair shoulder length, with the ends rolled.

Duke Charles was a person of impressive presence. When he entered a council hall, he made a grand entrance, after having kept great nobles waiting. His features were also impressive—he had a strong chin and long nose. He was faithful and deeply engaged to those he loved. His nature was one capable of profound attachment. His word was a bond upon which all could rely to the death, through thick or through thin. Very soon, events would show that he possessed also a peculiar dynamism that set him apart, as it were, from every person at the court. It was a mysterious quality that only the great seem to possess. Duke Charles of Orléans seemed endowed with the ability to fascinate both those around him and those who had never even seen him—those who had only either heard of him or who had heard at most some of his verses. For some strange reason even simple people who had certainly never met him face to face loved him.

In 1414 there were three chief cities held by the Burgundians. The king had resolved to recover them. They were Compiègne, Soissons, and Arras. When by Eastertime Compiègne had refused to surrender, although summoned by the Crown to yield, the king dispatched technicians with siege equipment, artisans and carpenters, whom he followed with the princes and their armies. Passing in review before the walls of Compiègne, the princes and the king went to lodge in the finest houses of a neighboring town. During that night they all barely escaped with their lives. While they were asleep, someone set fire to their various lodgings. Fortunately, one of the princes was able to give the alarm! All escaped. The mystery of this fire was never solved.

Around these beleaguered cities the Gascons from Armagnac fought like tigers. The rebels within the wall replied to the king that they were loyal to Burgundy and therefore enemies of Orléans. Bernard VII's men replied in their turn that they would guarantee to take the cities all by themselves if the king would allow them the right to the riches they would win. When the cities dispatched ambassadors to the king, instead of their distinguished citizens they sent barbers and surgeons whose rough language and insolent demeanor were insults to the Crown. Even so, the king hesitated to destroy his own cities. When the citizens of Compiègne saw that Burgundy, despite his fine promises, did not appear on the horizon at the head of his troops, they finally yielded. At this point the princes pleaded with the king to show clemency toward the rebels.

Soissons held out also until the end of May, refusing to recognize the Duke of Orléans as its master, and insisting that Burgundy would come to deliver it. This city was finally taken by storm. The Gascons swam the river and assaulted it from one side, while the dauphin and the Dukes of Orléans and Bourbon attacked it from the other. Since Soissons was entered by force, it was put to pillage. Its houses were ransacked from cellar to garret, its women raped, its bourgeois deported to Paris, its commander executed. This harsh lesson caused Burgundy's brother, the powerful Count of Nevers, to come in person and crave pardon. The king and the princes accepted his excuses and signed a treaty of peace with him. Burgundy's relatives were duly notified that the king had decided to confiscate all his lands—Flanders, Artois, and Burgundy—and to add them to the domains of the Crown.

Into Arras, capital of Artois, Burgundy had introduced soldiers by trickery, since he had begun to fear that its inhabitants might not be willing to risk for his sake the same fate that those of Soissons had undergone. Since the king had fallen ill again, this siege was commanded by the dauphin and the princes, who decided to take stern measures from the start. They therefore went to work at the siege without attempting to negotiate. This was toward the end of July. The princes were outraged to see that the besieged shot their cannons directly toward the king's tent. Until that time it was generally believed throughout France that the person of the king was sacred, since he had been appointed by God to rule. During the siege of Arras the Duke of Orléans must have felt very much like saying, "I told you so"; for again the Count of Richmond from Brittany switched his allegiance and went over to join the Burgundians.

At this point in the war Burgundy's sister, the Countess of Hainaut, arrived at the royal camp. Bathed in tears, she easily persuaded the dauphin in caressing tones to pardon Burgundy. The Normans under Alençon and the Gascons under Bernard VII were disgusted. Duke Charles naturally opposed the dauphin's decision. All the princes felt it was too rash. Despite their protests, however, Burgundy was pardoned again and made to swear that he would surrender Arras, return castles to Duke Charles, discontinue fomenting revolutions in Paris, not approach the royal family unless summoned, and abstain from further alliances with the English. This peace was ratified in Paris in February of 1415.

From the beginning of the siege of Arras until well into the spring of 1415, the weather was so bad that there were in all those months only three moonlit nights. The rivers throughout France were so swollen with torrential rains that their channels were no longer discernible. As a result all water transport ceased, and famine and discomfort plagued the disaffected areas. The runoff water from plowed lands carried the seeds with it. Reserves of wheat rotted in garrets and lofts. There would be only the most watery and savorless wine at the end of the summer. All this could bode no good. The morale of the country was low, and the princes themselves were weary from sleeping month in and month out in field tents. The land was full of deserters, disgruntled veterans who had grown so used to war that they could hardly conceive of another way of life.

Despite the bad weather, however, and despite the marauding bands that still infested the country, the war was over.

Duke Charles had won. John the Fearless had been chastised. The dauphin was safe in Paris. There remained only the ghost of Louis I still unpacified. This one last task remained to be accomplished before Duke Charles could ride home to Blois Castle and think about the arts of peace. Louis of France had never been properly buried.

Duke Charles, like Aeneas, could not allow his father to be snatched so quickly from the earth. This son, like Aeneas, longed for one more contact, for a final honor that would impress upon the world that Louis I had been not only a great prince but also a true lover of his country. Where in all France was that churchman who could do justice to such a burial? Where in the world was there a prelate who could comprehend such filial piety, a love so sleepless that it had persisted through seven years of difficulties and sacrifices? The prelate who came forward proved more than any subsequent words could ever do that Louis I had been an honorable man.

Jean Gerson was that prelate. Jean Gerson, whose ideas, mysticism, and vast love of humanity had so largely shaped this Charles of

Orléans, was the man who volunteered to write and deliver the funeral oration for Louis of France. Throughout the civil war the University of Paris had championed the Burgundian aims with all the might of their learning and prestige. Yet the chancellor of that university, the most eloquent, the most Christian scholar of the century, departed from their policy and appeared as an apologist for the dead duke. In so doing he risked the loss of his property, an event that swiftly ensued. He also risked his life as a result of this action. Jean Gerson was subsequently obliged to flee. With the Parisian mobs still in adoration before Burgundy, who had been Jean Gerson's patron and sovereign lord, the prelate's life was not worth a penny. Even so, he risked his life, preferring to champion Duke Charles even if his action caused him to leave his Church and flee for his life.

The funeral service for Louis of France was held in Jean Gerson's cathedral, Notre-Dame de Paris. Over the black and white stones of the worn floor, past the nests of gray pillars that rise slender and massive, holding the vaults of heaven throughout the centuries, passed the powerful nobles of France, garbed all in somber black. As they walked, they looked down carefully so as not to stumble, for the white stones in the floor were already more worn than the smooth black ones that met them in a diamond design. Entering the central portal, they passed by the Chapel of the Savior, the first one on their right, and took their places along the aisles to either side. Hatred did not enter with them. Under the rows of torches, in the flickering light of the thousands of tapers the king had ordered, they waited. Jean Juvénal, the chronicler, was there. King Charles VI was present. Duke Charles and Count Philip were present, and so were the Dukes of Berry, Bavaria, and Bourbon, and the newly created Duke John of Alençon. The Counts of Richmond, Eu, and la Marche were present. The king and the princes sat alone in the oratory to the right of the main altar. The light, passing through the brilliant storied windows, falling from the superb clerestory, stained the floors and splotched the pillars with pools of clear reds, blues, and greens. From behind the worshipers the rose window of the Virgin glowed, fusing red and blue. It flooded the massive cathedral with a wide beam of rose-colored light and made its sides widen until they were lost from sight, made the vaults rise and tower and grope through the gloom above, until the eye grew dizzy and the head whirled and the body dissolved into awe at the greatness of man's love.

Older than Chartres, darker and more solemn than Notre-Dame of Chartres, the Cathedral of Notre-Dame of Paris defies the tongue of man. Massive and gray, buttressed and towering, stalwart beside the flowing river, she is an ageless poem from the medieval heart. Inside, she is a prayer, a stillness in the heart and tears behind the eyelids. With the sunlight left behind and the noises of the street, with the huddling houses that caress her left outside, Notre Dame is the yearning heart of man in communion. Hatred cannot walk her worn stones. Violence cannot enter her portals. Only waves of peace rise to her cross vaults and breathe along her aisles.

Duke Charles knelt and heard, perhaps for the first time and certainly for the last time the earnest words of that man who had already given him so much, that man whose words could only fortify and sustain, through whatever more perils and sorrows were ahead, "the fortress of the heart."

Doctor Jean Gerson spoke so "profoundly and daringly" that those who heard him marveled at his temerity. He recommended Louis of France to the love and gratitude of the entire kingdom. He demonstrated how France had been better governed during the lifetime of this prince than ever it had been governed since. With an extraordinary courage Jean Gerson then attacked the Duke of Burgundy by name, saying that although he advocated neither destruction nor the death penalty for such a criminal, yet he firmly believed that Burgundy must be made to humiliate himself. It is not enough, said Jean Gerson, to force him to sign treaties! This proud duke is still a danger to the whole kingdom of France—and what is much worse, he is a danger to himself! If he does not admit his crime, if he does not do reparation for it, and if he is not absolved of it, then he is in danger of losing his immortal soul! Jean Gerson also spoke of the defense Doctor Jean Petit had made of Burgundy's crime. Such a defense was monstrous.

Said Jean Gerson: There is no excuse for murder, none whatsoever. No man has the right to kill his fellowman. The king had been amply justified in having such a blasphemous document publicly burned before Notre-Dame Cathedral. Even such an action was not sufficient to erase the shame of it, for the wicked words and fallacious arguments had sunk deep into public consciousness. The evil of this murder has bred a chain of evil that has continued after it.

Jean Gerson, a small man with deep-set, bright eyes, dressed in the simple robes of a monk, without the ornaments that his rank and position would have warranted; a small man with a sharp, slender face surrounded by a narrow halo of tonsured hair, standing clear-eyed before the great nobles of the realm in the pulpit of Notre-Dame Cathedral, still had not finished.

"I am ready and prepared," said Jean Gerson, "to uphold my words and my beliefs against all comers." What more can a man say? Duke Charles heard Jean Gerson, whether anyone else did or not.

At the conclusion of the service Duke Charles and his brother recommended Jean Gerson to the king's especial love and protection. Vast as it was, the church was so crowded that there was not an inch to spare. Even the Archbishops of Rheims and Pisa had come to hear Jean Gerson. Louis of France could rest in peace when the greatest scholar and perhaps the most influential thinker of the century had praised his name. Duke Charles had completed the first trial of his life with Jean Gerson by his side. Could the Master have known that the young prince who knelt at his feet was his intellectual heir?

On February 10, 1415, the king gave a festival to the princes. It was in honor of the war's termination. It served also to entertain ambassadors from England who had been arriving in France more and more frequently of late, always asking for the hand of the Princess Catherine. No one took them very seriously, for the new King Henry V, having become suspiciously pious since his accession to the throne, was making ridiculous proposals.

Once during the king's absence the old Duke of Berry told the English legates quite frankly that one does not ask for a wife in such terms. Catherine, plus cities in France? Catherine, plus *counties* in France? Catherine, plus entire *duchies?* It was laughable! One would think that Henry V was losing his mind! It couldn't have been more amusing if Henry V had upped the dowry to Catherine plus the Crown of France.

The king's festival lasted for three days. One of the principal events was jousting between Duke Charles of Orléans and the Duke of Brabant, brother to John the Fearless. The ladies showered favors upon Duke Charles. They were charmed to see such skill, such chivalry, and such cordiality between the two nobles. There was no longer any quarrel between them.

After the festival Duke Charles rode home to Orléans and to Blois. Bernard VII was busy administering his estates in Gascony.

Tanneguy du Chastel, a bold knight absolutely devoted to the royal family and therefore to Orléans, had become Provost of Paris again. John of Burgundy was apparently still in the North, hatching some scheme with the English, no doubt. However, Tanneguy was resourceful; he could keep the peace in Paris. The war was finally over!

Duke Charles went home and turned to the arts of peace while the wet west winds continued to blow. The roads were quagmires. But in between the showers the Loire River gleamed like a silver mirror bordered with fairyland castles . . . white stones set in a flat, green velvet valley.

During the summer of 1415, while the rains continued to fall heavily, a delegation of 350 French ambassadors called upon Henry V at Canterbury and then at Winchester. Henry V was flanked by his brothers of Clarence, Bedford, and Gloucester, and counseled by Henry Beaufort, the Archbishop of England. The French legates offered the Princess Catherine together with a staggering sum of money in exchange for a permanent peace. To their astonishment, Henry V, advised by his half-brother Beaufort, asked for the Princess Catherine plus Aquitania, Normandy, Anjou, Touraine, Poitou, Le Mans, and Ponthieu. Speechless at first, the French ambassadors then gave vent to their indignation.

Henry V moved down to Portsmouth and Southampton in August. His herald, Exeter, carried a letter to France. It was addressed to "the very noble prince Charles, our cousin, adversary in France. Henry by the grace of God . . . King of England and France" Desiring peace more than avarice, said King Henry V, we must drop the matter of the fifty thousand écus in gold you have offered us as a dowry. Let us not speak of marriage and money in the same breath! Rather we must claim our inheritance. . . . "Given under our privy seal in our castle of Southampton, at the sea shore, August 5, 1415."

King Charles VI replied that he would study the letter whenever he found the time and the place convenient.

After executing the Earl of Cambridge, Henry Scroope, and Sir Thomas Grey, King Henry V set sail in sixteen hundred ships out past the Isle of Wight and into the Channel. He landed on the north shore of the Seine estuary, where Harfleur faces Honfleur on the south side of the river. He pursued the siege of Harfleur so vigorously that, despite the cold rain, the fog, and the illness among his troops, it was apparent by the 1st of September that the chief port in Normandy would soon be obliged to surrender. The city of Harfleur had only two main gates, and the English were so numerous at the Montivilliers side that the king's relief forces could not enter Harfleur by land.

Early in September King Charles VI notified his vassals. Their vacation had been brief. It would clearly be necessary to throw the English into the Seine River. Henry V had gone too far. King Charles VI therefore sent ambassadors in person to the Dukes of Burgundy and Orléans, asking each vassal for five hundred knights-at-arms. The former replied that five hundred were by no means sufficient to show his great love and loyalty. John of Burgundy replied that he would send every knight in his vast domains and that furthermore he would lead them in person. Duke Charles of Orléans replied that he would gladly furnish the knights the king requested. However, there being that long distance between the cup and the lip, Duke John was "hindered" from keeping his promise. Instead, he had his oldest son, Philip, captured and shut up in a castle precisely so that he could not join the French forces. Duke John did not appear at all. Those of his vassals who reported did so on their own initiative.

Duke Charles of Orléans sent the five hundred knights to the king after the very briefest delay. Then he reconsidered, and within a few days stripped his fortresses and castles of men the length of his domains. He ordered them all to the king's side. After a few more days, he reconsidered again. Duke Charles of Orléans summoned his courtiers and his family. Turning over his power of attorney to his brothers, Count Philip of Vertus and the child Ferdinand-Jean, Duke Charles bade farewell. He kissed his sister Marguerite good-bye. He said farewell to his daughter Joan, who was then seven years old. He made the rounds of Blois Castle. Crossing the courtyard, he descended the steps in the cliff that led down the sheer rock to the level of the Loire River. He turned to the right and walked the two blocks to the abbatial Church of Saint-Laumer. He knelt in prayer at the tombs of the Duchess Valentine and the Princess Isabelle. It was not enough to send every knight from the heart of France. Duke Charles himself rode off to war against King Henry V. Duke Charles had married Isabelle and so thwarted this Henry. Duke Charles would never surrender France so long as a breath remained in his body. He would no more surrender France than he would allow the murder of his father to go unavenged. After John of Burgundy loomed King Henry V. Decidedly, his enemies were not shrinking! Neither was Duke Charles. He would be twenty-one years old in November.

By September 22nd, Harfleur, that ancient port of the Vikings, had surrendered to the English. Its inhabitants were cruelly treated. They were turned out of their homes half clothed. Women and children were allowed to take only five sous each from all their possessions. It was, as usual, very cold, wet, and damp in Normandy that September. The fog floated in from the Atlantic, gray and wet over the chalk cliffs that stretch for miles from Harfleur northward, past the Cape of the Hève, past the red, seaworn cliffs of Étretat, where the green meadows roll lush and fertile right to the verge of the precipice. Henry V sent his sick home to England and started northward across Normandy toward the English-held port of Calais. The bright intervals between the showers grew shorter. The "wild west wind" of fall drove the heavy rain across the beech forests and across the meadows. Meanwhile, the French forces collected. It was very late in the season for a major campaign, but the roads to the North were choked with volunteers. Henry V would be halted at the Somme River. Its bridges had been destroyed. Its fords were guarded. They would have to hurl him in the Somme instead of in the Seine.

The rains continued and the temperature fell below freezing at night as the English army groped its way northward and actually found, on October 19th, a place to ford the Somme. From Normandy they had passed into Picardy, where John of Burgundy could assist them freely. At his headquarters at Rouen, King Charles VI, the Dauphin, the eighty-year-old Duke of Berry, the Duke of Brittany, and the King of Sicily voted to send the French herald Mountjoy to notify Henry V that he would have to do battle shortly. Henry V's answer was a nonchalant acceptance of their challenge: "If any of your nation attempt once to stop me in my journey toward Calais, at their jeopardy be it; and yet I wish not to dye your tawny ground with your red blood."

Tens of thousands of French knights, squires, and servants poured northward to cut off the English on the Calais Road. By the afternoon of October 24th the enemy had advanced to within 250 paces of the French host. The battle would be joined in the morning. Both armies were in the County of Saint-Pol, a fief of Burgundy. The English host is reported to have lain silent while the French forces spent the night of the 24th in roisterous drinking and eating. Although it is certainly true that the French were well supplied with provisions and well known for their good cheer, it is also true that the English managed fairly well throughout Picardy, where their Burgundian allies sold them supplies.

Not all the French army, however, spent the night in heavy drinking and merriment. Duke Charles of Orléans, curiously prescient, spent his night in solitary vigil, kneeling in his tent before an altar. He had requested that his ordination into the order of knighthood be performed before the coming battle. It may have been William of Montaigu, the Archbishop of Sens, that old friend and champion of the Orléanist party, who officiated. The short Mass of the ritual of ordination began at dawn.

While Duke Charles, dressed in the white linen robe that preserved his body from impurity, his shoulders wrapped in the scarlet cloak of courage, knelt before the altar, the prelate prayed:

"Lord, you who allowed your servant David to conquer Goliath . . . in like fashion, today . . . grant this knight the strength and the daring required to defend faith, hope, and charity; give this young man in like measure both the fear and the love of You, grant him humility, perseverance, obedience, patience; dispose his heart toward all good things so that he may wound no one unjustly, neither with this sword nor with any other, but grant that he may use it in the defense of all that is just and equitable. . . ."

Then the archbishop extended the sheathed sword to the kneeling candidate.

"Receive this blade in the name of the Father and of the Son and of the Holy Ghost . . . and use it in your defense . . . and for the confounding of enemies; and insofar as human frailty may allow, wound no person with it unjustly. . . ."

The virgin knight then rose to his feet, drew the sword from its scabbard, held it straight before him—its point toward the roof of the tent—wiped both sides of its blade upon his left sleeve and replaced it in its jeweled golden case.

The prelate then bent forward to bestow upon the initiate the kiss of peace.

"Peace be with thee from this day henceforward."

Then the archbishop in his turn drew the sword. With its naked blade he struck the candidate three times upon the shoulders, saying:

"Be a warrior in peace. Be a warrior in vigilance. Be a warrior in fidelity."

As he intoned the final words, the young knight's sponsors came forward, knelt, and attached to Duke Charles of Orléans the two golden spurs of chivalry. One of the assistant knights or sponsors in this ordination was John, Duke of Alençon, who was not only the handsomest knight in France but also the most loyal to the House of Orléans-Valois.

"Thou, Charles, who surpassest in beauty the children of men, gird this sword about thy loins, O valiant warrior of France!"

Thus in the early hours of October 25, 1415, Duke Charles of Orléans was ordained. Had his father lived, this ceremony would have been performed in Blois Castle and witnessed by thousands; for an ordination into knighthood was the most important ritual of chivalry. Now it had to be much abridged. Outside the young duke's tent there was only the sound of distant voices and of the whine of the wind. The rain fell steadily upon the silken tent, streamed in wide rivulets over the frozen ground and down into the valley where the English army lay in dead silence. The Burgundian chronicler Monstrelet also noted an eerie circumstance: throughout that whole night not a horse whinnied or neighed in the French host.

When morning broke, the disposition of the opposing forces could be clearly seen even through the mist. The English—one thousand men-at-arms, six thousand archers, and a few thousand footsoldiers —lay to the south of a pass between the woods of Agincourt and Tramecourt. The French forces—at least four times as many, but practically without crossbowmen—stretched across the northern exit of the defile. Even by ten o'clock on the morning of the 25th of October, the French forces had not been able to extricate themselves from their sheer masses sufficiently well to take their battle stations.

There were all sorts of delays. The banners of some duke had not arrived, and how could he advance into battle unless his own knights could find him in the throngs? Last-minute disputes broke out over precedence, for every baron present felt entitled to a spot in the very front line. Others ordered their horses and gear brought up so that they could mount, only to discover that the Constable d'Albret had assigned them to a position in the center where they would advance on foot. Every nobleman required a certain number of fourteen-year-old pages, plus six squires—each with his own function—and his pursuivant-of-arms, who would accompany him into battle. The squires were forbidden to fight. Their function was to dress their lord and care for his armor, his weapons, and his horses; to defend him in combat; to keep him from being wounded; and to guard his prisoners. By ten o'clock in the morning there were at least five thousand French knights in the front line alone, milling about awkwardly and impatiently, squeezed together in the narrow land between the two forests. The ground where they wallowed had just been plowed that fall. At every step, weighted down as they were by their plate armor, they sank into the mud halfway to their knees. It was still drizzling and bitter cold.

Despite the slanting rain, despite the arguments, the scurrying to and fro of the harried squires, the angry tramping of the knights jockeying for position and half blinded by their massive helmets, the Gascons and the Netherlanders were heavily represented in the front line. Apparently no one had thought it necessary to summon Count Bernard VII of Armagnac. His Gascons were present without him. Even their belligerence, of course, had not taken precedence over the princes of the blood royal. Dukes Charles of Orléans was in the front line of battle and on foot, as King Henry V would be. On either side of the front line the cavalry was drawn up in wedge-shaped formations, their leader in front position, their gay banner blowing in the cloudy air. The mounted knights had been instructed to charge the English crossbowmen. In the very front line of battle were twelve French princes of the blood royal.

The French Constable d'Albret, "absolutely devoid of military ability," attempted to command the milling French forces. Even had he been a capable leader, it is difficult to see how he could have made himself heard above the hubbub, or how he could have communicated his plan of battle to the impetuous and rival barons whose tents and whose followers stretched for over a mile across the brow of the hill and to the north. Although the constable was the commanding general, each feudal lord commanded his own hundreds of vassals and was a strategist all to himself. D'Albret had ordered the French crossbowmen to the rear of the forces. His decision was heartily endorsed. Down to the most undistinguished French knight present, each one felt it his right of birth to have one chance at the English. A contribution of six thousand archers from Paris had been haughtily refused. The glory of this engagement belonged to the chivalrous. Besides this consideration, there were enough Burgundian supporters present without inviting more treachery. Even at this late moment, with the battle about to begin at any second, four thousand mercenaries withdrew from the French ranks and started streaming through the lines on their way homeward. Whoever had hired them had neglected to pay in advance.

Meanwhile, the enemy waited silently at the bottom of the hill. History was about to be repeated in a battle similar to that which Julius Caesar and Pompey the Great fought at Pharsala. While Caesar's meager and half-starved veterans waited quietly in perfect line, Pompey's vast forces—heavily filled with the perfumed young aristocrats from Rome—wavered and milled about in their thirst for glory and an easy victory.

King Henry V led his army in person. He was on foot but easily distinguishable by his jeweled crown set atop his helmet. This red Rose of Lancaster was, of course, not the only distinguished English knight on the field. The captain of his vanguard was Edward, Duke of York. With him were the Lords Beaumont, Willoughby, and Fanhope, and all the archers. The king commanded the second battle line. He stood quietly beside his brother, Humphrey the "Good," Duke of Gloucester, along with the Earls of Marshal, Oxford, and Michael de la Pole, the third Earl of Suffolk. With them were the "strong billmen." The rearguard—with its back to the village of Agincourt, which the English had occupied the previous night—was commanded by the Duke of Exeter. Their mounted knights "like wings went on every side of the battle" line.

King Henry V, with the courage born of confidence and desperation, did not rely on any accidental force to fight this battle. The French quite reasonably expected to overcome their enemies by sheer weight and mass. As King Henry had observed, the only way to get to Calais would be to walk there on the backs of the French! He had been unable to go around them.

Both armies had invoked the presence of God upon this field—with this difference: while each French baron relied upon God and his companions, each Englishman depended upon God and his own good right arm.

There were great lords of England and world-famous knights like Sir Thomas Erpingham, but there was a preponderance of commoners in the English ranks. All had suffered from the long overland trek from Harfleur. One chronicler later observed that the dysentery was so acute that many went out to fight that morning naked from the waist down.

A large contingent of Welshmen was present also. For one thing, Henry V himself came from the wild mountains of North Wales. No one had forgotten that this king had been born in Monmouth.

David Gam from Wales was there. So was the doughty Owen Tudor, who claimed descent from the last King of Wales. Owen Tudor later asserted his presence at Agincourt, at any rate, and he may very well have been there, though no doubt a great many men "then abed in England" later claimed to have been a part of the "happy few," the "band of brothers." Their proof of unity in the face of disaster, their refusal of despair, their brotherhood as men together on that field, characterized the English army that, having reasonably disposed their forces, awaited as one man the order to join battle. King Henry V waited courteously for the French to get set. Still they did not attack.

By ten-thirty in the morning the first French line of battle had swollen to include eight thousand men-at-arms. The Constable d'Albret commanded this wavering force flanked by Duke Charles of Orléans, the Duke of Bourbon, the Counts of Eu and Richmond, and the veteran Marshal Boucicault. The Duke of Vendôme commanded one wing of mounted knights. Clignet de Brabant, Admiral of France, commanded the second wing with sixteen hundred knights. Their assignment was to dislodge the English archers from their hiding place on their side of the woods.

The second line of battle, which included even more numbers than the first, was commanded by John, Duke of Alençon. With him were the Duke of Bar and the Counts of Nevers, Vaudémont, Blâmont, Salmes, Grandpré, and Roussy. The rear guard contained those thousands who had already been defeated that morning in that they had not been able to elbow their way into the first two lines of battle. This third corps was led by the Counts of Marle, Dampmartin, Fauquembergues, and contingents from Picardy, Artois, and Champagne. In other words, the rear guard was almost entirely made up of Burgundians.

Those among the French who could see down the hill into the English ranks were somewhat shaken to note that the enemy were standing there quietly, eating breakfast! Every now and then the English blew their trumpets, as they had been doing all night. Sometimes they blew in unison. It was disconcerting. While the French stamped their feet to keep warm and wished they had room to move their arms, they saw smoke rising behind the English ranks. Their foes had set fire to some haylofts and barns in the neighboring priory of Saint-George. The news was shattering to the French nerves. Saint-George was behind the English! And where was Saint-Denis? Miles to the south, in Paris! The French were facing toward home. Meanwhile, the sun broke through the fog, right in their faces, blinding and yellow.

Through its glare the French could see a rider before the English army. It was old Sir Thomas Erpingham, who rode up and down haranguing the Englishmen in the name of King Henry. Still the French did not advance. A hush fell upon their lines as they saw the old English knight wheel his horse, call for his squire, dismount heavily, and face the French army. Sir Thomas held a baton in his hand. He raised it in the air. A mighty cry, which sounded to French ears like "Ne strecke," and which the chronicler records as such, rose from English throats. It shrilled in treble waves through the sunlit air. Sir Thomas Erpingham had called: "Now! Strike!" The English advanced.

The blast blown by their trumpeters was earsplitting. Their volley of arrows curved through the air like a thick cloud. It darkened the day and stung into the French lines before the princes could even lower their visors. Then the French advanced, by spurts and starts, each contingent holding together and hurrying to strike the first blow. "Mountjoy!" cried the French. Finally they all got going, wallowing down the hill through the mud with their numbers falling in beside and urging them on from behind. Their very mass at first impact forced the English to fall backward; but the second and the third volley of arrows had found their mark, a solid wall of men. The first men who fell were trampled in the mud by those whose weight and momentum carried them over the bodies. Still the heavily armed knights lumbered down the hill in such numbers that they could no longer even get their sword arms free. The archers shot every few seconds into a solid wall of French chivalry. The fourth thousand French poured over the third, and fell. The sixth thousand, urged madly forward by the seventh, made a solid bridge in the soft earth—over which the eighth thousand knights clambered and struggled and still could not get across to the English. Those English knights who had advanced to meet them dropped their swords. Then they swung leaden war clubs, a surprise weapon, to and fro, cracking skulls at each swing until they had to stop and rest their arms. And still the French poured down the hill over the dead bodies.

While the French clambered over the bodies of the mountainous dead through all this, the cavalry spurred down the hill. Those on foot were spread out the whole width of the field and up to where the trees began on either side. Even so, the war-horses thundered down behind them. From the woods the volleys of arrows began a cross fire. The targets were large. The wounded horses reared and screamed in agony. They fell heavily, trapping their riders, who with the heavy armor could not disengage their feet from the stirrups. Out of Brabant's party of 800, not more than 140 ever reached the English ranks. There they were dragged from the saddle by the agile footsoldiers and hastily brained. The rest of the French horses trampled wildly through the living and the dead. Through this neighing, screaming mass the squires darted frantically. A few knights were found and dragged into the trees. The English were so busy wielding their clubs and maces that they let them go. Duke Charles of Orléans lay under a mound of dead. His squire had not even found his body.

At this lull in the combat the English looked up to see the second line of French ready to join combat. Sick at heart, desperate to be alive when the princes of the blood lay not only dead but buried deep under the pile of dead, John, Duke of Alençon, accompanied by eighteen of his own knights, led the second corps down the hill.

There was only one way to halt the English now. There was still one deed that could turn the tide of battle and save France from the blackest ignominy. King Henry V had not yet advanced into battle. John, Duke of Alençon, marked him out and made his way toward the King of England. In his first stroke Duke John aimed for the head. The blow was not quite perfect. Instead of killing Henry V, Duke John managed only to strike his crown in half and topple it in the mud. He had no second chance. In a flash he was pulled from his horse and rained with blows by those knights who surrounded the king. Within a matter of minutes the second line of battle had suffered a fate similar to that of the first. All were dead, except for those being taken prisoner. The English had kept their heads. They were now taking prisoners. There was a lull for a few minutes.

The third line of battle stood these two hours or so looking down the hill. They had still not moved to descend. When the order was given, they wheeled, almost to a man, and advanced toward the south. The third line of battle thus fled the field almost en masse. Not so their leaders! Overcome with shame, drunk with hopelessness, the last great nobles of France, in tacit accord, mounted their horses and charged singly down the field into the English ranks. They died one by one, without their feudal lord, the Duke of Burgundy.

The confusion on the field of battle was extreme. Rumors flew wildly; and undoubtedly the English, even had they heard a true account, would have had difficulty understanding the French. Their prisoners were not only French. There were also vast numbers of Normans, Netherlanders, Bretons, and Gascons who still survived.

One report was that the Duke of Brittany was just coming up the Calais Road at the head of six thousand knights. King Henry glanced anxiously about him. His prisoners far outnumbered the size of his original army. He could not be certain, either, that the rear guard had really retreated. Perhaps they had only wheeled out of sight in order to re-form ranks and ride into combat again. Then King Henry was informed that his baggage was being plundered in the rear. The report specified that a large French contingent was about to charge him from the rear. They would come as soon as they finished stealing his wealth and burning his supplies.

King Henry V was always a man of decision. He gave the order that all his French prisoners should be put to death instantly. Such an order was not only against all rules of humanity; it also ran counter to every code of chivalry and every regulation of medieval warfare. The French knights had handed over their swords. They had surrendered officially. They were unarmed prisoners of war standing quietly in long files according to instructions. King Henry's order was obeyed. There was no time for execution.

The English rank and file tore into the lines of defenseless prisoners with sword and club. As the French knights knelt in prayer, their heads were severed (and no time was taken for a clean job) or they were stunned or, if they were lucky, their skulls were cracked at the first blow. No man was ever able to give a coherent or accurate account of how many thousands of French knights died this cruel and useless death. Certainly no French chronicler was ever calm enough about it to be able to sit down and count. The Burgundian chronicler Monstrelet, on the other hand, gives a fairly detailed version. The Monk of Saint-Denis can only weep and cry out. No one will ever know how many thousands of French nobles King Henry V had put to death after the Battle of Agincourt was over.

It was not a very long battle. It was over when the French King-of-Arms Mountjoy, so named for the century-old battle cry of France, advanced to King Henry V and formally acceded the victory to him. It was then agreed that it would be known to subsequent ages as the Field of Agincourt, and to the French by the name of that village and castle where the English had encamped the night of the 24th, *Azincourt.*

As there had never been any close agreement as to the numbers taking part on either side—partly because the French were unable to count, so stunned were they—neither was there any agreement as to the respective losses. The English probably lost 13 knights and 100 footsoldiers. One French claim is that they lost a total of 1,600 men. The French lost between 5,000 and 10,000 noblemen on that field. This included the Constable d'Albret, 3 dukes, 5 counts, and 90 barons. The English held at the end of the massacre between 1,000 and 1,600 prisoners. Those who were never able to afford the high ransom had to die in English prisons. Jean Juvénal said that there were 14,000 prisoners and 4,000 French dead.

The second important issue still to be settled regarding the Field of Agincourt was who had precipitated the massacre by attacking and plundering the English camp. It seems certain that it was either the Burgundian deserters or other Burgundians. Monstrelet claims it was the latter. One bit of evidence seems to corroborate his assertion. The sword that the King of England had left in his tent when he rode out from Agincourt to do battle later turned up in the possession of the son of John, Duke of Burgundy—always a false friend and a doubtful ally.

The Duke of Burgundy lost two members of his immediate family at Agincourt—his brothers, the Duke of Brabant and the Count of Nevers. The Duke of Brabant heard of the coming battle too late to summon his vassals, but he went alone. John of Burgundy protested to King Henry that while he had every right to kill Nevers, because the latter was armed for France, he had no right to kill Brabant. King Henry V replied that he was innocent of their deaths. He affirmed that he stood ready to meet Burgundy at any time and prove to him that both nobles had been killed by the French! No doubt, King Henry insinuated, "by the Orléanists."

Such questions were never settled. All that was clear were the words of King Henry V: "We did not ourselves cause this great occasion to occur. It was God Almighty who did it, and we believe that He did it because of the sins of the French."

Charles d'Albret, the Constable of France, died at Agincourt Field. Dampierre, Admiral of France . . . Duke Anthony of Brabant . . . Duke Edward de Bar . . . Duke John of Alençon . . . William of Montaigu, the Archbishop of Sens, who was found still clutching his sword . . . Count Robert de Marle . . . Count Ferey de Vaudémont in Lorraine . . . and the Counts of Blâmont, Grandpré, Roussy, and Fauquembergues. The names of the noble French dead take up seven pages in Monstrelet. The Monk of Saint-Denis is too hysterical to list them. He was too ready to accept King Henry's dictum. The French, indeed, must have been very wicked.

John, Duke of Alençon, is said to have killed the Duke of York in person. The English also lost the Count of Oxford, the Earl of Suffolk, and David Gam, Esquire.

Evening . . . curling fog . . . and a fine mist fell early on the field of Agincourt. By torchlight and by the smoky light from bon-fires the English soldiers and the Burgundian peasants of the area furtively rolled over the dead knights and rapaciously stripped their bodies of armor and fine robes; of swords, coats-of-arms, and blazons, of gold collars, gold rings, and linen undergarments. Two or three strong men were required to haul one sprawled knight from the jumble of dead horses, legs, and mail-clad arms. Swords were pried from the jeweled gauntlets when dead fingers would not loose their grip.

In his tent the victorious King Henry sat jubilantly receiving the long lines of French barons whom he would order to line up in the morning and follow him along the white road into Calais. He was quite understandably in a joking mood. When Louis of Bourbon was brought in, King Henry greeted him cordially: "Welcome, Cousin. I hope that you will be kind enough to bear the expenses of this day for me."

The Counts of Eu and Vendôme were among the noble prisoners. So was Arthur, Count of Richmond. King Henry laughed when he saw him. There had been many prophecies about an Arthur who would come out of Brittany to outwit a King of England. Henry V and Count Arthur had much in common. They were more than "dear cousins." In a peculiar kind of way, one might say that they were brothers. That is to say, they had a mother in common.

Outside, in the swirling fog and fine rain that turned to sleet as it hit the ground, the rank and file were still hunting for more booty. They too had to wait in line, for they sold their prisoners to King Henry, receiving a few coins for a ransom that would run into the tens of thousands. It was an unthinkable humiliation for a medieval knight to be captured by a commoner.

Toward evening the somber and lanky Marshal of France was led in to King Henry. He had not managed to escape. His armor was too rich and too well known. The veteran Marshal Boucicault was frightful to see. His whole face was so red with blood and black scabs that he was almost unrecognizable. "I hope that you will be kind enough to bear the expenses of this day for me," said King Henry to the Lord Marshal of France.

Outside in the swirling fog the naked dead were dragged into piles all through that Friday evening. It would take the French five more days to collect them. Then Count Philip of Charolais, son of the Duke of Burgundy, would out of the kindness of his heart grant from his duchy a few feet of earth. Three ditches would be dug, each ditch the width of two men. Five thousand eight hundred French nobles would be shoveled into the trenches and covered with earth so that the four-footed wolves could not strip them any more. Some knights escaped and wandered through the woods to die in neighboring houses and monasteries.

As the fog rolled in from the sea all through that Friday night, scavengers tugged at the pile of bodies. Occasionally a wounded knight regained consciousness and, preferring to die alone, surreptitiously inched his way across the field until he found a bed of wet leaves under the dripping beeches. For weeks after the battle such pitiful corpses were found leaning against trees, still clad in armor, their visors still closed, for their hands had been to feeble to pry them open. No one can imagine how many hundreds died of suffocation on that field.

Occasionally through the long hours of that awful Friday—rarely, to be sure, but occasionally—the rank and file hauled out a knight who stirred when they yanked off his helmet, who sighed, or breathed a prayer in a language they could not understand before he drew his dying breath. When the plunderers reached the very bottom of the pile, they pulled out a knight who was a valuable prize. His armor was of the richest—heavily ornamented with three golden lilies on an azure field. His helmet was tightly stuck about his head. They pulled and tugged until it came off. His hair was long and black. His eyes were closed. When they unbuckled his armor and pulled off his sapphire-studded gauntlets, they saw that he wore the white robe and scarlet shoulder cape of a virgin knight. Around his neck was a curiously wrought collar of pure gold, with a heavy emblem of some animal that in the dim light and fog they could not identify. He must be a Prince of France.

The sentry was summoned. Someone brought a torch. Curious faces leaned over to see. The emblem was recognized. There on the ground at their feet, calm in the sleep of death, lay Charles, Duke of Orléans. The captain of the guard was summoned by excited voices. His identification was positive. The emblem was the Golden Porcupine. It was the young Duke of Orléans! The king must be notified! He would want to step out for a look at this proud prince. . . .

King Henry V did not have to disturb himself. Duke Charles of Orléans opened his eyes. He was severely wounded. Slowly, there on the ground of Agincourt, he came back that long, long way up the windy tunnels, away from the midnight gate of "easeful death," to the pain and humiliation of the living.

Duke Charles had mercifully been spared the sight of the carnage. He had not had to look upon the massacre. From the opening charge his eyes had been closed. He had slept the sleep of the unconscious throughout that whole, hideous day.

Duke Charles walked to meet King Henry V. "Greetings, dear Cousin," said the king. "I know that you, more than all others, will want to defray my expenses for this day."

Duke Charles returned no answer, not a word. Then King Henry himself, with his own hand, filled a goblet with wine and handed it to his most illustrious captive. "Dear Cousin," said the king, "refresh yourself with this wine."

Duke Charles still did not speak. Instead he reached out his hand and struck the goblet from the hand of King Henry V.

Part Two

ENGLAND

VI [*1415–1420*]   KING HENRY V DID NOT delay at Agincourt any longer than was absolutely necessary. He was overdue in Calais, where his prisoners from Harfleur had also been ordered to deliver up their persons. Duke Charles of Orléans refused to touch any food or drink for twenty-four hours. Finally he is said to have been persuaded by King Henry V to taste food again and to accept the king's theory that the war had been God's judgment upon France and God's reward to England because the English were less sinful. As the young Prince of Orléans jogged painfully along the road to Calais, no doubt he turned this thought over and over in his mind. He had been willed to live. God had spared him the sight of the French defeat. God had saved his life. God apparently willed him to go to England, to see before he was twenty-one years of age those famous castles and cathedrals the Princess Isabelle had so often described.

What must be my line of conduct? thought Duke Charles of Orléans. His head throbbed from his wound and from his thoughts. All he could do was to remain silent and watch how the cards fell. Did God really intend this proud English king to win all his battles? It could not be possible. Why had God then spared the life of Duke Charles of Orléans? For to the death—and King Henry knew this very well—the two would be adversaries. Perhaps another consolation occurred to Duke Charles. Perhaps, since he had not beaten the English on the field of battle, he might still defeat them by thinking more carefully, by using their own tactic, by demonstrating to them that God also loved France.

On the 6th of November, 1415, King Henry and his prisoners embarked at Calais. They were in Dover on the same day. With them they bore the bodies of the Duke of York and the Earl of Suffolk. The Lord Mayor of London and the aldermen, "apparelled in orient-grained scarlet," and four hundred handsomely dressed commoners met the king at Blackheath. The London clergy—for the English Church had financed King Henry—welcomed his triumphant return. Duke Charles of Orléans, as the most illustrious prisoner and as the one whose ransom would most enrich English coffers, rode behind the king. It was a dignified parade. No ballads were sung. No dented helmets or broken crowns were displayed. The astute King Henry stuck to his original line: God had given him the victory. Duke Charles of Orléans rode with bowed head. King Henry did not have a monopoly on piety, or on dignity.

It was not so very humiliating for the twenty-year-old to ride through the colorful streets of the strange foreign city. The crowds were pleasant. They congratulated their victorious king, but they did not insult his captives. France seemed very far away, indeed—much farther than the few sea miles. This was a whole new world full of unfamiliar faces and a babble of meaningless sounds. He heard a strange, guttural language spoken from the throat, hardly articulated at all, droning and horribly monotone. Much as he strained his ears to pick up a word, Duke Charles could not manage it. There were no words, or rather, he could not tell where one word ended and the second began. Everyone spoke very rapidly, much more quickly than in French. It was curious; these people could speak without gestures and without moving their lips!

The streets of London were muddy. The wooden houses looked shabby. The people's faces were pinched with cold. They stared at him from their curious deep-set eyes. They were very different from the open-faced people in the Duchy of Orléans. It was not so bad after all. At any rate, he would probably see his brother soon. In any case, he would pay whatever ransom they wished. It would not be so bad. He would soon be home. Better not think of home. Better keep one's head bowed, one's face neutral.

Duke Charles looked up curiously at the yellow stone castle where he was escorted. He saw its four towers and the pennant of Lancaster. He rode over its drawbridge, dismounted, looked about him in the courtyard, and acknowledged the greetings. People seemed to think he would understand them if they shouted! Curious people, the English!

It was a very old castle beside a river. That would be the *Tamise*. Yes, *Thames* in English. The castle was very impressive: a Norman edifice. Duke Charles studied it as a specialist in castles would do. As he followed his guide up several flights of stone steps, he was trying to recall the Princess Isabelle's words. Then he remembered her description with a start! He was in the Tower of London!

It was not until the heavy metal door clanged shut behind him; not until he saw the narrow, barred windows; not until he looked with a growing horror at the crude bench in the corner and the straw on the floor that Duke Charles realized that the door was being locked behind him. He was in prison. He was a prisoner. Perhaps no one would ever come to unlock the door! He stepped toward the windows. They were very high. All he would ever see was that thin vertical line of blue sky or white cloud. His second impulse was to call aloud, to cry for his chamber valet. For whom? He was alone. There were no servants. He was in England. He might never see France again. His throat tightened in desperation.

Then, in the midst of his agony, somewhere . . . from a church across the city, he heard the sound of a bell, with a note like that of the little bells in the Convent of the Celestine Monks in Paris, not far from where he had been born. And comforting words he had not realized he knew by heart sounded in his ears at the same time:

"In especial you, Saint Gabriel, by your holy inspiration, announce to me good tidings as you did to our Mother. . . . And you, Saint Michael, you who are guardian and Prince of the Church, who vanquished the dragon—which is to say, the enemy from hell . . . you, angels in Heaven . . . when I am in cruel sadness, come to console me. . . . And afterwards, if it were not for the aid of the angels, who could conquer or elude the frauds and the crimes of the enemy? Certainly, no man! . . . *My poor, my sick, my emprisoned, my miserable soul put out as a hostage far from its native land.*"

The words went on and on in his mind, beautiful words that seemed at such an hour to have been written especially for himself. It was indeed his poor and imprisoned soul. And he *was* the hostage put out of his home and far from his native land. And the angels would console him as the beautiful words had already done. The more he let their healing beauty sink into his heart, the more Duke Charles could believe that Jean Gerson stood beside him and recited them. He could almost hear that voice he had heard in Notre-Dame of Paris. But they were words from Jean Gerson's books.

By the time his jailer came to fetch him, Duke Charles was calm again. He could be alone among many, or with Jean Gerson when alone. The English could do what they liked. They could not destroy his solace. The main thing, the first thing, to ask for from Blois would be some of his books.

It also seemed that King Henry did not have a monopoly on charm. Not long after the king's triumphant return, his illustrious prisoners were presented to the Queen Regent Joanna, probably in Westminster Hall. During the king's absence England had been governed by Queen Joanna, the widow of Henry IV, and by the king's second brother, John Duke of Bedford. The story of Queen Joanna was one that Duke Charles of Orléans had very personal reasons for remembering.

When, back in 1399, Louis of France had allowed Henry of Lancaster to go on a visit to Brittany, a visit that had allowed Lancaster to escape from the Continent to Yorkshire, the House of Orléans had been nicely hoodwinked. John the Valiant, the aged and choleric Duke of Brittany, had furnished the ships that made the conquest of England and the deposing of Richard II possible. Henry of Lancaster had not only visited Brittany and escaped from there to Yorkshire; he had also been smitten by the splendid beauty of the Duke of Brittany's wife, Joanna, already a mother of numerous children. Therefore, in 1403, much to the amazement of France, Henry IV had called the Duchess of Brittany, who was by that time a widow, into England. He had married the Duchess Joanna in Winchester Cathedral. This was the Queen Regent of England, stepmother to Henry V and to his brothers of Clarence, Bedford, and Gloucester. This was the lady who had nursed Henry IV during his leprosy and who now celebrated his son's victory at Agincourt.

The honor of being Queen of England was for Joanna a very mixed blessing. On the one hand it was her duty and privilege as regent to rejoice with her stepson Henry V. On the other hand, the Constable d'Albret, who had perished on the field at Agincourt, was the lady's brother. The handsome and heroic John Duke of Alençon, was her daughter's husband. Fortunately, her oldest son and heir, the present Duke of Brittany, always wavering in his affections over the past few years, had remained at Rouen with King Charles VI and the ailing dauphin. Her second son, Count Arthur of Richemont, or Richmond, who held his title from Henry IV, had fought at Agincourt and had been captured. This Arthur had not seen his mother for twelve years. At the age of nine he had journeyed to London from Brittany, had knelt before his mother and her second husband Henry IV, had placed his hands between the hands of King Henry IV, and had received from him the Earldom of Richmond.

King Henry IV and Queen Joanna had not had children of their own. Twelve years had elapsed since this queen had seen her son

Arthur. Her daughters had returned to France. Another of them had married the son of Bernard VII of Armagnac. The queen was therefore personally allied with the enemies of King Henry V.

Imagine the feelings of Queen Joanna of England, sitting on her throne under the lofty wooden rafters of Westminster Hall, to see, walking down the aisles between the great lords of England, her own son Arthur, and beside him Duke Charles of Orléans. This queen dowager of England could not have failed to hear their story. Count Arthur, aged twenty-one years, had been found at Agincourt under a pile of dead bodies. He was "riddled with wounds." Duke Charles had been revived, been brought back from the dead! A mother's love for a brave and defeated son caused the queen to act strangely.

Queen Joanna slipped from her throne as the two young prisoners walked the length of Westminster Hall. Instead of greeting her son, the queen hid among her attendants. The young Count Arthur, standing beside his fellow prisoner, greeted her ladies-in-waiting. Then his mother burst from their midst. "Unhappy son," she cried in tears, "do you not recognize me?"

Count Arthur of Richmond also burst into tears. It was he who through his sobs presented the Duke of Orléans to Queen Joanna. This meeting was also a strange one, for Queen Joanna had many things in common with the young dark-haired duke. Both of them were descended from King John of France. The name *Charles* was common to both their families. The lady's father had been named Charles. Although that Charles of Navarre had been a very wicked southerner indeed, his daughter Joanna had loved him dearly. Then after her marriage to the Duke of Brittany, Queen Joanna had been involved with the House of Orléans. It was because of his pursuit of Clisson into the territories of Brittany, then ruled by Joanna's first husband, that King Charles VI had lost his mind in the forest of Le Mans. Louis of France had been subsequently disgraced and insulted because of the aid he had given Henry IV.

Queen Joanna looked through her tears at the two young heroes who stood quietly and also in tears before her. How could she ever have thought to see her son Arthur brought before her as a captive? In point of fact, given the vindictive temper of Henry V, Arthur of Richmond's life was in great danger.

Duke Charles of Orléans had broken no feudal oath at Agincourt Field. Arthur of Richmond had sworn fealty to the Crown of

England and then borne arms against it! Queen Joanna was endangering her own position in even welcoming her son. Her love, however, was stronger than her sense of danger. She kissed him. She also kissed Duke Charles of Orléans. Then she handed the two youths her purse, containing one thousand nobles! Before the young men left Westminster Hall, they had enough gold to buy all the comforts to which they were accustomed. Queen Joanna did more than that. She gave them also gifts of rich apparel and furs. Like any mother, she thought of feeding and clothing her child before anything else. She not only rejoiced to see her own son; she had also been charmed by Duke Charles of Orléans.

Both Arthur of Richmond and Charles of Orléans were subsequently lodged together in the Tower of London, but it is a moot question whether or not they spent all their time shut up there. It is hard to keep attractive men in prison. The ladies of King Henry's Court could hardly have been expected to be satisfied with a brief glimpse of such distinguished captives. In particular, Duke Charles of Orléans quickly found a way to their hearts. He was young, and he had suffered so dreadfully! He had also been defeated. There is perhaps nothing so appealing to ladies' hearts as a glamorous French prince who is to be pitied. This was not all. English beauties soon discovered that he loved to dance and that he danced divinely! They swooned at his French accent. They adored his French manners—his elegance and his courtly charm. Then they also learned that he wrote poetry, the very sort of poetry ladies most appreciate—love poetry. He was a lyric poet.

Poems, perhaps to his Lady Bonnie who lay across the ocean, who lay across the sea, welled from his heart. He wrote poems so delicate and so amorous, so refined and so clever, that they could not wait until the day when he would write one to them. Perhaps one day he would even write a poem in English. Queen Joanna, of course, had an advantage over the ladies of her court. She spoke French. She was also a connoisseur of poetry, particularly that of Geoffrey Chaucer. Duke Charles could quote Chaucer by heart. The Queen of England probably told him that she had only recently bestowed two manor houses upon Chaucer's son Thomas. How could such a lady, who had been twice so beloved, fail to appreciate the love lyrics of Duke Charles?

A contemporary manuscript shows Charles of Orléans in the Tower of London. The young duke is splendidly attired in a long velvet cassock trimmed with ermine. His dark hair falls to his shoulders and curls in a roll at the ends. On his head he wears a velvet bonnet with a brim made of matching white fur. He is sitting at a long bench, sitting very straight, for the bench has no back. His hands are turning the pages of a very large, thick book, the pages perhaps two feet by a foot and a half. He seems very busy with what he is reading—oblivious, in fact, to the guards who stand inside the open Gothic door. Their pikes are placed on the floor before them in readiness. Through the open vaults of the doorway a crowd of curious onlookers tries to peer over the shoulders of the guards. There are many women's faces among those who have apparently come to crane their necks for a look at the handsome Frenchman. The ladies of the court were not the only ones who heard of him. The women of London were also fascinated. And no wonder. Such a gallant prince! A prince and a poet.

Duke Charles of Orléans had begun by charming the first lady of England, but he did not stop there. Overnight the reputation of this handsome grandson of King Charles V traveled through high society in London. Surely Henry V had nothing to fear from so debonair a prince! Everyone could see that this prince was interested only in his books, in his poetry, in the songs he composed, and in dancing with the loveliest of English ladies. What a shame to keep him in the Tower! The ladies set about making their own plans. By next summer he must be brought down to Windsor. There in the lovely gardens along the Thames he would recite *The Romance of the Rose* to them, and they would teach him English. Let Henry V raise money and troops. Let the sanctimonious Henry V go wife-hunting in France. The English ladies could more than console themselves with the attentions of the French prince!

During those first months of his captivity at the Tower of London, Duke Charles seemed concerned with only one thing—making friends in England. First and foremost, he spent long evenings with Count Arthur of Richmond. It would have been natural for them to discuss Agincourt together. Little by little they began to understand their errors of strategy. It was too late, of course, to do anything about that now. Second, they discussed the precarious position of Count Arthur's mother, the Queen Joanna. Surely Henry V would not dare punish her on Arthur's account. She was well surrounded by servants from Brittany. The English could not speak Breton. Furthermore, Queen Joanna was exceedingly wealthy. Her late husband, Henry IV, had showered her with revenues, and she had a large annual income from Brittany. Meanwhile, Count

Arthur's hands were tied. He could not make a suspicious move without endangering his mother.

Duke Charles had many reasons for wishing to converse at leisure with Count Arthur of Richmond. The House of Orléans had long wished to make the Bretons feel that they were French rather than English. Of course, Duke Charles would have observed, Count Arthur was a feudal prisoner. He had pledged his word to Henry V. One does not break one's knightly pledge. Count Arthur thought it over thoroughly. Of course, mused Duke Charles, there is always a papal dispensation. Feudal word, thought Count Arthur: if I broke my word to Henry V, it would not be the first time. After all, my feudal oath did not keep me away from Agincourt Field, did it? Duke Charles sat musing. The two also discussed the question of escape. Even if he were able to escape, reflected Duke Charles, he might find it more advantageous to remain in England. King Henry might be made to rue the fact that he had an adversary in England when he returned to France to pursue the war. What the two young nobles chiefly needed on such nice decisions was legal advice from home. In time they would be instructed what to do.

England was to them a strange country. The chief idea was to make friends. This was Duke Charles's strategy. Hardly was there a noble lord or lady in England but had close connections in France. Many had been lavishly entertained by Louis of France. Many had seen the Duchess Valentine Visconti. They knew this young duke was the possible heir to northern Italy. Many had known and done homage to Queen Isabelle. This duke was her widower, and the father of her child. Therefore Duke Charles was no stranger in England.

Many English lords and ladies could see that there was no harm in the young duke at all. Henry V might glower as he liked. As far as that went, Henry V, after youthful pleasures that had been far from innocent, had become far too austere. This French prince cared only for study, poetry, dances, and gay parties. The world had used him cruelly indeed. Humphrey, Duke of Gloucester, might storm and frown in disbelief. He was probably only envious. One had only to hear a ballad composed by Duke Charles to see that he was no dangerous adversary. His war was ended. And that was good.

In such swift days had life changed utterly for Charles of Orléans. While he waited to establish contact with Blois and his family, allowed himself to be solicited by new English friends eager to know him, and won the confidence of Count Arthur and the queen, the duke was also making plans for his private life. Jean Gerson had often remarked that the man who wished to lead a life of contemplation must first have led one of activity. This had been forced upon Charles. For the first time in years he had leisure for reading, study, and writing. One of his purchases in England was a book.

This was not an unusual order. Duke Charles desired a book of several hundred pages, not a large book, but a thick one. It was to be bound in the shiniest green leather. Its pages would be the most expensive vellum. Its pages would be left blank. The duke also required two colors of ink—brown for the verses and red for the capital letters. He also purchased a ruler so that he could make thirty or so lines to a page, for his handwriting was small, rounded, regular, and meticulous. Once the book arrived, he began to fill it with his poetry, carefully copied and numbered. This would be his diary, the book "which Duke Charles made in exile."

Occasionally he may have taken a copy of one of his poems to his new friends. Perhaps the Queen, and certainly her young ladies-in-waiting, would enjoy hearing a love poem. They would like to listen to a poem set to music by Duke Charles himself. In English, one of his early poems would sound something like this:

BALLAD XXXII

"Belle, if you please, hear me say
　　How I treasure tenderly
Your heart that you gave away;
It's with me, by your bounty.
How I keep it warm today
In the handkerchief of Joy
And enclosed for surety
In the coffer of my memory.

　　"So it shall not feel dismay
　　　Often bathe it lovingly
With tears I cannot gainsay;
For I miss your bright beauty!
Then each day without delay
Dry it at the hearth fondly,

And replace it carefully
In the coffer of my memory.

"Now, dear Lady, let me pray
For my heart I left gladly
In your hands just yesterday:
Keep my love in loyalty.
My sweet heart, do not betray;
Keep the key most faithfully
While I your heart guarantee
In the coffer of my memory.

"Lady, word to you relay
How I treat your heart kindly;
Ever shall be, as I say,
In the coffer of my memory."

⚜ ⚜ ⚜

Duke Charles remained not more than a month in London without making direct contact with his Duchy of Orléans and with his family at Blois. As soon as the news of his capture at Agincourt reached Paris, the duke's personal lawyer in that city, William of Mountjoy, sent a messenger riding night and day to Blois Castle. The rider's name was Hennequin de Werde. Once the dreadful news was known, a party set out from Blois immediately. Destination: England. The Parliament granted them, on November 17, 1415, a safe-conduct for a month. The order covered Master Robert de Tuilliers, Advocate for the Duke of Orléans; Master Hugo Perriez, Secretary; John Benoît and Jeum. Le Breton, French servants. They were allowed to bring with them "horses, harnesses and trappings, goods, belongings, affairs, personal effects whatsoever." Fortified with a first-rate lawyer from the University of Orléans, the young duke felt confident in his strategy. Now he could advise Arthur of Richmond about feudal oaths. So far the English had been very evasive about his own ransom. Meanwhile, let the nobles of the social set take him for a butterfly. That game was well worth the candle!

The tragedy of his personal situation came home to Duke Charles when he saw the first faces from France, when he heard their accounts of his grief-stricken duchy and all the other duchies of central France. His brother, Count Philip of Vertus, had not been well. The first dauphin was about to die. The second dauphin was sickly; he would not live long. Every day, and every messenger from France, brought Duke Charles the certainty that he was drawing closer to the throne of France—a fact that had by no means escaped King Henry V. Therefore the passing days served to increase his mythical ransom to the point where it appeared more and more unfeasible.

France mourned. Spirits were crushed. Marguerite of Orléans wept in Blois Castle. The little Joan hardly understood what had happened to her father. In the neighboring Duchy of Alençon a six-year-old boy, named John for his father, opened his eyes wide with incomprehension. People kissed him and told him that his father had died a great hero. Little John, the future Duke of Alençon, learned in early childhood that he would have to grow up fast in order to drive the English out of France.

In Blois Castle the Bastard of Orléans, Count Ferdinand-Jean, was twelve years old. His face was characterized by a stern lantern jaw. When he set his teeth, he looked very fierce indeed. Louis of France and Valentine Visconti had done well to raise this youngster. Even at the age of twelve the boy asked for a sword. His tutors, too, probably sensed the determination that his older brother Charles possessed to such a high degree.

Agincourt Field had decided the missions in life for most of the young boys in France, and for most of the young girls. France had not yet reached her darkest hour. They had still to see the worst, for King Henry V would return shortly. One consolation was the fact that Duke Charles of Orléans was safe. That was good news.

Furious with anger and grief, Bernard VII of Armagnac leaped on his horse and tore up the roads to Paris. Henry V had not yet entered Paris. When he did so, it would be over Armagnac's dead body!

The race for Paris was on, with three contenders in the front of the running: Bernard VII, John of Burgundy, and Henry V. While the third raised money in England and levied another victorious army, the Duke of Burgundy—rather better prepared—marched southward at the head of his troops. The violent southerner beat him in the first lap. Arriving at the Hôtel Saint-Paul, Bernard VII had himself appointed Constable of France. His first act was to close Paris to the Duke of Burgundy. Then he set about hiring a Genoese fleet to deliver Harfleur. Moderation, in the person of Duke

Charles of Orléans, had left the country. There would no longer be any respect for law or regulation or procedure. Armagnac and Burgundy had met face to face: cruelty versus cruelty, murderer versus murderer, captain versus captain—with one difference. Armagnac acted also out of love for his country. Whatever he did could be construed as defense of France and of its king. Each baron privately desired nothing so much as the death of the other.

The first dauphin had died before the new constable, accompanied by Ramonet de la Guerre, one of his best captains, had entered the city. Within a few months the last moderate, the Duke of Berry, had also died at the age of eighty-five. The first English ambassadors to arrive in France concerning the ransom of Duke Charles departed without beginning to reach an agreement. The new constable at once laid siege to Harfleur. The ambassadors therefore signed a separate treaty with the Duke of Burgundy.

From his prison in the Tower, more often from his frequentings of English society, Duke Charles kept informed of all that happened in England and at home. Little by little he was learning to know the characters of his enemies. One story he heard was enlightening.

Henry V had gone to Calais with his brother Humphrey of Gloucester. The Duke of Burgundy and his son Count Philip arrived shortly thereafter to pay their respects. Count Philip went in person to the Duke of Gloucester's lodgings. At the entrance of the Burgundian count and heir, the Duke of Gloucester did not even turn his head! After continuing his conversation a while, he bade only a casual welcome. He did not advance to greet the Burgundian scion. Count Philip said nothing of this at the time, but it was an outrageous affront. With good luck such a wound might be made to fester. This Duke of Gloucester had already shown himself an enemy of Duke Charles. There might be a way to bait him. There might be a way to turn Burgundy against Gloucester, and thus against England. One thing was clear: the English dukes had no respect for traitors. Count Philip had seen that. If John of Burgundy were out of the way, there might be a chance of winning Count Philip. Sooner or later the Burgundians would grow tired of having the English so near Flanders.

On April 7, 1416, the name of Charles of Orléans appeared again in the Archives of England. On this date he was granted another safe-conduct, this time for Hugues Ferrier and his brother Rudolf, both "servants." *Veniendo et ibidem morando,* says the document. In other words, these servants were to journey to England and stay there. In February of that same year Duke Charles paid an astonishingly large sum of money from his Paris attorney for the ransom of his brother John d'Angoulême. Who received this money is, of course, not stated. Nor was Count John set free. By the second day of May, Duke Charles was at Windsor Castle, where he dated a payment order for some new clothes. No doubt he also wrote a poem, in his inimitable way, about the return of spring when a young man's thoughts turn to beautiful and so kind English ladies. However, with his usual discretion he failed to name them. The poems that already filled many pages of his new book might have been addressed to anyone. Perhaps that was his idea.

Meanwhile, the news from France was disquieting. Bernard VII and his trusted subordinate, the Breton Tanneguy du Chastel, ruled Paris with hands of iron. When they needed money, they levied it from the city's tradesmen, particularly from those guilds that had so long championed Burgundy with cleaver and butcher knife. Henry V had spent almost a year idly in England, or rather in negotiating for money and troops. Not all had gone well for the English king. There were troubles about religious matters; dissenters from the Church—some of them old cronies of Henry V—would have to be executed if the king was to draw again upon Church funds. His chancellor was Henry Beaufort, surnamed "Henry the Rich." This prelate had always been devoted to his king—had even, in fact, wanted Henry IV to abdicate in his son's favor. However, Henry Beaufort was hated in London. Then, too, he was an enemy of the Duke of Gloucester. It is not certain when Duke Charles first met Henry Beaufort or how he managed to win his friendship. It is certain that Beaufort had high ambitions of which the king did not approve. While the Duke of Orléans was a prisoner, he had friends in high places—friends more powerful than the King of England. Henry Beaufort listened, and received rich gifts from the Duchy of Orléans.

By April of 1417 the friendship of Duke Charles was even more to be sought. The third dauphin of France had died quite suddenly, an event that moved his cousin in England to within one step of the throne of France. The only person between Duke Charles and the throne—if King Charles VI were to succumb to his insanity—was the last Dauphin Charles. This last prince of the House of Valois was a shy, dark, thin, and nervous lad of fourteen. Tanneguy du Chastel redoubled his guard at the Hôtel Saint-Paul. John of Burgundy roamed about the City of Paris. His principal pastime was forays upon the Duchy of Orléans: assaults on an isolated castle, surprise raids upon a village, the burning of crops and haylofts, the terrorizing of anyone suspected of Armagnac leanings.

In April of 1417 Duke Charles managed what must have been a complicated negotiation. He was granted permission to have his same advocate return, the Robert de Tuilliers who had visited him in 1415. The lawyer was not only to be accompanied by a secretary, a new one named Chomery. This time the advocate was to conduct with him "thirty men, whether sailors or experts in the use of catapults, or other men of war, in a craft or armed vessel." Duke Charles was to have his personal bodyguard; these thirty-two men were to remain in England. Permission was also granted for the entry of goods and clothing for the captive. The safe-conduct did not specify what sort of "provision" they were to bring their lord. His fiefs in Touraine and Champagne were already well known for the type of "provision" they might be expected to supply someone in England, the many new friends of Duke Charles.

By the summer of that year the new and last Dauphin Charles had shown some initiative. During one of King Charles VI's lucid moments, the two had rid Paris of what had become a perennial scandal, Queen Isabeau. One of her gentlemen had, in fact, met the king in person on the road leading from the queen's summer residence at Vincennes. The gentleman in question, after a private interrogation by the king, was summarily sewn in a leather sack and dropped into the Seine. Then the queen was ordered into solitary quarters, first at Blois Castle and then in Tours. Her Majesty was furious. She vented her wrath upon her last son, the Dauphin Charles. Perhaps her hatred of this particular youngster had its origin in his hatred of her.

The circumstances of the dauphin's birth, although never openly questioned in a court of law, were a thorn in his side. It was true that he did not resemble King Charles VI. This dauphin had been born in the same year as the Bastard of Orléans. These two, however, had probably not yet met each other. The dauphin's known suspicions of his illegitimacy were very painful to him. Four centuries before, William the Conqueror, who was an illegitimate son, had had the ears cut off everyone in a Norman village for one taunt concerning his birth, for one voice calling "Bastard." Yet, throughout this century the youngest brother of Duke Charles is always referred to as the "Bastard of Orléans"—from his birth until 1440, at least. In the case of the Dauphin Charles, there were no taunts to his face. Their absence did not cause the frail dauphin to suffer any less acutely. How could he ever put his mind to rest on such a subject? In whom could he confide such dreadful suspicions? Who in the world could ever reassure him?

While Duke Charles studied the situation at home and discussed it with his lawyers and his fellow prisoners, he continued to keep up an appearance of gaiety, to frequent the society of the ladies at Windsor, and to dance whenever they so willed. At Windsor he met another illustrious prisoner, Sir James Stuart of Scotland. The future King of Scotland was the same age as Duke Charles. He had been captured while on the way to France to be educated. For the past eleven years he had remained at Windsor Castle, being carefully educated, while the Duke of Albany gladly ruled Scotland for him. The future James I was a poet, from which one might suppose that he and Duke Charles had a bond. No doubt the French prisoner desired such a friendship. No doubt he had already formulated plans concerning Scotland, the old and faithful ally of France. However, James I seems also to have been the especial protégé of Henry V. If there had been a way to suborn this poet-musician, Duke Charles would probably have found it. Although James I was vigorous and healthy, he was also very corpulent, and satisfied to be so pampered at Windsor.

Duke Charles's intimacy with Arthur of Richmond and Sir James Stuart was of short duration. The changed situation in France caused uneasiness in England. Duke Charles had made too many friends. Meanwhile, he had become even more valuable. The decision was made on June 1, 1417. Its blow was bitter and very frightening:

"Robert Waterton, Esq., to convey Charles of Orléans from our castle of Windsor all the way to our castle of Pontefract there even to delay up to a certain time. By order of the King himself."

On June 2nd a further order provided for "moneys and the hiring of horses" to convey Duke Charles to Pontefract—again by order of the King himself.

Pontefract! The very word was enough to strike fear into a stout heart! What would they think in France? What would they say? What but that the young duke had just received his death sentence from Henry V, even as King Richard had received his, openly or by implication from Henry IV? No one who entered Pontefract as a prisoner lived to ride forth from its massive walls! It was the black castle of England! Of all the castles of England, its reputation was the worst.

Robert Waterton, Esquire! They would recognize the name in France. The name was, in fact, familiar. He had been among that small party of ardent Lancastrians who had escorted Henry of Lancaster from Brittany to Yorkshire in 1399. As soon as Pontefract Castle had opened its wide gates to Henry of Lancaster, Richard II was as good as deposed!

In June of 1417 the debonair Duke of Orléans was torn from his round of parties at Windsor. He was removed from the proximity of the other hostages. The Duke of Gloucester suspected Charles of Orléans. King Henry V suspected him even more. Under heavy guard the gallant, dashing young duke traveled the length of England, from Windsor up to Yorkshire.

There was a very noticeable change between southern and northern England, and one that was not due to temperature alone, although that variation was certainly appreciable. From Windsor, Duke Charles was not far from France—down the winding Thames, into London, and out into the Channel.

Pontefract was hundreds of miles farther away from France. Southern England was sunny. The estates and manor houses and castles of Surrey were set among the most beautiful gardens of the world. The area was wooded and rolling, with open fields and tiny cup-shaped valleys that dipped out of sight as one rode south of the Thames. The fields and hedgerows were green in daylight and a soft blue at twilight. Life seemed easier for everyone. Faces were friendly. In southern England the showers gave way gracefully before brilliant sunlight over gentle, flowered fields.

The farther north he rode, the more Duke Charles could feel the northland. The country became more open to sky and to wind; more barren, colder, more unprotected. There were fewer trees and larger areas of cultivated fields as he approached the Ridings of Yorkshire. He had an impression of height, as if the sea were very far away, indeed; not at all as if it were just over that plateau to the east and beyond that narrow strip of flat coastline. The air was wet and sharp. The hills were higher and more pointed. The valleys were wider, often more than a quarter of a mile across. The faces were sharper. The people were thinner and sterner. They looked coldly at him from deep-set eyes that were a paler blue. They looked even less French than the southerners.

Duke Charles was surprised at Pontefract Castle. He had imagined a huge, sprawling black mass of masonry like Chinon in France, or a squat black pile like the Duke of Brittany's castle in Nantes. Sad as he was, frightened as he undoubtedly was, his poet's heart could not have helped surging in his chest at the sight of Pontefract Castle! Such is the nature of a poet.

Even at the point of death—perhaps especially at the point of death—a born poet has an eye for true beauty when he sees it. Duke Charles must have reined in his horse as the party reached the summit of a round hill and looked across the valley to a higher hill just north of them. His heart must have filled with wonder.

Pontefract towered into the blue sky of Yorkshire. Very few architectural wonders of medieval England could equal its lofty splendor. The slender round towers of its donjon fingered the sky itself. Pontefract rose splendidly against the bare horizon like a castle in a dream. It was not black at all! How could its epithets be explained? Perhaps the medieval and later writers who described it transferred to the castle the black deeds of the Dukes of Lancaster.

Pontefract Castle was yellow, tall, and golden in the sunlight; blond except for the dark curtain walls that blended into the eastern ridge upon which it had been piled, wall upon encircling wall. From its southern side Pontefract presented five walls of defense, with square towers, forts, and star-shaped towers placed at intervals around its main line of fortifications. Each encircling wall was smaller in circumference and farther up the cone-shaped hill. There were four main gates, each a fortress in itself, to pass before one reached the summit of the hill and the crown of inner castle.

As one entered the courtyard from the south, the porter's lodge, a heavy stone building, was on the left. The western wall of the courtyard was the highest. At its southwestern corner towered a group of turrets called the Round Tower. A curving flight of fifteen to twenty steps led up to their main entrance. The base of these towers was on the top of a wall at least some twenty feet above the level of the main courtyard. The central turret in the nestlike structure, or Round Tower, rose another good five stories above the base of the wall, or promenade. There were narrow, vertical windows in all sides of the turrets. At such a height one could see for miles and miles in all directions. Continuing along the west wall, the next tower was the Red, or Gascogne, Tower, which formed an angle with the north wall. Underneath this huge mass of masonry were rooms built into the thickness of the wall, and under them the dungeons—thirty or so feet below the surface of the courtyard.

Below the Gascogne Tower and to the left of it was a room about twelve feet by twelve feet. There, learned Duke Charles, Richard II had starved himself to death. Did Robert Waterton, Esquire, realize as he did the honors, showing his royal prisoner the various points of interest of Pontefract Castle, that he was speaking to one of the very few men of the fifteenth century who really knew what had happened to England's King Richard? Undoubtedly he did not. Duke Charles told no secrets, ever.

There were altogether eight towers inside the castle proper. To the north were the Treasure Tower and Swillington Tower. On the east wall were the King's Tower and the Queen's Tower. The Constable Tower, where Robert Waterton sat while on duty, formed the angle of the east and south sides. In the courtyard itself was the Great Hall with its storerooms and dungeons below ground level, cut out of the solid bedrock of the hill. In the eastern end of the courtyard were a cemetery and a Norman chapel. Pontefract had been built by the Norman French centuries earlier. Situated as it was in the border country, in the ancient Danelaw, between England and Scotland, it had been constructed to serve as a tower of strength. Duke Charles could see even at a glance that it was virtually impregnable. The wild Scots might drive their lightning raiding parties well to the south of it. Pontefract could be taken only by a long and extensive siege. Only a full-scale war waged over two or so years could cause Pontefract to yield. A person could escape from Pontefract into Scotland, however. Duke Charles had already begun to gain the confidence of Robert Waterton and his family.

The French prince climbed the steps to his round chamber in the Towers. He would have to begin all over again. Whatever friends he had made in the South could not help him so easily now. Henry Beaufort must still be made to hear his blandishments, however. He would know soon enough if Robert Waterton had a price.

Duke Charles was far from everyone there in Yorkshire. He had in his turn come to that very isolated spot where the Princess Isabelle's first husband had suffered and died. The chief idea now was just to stay alive himself. He must stay alive, and he must look northward, since Henry V had been so disobliging. He must find a way to get in touch with Scotland. He must make use of catastrophe if possible.

North of Pontefract was the royal City of York. Duke Charles thought until he remembered what he knew about York. He recalled that the chief primate of England was the Archbishop of York. A little farther north than Yorkminster Cathedral was the Kingdom of Scotland. In Scotland the House of Orléans had many loyal friends.

The proof that Pontefract's lofty towers and multiple curtain walls had not depressed Duke Charles or decreased his sense of policy is corroborated by none other than King Henry V himself. In a letter to the Privy Council, dated the end of November, 1417, King Henry says:

"Furthermore I would that ye commune with my brother, with the chancellor, with my cousin of Northumberland, and my cousin of Westmoreland; and that ye set good ordinance for my North Marches, and especially for the Duke of Orléans and for all the remnant of my prisoners in France, and also for the King of Scotland.

"For as I am secretly informed by a man of right notable estate in this land, that there hath been a man of the Duke of Orléans in Scotland, and accorded with the Duke of Albany that this next summer he shall bring the mannet [Sir James Stuart] of Scotland to stir up what he may; and also that there should be found ways of having away specially of the Duke of Orléans, and also of the King, as well as of the remnant of my said prisoners, that God do defend!

"Wherefore, I will that the Duke of Orléans be kept still within the castle of Pomfret [Pontefract], without going to Robert's Place., or to any other disport; for it is better he lack his disport than we be deceived."

It is to be assumed after such an order that Duke Charles found his merriment curtailed. It is further to be assumed that the ladies of Yorkshire were grieved. Henry V might still be made to rue the day when he had carried this French noble into England. Ostensibly the duke was chiefly concerned with ransoming his poor brother John. The orders from Parliament allowing safe-conducts came regularly, one after the other. Someone in a high place was being sorely tempted and was yielding to more than blandishments. In July of 1417 Duke Charles was actually allowed to import into England a shipload of lawyers, secretaries, servants, and a cargo of gold, silver, and precious gems. Parliament even ordered that good care be taken of this shipment.

During this same summer Duke Charles also ordered a present for his young brother, the Bastard of Orléans. It was a suit of splendid gray clothes lined with black Lombardy lamb.

News from home was particularly bad. Events had taken a turn for the worse that could mean total disaster. Queen Isabeau, in

solitary confinement in Tours, had requested the help of John,
Duke of Burgundy. If Burgundy once got his hands on the Dauphin
Charles, the game was finished! Duke Charles instructed Bernard
VII to negotiate immediately. His suggestions, his reasons, and
his orders were countermanded. Bernard VII had the bit between
his teeth. Henry V would have to take one city in Normandy after
the other—each one after a year of siege—before he could work
his painful way up the Seine to Paris. Burgundy would enter Paris
only over the constable's dead body.

By May of 1418 Queen Isabeau and Duke John of Burgundy tried
a new tack. Instead of attacking the constable in Paris, they sent an
army to lay waste and conquer Gascony. Years later Frenchmen were
still repeating Count Bernard's witticism. When he was informed
that his home city of Rodez might rebel, Count Bernard VII of
Armagnac answered laconically, *"Se ley dabale"*—If I give permission.

On the 12th of June, 1418, Duke John of Burgundy was free to
enter Paris over the dead body of Bernard VII, Count of Armagnac,
Constable of France.

During the previous night Paris had been handed over to the
most cruel and bloody violence. Blood ran in the streets. The butchers
and the hangmen were second in popularity to John of Burgundy.
The city had been betrayed by an ironmonger's son.

During the night a young man had stolen the keys to the city
gate at Saint-Germain-des-Près. Eight hundred Burgundian troops
had crept into the city in the dead of night. Dividing into groups,
one band had headed for the dauphin in the Hôtel Saint-Paul. A
second had lunged for Bernard of Armagnac. The Gascon constable, alerted in the nick of time, had slipped in his nightclothes
out into the dark streets and found refuge in the house of a mason.
His host then betrayed him. Count Bernard was handed over to
the mob. Before killing him, the Parisians flayed a band of flesh
from his right shoulder down across his back to his left hip.

The Provost of Paris, Tanneguy du Chastel, made a sortie with
whatever troops he had near him. One short battle was fought in
the outer court of the Hôtel Saint-Paul before the provost wisely
withdrew. It was too little and too late. The mobs would rule Paris.
Duke Charles, sitting in his lonely tower at Pontefract, must have
held his breath as he came to the end of the letter. He must have
wondered if the young Dauphin Charles had survived.

All had not yet been lost. Let John of Burgundy and Queen

Isabeau enter Paris in triumph. Let them congratulate the butcher Caboche and the hangman Capeluche. Let Henry V starve the 100,000 people inside the ancient capital of the Dukes of Normandy. Let the queen city of Rouen fall. That—even all that—still did not mean that France was lost! Duke Charles of Orléans must have gripped the edges of his wooden lectern until his knuckles were bone white. The last sickly Dauphin of France was safe in the Duchy of Orléans!

At that moment of pain and desperation, Tanneguy du Chastel had not lost his head. He had darted through the dark streets into the Hôtel Saint-Paul, down its vaulted passages, up flights of steps, breathlessly, and found the frail dauphin, the Prince of Vienne, asleep in his bed. Without an instant's hesitation Tanneguy du Chastel had grabbed a blanket, wrapped it around the little boy, lifted him easily in his arms, and darted down passages, bolting doors behind him as he ran—just seconds ahead of the mob and the Burgundian troops. The old King Charles V had been wise indeed to erect his palace by the edge of the river. It was the Seine that had saved both their lives. Tanneguy du Chastel tossed the child into a rowboat, jumped aboard, and shoved out into the dark river. Duke Charles was well served in France. France was well served by such a doughty Breton. The dauphin was "home" in Orléans.

From his prison in Pontefract Duke Charles sent letter after frantic letter. Negotiate. Negotiate. It is the only way. As long as we hold the dauphin in our duchy, John of Burgundy will come to terms. Paris will become untenable for him.

Rouen fell after one-third of its people had starved to death. The English king allowed the women and children to leave the city. Then, according to Michelet, he let them die in the snow between the city walls and the river. John of Burgundy made a few feeble attempts to save Rouen.

Pontoise was about to fall. The English king was growing weary of such long sieges. When he had condemned Lord Cobham to death on Saint Giles's Field, London; when he had allowed this religious dissenter to be put to torture, causing his intestines to be drawn out of his opened abdomen and slowly burned before his eyes, why should he show compassion to stubborn French provincials? Had he not styled himself their king? While in Rouen, King Henry consecrated John Kempe as Bishop of Rochester. Duke

Charles did not miss this fact either. This was a man who, like Henry Beaufort, wanted a cardinal's hat.

That year in Paris 80,000 people died of the plague. The Gray Friars preached openly that this was God's retribution.

Duke Charles commissioned four ambassadors to represent him in France. One of them was another member of the Cousinot family who had defended his mother so ably in her lawsuit. Their orders were to negotiate with Burgundy before it was too late.

Early in 1419 a meeting was held between King Henry V on the one hand and the Duke of Burgundy and Queen Isabeau on the other hand. The Princess Catherine of France was present. Since Henry V was so determined to marry this princess, her mother had decided that the English king should be allowed to see her—should, in fact, be allowed to kiss her once. Then the French queen, after seeing how smitten King Henry was, withdrew her daughter from the council. Let King Henry languish for a second look and another kiss!

During this session there was a sharp exchange of words between John of Burgundy and the King of England.

"Dear cousin," said King Henry to Duke John, "we wish you to know that we intend to have your king's daughter, and everything else we are asking for along with her, or we shall boot him out of his kingdom, and you along with him, out of the kingdom also."

"Sire, you speak according to your pleasure; but before you boot our sovereign and ourselves out of his kingdom, you will be very weary—and of that fact, we have no doubt."

Such an exchange of threats prompted Duke Charles to urge his ambassadors to negotiate with Burgundy. In accordance with their pleas, this council between King Henry and Burgundy was followed by a treaty signed on July 11, 1419, between the Dauphin Charles and Burgundy. That was, to Duke Charles's way of thinking, a great victory.

Meanwhile, the Orléanists were besieging castles on the periphery of the two territories. Both brothers of Duke Charles, Philip of Vertus and the Bastard Jean, had taken to the field. The latter, although still only a boy, had already been captured by the Burgundians. From his prison in England Duke Charles paid a stiff ransom for the young firebrand Jean. Had the Burgundians realized what an extraordinarily good warrior the Bastard of Orléans was becoming, they would probably never have let him go free.

King Henry, very angry at this new attempt to arbitrate the differences between the Orléanists and the Burgundians, stepped up his siege operations in Normandy. In short order he took Pontoise, Gisors, Roche-Guyon, and the Château Gaillard on the Seine. This last castle had been the celebrated stronghold of Richard the Lion-Hearted.

The peace between the dauphin and Burgundy was still not permanent. Therefore in August and the first days of September, Tanneguy du Chastel rode back and forth between his master and the duke. Would the latter consent to another conference? He would not. Why would he not? Let the dauphin come to him. That would be most unseemly. Did the Duke of Burgundy really want this English king to conquer Île-de-France?

At this point the Lady of Giac, Burgundy's mistress, also interceded. Would not Burgundy ride down to Montereau? The dauphin had something new to propose. Would not Burgundy care to listen, at least, to a new proposition? Did he not see that the situation was critical? The dauphin awaited His Highness of Burgundy at a bridge over the Yonne River near the castle of Montereau. To prove his good faith the dauphin had put Montereau Castle at the disposal of his uncle of Burgundy. Tanneguy du Chastel sedulously neglected to mention that the dauphin awaited his dear relative with twenty thousand troops from Orléans, Berry, and Touraine.

Yielding finally to the insistence of his dear friend, the Lady of Giac, and to the clever importunities of Tanneguy du Chastel, John the Fearless rode down to Montereau on the Yonne on or about the 10th of September. He was flanked by his nobles of Bourbon, Noailles, and Saint-George, plus five hundred soldiers and two hundred archers. At three in the afternoon he was met on the road by three lords. They told him that they came from Montereau. They said they came to warn him. They described barricades and a pavilion that the Orléanists had constructed on the bridge itself. Duke John halted to take counsel.

"We will go forward," decided the Duke of Burgundy, "and await whatever fortune it shall please God to send us. Let it never be said that peace shall fail to come to this kingdom because of our delays."

The duke and his suite lodged in Montereau Castle where a side entrance opened into a small meadow beside the bridge. There he met Lady Jane of Giac, who had already consulted several times with the dauphin. She assured her friend of Burgundy that he was in no danger. Then Tanneguy du Chastel arrived to remind Burgundy that the dauphin was sitting on the bridge awaiting his good pleasure. Duke John chose ten noblemen from his retinue and strode across the meadow. As he set foot on the bridge, he waved a part of his escort to precede him.

When they came to the first wooden stockade on the bridge itself, several of the dauphin's party threw open the gate. "Advance toward His Highness," they said. "He awaits you, Sire."

"I am going before him," replied Duke John. After he had entered this first stockade, the gate was locked behind him. So was the second gate.

Then he was ceremoniously welcomed by Tanneguy du Chastel. Duke John slapped his Lord of Saint-George on the shoulder. He said of Tanneguy, "There's the man I trust."

Duke John came up to the Dauphin Charles, who was fully dressed in sword and armor, and leaning casually on the last wooden enclosure. Duke John fell on one knee. Then the dauphin spoke to him coldly. "We reproach you, Uncle, for having broken your word, for having prolonged and incited war in our kingdom, for having kept your domains in a state of war instead of having withdrawn your troops as you swore to do."

Then an Orléanist lord named Robert de Loire tugged at Duke John, or pulled at his left shoulder. "Get up, Sire," he said, "you are only too honorable!"

At this point Duke John is said to have tried to adjust his sword, which had fallen too far behind him as he knelt. Sir Robert then asked him sternly, "Do you put your hand to your sword in the very presence of His Highness the Dauphin?"

As Sir Robert spoke, Tanneguy du Chastel, stepping up to Duke John from the right, nodded his head to the Orléanist noblemen. He said, "Now is the time."

Monstrelet affirms that it was Tanneguy du Chastel who struck the first blow, with an ax stroke that cut off Burgundy's chin. He also adds, however, that each Orléanist lord present also struck— one through the chest, one through the belly, and so on. The idea was that each one took equal responsibility.

The dauphin was carried away from the ensuing short struggle by a southern lord who was there present. John of Burgundy was thus murdered in broad daylight. His retinue were also slaughtered, except for one who managed to escape by leaping over the stockades. The greater part of his attendants who subsequently made a

dash out of Montereau Castle were killed along the main road
north. Louis of France's murderer had been murdered in his turn.

Count Philip of Charolais, only son of Duke John, became the
next Duke of Burgundy. He always blamed the dauphin for this
murder. It did not halt the war. On the contrary, it threw Duke
Philip into the arms of King Henry V. Not more than two weeks
after the death of John the Fearless, King Henry wrote another
strong letter home to England. It concerned the Duke of Orléans,
whom no one ever connected with the assassination of Duke John
of Burgundy.

"Given under our Signet in oure Town of Gisors, the first day
of October. To the Worshipful Fader in God, our Right Trusty
and Well Beloved, the Bishop of Durham, our Chancellor of England . . . We Greet You Well . . .

"And we will and pray you and also charge you that, as we trust
unto you, and as you like to have our good Lordship, you see and
ordain that good Heed be taken unto the sure keeping of our
French Prisoners within our realm of England; And in especial
of the Duke of Orléans. . . .

"For their escaping And principally of the said Duke of Orléans
might never have been so harmful and prejudicial unto Us, as it
might be Now, if any of them escaped, and Namely the said Duke
of Orléans, which God forbid.

"And therefore as we trust in you, you see that Robert Waterton
for no Trust, fair Speech, nor Promises that might be made unto
him, nor for none other manner Cause, be so blinded by the said
Duke that he be the more reckless of his Keeping; but that in
eschewing of all Perils that may fall, he take as good Heed unto
the sure keeping of his person as is possible.

"And enquire if Robert Waterton use any reckless governance
about the Keeping of the said Duke, and write to him thereof,
that it be amended."

The urgent instructions of King Henry were put into effect.
During the larger part of 1420 there were no safe-conducts issued
to the Duke of Orléans. The prisoner was very quiet, and for many
obvious reasons. First of all, he suffered because of the blunder committed in Montereau. Then, too, he grieved for his fellow prisoner,
Arthur of Richmond.

Queen Joanna had not been safe despite all her wealth—or rather, because of it. She had felt King Henry's rapacity and his vindictive-ness. Her wealth and estates had been summarily confiscated by the king. To obviate any recourse on the part of her friends or her sons, the handsome lady was charged with witchcraft. She too was in prison, and in the direst poverty.

Duke Charles had still another reason to be very quiet during these months. He *had* been in touch with Scotland. His negotia-tions with the Duke of Albany, Regent of Scotland, were proceeding in a very satisfactory manner. If his party committed a major error in France, Duke Charles was about to complete a major triumph in England.

Perhaps an excellent soldier who also hated the English, someone like Archibald, the fourth Earl of Douglas, might be persuaded to command French and Scotch troops in France under the Dauphin Charles. Could Archibald of Douglas forego his old friendship with Burgundy now that Duke John was dead? Could the Earl of Douglas be tempted by one of the duchies belonging to Duke Charles—the Duchy of Touraine, for example? Such negotiations required the greatest secrecy.

Just to show them that he was still alive, however, in February of 1420 Duke Charles surprised his sister Marguerite with one of the loveliest presents conceivable—and one of the most costly. He ordered a *Book of Hours* written, illuminated, bound, and decorated with gold. It was made for "our very dear and very beloved sister in Blois" so that she could recite her prayers and her Church services from it. It is not known what thoughtful presents the family at Blois prepared for their liege lord and brother, but there were probably many. This was a close-knit family.

In 1420 this family grew even closer when the sad news reached them all of the death of Count Philip of Vertus. Duke Charles re-acted immediately; his powers of attorney were to be entirely vested in his half-brother, the Bastard Jean of Orléans. He also gave Jean the lands and the title of Vertus, but the chroniclers of the century continue to call this Jean the Bastard of Orléans. The name *Orléans* was the magical part of it.

The Treaty of Troyes, June, 1420, repudiated the ancient constitu-tion of France by which the Crown could not pass through the female heirs. The treaty read:

"I Philip Duke of Burgundy for mine and my heirs . . . to Lord Henry, *King of England and of France* . . . And immediately after the death of Lord Charles [VI], our King, we shall pledge our faith to Lord King Henry and to his successors in perpetuity, nor shall we have or suffer any other whatsoever for our supreme Lord, King of France, than thou [this] Henry and his heirs."

King Henry V swore that he would henceforth call King Charles VI his father and Queen Isabeau his mother and that he would honor them; that he would have the virgin Catherine to wife; and that he would reduce the Armagnacs and "those who follow the Dauphin" to obedience.

The Dauphin Charles was subsequently disinherited and declared a rebel.

Then Queen Isabeau, accompanied by her beautiful daughter Catherine, so swore.

Then Philip of Burgundy so swore . . . thus handing France to the King of England.

VII [*1420–1427*]   HENRY V, GRANDLY AC- companied by two of his broth- ers, by the Earls of Warwick and Huntington, and by sixteen hundred archers, married Catherine of France in Troyes on Trinity Sunday, June 3, 1420, thus sealing the treaty that declared him heir to the throne of France. The new Archbishop of Sens officiated.

After the ceremony there were such festivities and displays of pomp and magnificence that one would have thought King Henry was "about to become king of the entire world." King Charles VI was not present at the wedding. If his daughter Catherine was one of the poorest brides an English king had ever won, she may also have been one of the richest in promise. Duke Philip of Burgundy, who was present in full panoply, remarked that Catherine had fallen passionately in love with Henry at their first meeting in 1419, that she was determined to marry him, and that she had

teased Queen Isabeau until the latter signed the Treaty of Troyes
out of sheer fatigue. That was his version.

King Henry, superbly attired in burnished armor with a jeweled
fox's tail hanging from his helmet, presented his bride with a live
eagle that wore some verses praising himself. Catherine was eighteen
years old, and King Henry was thirty-two. Their honeymoon was
spent at the siege of Sens. "You gave me a wife," said King Henry
to the officiating prelate, "and I shall now return yours to you."

After the siege of Sens King Henry took Catherine and her
parents to the siege of Montereau and then to the siege of Melun.
His reasons were sound: he wanted an heir as quickly as possible;
he could not commute back and forth while prosecuting the war
to win France; he needed King Charles VI's presence in the hope
that the French would surrender to their king; and he believed
that the French would hesitate to attack an English camp where
so many members of the French royal family were quartered. Like
a good son, King Henry ordered that martial music be played
outside King Charles VI's tent every evening in the expectation
that such loud and stirring strains would be therapeutic.

The four to five hundred defenders at Montereau were hardly
pressed by the king and the Duke of Burgundy. When only the
central fortress still resisted, the French prisoners were hanged on a
gibbet in plain sight of the besieged. King Henry's valet, who used
to ride into battle beside him daily, was hanged along with them.
This valet had killed an Englishman by mistake. After the last
defenders had capitulated, the body of John the Fearless was ex-
humed and sent in state home to Burgundy. Montereau was punished
because the murder had been committed there. The persons Burgundy wanted most were Tanneguy du Chastel and Robert de
Loire. So staunch was the pact between those lords who had killed
Burgundy, however, that each one stoutly maintained that he
could not have struck down Duke John. Each one claimed that it
was he who had carried the dauphin away from the sight of so
much blood!

No such pact protected the Lady Jane of Giac, who had become
the mistress of Duke John around 1419 but who had helped the
Orléanist lords betray him nevertheless. This lady suffered a fate
even worse than that of many prominent ladies of the century.
After the murder on the Montereau Bridge, her husband found himself in love with another noble lady whom he wanted to marry. In
order to free himself from his wife, who was pregnant, he forced

her to drink poison. Then he lifted her to the croup of his horse and galloped with her until she died. For this murder, and also for the misappropriation of dauphinist funds, the Lord of Giac was tried, sentenced, and drowned. Aside from this execution, however, the lords who had killed John of Burgundy kept faith with each other and continued to deny the dauphin's guilt.

By November of 1420 King Henry, King Charles VI, and Duke Philip of Burgundy were laying siege to the city of Melun. King Henry, realizing that his money was running low, grew more and more short-tempered. At Melun he stripped the Marshal of France of his function because the latter had dared to look at him.

"How dare you look a prince in the face when you speak to him?"

The Lord of Isle-Adam replied, "Sire, the custom of the French is such, no matter what their position or authority, that if they lower their eyes, they are considered evil men."

King Henry retorted, "That is not our fashion in England."

While it is true that he was conquering France, he was still proceeding bit by bit. The English troops were decimated by epidemics. The weather was raw and bitter. The fall rains had set in heavily. Still the French, reduced long since to eating dogs, cats, horses, and other nourishment not fit for human beings, held out at Melun. By the time the town surrendered, the English king was in a foul mood. His money was gone. His soldiers were ill. Henry V even had two monks decapitated.

A Frenchman who had switched sides at Agincourt and subsequently recognized the English sovereign was also decapitated. This man had aided a wealthy merchant implicated in the murder of Duke John to escape from Melun. King Henry would not even grant appeals for mercy from his oldest brother, the Duke of Clarence, or from Duke Philip. There is no mention of Queen Catherine's asking for clemency for any French man or woman. King Henry was generally accounted very handsome. Perhaps she *was* passionately in love with him. Perhaps she was ashamed and cowed.

Passionately in love, or terribly afraid, whatever her emotions may have been, Queen Catherine was still not pregnant. As soon as Melun capitulated, King Henry and King Charles made a solemn entry into Paris, where they were so well received that the next day Queen Catherine and Queen Isabeau took their turn. The Bourgeois of Paris noted in his journal a similar entry of Queen Catherine. He says there were "displayed in front of her litter two robes of ermine. The people did not know what to make of them unless it was a sign that she was Queen of France and of England."

Christmas was celebrated in Paris, King Henry in great pomp at the Louvre, where the rich and important people of northern France gathered, and King Charles alone except for a few old servants and courtiers of no standing. "Nobody," says Monstrelet, "could recount the great receptions, the pomp and the splendor which were done" in the Louvre Palace. After Christmas King Henry, desperate for money and troops before spring, decided to take his queen to London. The Bourgeois of Paris very fortunately noted in his journal: "*Item,* today departed the daughter of France, named Katharine, whom the King of England had wed, and she was led into England, and it was a pitiful leave-taking, especially between the King of France and his daughter." In his "Memoirs" Pierre de Fenin tells of seeing Catherine. He observes that she was very beautiful, noble in appearance, and modest.

Queen Catherine was crowned at Westminster in February of 1421. Her husband was quite rightfully in his glory, for he had been welcomed in England "like an angel of God." The ceremonial dinner was held in Westminster Hall, says Holinshed. The Archbishop of Canterbury and Henry Beaufort, Bishop of Winchester, sat on the queen's right. On her left side sat Sir James Stuart, the future James I of Scotland. This prince had advanced in the world. A Scotch army under the command of Albany's son had recently landed at La Rochelle in France. They were reported thirsting to kill Englishmen. They had already joined the Dauphin Charles. This news was behind the lavish dinner in Westminster Hall. Notwithstanding, the haughy Duke of Gloucester was master of the ceremony. He stood bareheaded before the newly crowned queen.

Since it was Lent, the feast consisted principally of fish. The first course featured dead eels stewed. The second course was jelly colored with columbine flowers, cream of almonds, sea bream, conger, sole, chub, barbel, fried smelts, crayfish, and baked eels. The third course was "white leche" garnished with hawthorn leaves and red haws, compost of dates, mottled cream, carp, turbot, tench, perch, sturgeon with whelks, and roasted "porporous," or porpoise. These delicacies were followed by shrimps, prawns, eels roasted with lamprey eel, and marzipan.

The table decorations were called "subtleties." Each one was designed as an intricate culinary compliment to the sovereign. One represented the queen as Saint Catherine disputing with learned doctors and a pelican holding in its bill a poem complimenting the king. The king's motto, *Une Sans Plus,* or "One Without More," was featured. There were, of course, the golden fleurs-de-lis of Valois-Orléans. Another masterpiece was a candy panther representing the queen. Then there were angels wishing the couple a marital bliss unmarred by domestic wrangles. The last "subtlety" was perhaps not in the best taste. It showed King Henry holding a tiger's whelp in his hands and looking into a mirror. It said, "By force and not by reason have I conquered the Beast"; and just in case the meaning was not clear, a second explanation:

> "The sight of this mirror
> Tames wild beasts of terror."

If Queen Catherine was passionately in love, she would not mind her young brother's being called a tiger's whelp. It is to be hoped that someone in England smuggled the news to the poor timorous dauphin that English cooks had likened him to anything resembling a tiger. The Dauphin Charles would have been flattered.

While Queen Catherine is not known to have made any request for clemency in France, she did present Sir James Stuart with her gilt wine-cup. She also asked that he be liberated. However, viewing the political expediency of such a request, her words were perhaps not unprompted. On the other hand, she may very well have admired the Scotch poet whom she was to see frequently during the next year or so. As a direct result of Catherine's coronation, Henry Beaufort lent King Henry more money. He accepted another golden crown as security. Then his niece was betrothed to Sir James Stuart. A tender and touching story has it that this match between Sir James and Joan Beaufort was made through the bars of Sir James's prison at Windsor. It is not supposed to have been a political alliance.

Another story has it that while in England Queen Catherine went to visit her cousin, Duke Charles of Orléans. Such a meeting belongs to the domain of the novelist, who alone could do justice to such a scene in Pontefract Castle. The cousins had not met for at least six years. One had endured cruel vicissitudes. The other was now the queen and the wife of Henry V. One had defended France with his life. The other had sold her country for a husband. However, in physical features Queen Catherine resembled her oldest sister, Isabelle, in almost every detail. The poet-prisoner at Pontefract could not have failed to view her with emotion.

King Henry's purpose in conducting his queen through England was to display her as irrefutable proof that he had become, or would soon become, actual and legal King of France. Since he was everything he claimed—a great warrior, a stern and capable ruler, a handsome and youthful prince—and since he was also an accomplished orator, King Henry rapidly collected the necessary troops to return to France shortly. By the time they started south again in May of 1421, his queen was pregnant. Therefore the disrespectful joke they told all over England that summer was true: that between Saint Denis and Saint George Henry V had got the daughter of France with a child who would be one-half English and one-half French and who would leap into Egypt one fine day and pull the Great Turk's beard. Well, it was partly true.

Duke Charles, whatever he may have thought of his cousin Catherine, must have felt that a part of his years in prison had been worthwhile. He had, in fact, sent two Scotch lords into France with an army of four or five thousand men. One of their commanders was another James Stuart, the Earl of Buchan, an experienced soldier and a man around forty years of age. The second was Sir John of Darnley, a man in his middle sixties. Both were eager to fight—so eager, in fact, that their Scotch troops would often run to meet their enemies instead of advancing in an orderly fashion. The soldier the dauphin needed the most was Archibald the "Tyneman," the fourth Earl of Douglas. Under such commanders as these, fighting alongside the celebrated Gascon captains from Armagnac, the young Bastard of Orléans and John Duke of Alençon would be able to finish their apprenticeships.

Duke Charles did not hear regularly from the dauphin. He was too far away to act quickly in an emergency. He was very angry to learn that his sister Marguerite had been married to Richard of Brittany, who therefore acquired her dowry, a rich county. By the time Duke Charles heard of this marriage, it had already taken place.

In March, just before Easter Sunday, while Henry V was still in England, his brother of Clarence made an attack on dauphinist forces at a town called Baugé in Anjou. Very confident in his prowess, the Duke of Clarence had forged ahead with his main body of troops and been surprised by some of the new Scotch reinforcements. The English lost two or three thousand of their best knights. The Duke of Clarence was killed. Two hundred prisoners were taken, including the Earls of Somerset and Huntington.

Robert Blondel, a Norman reporting this engagement, tells how the Duke of Clarence was killed. He says that as the English duke fell to the ground, a vassal of Duke Charles of Orléans, a man named Charles Pincerna, hurled himself over the body of the fallen English duke. The man from Orléans wanted to take him prisoner, "thinking to preserve him from death in order that his liege lord of Orléans might be returned to France from his English prison as an even exchange." However, a certain Scotsman more fierce than the "cruel English" killed both men at once, both duke and soldier, *uno gladii ictu*—with one blow of the sword.

Shortly after this unexpected reverse, King Henry arrived at Calais with troops that had been paid for eight months.

Since October the English had been besieging Meaux. King Henry brought to this siege his captive Sir James Stuart, heir to the throne of Scotland. He had arranged for the Scotch prince to order his vassals to return home in peace. No doubt, since such a trick had been expected, the Scotch lords made no bones about replying to their future sovereign. They said they appreciated his solicitude for their welfare. They said they would not dream of disobeying him. They added that they understood he was being forced to give them such an order because he was Henry V's prisoner. They understood that he didn't mean a word of it. Therefore, they would do his will by remaining in France.

This was not the only idea that King Henry had. He next brought forth from England Count Arthur of Richmond, whom he had again caused to swear fealty to the throne of England. To make doubly sure of his sincerity, King Henry had the young count marry Burgundy's sister. King Henry did not release Queen Joanna until June of 1422. As long as he still believed his mother to be in prison, Count Arthur remained faithfully in the English ranks.

That summer Duke Charles had a lovely gold ring with a diamond solitaire sent to Blois from a jeweler in Bourges. The ring was for his daughter Joan to keep secretly until the wedding day of the Bastard of Orléans. The youngster was to marry one of the dauphin's favorites.

On December 6, 1421, a son was born in Windsor Castle to King Henry V and his queen, Catherine of France. When at the siege of Meaux he heard this news, he was both delighted and infuriated. He had consulted his astronomers months before, and they had given him prognostications that were not at all clear. One thing was certain: the child should not under any circumstances be delivered at Windsor Castle! Henry V had grown up in the beautiful mountains of Monmouth in Wales. He had instructed his queen to proceed into Wales for her confinement. However, Queen Catherine, who was in her lifetime to have such an intimate relationship with Wales, disobeyed his command. At the news of his son's birth, King Henry is reported to have made his prophetic remark, in verse, that "Henry born at Monmouth shall get much, but Henry of Windsor shall reign long and lose all."

The sponsors at the baptismal ceremony of the future Henry VI were the Duke of Bedford, Henry Beaufort, and the Duchess Jacoba of Hainault. This lady was a personal friend of Queen Catherine, and a dashing young lady if there ever was one. She had recently run away from her second husband. She was temporarily in England trying to find an army to attack her liege lord, the Duke of Burgundy. Duke Charles of Orléans must have hoped ardently that she succeeded. He had met the young lady at his wedding. She had been married in the double ceremony that had united Duke Charles and the Princess Isabelle.

After her purification Queen Catherine left her infant in England and rejoined her husband in France the following May. Much to her surprise, the vigorous King Henry was ill. It was not so serious, however, that he could not wear his armor and march against Senlis. Queen Catherine retired to be with Queen Isabeau at Vincennes. Thither King Henry was brought on a litter. By August 30th he realized that he was dying. His brother of Bedford, always the most reliable of the three, attended his deathbed.

"How long have I to live?" asked King Henry on August 31st.

"Without a miracle," replied the doctors, "two hours at the most."

Clearheaded apparently until the end, King Henry made his will. He left his Queen a gold scepter. His dying remarks concerned his old adversary. Coming back from death's door for one last look at his short life, King Henry V ordered distinctly that the Duke of Orléans should be kept a prisoner until his son, the future Henry VI, reached his "lawful age." Let this duke not return home again to France, warned King Henry, "lest he kindle more fire in one day than might be quenched in three."

The real malice of the French was obvious in the ways their chroniclers chortled over the unexpected good news of the great king's death. They gleefully spread variously that he had died of a rectal fistula, of "Saint Anthony's fire," and of "Saint Fiacre's disease." The English chroniclers hastened to call them "liars." He died "positively" of a pleurisy, or of a fever. He definitely did not die of "Saint Fiacre's disease;" he died on Saint Fiacre's Day! He had been very weary of long sieges and the bad climate in France. He simply came down with a fever or a distemper during the dog days. The English were in a better position to state the truth; they had it from the chief man of King Henry's bedchamber, a certain Peter Basset.

The Queens Catherine and Isabeau had nursed King Henry. They naturally made no comment—none that reached a manuscript, at any rate. The future James I of Scotland accompanied Queen Catherine and the body back to Westminster Abbey. He was the chief mourner at the funeral. Queen Catherine subsequently removed to Windsor. The young widow had a few revenues still confiscated from Queen Joanna, but she was very poor, golden scepter notwithstanding. Her martial husband had ruled England for nine years, five months, and eleven days.

Throughout France people were grateful to their insane old king, Charles VI, who had managed somehow to hold to his life while his self-styled heir conquered city after city. By virtue of the old king's persistence, Henry V had never been able to crown himself at Rheims Cathedral. He had never been anointed King of France. No one begrudged the pitiful old man the right to his ease when, less than two months after Henry V, King Charles the Beloved died in the Hôtel Saint-Paul. He had always been cherished because God had visited him all his life with severe afflictions. France mourned. The Dauphin Charles, who had a terrible fear of death, a fear so intense that since he had seen the blood on the planks of the Montereau Bridge he would never again walk on wood, bowed his head in deep affliction. His father had declared this last son an outlaw. Far away in Pontefract Castle the next heir to the throne of France was sorely grieved. He also had loved the gentle, mad king, his father's only brother.

France in 1422 was without a king. The King of England was a fretful baby.

By the first of November the wind came whistling down across the ridings of Yorkshire. Duke Charles was twenty-eight years old. He had been in prison for more than eight years. It had begun to be more than he could bear. At times he had to force himself to speak French, and even more to understand it. He spent longer hours at his poetry, reworking it and polishing it. He had also begun to

write poetry in English. The long winter days dragged by endlessly, cold and monotonous. From time to time he received a new
book, such as Alain Chartier's interesting but not brilliant poem
called *La Belle Dame sans Merci*. It had raised a storm of controversy in France. Duke Charles read it and liked the first few
verses enough to rewrite them in one of his poems. Alain Chartier
wrote well, but his gift was not that of a real poet.

Duke Charles had begun to enjoy English. He liked to learn new
words such as "fiddle-faddle." They almost made him smile occasionally. Early in the afternoons, when the sun warmed a corner
of the courtyard, he would walk up and down, back and forth, an
hour or two. The view to the south was lovely, especially when
the sun chased the cloud patterns along the earth. His eye leaped
over the valley, past the houses that clustered close on the castle
slope, across to where the fields of oats had lain blond in the August
sun. The opposite hill was not really a hill, but a rise in the downs
that sloped down in rolling undulations from York on the northeast. The courtyard at Pontefract was always protected from the
wind. Above his head it whistled and shrieked and wore at the
limestone to keep it yellow and clean. Sometimes he sat under the
espalier fruit trees that he had been sent from home. At his feet
were flowers very similar to the ones in the courtyard at Blois
Castle—*pensées,* which the English called pansies; *roses tremières,*
which they called hollyhocks; and roses, which everyone called
roses.

"Many times I wished for death," Duke Charles said. It was often
a sadness more than he could endure. Tears came to his eyes as he
thought of home across the sea . . . the gray slate roofs of the Loire
castles, the pleasant days when he and the Princess Isabelle were
young and in love. At night he could not sleep. He tossed to and fro
on his pillow and was driven deeper and deeper into his own mind.
It was almost the only amusement, the only recourse that remained
to him. Even the thought of Henry V alive and decisive had given
Duke Charles a kind of stimulus to live. No one would know him
in France by this time. No one would recognize him. He was growing old. He was a forgotten man. "The weather has shouldered its
winter coat . . . of wind . . . and cold . . . and icy rain. . . ."

No one but a poet could explain the mental processes that drove
Duke Charles in his homesickness and his solitude to creative literature. No ordinary mind would have functioned quite that way.

Only the man who was himself a consummate poet would understand a prisoner in Pontefract Castle and would realize how his thoughts worked. Shakespeare has explained it so well:

> "I have been studying how I may compare
> This prison where I live unto the world:
> And for because the world is populous
> And here is not a creature but myself,
> I cannot do it; yet I'll hammer it out.
> My brain I'll prove the female to my soul,
> My soul the father: and these two beget
> A generation of still-breeding thoughts,
> And these same thoughts people this little world
> In humours like the people of this world. . . ."

Thus making the brain and the soul combine to generate still-breeding thoughts, Duke Charles did not die. Once the news of his death spread through France, and he refuted the rumor in a very beautiful poem in which he compared himself to a mouse. Why a mouse? Who could be sure?

During the last few years he had undoubtedly been sending poetry back to France. It had not all remained within his personal book. There is something about the creative process that likes company. The poet writes from himself, but not *for* himself. Poetry is the desire to hold the whole world closer. It may appear to be a solitary pursuit. It is more properly a desire to communicate beauty. Without the poetry it seems probable that Duke Charles of Orléans would have been forgotten. It must have been the poetry that kept his name so alive that somewhere in France a simple child who had never seen him, who would never see him, came one bright day to deliver him from Pontefract Castle in the West Riding of windswept Yorkshire. As Duke Charles sat alone in a warm, sunny corner, turning back and forth on his pillow throughout the endless, solitary, northern nights, somewhere in France his champion was preparing to come to his assistance. He did not even dream of it. He did not even know.

His letter writing kept him busy during certain hours of the day from December of 1422 until the end of May in 1423. The safe-conducts then graciously referred to him as "our most beloved relative near to us in blood." The treasurers and secretaries, with six new servants and twelve horses, were still forbidden to stay more than one night in any of the English fortresses along the way to Pontefract. In February more lawyers and parliamentarians were allowed to join him while awaiting a "definitive treaty of peace." Messengers continued to arrive almost daily through May. At the end of the month Duke Charles was removed to Knaresborough from Pontefract Castle. The distance was only a few miles. His warder was now a Thomas Combeworth. The new safe-conducts were signed from Westminster on "behalf of the King." The latest document began: "Having been favorably disposed by the supplication of the aforesaid Duke . . . in this matter . . ."

The matter here referred to is Duke Charles's desire to confer with the Abbot of the Abbatial Church of Saint-Laumer in Blois. It was an odd request, indeed. It is a strange and beautiful church with a Gothic choir and transept erected by Benedictine monks between 1138 and 1186. The choir is simple and lovely with huge cylindrical pillars. Its semicircular apsidiole rests on six slender columns. Its nave rises three stories and is reminiscent of Chartres. Its transept is very well lighted, and vast. Above it rises a cupola that gives the structure an Oriental appearance. Its architects were bold and imaginative. Duke Charles remembered that as he approached Blois along the Loire River, what he saw first was the square cupola rising to a point. His castle stood on a cliff just above the church. Duke Charles had sent for the Abbot of Saint-Laumer in person.

The matter they discussed shows what Duke Charles had been thinking recently. He had made long and complicated arrangements beforehand, for what he entrusted to the Abbot of Saint-Laumer was very near his heart. He had decided that the Princess Isabelle should be taken from "the minster of our love" and reinterred at the Convent of the Celestine Monks in Paris. This was the chapel that his father had redecorated and endowed and the one where he was buried. Duke Charles must indeed have been thinking of Isabelle during the long winter nights at Pontefract. After his own death he hoped to be buried at Paris beside her. Perhaps he also made arrangements at this time for the approaching marriage of his daughter Joan.

The Duke of Orléans was removed to Knaresborough, another old castle in Yorkshire that had been a part of the Duchy of Lancaster since the days of John of Gaunt. It was only a few miles to the north of Pontefract. The castle was on the brow of a rock two hundred feet above the brown water of the river Nidd. Its twelve towers were further defended by a deep moat hewn out of the rock on the side toward the town. From its terrace the view was splendid, and a south wind blew strong in his face. Duke Charles was lodged in the keep behind walls twelve feet thick.

This keep, or donjon, rose three stories above the celebrated dungeon, the construction of which was unique. The whole structure was supported on a central pillar only nine feet in circumference and had twelve arches springing from it. Circular stairs, so narrow that they could be guarded by one armed sentry, led up to the State Room, which was fifteen feet square. The height of the tower from courtyard to parapet was fifty-three feet. Subterranean passages ran under the courtyard to exits over the moat. The whole castle area contained between two and three acres.

Inside the castle yard was a courtroom complete with raised wooden floor, partitions for the prisoners, benches for the lawyers and their secretaries, a judge's seat about four feet above them, and a platform than ran the whole side of the room. Knaresborough Castle had also welcomed Henry of Lancaster upon his arrival from France. However, it did not have the black reputation of Pontefract. King Richard had gone from Knaresborough to Pontefract. Duke Charles of Orléans had already seen the worst prison England had to offer him. Knaresborough was a much more pleasant seat. From the castle terraces he could overlook the river and see more of the outside world. Perhaps he took his new prison as a sign of hope. Perhaps he was drawing closer to freedom.

If this change of prisons at first brought some relief to the prisoner, he was soon to understand that he was wrong. The summer wore away. The leaves fell. The fall winds blew about the towers of Knaresborough even more violently than about lofty Pontefract. The only sheltered area was near the donjon, and there the afternoon sun did not reach.

Henry V was dead. His brother of Bedford was Regent of France. City after city throughout Normandy still fell to the English, who efficiently enlisted the conquered Normans in their ranks. The news could not have been worse. Tanneguy du Chastel and Lord Buchan were badly beaten at Meulan. Duke Charles of Orléans turned inward again. He studied. He continued his poetic invention. The silent years of his life begin in 1423. If he was alive, he gave only few signs for a period of seven years.

In France the war was being very successfully prosecuted by the Duke of Bedford, the "so-called" regent, said the French. On every front, before the important town of Meulan, the "so-called" regent was victorious. The Earl of Buchan and Tanneguy du Chastel had run to its defense in vain. The Duke of Bedford therefore drew Duke Philip of Burgundy closer into the English alliance and tempted the Duke of Brittany to join them. On October 10, 1423, they married Count Arthur to the Duke of Burgundy's sister Marguerite. The Duke of Bedford wedded Burgundy's other lovely blonde sister Anne. This lady, however, did ask for clemency on behalf of French prisoners whom she saw led in chains into Paris; and it was granted.

France hung by a thread. In Knaresborough Duke Charles held his breath. He made no sign, and not a move to surrender Orléans to the English.

Meanwhile, in England, the Bishops of Durham and Winchester were having their own difficulties with Henry V's youngest brother, the Duke of Gloucester. This powerful nobleman, who had been Lord Great Chamberlain of England since 1413, commanded at Harfleur, and performed distinguished service at Agincourt, had married—very much as he pleased!

His wife was Jacoba of Hainault, Duchess of Holland, the same young lady who had run away from her second husband. Her first husband had been the Dauphin Jean, who died in 1417. By his death she had therefore lost the crown of France. John the Fearless had subsequently forced her to marry one of his vassals, the boy Duke of Brabant. By this time Jacoba was nineteen years old and ready for a real husband. On the grounds that they were first cousins, she had vigorously repudiated her second husband and flown merrily away to England. There she had been welcomed by Queen Catherine, been godmother to Henry VI, and captivated Humphrey, the "Good," Duke of Gloucester.

The Bishops of Durham and Winchester took a second look at this love affair. Not all the world loves a lover, especially when the bride intends to make her new husband Duke of Brabant while her second husband is still Duke of Brabant. Not that Duke Humphrey could not whip his predecessor; quite the contrary. The catch was that the first Duke of Brabant was a loyal vassal to Duke Philip of Burgundy. Surely Duke Humphrey was not seriously considering an invasion of Burgundian territory from the north while Duke Philip was otherwise engaged in helping the English conquer Normandy!

Duke Humphrey was thirty-two; his bride was twenty-one. Love is a powerful persuader. Therefore Duke Humphrey prepared to invade Burgundy and take his bride with him. Jacoba, or "Dame Jake," as she was called in England, seems to have been not only determined but resourceful.

While this love affair was the main topic of conversation in England, another wedding occurred in Blois Castle. The chronicler Cousinot of the House of Orléans records the marriage of Duke Charles's only child, Madame Joan, to the young Duke of Alençon. About this second wedding celebrated in Saint-Laumer's, one is tempted to think that happiness could not have come to two more promising young people.

Thus were united those two houses that had always shown more than the bonds of chivalry and political expediency required: a true love for each other. The former Duke John, the hero of Agincourt, had been prompt to protect the boy Charles after the murder of Louis of France. Fifteenth century chroniclers rarely commented on physical beauty, but they had noted the extraordinary good looks of the Alençon dukes, father and son.

Joan of Orléans had a young husband whom even the chroniclers had to remark was, like his father, the handsomest French knight of the century. He is generally called "John the Fair," the "gentil Duc" of Alençon. Before his wedding day he had demonstrated his courage against the English. He was a young man to watch. For the next fifty years he would be on the tip of everyone's tongue. All that is known of Madame Joan's feelings is that she worried a good deal about him. It is also known that he visited her frequently and that he was careful to reassure her. Duke John did not expect to die in battle. He had no fear of death at all, as his military career and his presence at the two most famous trials of the century attest. His testimony also reveals his sensitivity and his right to have been called "gentil" or "nice" by his companion-in-arms. No duke of the century, English or French, has a more unusual claim to fame than this John, Duke of Alençon.

Around Eastertime the French and Scotch soldiers of the dauphin suffered a severe reverse at a castle named Cravant. Four great English lords were present: Bedford, Suffolk, Willoughby, and Salisbury. Sir John Stuart, Constable from Scotland, lost an eye at this encounter. The Armagnac Captain Xaintrailles was taken prisoner and put up for ransom. Three thousand Scots died on that April 4th. When the French forces saw that the battle was lost, a great many retreated, leaving their compatriots and allies still engaged on the field. They "fled very dismally," says Cousinot, "which caused a great harm to the King of France; and if they had stopped and done their duty, the engagement, as seems possible, would have been otherwise."

It is to be noted that this official of Duke Charles of Orléans refers to the Dauphin Charles as king, although he had not at the time of Cravant been so sanctified. Not long after this battle the hasty and amorous Duke of Gloucester landed in Holland with his army and his bride. During that summer also a dauphin named Louis was born to the Dauphin Charles. The baby's godfather was John, Duke of Alençon. If Duke Humphrey had not landed in the North, the war would have been won by England that summer.

During January of the following year, as the Orléanists continued to suffer one reverse after another, the Dukes of Gloucester and Brabant were negotiating, preliminary to a private war in the North. By virtue of extra persuasions exerted on Scotland during a personal visit by Reginald of Chartres, Archbishop of Rheims, the "Tyneman" of the Douglas family arrived in France. He had been long expected. It is to be hoped that the Orléanists' first joy was not dimmed by any suspicion that Tyneman means Loser! The English countered this move by finally releasing her king to Scotland. Sir James Stuart became King James I.

Throughout that summer the victorious troops of the Duke of Bedford looted and raped. Their cruelty was so frightful, and the dauphin's position so alarming, that several Burgundian vassals decided to switch allegiance and join the losers. The combat became so unequal that there was no more chivalry in it. By the 16th of August a major engagement was coming to a head at Verneuil.

This town had once marked the frontier between Normandy and France. By evening 18,000 English and Burgundian troops were in position along with 8,000 archers. This time the lords of Bedford, Suffolk, and Salisbury were joined by another unusually famous knight. This was the formidable Richard de Beauchamp, Earl of Warwick. He had an astonishing military record. He had not only commanded at Harfleur. He had received the surrender of Rouen. He had also been Captain of Calais and Pontorson. Just the sight of the two fierce bears on his coat-of-arms was enough to frighten the French.

The Orléanists were represented by scores of minor barons from central and southern France. Among them as leaders were the Earls of Douglas and Buchan from Scotland, the Duke of Alençon, the Gascon Captain La Hire, and Marshal de La Fayette. The older French knights were of the opinion that they should withdraw inside Verneuil and let the English sit out a siege.

The Scotch commanders, seconded by the great numbers of young knights, vetoed this suggestion. They would not heed what happened at Agincourt, says Cousinot. Both sides drew up for combat. "Then," says Cousinot, "they began to march the ones against the others; but the English set their feet down heavily and carefully, without getting overheated at all; and, on the contrary, the Scotch tripped forward nervously and too hastily, so eager were they to get to their enemies, and likewise the French, so much so that most of them were already out of breath before even making contact with the enemy."

The horsemen from Lombardy in Italy who were riding for the dauphin made one charge, wheeled, and abandoned the field. Monstrelet says that the French lost because the English had tied their horses' manes and tails together so tightly that the French could not wheel and strike them from the rear.

On that Thursday at Verneuil the Earl Archibald of Douglas, the Earl of Buchan, and eleven French noblemen died. Monstrelet says the French allies lost between 4,000 and 5,000 men. The Orléanist chronicler Cousinot says 7,000. John Duke of Alençon, was taken prisoner, as was the Marshal de La Fayette. Most of the French dead were Scotsmen. The English lost 1,600 men, most of whom were Normans. The French lost another 200 who were taken prisoner.

The Duke of Bedford showed unusual generosity. He allowed those French who had sought refuge inside Verneuil to go free and to take their belongings. He also permitted the Orléanists to recover their dead. Cousinot adds that the English losses were so substantial that the Duke of Bedford expressly forbade any celebration or even any announcement of victory.

The two Scots lords were interred with great honor at the Cathedral of Saint-Cross at Orléans, with the following inscription carved on their tombs: "Fallen at Verneuil in 1424 in the Defense of France against the English. In Peace."

That fall the Dukes of Bedford and Burgundy met in Paris to discuss the Duke of Gloucester's outrageous claim to Holland. Duke Humphrey the "Good," the darling of the Londoners and of his young wife, was still in Holland with his army. What is more, he showed no signs of flagging. He intended to recover and then rule his wife's domains. He sent furious letter after letter to his older brother of Bedford and to his "beloved cousin" of Burgundy. The Duke of Bedford was greatly embarrassed. The Cardinals of Winchester and Durham appealed to the Pope. Duke Humphrey could cause England to lose the Hundred Years' War all by himself.

Meanwhile, the Duke of Bedford was being pressed to accept a ransom for the young Duke of Alençon. The Duchess Joan of Alençon was ready and eager to despoil herself, even to the point of destitution, to obtain her husband's release. Duke John was by right of birth one of the first noblemen of France. The Duke of Bedford, far from wishing to mistreat so noble and charming a prisoner, had a better idea. He saw to it that Duke John was offered every enticement, every honor, and great riches if he would forswear his allegiance to the dauphin and join the English-Burgundian forces. They pointed out to the prisoner all those facts that were demonstrably true: that the Dauphin Charles was surely losing France and that to return to him then would mean certain defeat, ruination, and disaster. None of their words had the desired effect. Duke John refused to budge. He answered only that the dauphin was his king, whom he would follow, regardless. He preferred to be ransomed even if it meant stripping himself of all his domains and riches.

After the Battle of Verneuil, when it seemed clear that France was lost, quantities of lesser Norman nobles deserted their homes and families and rode off to war on the dauphin's side. They were ashamed because of the dauphin's youth, the hopelessness of his cause, and his extreme poverty. Although they had consented to join the English in the hopes of great riches, they now went to die for the dauphin—for nothing. The powerful and vacillating Duke of Brittany, however, joined the Burgundians again.

Then all Europe was surprised when Count Arthur of Richmond came quietly down across France to knock humbly at the dauphin's door. The Breton count said that he felt released from his feudal oath; after all, Henry V was dead. It was not, of course, that he had just awakened to that fact. He had tried, he said, to get along with the Duke of Bedford, but couldn't. He knew he was not a Frenchman. He realized that he was a Breton, but he felt more French than English.

The Dauphin Charles was overjoyed. Overcoming Count Arthur's reluctance, he made him accept the constable's sword. That office had been vacant since Verneuil. He also gave Count Arthur his three castles. It was all the Dauphin had left: Lusignan, Loches, and the black and massive Chinon. The French were all delighted. Count Arthur would make a brilliant constable. He gave them new hope when all seemed lost. We still have Orléans, they remembered. We can stop the English at the Loire, in the heart of France.

The English advance was slowed up by the winter weather and by the prolonged absence of the Duke of Bedford. Duke Humphrey of Gloucester, the troublemaking younger brother, had been ordered home to England. Once there, he was publicly censured. Nothing could make him relinquish his bride. Therefore, the Duke of Bedford had to return home also to arbitrate. The long war between the Bishop of Winchester and the Duke of Gloucester had commenced in earnest.

The bishop, Henry Beaufort, was serving his third term as Chancellor of England. Since the Londoners sympathized with Duke Humphrey, there had been serious riots in the city. The Duke of Gloucester wanted the guardianship of his nephew, King Henry VI, which had been bestowed by Henry V upon the Earl of Warwick. The duke was also trying to borrow the 9,000 pounds he needed for his duchess in Holland. He caused Henry Beaufort, Bishop of Winchester, to resign his post as chancellor. He became all the more abusive when the bishop suddenly realized his lifetime ambition—a project that Duke Humphrey opposed on the grounds that his oldest brother had always opposed it. The Bishop of Winchester became the Cardinal of Winchester, or of England.

The Pope also declared Duke Humphrey's marriage annulled. The duke would have to remain in England. In consolation, while his Duchess Jacoba wrote him pleading letters from Holland, Duke Humphrey married his mistress, Eleanor Cobham. But he had by no means forgiven the cardinal.

While the Duke of Bedford spent seven or eight months in England, the Earl of Warwick and the Duke of Suffolk suffered one defeat that raised the morale of the dauphin's men. This victory was due to the courage and intelligence of the Gascon Captain La Hire, but he was ably seconded by the Bastard of Orléans.

On April 20, 1427, the two English lords laid siege to the town and castle of Montargis, which its citizens wanted very much to defend. The English tried first to find a traitor who would let them in the fortress. When this plan failed, they constructed trenches, battlements, and barricades, and cut off the town completely. Then they showered it with cannon fire and arrows. The Constable of Richmond granted La Hire and the Bastard of Orléans permission to take a Scotch captain named Kennedy and about 4,000 foot-soldiers and advance to relieve the town.

La Hire, since he had been well trained under Count Bernard VII of Armagnac, advised the Bastard of Orléans to remain hidden with the main body of the French troops. Then, with a few other nobles, La Hire reconnoitred the English camp until he found one weak spot through which he hoped to force a spearhead into the town. Before gathering his men and launching his lightning attack, La Hire hunted for a chaplain who could give him absolution. He found one, but the chaplain could not forgive him his sins until he had confessed them. La Hire argued with the priest, saying that an exception ought to be made in his case, first because they were in the middle of a war, and second, because he had to lead his attack right away, while the English were having dinner, if he was to have any chance of success. The chaplain consented to absolve him "such as he was," for La Hire assured him he had only committed those sins all soldiers commit.

Then, before spearheading his attack, La Hire knelt and "in his Gascon tongue" recited a prayer that the chronicler Counsinot admired. "And La Hire understood very well how to make a prayer and how to say one."

"God," prayed La Hire, "I beseech Thee to do unto La Hire today what Thou would want La Hire to do for Thee if he were God and Thou wert La Hire."

Then La Hire, an abbot, and Kennedy led their men through the English fortifications, setting fire to the tents and the brush obstacles. The English rushed for their armor, thinking it was only a skirmish. When the lords of Warwick and Suffolk heard the main French force thundering in behind them, they ran for safety across the river. It was only a minor engagement, to be sure. However, La Hire and the Bastard of Orléans could be proud to make such great knights run before them. The French also captured some foodstuffs and a few cannons, which they sorely needed.

Later that year, 1427, John Duke of Alençon was ransomed. The terms were cruel. He had to pay 200,000 écus. He was obliged to sell his domain of Fougères, one of the loveliest castles in France, and all the jewelry, furniture, and tapestries that he could collect. He rode home to his wife in very good spirits, handsomer than ever.

The Duke of Bedford was finally able to return to France. He was determined to finish with the dauphin once for all. His mind was not at rest, however, for he could not be sure of his younger brother. Duke Humphrey had a score to settle. He was set on ruling England, especially now that he had been so thwarted by the cardinal. In 1427 something came to his attention at Windsor.

Queen Catherine had been a widow for five years, and a poor one. Aside from having to accompany her small son up to the opening of Parliament a few times, the young queen-without-a-court was left much to her own devices. No doubt she had followed the first part of her friend's love affair with some stirrings of envy. Dame Jake had ended badly, in a Burgundian prison for the past two years. Despite a fourth husband, this lady would never bear a child and would never recover her position or her wealth. She would die at the age of thirty-five. She and Queen Catherine had been born in the same year. Queen Catherine would live to be only thirty-six. Both ladies would die of broken hearts.

Whatever Catherine of France felt about her marriage with King Henry V, it is quite certain that she remarried for love and only for love. The story told about her great love affair became a legend during her lifetime, and grievously, indeed, did she answer it for centuries after her death. Not everyone in England loved a lover, especially if she was a queen-mother, and a French one at that.

Queen Catherine at the age of twenty-six fell in love with the Master of her Wardrobe, a young Welshman named Owen Tudor, who, if he was at the Battle of Agincourt, must have been there at the age of eight. The queen had singled him out because of his sturdy, healthy good looks. She asked him to dance a Welsh jig for her. He danced so gaily that he lost his footing and fell in her lap. He begged her pardon in broken English, for very few Welsh-man of that day spoke English at all. Queen Catherine forgave him in broken English. They met often afterward "by private arrange-ment." The queen resolved to marry him. She did so, without permission from Parliament or from the Duke of Gloucester.

The duke, not quite knowing how to handle the situation, had a law passed to the effect that a queen-mother could not marry without permission. Therefore the poor Queen Catherine and her handsome Owen had to keep their marriage a secret. Owen Tudor was not a knight. He was unbonneted, without title or coronet. Their relationship was therefore "winked at" but not really believed. Queen Catherine must have known that her sister Isabelle had once owned Pembroke Castle in Wales. She also must have known or been reminded that, in Owen Glendower's long war against the English all through the first part of the century, her father had once sent him aid in the person of the French Marshal de Montmorency, who had landed in Milford Haven near Pembroke Castle with a fleet of 140 ships and 12,000 men. Perhaps Owen Tudor told his bride that he was descended from Cadwalader, the last King of Wales, and that his name should have been written *Twdwr*. In Welsh Twdwr means "tower of strength." It is said that he sent for two of his cousins out of Wales, John ab Meredith and Howel ab Llewelyn. Both were stalwart mountaineers and very handsome to look at, but knew not a word of English. Catherine is supposed to have remarked, "They are the goodliest dumb creatures we have ever beheld."

A modern Welsh historian, still resenting the slurs cast upon the Welsh because of this marriage and its secrecy, has informed us that Owen Tudor always stressed his remote ancestry because of a skeleton in his family closet. Years after Queen Catherine's sad death there was a great deal of research done into the origins of the obscure Owen Tudor from Usk Castle. Long after both their deaths, it was discovered that his genealogy was given in the Welsh chronicles of antiquity and that he could have claimed his descent from the kings of North and South Wales, from two lines of rulers, like Darius the Great.

Satirists have amused themselves no end with this mésalliance of a royal princess and a Welsh commoner. They have claimed that Queen Catherine sent a commission into Wales. The investigators, after much walking, climbed up to the hill farm of Penmynydd on the island of Anglesea.

Owen had hurried home ahead of them and was in the woodshed stropping his razor. Sitting in her "beehive pattern armchair" was his venerable mother, eating her supper of milk and flummery with a horn spoon. Her wooden porringer rested on her knees. An ancient patriarch who was also descended from the rulers of those mountains sat in the cottage beside her. Suddenly the oldster took it into his hoar head to resent the unsolicited intrusion. He charged, and spun them out the open door.

"What's all this great rumpus?" cried Owen, who burst into the room half shaved.

The royal commissioners did not fail to note the birch broom that rested beside the doorjamb. They heard the nanny goats bleating for their kids. They saw the hens pecking at the manure pile or roosting in the kitchen rafters. Their eyes stung from the smoke of a turf fire. The kettle sang. The iron dinner pot was black with soot. The bakestone was warm. It was a palace fit for a French princess.

The royal commissioners decided that the Welsh did "belong to the human race" and that Queen Catherine had married a fine gentleman.

While the Cardinal of England feuded in London with the Duke of Gloucester, Queen Catherine lived the last years of her life with her second husband. One child after another was born to them in fairly rapid succession: three sons and a daughter in less than ten years. Owen Tudor was quite different from the stern King Henry V.

Aeneas Silvius, the Italian writer and papal legate who later became Pope Pius II, says that King Henry V had forbidden the use of featherbeds in England and intended, if he became absolute master of France, to have all its vines pulled out by their roots. He said that nothing excited men more than feathers and wine.

VIII [*1428–1431*]   IT WAS 1428. THE WAR was almost over. From Knaresborough in England, Duke Charles of Orléans had put his own duchy in a state of defense. His vassals still rode forth with the Bastard of Orléans, with John, Duke of Alençon; with La Hire, Xaintrailles, and Count Arthur of Richmond. His officers mounted guard in one castle after another the length of the Loire River. The war had come to Orléans.

Since Agincourt, Henry V and his brothers of Bedford and Clarence had led their invincible armies the length of the Atlantic seaboard. They held western France solidly from Gascony northward to Guyenne, northward through Normandy. Only that sea-bound fortress of the Mont-Saint-Michel remained unconquered. No matter,

the English had bypassed it after having failed to wrestle successfully against its defenders, its riptides, and its quicksands. Other
than the Mont, nothing in Normandy remained to the dauphin.

The Duke of Burgundy had brought his English allies northern
and northeastern France—Artois, Flanders, Picardy, and Champagne. Paris had long been theirs. North of Orléans and Blois not
an inch of French soil remained French.

Said the Monk of Saint-Denis: "Treading under their feet alike
the fear of God and man's fear the English have swept over our
land with the fury of the tempest. Their only thoughts have been
of plunder, of fire, and of bloodshed!"

Northern France had returned again to a wilderness. Where the
furious armies had fought and eaten, not a granary remained full.
Farms had been looted and burned as the tide of war swept back
and forth across them since the death of Louis of France in 1407.
Starvation and epidemic were the crueler aftermaths. Children could
not be fed and could not survive in a ravaged countryside where
no fields could be tilled. Deserters formed into marauding bands
that terrorized, patrolled, and hid in the forests. There was no
king in the land. The "so-called" regent was a brilliant man and
not an unkind man, but he could not reign until he had finished
conquering. The French had lost the war.

In England Duke Charles spoke long about peace and made no
move to surrender. Instead, he ordered his duchy to prepare for
the final onslaught. The war was over but not ended while the
Queen City of Orléans stood white and magnificent spanning the
Loire. This was the last frontier.

From the Loire northward the fertile fields had grown up to
weeds and nettles. The few farmers who still survived hid in the
English-held castles. Whenever they ventured out to dig roots or
gather grasses for their families, the long notes of the war trumpets
warned them to take cover. From Loire to Seine, from Seine to
Somme, France had become a desert.

The dauphin was considering surrender and escape. Aside from
the Duchy of Orléans, he held only parts of Languedoc, Dauphiné
in the Alps, and Lyons on the Rhône. His Scotch allies had died
gallantly at Verneuil, that second Agincourt. He controlled no sea-
port, had no navy, had no army left, and no money. In England,
Henry Beaufort, the Cardinal of Winchester, had not only arranged
a truce with Scotland but had also generously supplied the Regent
Bedford with money enough to capture Orléans. Only two leaders

still held for the dauphin, but both were exerting themselves to the utmost. They were Pope Martin V in Rome, and Duke Charles of Orléans in England.

The strategy of these two leaders was identical: to separate Burgundy from his English alliance and maintain the dauphin's legitimate right to the Crown of France. Therefore, prepare Orléans for defense! Fight to the last minor fortress on the Loire River. Never surrender.

Duke Charles of Orléans had been trained from childhood to adhere to his duty, to bear discouragement, to trust in God, to find in himself the power that would enable him, as he says, "to come first to our own aid." Was this all that he could do—to put his duchy in a state of defense? It was not.

The reasonable and urgent pleas of Duke Charles of Orléans were heard in London by the "protector and the Council." As was his unfailing custom, Duke Charles appealed to England upon a point of law. He asked that justice be done him. It was well understood throughout western Europe that if a feudal lord was a prisoner upon his word, his lands and domains should be allowed to plead neutrality as long as their feudal master did not violate his oath as a prisoner and as long as he remained imprisoned. As soon as Duke Charles learned that the Earl of Salisbury had been ordered to attack Orléans, the duke appealed again, this time to the Earl of Salisbury himself.

He was assured by his English "cousin" that the neutrality of Orléans would be respected. No doubt neither lord expected this guarantee to be honored. However, its propaganda value was inestimable. Such a promise given and then broken could not fail to raise the prestige of Duke Charles.

Pope Martin V, ardently negotiating to shame the Duke of Burgundy, could use this breach of promise as a further argument. The new Cardinal of Winchester could also be made to feel its ignominy. Duke Charles had duly stressed the fact that no nobleman, no knight, would attack his unarmed civilians in Orléans while their feudal lord was so bound that he could not honorably go to their defense.

Duke Charles had by this time been moved even farther south, to Bolingbroke Castle. This promising change, which put him nearer London, occurred at about the same time that Henry Beaufort was created cardinal.

Duke Charles studied the situation, weighed the pros and cons, and tested the English lords. His pen became busy again. For some time now he had been writing English and translating some of his poems into that language. However, only a rapid examination of his English poems reveals an astonishing divergence between them and the French poems with which he was filling his private book. The English poems fill a scant 225 pages, and there are easily three times as many in French. An even more interesting comparison gives food for much thought. The English poems, all but two, deal with love. The French poems treat love and a variety of subjects such as the weather, politics, and war. In other words, Duke Charles wrote of the war in French, for French consumption. He was careful to let no English eyes pierce his real thoughts. His French poems also are allegories, perhaps in code. If the key to their meaning were ever discovered, they could very easily read: The Earl of Salisbury will attack Orléans shortly!

In only two instances has Duke Charles translated his own war poems. It is indeed a rare privilege to see how a French poet writes when he writes in English.

The following poem, slightly modernized in spelling, comes from the pen of Duke Charles. Its French original is far more terse, more nervous, and more belligerent:

ROUNDEL XVIII

"Refresh the castelle of my poore heart
    With some supplies of joy or of pleasance,
  For false danger with his alliance
    Besiegeth it with woe and grievous smart.

"That it may not long hold you may avert—
    Which woe forbeateth so with ordinance—
  Refresh the castelle of my poore heart
    With some supplies of joy or of pleasance.

"Not suffer him to lord, this false coward,
    In conquering unto his obeissance
  Which that you have under your governance.
  Advance you now, and keep you low covered;
    Refresh the castelle of my poore heart."

The French original of the above poem speaks not of "danger," but of "Danger" in verses 3 and 9. In Verse 5 Duke Charles says in French "raise the siege or break it," and in Verse 12 "uphold your honor." The English translation is mild by comparison. Duke Charles was playing a dangerous game. The English were meant to think of him under two images: as a helpless and injured lord, and as a lovesick scholar. His French poems, carried into France and spread about among as many people as possible, were intended to urge his allies and friends to fight even to the bitter end.

France in 1429 was undergoing a strange ferment. As Jean Gerson had pointed out to King Charles VI long before, it was not only the nobility who suffered in a war but also the helpless people in the towns and cities, who starved and died by the thousands. The people had no defense whatsoever. King Charles VI had even forbidden them to possess crossbows or learn how to use them. The people of France had also watched this war. They too had opinions and ideas of their own, even if they could neither read nor write, even though they had been puzzled by Queen Catherine's two ermine robes. Without doubt they only partially understood what trickled down to them. They were not present at the conference table or on the battlefields, except as servants. But they were present at the surrender of one French town after another. They understood one thing: that when Orléans fell, the kingdom fell. They had no love for an English infant who would then become their king. No doubt they grasped at straws and struggled to comprehend, much as anyone, even the most learned, struggles to comprehend history in the making.

Throughout 1428 and the spring of 1429 the people of France were in turmoil. Their only access to facts, their only interpreters, were their preachers. Therefore they listened to the Gray Friars and the other mendicant orders who appeared from nowhere, harangued the crowds, and vanished overnight, either into retirement in Brittany, or into thin air. The religious revival was intense. Monstrelet speaks at length of a certain Brother Thomas, a Celt and not a Frenchman, who enthralled his congregations by the thousands, week after week. Brother Thomas preached hellfire and damnation. He preached that the wages of sin are death. He stormed against evil, vanity, adultery, ostentation, and wealth.

Ladies, terrified in the presence of Brother Thomas, raised trembling fingers to remove their elaborate winged headdresses. Brother Thomas urged all France to fall upon its knees and pray God to come to its aid. Repent, or you are lost! Mend your evil ways, or the Lord will forsake you! Pray for France, wretched people, or you are surely doomed! Where among you is the pure-in-heart? Brother

Thomas was a seven-day wonder—until he vanished or went home to Celtic Brittany.

As in England from 1399 until long after the death of Richard II, weird and mysterious prophecies accompanied this resurgence of religious fervor. The Bretons had their own beloved Arthur, now the Lord Constable of France in the ranks of the despondent dauphin. They remembered the legends of an Arthur who would come again, bearing a boar as his device, to expel the English and re-establish the ancient kings of the Celts.

By July of 1429 even Christina of Pisa, the lady writer and biographer of King Charles V, had heard some of these prophecies in Paris, where she was living in poverty. In her poetry she speaks of them.

The prophecies concerned a Virgin like the Celtic fairy Vivian, who vanquished the magician Merlin and held him enchanted in the Hawthorn Wood. Or like the Christian virgins and martyrs, Saint Catherine and Saint Marguerite.

A white virgin, the pure-in-heart, from the White Wood, clad in white armor and bearing a white banner, was mounting a white war-horse to ride for France! She would wear white like Roland! The healing maiden would fill the wind with her sighs. She would dry up rivers before her and kill the fierce stag with its diadem of royalty; and the Celtic forest would rise before her and say: Daughter of Gaul, admirable virgin, Druid priestess from the mistletoe groves, comfort your people, for here before the English cannons they die. Succor the fair city of Orléans. O pure-in-heart! O virgin of Orléans!

Little pieces of vellum, lines of Latin verse reported to have come from Bede's histories and lives, were passed from hand to hand. The Latin letters, which were also numerals, made a nice sum:

bIs seX CVCVLLI, bIs septeM se soCIabVnt
1 10 100 5 100 5 50 50 1 1 1000 100 1 5 = 1429.
Ecce beant bella, tum fert vexilla Puella.

* * *

Twice six hooded ones, twice seven will band together
[In 1429]
Behold! Wars yawn wide, then the Maid bears the banners.

The fleur-de-lis, the heraldic symbol of Orléans, was the more ancient sign of the Virgin. This would be the virgin of the fleur-de-lis—the Maid of Orléans.

No one knows the origin of these prophecies, but they circulated, perhaps at the hands of the Franciscans, perhaps from unknown hands.

Duke Charles of Orléans meanwhile had taken one last precaution. He sent word into France that his treasures—the archives, the priceless tapestries, and in particular his precious books—be removed entirely from Blois Castle. They were to be put under heavy guard and taken first to Saumur in Anjou and then to the port of La Rochelle, there to be carefully preserved from theft and fire until the Duchy of Orléans was safe from the English. He sent eighty books, each one worth between $4,000 and $5,000.

Even this was not his last precaution. The Earl of Salisbury had been ordered to the siege of Orléans, and he had obeyed. In doing so, he had broken the feudal code. Duke Charles would not like to say what Salisbury's fate would be!

Duke Charles then shrewdly perpetrated one of the master strokes of his career. Its audacity was so enormous that its ingeniousness was not understood. The English, however, understood it. Decades later Parliament was still thundering about the "wily, subtle" Duke of Orléans and quarreling about who had allowed him to come down to the London area.

The prisoner ordered the Bastard of Orléans to hand over the Duchy of Orléans, entire and undamaged, to Duke Philip of Burgundy! The Papal legates also understood. They urged Duke Philip to accept this charge, this unparalleled honor, to bow before the generosity and the Christian confidence of the sovereign Duke of Orléans. Here he was, entrusting the stewardship of his duchy to the sure care of his enemy, for the duration! The citizens of Orléans waited upon Duke Philip with tears in their eyes. The burgesses pleaded with him to become their guardian.

Duke Philip of Burgundy swallowed the bait. Ordering his vassals to halt all military operations until his return, he rode hastily from Orléans to Paris to announce the good news to the "so-called" Regent of Bedford. Let the English armies retire! Orléans was Burgundy's before a shot had even been fired!

John Duke of Bedford replied coldly, "We are not of a humor to beat the bushes while others run away with the game." His answer was a categorical "No." Duke Philip was so disgusted that he recalled his forces from the siege of Orléans! He could no longer fight Duke Charles. His sense of chivalry prevailed. Let Orléans fall to the English—but not to him.

France had reached its darkest hour. Only one chink of hope shone through the blackness. Now even the Burgundians, deprived of immense revenues and of even greater honor, had reasons to say also, "the poor Duke of Orléans!"

If Ballad XXV, the only other war poem Duke Charles translated, reached France in its original French form in 1429, it could have left no room for doubt as to the instructions of the duke to his vassals and subjects. In the French original of this ballad, Duke Charles says more daringly: "Loyalty, unfurl your banner, I beg you. Mourning and Melancholy are holding Joy a prisoner. I pray God to curse them! Danger and Distress boot my pleasure out. If Reason were not corrupt, I would win my case against Fortune and her lawyer Hardness. If I had the mastery of that false house, I would put them in their coffins! That is my prayer. I beg God to damn them!" In plain words, I beg God to send Salisbury to hell!

BALLAD XXV

"O steadfast truth, display thy banner,
Support my right, I pray thee heartily,
And fresh assail this new and strong frontier
Where painful thought and woe do now ally,
O welaway! to hold feloniously
The little joy I had as prisoner
So that to me they make him a stranger.
I beseech God accursèd might they die.

"When that I ought bear forth a gladsome cheer
In places strange or else in company
Naught can I say but what is a manner,
For though my mouth out-show a laughter dry,
Or speak a sportful word, yet verily,
Distress and Danger with pain confer
Aback to thrusten my poore pleasure;
I beseech God accursèd might they die.

"Of cheer, alas, who had there here
Or made of joy, methink, so much as I?

171

Wherefore, of right, as reason doth me hear,
Yet at the least I should have some party;
In banishment as now thus doth he lie
Far from my heart as by the false treaty
Of faithless fortune and woe her counsellor;
I beseech God accursèd might they die.
But and I had as of them the mastery,—
As would God the term that it were nigh,—
I should not miss to bring them to their bier;
I beseech God accursèd might they die."

The Master Chancellor of Orléans, William Cousinot, recorded with accuracy the events that followed. His chronicle, written for Duke Charles and Count John of Angoulême, is an eyewitness account. All words within quotation marks in the following are from him of words he actually heard.

Tuesday, October 12, 1428. The Earls of Salisbury and Suffolk, and William Glasdale, plus many English and false French, with others from Paris and Chartres and Normandy came with all their might to besiege the city of Orléans. The Bastard of Orléans and the people of the city worked day and night to rip down the suburbs and to barricade the main thoroughfare into the city.

October 21, 1428. Around twelve-thirty the English delivered a marvelously powerful assault against the boulevard leading from the bridge. The brave women of Orléans helped to topple the scaling ladders into the moats, while others poured down on the enemies's heads hot coals, lime, hot grease, and boiling water. And to refresh the French, the women carried them wine, meat, and fruit. Others lugged rocks and anything that could be used in their defense. Some women were even seen to grasp the points of English lances in their bare hands and to topple the knights over backward. Xaintrailles was wounded, but he later recovered.

October 23, 1428. The French set fire to the boulevard in plain sight of the English, retired over the bridge, and raised it after them.

October 24, 1428. The English captured the Tournelles fortresses, from which they began to bombard the town day and night. The citizens despaired, but the Bastard of Orléans rushed forth to fortify the drawbridge that they had raised. William Glasdale, a braggart and a proud man, called to the people inside the city that he would murder every living soul once he got in—men and women alike, without sparing anyone.

November. The Earl of Salisbury, who had gone up to the Tournelles to reconnoiter, was struck in the eye by cannon shot. He fell to the ground beside Glasdale. He was laid low "by the just judgment of God who knows all and who treats and rewards man according to his deserts."

The courage of the English was weakened. They sent messengers hastily to the Duke of Bedford, who "calls himself the Regent of France," asking for another commander, reinforcements, food, and silver. He sent them William de la Pole, Duke of Suffolk, and Lord Talbot among many others.

The lords of France had pity and compassion upon the inhabitants of Orléans, who swore never to surrender; for their feudal lord, so long a prisoner in England, trusted in their loyalty.

The besiegers numbered ten thousand.

December 29, 1428. The English finished their chain of forts, thirteen in all, that by this time encircled the city and cut it off both by land and by water.

February 12, 1429. The Duke of Burgundy, who was in Paris, sent his herald to order his vassals to return home to Burgundy. The citizens of Orléans demolished their beautiful suburbs, which were as large as the city proper. They also razed twenty-six churches, including the collegiate church, the cloister for the canons, and the presbyteries. The inhabitants, in immediate danger of perdition, heard that a virgin was riding toward the dauphin. She claimed to be able to raise the siege of Orléans.

Easter, March 27, 1429. There was a girl, a native of Domrémy, a simple village girl accustomed to tending animals, and when she was not tending them, she was learning to sew and to spin. She was about eighteen or nineteen years old. She went to Sir Robert of Baudricourt. Joan said simply to him the words that follow: "Sir Captain, know that God, for a long time past, has made me know and has commanded me to go to the gentle dauphin who ought to be and who is the real King of France; and that he should give me men-at-arms and that I would raise the siege of Orléans and that I would take him to be crowned at Rheims."

CHINON CASTLE

JOAN: "Gentle Dauphin, why do you not believe me? I tell you that God has pity on you, and on your kingdom, and on your people; for Saint Louis and Saint Charlemagne are on their knees before

Him, praying for you. And I will tell you, if you please, such a thing that it will give you to understand that you should believe me."

JOAN IS QUESTIONED BY DOCTORS AND PARLIAMENTARIANS AT POITIERS

QUESTION: "We are here assembled because you have told the dauphin that God has sent you to him. The Holy Scriptures forbid us to believe you unless you show us a sign."

JOAN: "I do not want to tempt God. The sign he ordered me to give was that I should raise the siege of Orléans, and lead the dauphin to be crowned at Rheims. If you come, you will see it too."

QUESTION: "Joan, you are asking for soldiers? If such is God's will, then you have no need for men-of-war; for God's pleasure alone can send the English back over the seas to their own land."

JOAN: "I am only asking for a few soldiers, none in any great numbers. The soldiers will fight, and God will give the victory."

On the second day of examination many notables attended. Before the hearing, they said the whole affair was only daydreams and fantasy, but when they came from the chamber they were weeping "hot tears."

QUESTION: "Why do you wear men's garments?"

JOAN: "I can see that this appears strange to you, and not without cause; but it is necessary for me to dress in men's clothing in order that I arm myself and serve the gentle dauphin; and also when I am thus among men, they will not have any carnal desire for me, and so it seems to me that thus I shall better preserve my virginity in thought and in fact."

Joan was examined by three noble ladies who found her to be a virgin with no "appearance of corruption nor any trace of violence." She had never menstruated. In Poitiers, Joan was fitted for a coat of mail and armor. A white horse was purchased for her. Meanwhile, the dauphin had decided to test her by seeing if she could lead a supply train into Orléans. The dauphin sent one of his officers to ask her:

WILLIAM COUSINOT OF MONTREUIL: "Joan, we want to try to put some supplies inside Orléans; but it seems that this will be a hard task, considering the bastions that are before it and that the English are strong and powerful."

JOAN: "By God, we shall put them inside Orléans at our ease, and also not an Englishman will sally forth, nor none shall make a move to hinder us."

Then Joan went to Blois to await the convoy. During her visit she had a white banner made on which she had portrayed an image of the Saviour and of two angels, and she had it blessed. While in Blois, Joan had a herald take a letter to the English at Orléans.

JOAN'S LETTER

"Jesus.   Mary.   [March 29, 1429]
"King of England, have respect for the King of Heaven and for His royal blood. Give up to the Maid the keys to all the good cities you have forced. She has come through God to uphold the blood royal, and she is ready to make peace if you will do the right thing and pay for what you have damaged. . . . She comes from the King of Heaven, body for body, to boot you out of France, and she promises and guarantees, this Maid, that she will make such a hubbub that France shall not have seen its like in the last thousand years.

"Archers, men-in-arms, who are valiant and fine, return to your homes in peace, all you who are before Orléans, and, by God, if you do not do it, the Maid will give you some injuries to remember. . . .

"William de la Pole, Duke of Suffolk, John Lord Talbot, and Thomas Lord Scales, answer if you want to make peace at the city of Orléans. . . .

"Duke of Bedford, who call yourself Regent of France for the King of England, the Maid begs you and requires that you make no more destruction. If you do not do her justice, she will so do that the French shall accomplish the most brilliant deed that was ever done in Christendom.

"Listen for news from God and from the Maid."

April 28, 1429. When the convoy was ready—livestock, wagons loaded with grain, ammunition, firearms—Joan sent her host to confession. Then they set out for Orléans, sleeping one night en route. When they had arrived outside the city, there was a contrary wind so that they could not sail their boats on the Loire. Joan said, "Just wait a bit, in the name of God, all will get into the city."

And suddenly the wind changed so that the ships and barges came easily up to them. The Bastard of Orléans and several burgesses who were particularly curious to see the Maid had come out to meet her and to request her to enter their city:

JOAN: "Are you the Bastard of Orléans?"

JEAN: "Yes, Joan."

JOAN: "Who counseled you to have us come in this way instead of by the other route close to the English? From the other side the supplies could have easily passed down the current."

JEAN: "Pardon me, but it was at the advice of our council and of our captains."

JOAN: "The council on high is better than yours and your men's, and is more certain and more wise. You thought to deceive me, but you only deceived yourselves, for I bring you the best aid that ever knight, town, or city ever had, aid that proceeds not for the love of me but purely from God; who, at the request of Saint Louis and Saint Charlemagne, has had pity for the City of Orléans, and has not wished that his enemies keep the body of the Duke of Orléans and also his city. As far as for entering your city, let me also take my followers who have all confessed their sins, and I should not fear the entire might of the English while in their company."

CAPTAINS: "Joan, enter in all security, for we swear to be shortly beside you."

Then Joan entered Orléans, where she was lodged in the house of the Duke of Orléans's treasurer, Jacques Boucher. True it is that she had been riding all that day without once dismounting, without drinking or eating. Although a good supper had been prepared for her, she took only five or six soup-spoonfuls of wine in a silver cup with an equal amount of water. She went to sleep in the chamber that had been made ready, with the treasurer's wife and daughter for company.

When the herald who had carried her letter to the English returned, he told Joan that the enemy considered her a heretical witch and that Lord Talbot and the others reviled her as much as they could, saying that if they caught her they would burn her at the stake.

JOAN: "Tell Talbot that if he will arm himself, so will I also, and let him take his stand before the city, and if he can get me, let him burn me. But if I vanquish him, then he shall raise the siege and return to his own country."

May 4, 1429. Early in the morning the Bastard of Orléans and Joan sallied forth with banner unfurled to meet La Hire, who was bringing in a convoy from Blois. They escorted La Hire back into Orléans right in front of the English, who sat in their bastions without daring to come forth and attack them. They were all inside the city by 7:00 A.M.

Around noon a party of French noblemen attacked one of the thirteen strongholds. Joan was asleep with only her page and her hostess in the house. Suddenly she awoke.

Joan said: "Go saddle my horse. In the name of God, men from the city are fighting before a bastion and there are wounded." Joan rode straight through the city to the fortress, although she had never been there before. The battle waged fiercely until Vespers, by which time the English retreated from that tower, leaving all their food and military equipment.

May 6, 1429. Carrying her banner and on foot, Joan led her soldiers against the English under Glasdale. An alert at her rear caused her men to turn and run. When Joan started to follow them, the English ran after her, taunting her. Suddenly Joan turned, and although there were only a few soldiers with her, started walking directly toward the enemy. When the English saw her charging them, they turned and fled from her. During the following battle Joan's soldiers captured another English position. When Joan saw them looting this fort, she ordered it to be burned. That day she was wounded in the foot. During the night the English retreated to another position across the Loire.

May 7, 1429. On this day, with the full approval of the burgesses but against the advice of the dauphin's captains, Joan crossed the Loire. While she was deliberating as to how she should proceed, someone brought her host a present—a splendid shad.

JACQUES BOUCHER: "Joan, let's eat this shad before you leave."

JOAN: "In God's name, we'll have it for supper when we cross back over the bridge, and we'll bring one of the God-damns with us who'll want his share."

The main assault on the Tournelles, over the broken arches of the bridge, lasted all day. Although Joan got an arrow through her shoulder early in the morning, she pulled out the shaft herself, stuffed some cotton on the wound to staunch the flow of blood, and kept going. Toward evening the French despaired of dislodging the English.

JEAN OF ORLEANS: "We must retreat, draw our cannons back into the city, and wait for morning."

JOAN: "In God's name we shall pierce through any minute now. Have no doubt of it. . . . Watch my banner carefully, and tell me when I have come to the Boulevard."

A KNIGHT: "The staff of your banner is there."

JOAN: "Now forward. All is ours, and enter."

Then were the English assailed from two sides with a cross fire of cannons, culverins, and crossbows. It was a proud and a marvelous attack, more so than had ever been seen in the memory of any living man present. Meanwhile, the carpenters were repairing the spans of the bridge across the Loire, taking cover always so that the English could not see them. By 6:00 P.M. the English were so weary that they could no longer fire. Then Glasdale tried to escape down the Boulevard, but the drawbridge collapsed as he passed. He and his men were all drowned in the Loire.

In plain sight of Talbot and the veteran warrior Suffolk, the French poured over the Boulevard. Five hundred of the proudest knights and squires of England were killed that day. In afteryears the French could never understand how they had managed to capture the Tournelles—if not by divine intervention. Before Joan returned over the bridge night had fallen.

Joan asked that all the church bells of Orléans be tolled in rejoicing.

May 8, 1429. (Sunday). On this day the English sallied forth from their forts with their prisoners and all they could carry with them. They converged at the road east leading into Meung-sur-Loire. As they filed past the city, Joan asked that the gates of Orléans be thrown open. Wearing only a thin jerkin because of her wound, she followed them out into the fields. Priests in their vestments formed a long procession after her. An altar was set up in the meadow. Mass was begun.

JOAN: "Look toward the English. Are their backs facing us or their faces?"

REPLY: "Their backs are turned. They are retreating."

JOAN: "Then let them go. God would not be pleased if we were to combat them today. You will get them another time."

La Hire took out a company of knights who followed the English for a few miles to be sure that they were not returning. They were not. Orléans was delivered! The tide of battle had turned!

Joan returned to the dauphin at Tours. He entrusted the mopping-up operations along the Loire River to John, Duke of Alençon, who requested that the Maid accompany him. They set siege to Jargeau, and won it.

June 12, 1429. During the night Alençon and Joan returned under cover of darkness to Orléans, bringing with them their prisoner, William de la Pole, Duke of Suffolk, whose life was in danger. The French were so violent that they no longer accepted prisoners. They killed close to five hundred Englishmen at Jargeau, and there Joan had saved Alençon's life.

June 15, 1429. Alençon and Joan captured Meung-sur-Loire. The two became friends, and Joan called him the "Gentle Duke."

ALENÇON: "Joan, there are the English in battle stations. Shall we fight?"

JOAN: "Are you wearing your spurs?"

ALENÇON: "Speak up. Should we withdraw and flee?"

JOAN: "No, in God's name, go at them, for they will flee, and they won't stop running, and they will be undone with hardly the loss of one of your men; I meant only that you would need your spurs so you could chase them!"

June 18, 1429. Alençon and Joan not only took Beaugency next, but following that triumph fought a pitched battle against the English at Patay. The Bastard of Orléans and Alençon had hesitated to meet the English in the open field because they remembered Agincourt and Verneuil, but Joan promised them the victory. At Patay they killed Sir John Fastolf.

After these successes the dauphin and his council wanted to attempt the siege of the large city of Troyes where Henry V had been wed. However, they dared not attack it. Joan was summoned to their session.

July 10, 1429.

CHANCELLOR: "Joan, the king and his council are perplexed to know what to do."

JOAN: "If I talk, will I be believed?"

DAUPHIN: "Yes, you may speak."

JOAN: "Gentle King of France, Troyes is yours. If you can wait for two or three days, it will be under your rule for love or by force. Have no doubt as to this."

CHANCELLOR: "Joan, if we were sure to have it even within six days, we could still wait. But I do not know if what you say is true."

Even at that very hour Joan called her men, mounted her horse, and began the siege operations. The inhabitants of Troyes, looking down from their high walls, were awed. As Joan on her white war-horse moved about her men and directed the placing of the cannons and siege batteries, a cloud of white butterflies flew above and around her. The people of Troyes hesitated no longer. It was the Maid of Orléans! Tearfully they threw open the gates of Troyes, and surrendered. The English garrison quietly withdrew. They also were awed.

July 17, 1429. On Sunday, in the Cathedral of Rheims, was anointed and crowned King Charles VII of France. The ceremony was performed in every detail, according to rites established in antiquity, by Reginald of Chartres, Archbishop of Rheims. Beside the king stood Duke John of Alençon and Joan of Arc holding her banner. After her dauphin was crowned, Joan fell to her knees weeping, and embraced his knees.

Joan said: "Gentle King, now has been performed God's pleasure, for he willed you to receive this honored sacrament at Rheims, showing that you are our true king and he to whom this kingdom rightfully belongs."

In August at Château-Thierry the poor people of France crowded about Joan wherever she went, and wanted to touch her.

JOAN: "In God's name, look at these pious people. When I come to die, I hope that I die here among them."

JEAN OF ORLEANS: "Joan, do you know when you will die and in what place?"

JOAN: "I have already accomplished what my Sovereign Lord commanded me to do: raise the siege of Orléans and have the gentle king sanctified. I wish he wanted me to return to my father and my mother's home so I could care for their animals and do again the tasks I used to do."

When the knights heard Joan speak such words, when they saw her kneel so often alone in prayer—even in the midst of battle—when they saw her, as often, raise her eyes to Heaven, "then they thought that she was rather a *thing come from God* than otherwise."

One month before Joan uttered these words, on July 12, 1429, Jean Gerson breathed his last in the dauphinist city of Lyons in eastern France, where he had been living in seclusion for the past ten years in his brother's monastery. Aside from writing several immortal hymns and his last words on education and religion, Jean Gerson, unable to return to Paris because of the enmity of the Burgundians, had lived the peaceful life of the monastery. The wandering monks kept him in touch with the outside world. Just a few months before his death this great man had requested a secretary to attend his bedside. As he lay dying, he wanted to dictate one last work.

While Joan of Arc was leading her first soldiers during the siege of Orléans, Jean Gerson was thinking of her and writing about her. He was the only French writer during her lifetime, or for two hundred years afterward, who devoted an entire work to Joan of Arc.

The gist of Jean Gerson's *Treatise,* written on the point of death, is this:

The King and the noblemen of France have fallen in behind the white standard of this child. Their risk and their shame would be unthinkable if she were an impostor. Throughout the kingdom ordinary people praise Heaven because of this Maid; for, in very fact, her enemies are continuously undone before all eyes. The adversaries run and cower before this girl. They shake and tremble like pregnant women at the sight of her. Does this Joan violate the dictates of prudent conduct? What does she claim? Only that she is inspired of God.

Let us be concerned for the king and for the princes of the blood royal. Let us also look to the king's soldiers and to all soldiers who have been in contact with her. Let us weigh her effect upon our learned clergy, upon our people. Let us consider this Maid of Orléans.

Everyman's goal in this world is the same: to lead a good life, to love God, to be just toward his neighbors, to be abstemious, moderate, and virtuous in his personal habits. This, and only this, is her goal.

Let us beware lest the special grace which God has granted this Maid be not used in consuming vanities, nor in retribution and revenge for old crimes, nor in selfish glorifications. Let her rather turn us toward humility, toward Christian forgiveness, toward prayer. Let each man rather assist her by a generous contribution of his earthly goods toward the sacred cause of peace so that instead of slaughter and cruel war, Justice may once more prevail in our land, so that delivered from the hands of our foes, God willing, we may once again raise up our voices to serve Him in holiness and truth.

This Maid is in danger. It is said that she is wicked because she wears men's clothing. While it is perfectly true that there is an old law forbidding such attire, that law is superannuated and superseded. It was an old law aimed at checking immodesty in public places, an attempt to safeguard public morality. The case of the Maid is other. She wears masculine attire so that as standard-bearer to the King of Heaven she may better trample underfoot all enemies of law and justice. . . . History is full of precedents. Consider the case of the warrior maiden Penthesilea in Homer. . . . Remember how the warrior-maiden Camilla in Vergil came down from the hills of Latium to lead her soldiers to battle, and how she died.

I pray for the Maid of Orléans.

Lyons. May, 1429 JEAN GERSON

The opposite school of thought concerning Joan of Arc during her lifetime may be seen in a letter written, according to Rymer, in 1428–1429 by the Duke of Bedford to King Henry VI:

"All things have prospered for you till the time of the Siege of Orléans, undertaken by whose Advice God only knows. Since the Death of my Cousin of Salisbury, whom God absolve, there fell by the Hand of God, as it seemeth, a great Stroke upon your People, that was assembled there in great number, caused in great part, as we trow, by the Confidence they had in a Disciple and Limb of the Devil, call'd Pucelle [Maid, or Virgin] that us'd false Inchantments and Sorcery.

"The which Stroke and Discomfiture not only lessen'd in great part the number of your People here, but also sunk the Courage of

the Remainder in a wonderful manner, and encourag'd your enemies
to assemble themselves forthwith in great number.

"JOHN DUKE OF BEDFORD. PARIS."

July 18, 1429. King Charles VII, accompanied by the Bastard of
Orléans, Alençon, La Hire, and Joan, decided to advance toward
Paris. It had come to the attention of King Charles that the Duke of
Bedford's army had been increased by an additional four thousand
fighting men the Cardinal of Winchester had just brought over into
France. This cardinal had recruited these men at the Pope's com-
mand and with his funds. They were intended to be used on a
crusade against Hussites in Hungary, but "he made them stop to
war against true Catholics in France." The French were angry.
They heard that the Duke of Bedford was setting out to meet them.

August 18-22, 1429. The French took Compiègne, Senlis, and
Beauvais. After skirmishes that lasted several days, the Duke of Bedford withdrew before the French advance.

August 26, 1429. The English partitioned their forces in order to
fortify the Norman cities to the west of Paris. King Charles and his
army entered the Saint-Denis area.

September 8, 1429. Joan and the Lord Marshal Gilles de Rais attacked Paris at the Saint-Honoré Gate. Joan, not realizing the depth
of the water between her and the walls of the Louvre at this point,
tried to fill up the moat so that she could make a breach in the wall.
Both her thighs, "or at least one," were pierced with an arrow. When
her men retreated, she refused to go. They dragged her behind a
mound and left her there that day. After it was dark, the French
sent word to her several times. She refused to leave. It was finally
necessary for John, Duke of Alençon, to go in person. He carried
her back to the French camp.

The Cousinot Chronicles, eyewitness accounts that report conversation verbatim, end at this point. It would seem that they were
destroyed.

October 13, 1429. The Duke of Bedford arranged to give Duke
Philip of Burgundy the Lieutenant-Generalship of France, reserving
for himself the regency of Normandy. The English troops began to
evacuate Paris.

December, 1429. Joan asked that her native village of Domrémy
be exempted from taxation. Her request was honored by the king.
He also raised her to the nobility under the name of Du Lis or

Dulis (of the Lily). The year 1430 was to be, according to the prophecies, the decisive year when the English would be driven out of France and when Charles VII would rule supreme.

As usual the prophecy was in Latin:

angLIa CVMpVLsa, reX franCUs prInCIabIt = 1430

April 25, 1430. To counter the coronation of King Charles VII, the boy king of England, already crowned at Westminster as Henry VI, was brought over to France. He was lodged in Bouvreuil Castle in Rouen. He was still in the care of his tutor, Richard de Beauchamp, Earl of Warwick. This nobleman had carried the child into Westminster for his coronation. Henry Beaufort, Cardinal of Winchester, called Cardinal of England because of his royal blood, also attended Henry VI.

May, 1430. The Duke of Burgundy descended from Flanders to lay siege to Compiègne where Joan was with two thousand French soldiers. Joan told the people of the city that Saint Catherine had revealed to her that here she might capture the Duke of Burgundy in person. Joan wore a crimson cloak, a gift from the burgesses of Orléans—or, some say, from Duke Charles of Orléans himself. Crimson and dark green were the colors of Duke Charles. This day Joan rode a powerful, dappled-gray war-horse.

May 24, 1430. Joan was captured by the Burgundians. As she fought a retreating action, being the last, says the Burgundian chronicler Georges Chastellain, to retreat, she was pulled from her horse by a valiant Burgundian who caught her by the cloak. She was held down on the ground until the skirmish was over. Duke Philip, alerted by his men—who were more joyous than if they had captured a king—hastened to talk to her. Chastellain says that, hard as he tried, he was never able to find out what his master said to Joan or what she said to him.

May, 1430, to May, 1431. Joan was lodged in Beaurevoir Castle as a prisoner of John of Luxembourg, vassal of Duke Philip. Joan tried to escape, once leaping out her tower window to the stones below. When the English had finally collected the king's ransom that the Burgundians asked, she was turned over to the Duke of Bedford and transported to the same castle at Rouen where the young King Henry VI and his tutor lodged.

Joan of Arc was to be tried for witchcraft. The judges were the Bishop of Beauvais, whom Joan had expelled from his diocese only

recently; the Cardinal of England, and the Earls of Warwick and
Bedford. Both chroniclers, Monstrelet and Chastellain, saw Joan in
1430; but their narration also has been either lost or suppressed. It
is said that the Lady of Luxembourg begged her husband on her
knees not to sell Joan. Joan's ransom ran into millions of dollars.

The public hearings began on February 21, 1431, and lasted till
May 29th of that year, when the Bishop of Beavais condemned Joan
to the stake as a relapsed heretic.

May 20, 1431. The sentence was effected. The executioner was
ordered, after Joan had cried her last "Jesus!", to let the fire die
down a bit so that the crowds could see that the victim was really
burned to death.

In such an important and expensive execution, it was essential that
no stories of substitution, or rescue, or resurrection start. The executioner was also ordered to throw her ashes into the Seine River,
and this was done.

There is no evidence that King Charles VII protested her trial or
her execution. Reginald of Chartres, always her enemy, announced
her capture to his diocese of Rheims laconically enough. The Earls
of Bedford and Warwick and the Cardinal of England had managed
to bring to a satisfactory conclusion what was a master stroke of
diplomacy. They should have no more trouble enlisting soldiers in
England, where people were so frightened of Joan that soldiers
simply would not go to France. Since Joan was a witch and burned
as a witch, they could now explain their past defeats. Who could
fight a witch? Best of all, the new King of France could now wrestle
under a second stigma: he had been crowned by a witch! The joke
was definitely on him.

So that all should be done according to law, a letter was sent by
the King of England to the Duke of Burgundy, summarizing the
trial and explaining how the Bishop of Beauvais had insisted upon
trying Joan, since she had been captured in his diocese, and further
how he had rid the world of her—he and the learned doctors of the
University of Paris. The court had duly sat and had found, after
sedulous examination, that Joan was not only a corrupter of public
morals and a cruel murderess, but a "superstitious witch of the devil,
and a blasphemer of God and the saints, schismatic and much wandering away from the faith of Jesus Christ." The letter further
stated that "she, seeing her end approach, fully recognized and confessed that her voices . . . were evil and lying . . . and that their

promises that they would deliver her were false . . . and further confessed that her voices had mocked her and deceived her. . . ." No mention was made in this letter either of King Charles VII or of Duke Charles of Orléans, except that Joan and her brothers were censured for having adopted the gold-and-azure lilies of France as their heraldic charge.

In his prison Duke Charles of Orléans read this letter. He did not read the minutes of the trial, for they were not available. He would have heard, however, her several famous answers from each interrogation. Too many people had been present at the open sessions for them not to have become public knowledge among the doctors and priests. The duke certainly learned, both from friends in England and from his own messengers to and from Orléans, that his name had come up several times during the trial. He had also received a poem praising her from one of his vassals in Italy, a Professor Antonio Astesano of the University of Pavia.

Duke Charles knew more than this, of course. As the most interested party, he knew every move Joan had made at Orléans and at the coronation. She could not have worn her crimson-and-green costumes, his own colors, without his express permission. He is said by some historians to have presented her with these clothes, and also to have paid for her banner. In Orléans she was lodged with his officer. Duke Charles was also in close contact with his brother and with the Duke of Alençon, for whom he had an almost fatherly affection. Even more than this, Joan of Arc had corresponded with another devoted Orléanist who believed in her unswervingly, the new Count of Armagnac.

Another association had brought Joan of Arc closest of all to Duke Charles. The Duke of Alençon had taken Joan of Arc to meet his wife. The Duchess of Alençon, this daughter of Duke Charles and the Princess Isabelle, had told Joan of Arc how worried she was about her husband.

"He was captured once," said the Duchess Joan.

"Never worry about him, Lady," answered Joan of Arc. "I promise to take care of him for you, and I swear to send him back to you safe and sound." And she had done it, too.

"Gentle Duke, step away from that window," warned Joan of Arc. Duke John of Alençon had moved aside just seconds before a shell came crashing through the window. Everyone knew that Joan of Arc kept her promises. The voices may not have kept theirs, for they moved in more mysterious ways their wonders to perform; but Joan kept her word always.

In England, Duke Charles must not have known what to believe. The English believed that she was a witch. Duke Charles and the King of France must have wondered just how much she had said at the trial. Everyone in high places kept silent. They had food for thought.

Joan of Arc had promised to do three things: to raise the siege of Orléans, to crown the Valois king, and to deliver Duke Charles from his English prison.

The white dove that an English soldier had seen fly out from her charred body had hardly cleared the black smoke of her pyre, the Cardinal of England had hardly dried his tears and climbed down from his platform opposite the scaffold, the Dukes of Warwick and Bedford had hardly finished their mutual congratulations, when already certain people were busy whispering . . . Duke Charles will be delivered from his English prison. Joan of Arc said so. The Maid of Orléans said so. Wait and see.

IX [*1431–1435*]   IN THE NAME OF KING Henry VI open letters were sent throughout Europe stating that the court at Rouen had burned a relapsed heretic. John Duke of Bedford could breathe more easily. The "limb of the fiend" was no more. The newly crowned Charles VII could feel properly ashamed of himself. His personal chronicler, Jean Chartier, says that the English in France continued to spread stories of the king's illegitimacy, in addition to which they reduced his mother, Queen Isabeau, their old ally, to virtual poverty in Paris. The one person who had dared to say that Duke Charles would be released from his English prison was the "relapsed heretic." Parliament in England refused categorically to discuss the possibility of any ransom negotiation. The only people who still remembered the Maid of Orléans were the simple, the uneducated inhabitants of Orléans itself. Only they still shed tears for her fate, and they were of no consequence.

Then in the same year that Joan died, a new princess entered the scene; and, strangely enough, this lady *was* touched by the "life and death of Joan of Arc."

In 1430 Duke Philip of Burgundy remarried for the second time. His third lady was chosen with the view to strengthening the Burgundian-English alliance. Although she was the daughter of King John of Portugal, she was also the daughter of Philippa Beaufort of Lancaster, the fourth child of John of Gaunt by Catherine Swinford. The lady Isabella was therefore the niece of the very Henry Beaufort, Cardinal of England, who had watched Joan's death, and wept. The Portuguese princess, coming up into Flanders, felt some strange tie to Joan of Arc. She said that she would very much like to be the instrument by which Joan's last prophecy came true. The Duchess of Burgundy was a brilliant lady herself. She had also a brilliant brother who was the same age as Duke Charles of Orléans. Her brother was Prince Henry the Navigator.

Although the new Duchess of Burgundy was most splendidly received by her husband, who created an Order of Chivalry in her honor and outdid himself to make her feel at home, the duchess realized soon enough that her position was embarrassing, if not false. Wherever she went in France, noble ladies fell to their knees before her and beside her. They wept, they sobbed, they clutched at her garments. They pleaded that the Duke of Burgundy withdraw from his English alliance and that peace be returned to the kingdom.

Not only the Duchess of Burgundy was so importuned. The Duchess Anne of Bedford was also entreated wherever she went, and this sister of Burgundy had seen Joan of Arc, examined her in Rouen to ascertain her virginity, sent her own physician to treat Joan, and doubtless heard the ugly slander to the effect that before her death Joan had been raped by an English "milord."

Through all these months Duke Charles had maintained a discreet silence. His greatest weapon and his only protection was a dignified withdrawal from the whole affair. In years to come he would perhaps see what could be done about Joan of Arc.

The opinion of Duke Charles was not needed at this time. His advice had not been asked. By the time he was thirty-six years of age most people in France had forgotten him. During these years he withdrew into books. He and his brother John of Angoulême were spending large sums of money to recover the books from their grandfather's library that Henry V had taken from Paris to London. Duke Charles found in books a compensation for the active life he could not lead. He had written in French and in English to his heart's content. During these years he withdrew even further, as if what he longed to express could not be said in either language. His was an experience familiar to all people who speak more than one language. Duke Charles wrote of love in English. In French he wrote of Isabelle, of the war, of his prison, of his insomnia, of his illness, of his homesickness, of the seasons, and of his sadness. During this long period of withdrawal the poet wished to turn to God. He did it neither in French nor in English. When he spoke of his soul's longing, he began to compose in Latin.

The Latin poem of Duke Charles is, so far as is known, the only major composition he ever wrote. It is called *Canticum Amoris,* or song of love. He also wrote hymns in Latin.

Churchmen and scholars in England to whom he lent the works of Jean Gerson, and from whom he also borrowed Latin treatises, began to dedicate their works to him. Therefore, despite his withdrawal from the world, the reputation of Duke Charles grew tremendously. He began to have friends among the prominent prelates of England. He had never been mistreated there. The Cardinal of England had always been amenable to suggestion and request. Now, because of his learning and his piety, he began to be greatly honored. Before long, Parliament would decide that he was being charged too much for his jails. It also happened, and at the same time, that English people in high places needed friends among the French nobles.

The death of the Maid had not turned the tide of battle. Raw recruits in England still showed the same reluctance to embark for France. The French and Gascon captains almost to a man still forged ahead, castle by castle and town by town. The Bastard of Orléans, La Hire, Xaintrailles, and the Constable of Richmond were still riding the tide of victory.

In a splendid and united effort to stem this tide, the nobles of England conveyed Henry VI to Notre-Dame Cathedral. As the boy king entered Paris, he received from the Duke of Burgundy the shield of France and from the Duke of Bedford the shield of England. The Earls of Arundel, Somerset, Suffolk, Huntington, and Warwick were also present, along with many prelates, including the Cardinals of England and York.

A huge scaffold of wood eighty feet long had been constructed for the coronation of King Henry VI in the cathedral. All was not harmonious, however, for the Bishop of Paris felt that he instead of Henry Beaufort should have crowned this King of France. The wine for the Mass was served in a valuable silver bowl belonging to the cathedral treasure. After the ceremony it was appropriated by the king's officers. Angry recriminations ensued until it was returned.

One of the guests at the following dinner was the Bishop of Beauvais, the magistrate who had presided at the trial of Joan of Arc. Among the "subtleties" were an image of our Lady beside a little king crowned, a fleur-de-lis crowned in gold and upheld by two angels, then a lady and a peacock, followed by a lady and a swan.

Despite the increased prestige that the English felt they had gained from this ceremony, their French subjects still knew that Kings of France were crowned, not at Paris, but in Rheims. They also wondered that neither queen mother attended. Queen Catherine remained in England and Queen Isabeau was in poverty in the Louvre, in the very city where her grandson was so fêted. Monstrelet says that Henry VI did pay his respects to her, but other sources claim that she saw him only from her window and that he had been taught to hate her.

All this could have made very little difference to Duke Charles in England. The poet, withdrawn into himself, had new sources of grief. Bonnie of Armagnac died at about this time, although, because of the confusion of the war, there is no record of her passing. Then in 1432 the son-in-law of Duke Charles, John, Duke of Alençon, seemed to undergo a change of nature. He was involved in a bitter quarrel over moneys owed him by the Duke of Brittany. The two dukes took time off from their war with England to fight a private war of their own. John, Duke of Alençon, along with his mother and his wife, was besieged in one of his castles. Those inside the castle had begun to suffer from lack of food and water. At the end of seven days John of Alençon daringly escaped in broad daylight, leaving the Bastard of Orléans behind with the ladies. By the time the Constable of Richmond had settled the dispute and raised the siege, the ladies were very weak indeed. This prolonged misery may have been what caused the death of Duke Charles's daughter, whom he had not seen for seventeen years. Thus, having lost two wives, he now lost his only child.

No doubt his grief was further increased by the news that the Duke of Alençon reacted more violently to his wife's death than could have been expected. It is not certain when he became an alcoholic, but the deaths of the two Joans were a contributing factor. It is amazing to note the list of catastrophes and the sudden changes in personality that occurred directly after Joan's death.

Then in 1432 came the death of the young Anne, Duchess of Bedford. Some say she died in childbirth, but Monstrelet asserts that she died from an illness that had undermined her health over a long space of time. In any case, the Duchess Anne was the last link between Duke Philip and the English. Her husband attempted a new treaty with Burgundy, but the latter was now openly reserved. The Duke of Bedford was hard pressed on all sides by French troops. Then, too, there was the trouble with King Henry VI.

Even in infancy, while his mother had held him on her lap during sessions of Parliament, this had been a turbulent and unhappy child. By 1432 his tutor, the formidable Earl of Warwick, requested permission from Parliament to chastise His Majesty. The permission was granted!

There were commotions in England also. Duke Humphrey was still impatient to fly at Burgundy's throat. His bitter and avowed enemies by now were the Cardinals of England and York. In 1432 Duke Humphrey forced the resignation of the latter from his post as chancellor. Both cardinals had begun to hear a good deal about Duke Charles. They had perhaps received a copy of his Latin poetry. They wondered why so fine a nobleman should not serve the cause of peace before England lost all of France. By 1433 Duke Charles had begun to negotiate directly with them.

On August 14th the duke drafted a fifteen-page reminder to the Privy Council. It was not the first such document he composed, nor would it be the last. He offered peace if only the English Council would deign to use his services. He claimed that he held a commission from King Charles VII, his nephew, to treat terms of peace directly. He pointed out that England could have nothing to lose by negotiating, or rather by allowing him, as an *impartial observer,* to negotiate in their names. All knew how disinterested he was, said Duke Charles. In the event that the Privy Council was disappointed in the terms he could arrange for them, he would guarantee to deliver up to them all the possessions in France that King Henry V had won. He personally would be willing to give up Orléans, Blois, La Rochelle, and the Mont-Saint-Michel!

The English Council was dazzled. The Cardinals of England and York were pleased as much by the elegant Latin as by the proposals, for they must have known that Duke Charles had no jurisdiction over most of the territories he so graciously proposed to bestow upon them—certainly not over La Rochelle or the Mont-Saint-Michel.

Surely no more treacherous or false document could be read than this peace letter of Duke Charles of Orléans. If a clever man like Henry Beaufort did not see through it, then it was because he too had suffered a change of personality, or because he did not wish to see through it:

"We have promised and we do promise, we have sworn and we do swear on our Word as a Prince and on the Holy Writ of God, that we Charles Duke as above-named will do, will implement, and will observe all and every single one of the above-named conditions . . . and we shall do so that our above-named friends of Alençon, Anjou, etc., etc., shall deliver and abide by our word, . . . and also that we shall at no time whatsoever run counter to our promises, nor none of them either, in Legality or beyond the pale of Legality, directly or obliquely, or in whatever exquisite shade whatsoever.

"And so that your Confidence and Faith in ourselves may be all the greater, and in Witness of the same, We, from our entire and spontaneous free will, do cause our Great Seal to be affixed to these letters and do further fortify them with our own Signature given by our Own Hand."

As the English archivist Rymer said later in great disgust, Duke Charles of Orléans "was reckoned the fittest Tool to decoy the English into the intended" trap. The strange part of such a move was that it succeeded!

The council asked for a meeting with King Charles's officers at Calais. For the first time in eighteen years Duke Charles had real reason to hope for his release. The principal voice raised in objection was that of Duke Humphrey of Gloucester. If Duke Charles had once seen himself as the "mouse," then Duke Humphrey was the "cat." The latter's credit, however, had fallen into abeyance. Let him storm and rant and try to warn his fellow peers that Duke Charles was false! Who cared to listen to Duke Humphrey? Certainly not the two cardinals whom he had robbed and demoted.

In July of this year Duke Charles was remanded from the custody of the Baron of Fanhope to that of William de la Pole, Duke of Suffolk, at the latter's request. William was the brother of the Third Earl of Suffolk who had died at Agincourt Field. He had received the Order of the Garter from King Henry V and remained in France under the command of Salisbury at Henry's death. In fact, William de la Pole had been fighting in France for fourteen years without once returning home to England.

He had been present at the resounding English victories at Cravant and at Verneuil. At Salisbury's death the Duke of Bedford had entrusted Suffolk with the command at Orléans where the tide of battle had first changed. After his defeat at Orléans he was subsequently taken prisoner by Joan of Arc at Jargeau. In order to save her prisoner, Joan and Alençon conveyed him to the safety of Orléans during the night. As Joan later testified, she expected to exchange him for Duke Charles. However, in June of 1429 the Dauphin needed the ransom more than he needed his royal cousin. Therefore the Duke of Suffolk, upon the payment of 20,000 pounds sterling, was released in time to attend the coronation of King Henry VI in Notre-Dame Cathedral. He finally returned to a much-deserved rest in England in November of 1431. Without doubt, his request for the custody of Duke Charles was expedient politically, but it is true that he owed his very life to the Orléanist party.

Duke Charles was therefore removed to the Duke of Suffolk's town house in London. The two lords had much in common, although they were divided by their patriotism. Each was a poet, and each was conversant with both French and English. Then, too, the Duke of Suffolk's wife was a former Alice Chaucer, perhaps the granddaughter of the famous poet whom Charles and his brother John of Angoulême so much admired. This connection may explain the otherwise curious fact that certain English poems of Duke Charles appear in the manuscript of Geoffrey Chaucer.

At about the time that Duke Charles was drafting his peace proposals to the Privy Council, certain ambassadors from Philip of Burgundy, in London on matters of high policy, had two occasions to see the Duke of Orléans in Suffolk's home. Affairs in England were so critical at this point that Parliament had been convened that summer. Many of the greatest peers of the realm were in England attendant upon King Henry VI: the Dukes of Bedford, Suffolk, Warwick, Gloucester, York, Norfolk, Northumberland, and Salisbury, and, of course, the Cardinals of England and York.

The ambassadors from Burgundy were there to offer their master's best advice: that the English should try to bribe the Duke of Brittany and Count Arthur of Richmond to switch allegiances and that they should also try to alienate the Duke of Savoy from the

Orléanist camp. Otherwise, counseled Duke Philip, they should sue King Charles VII for peace, realizing that he held to two stipulations without which there could never be any consideration of peace. King Charles VII and the Bastard of Orléans were adamant on these two conditions, namely, that the King of England must renounce his claim to the title King of France, and second, that the English must release Duke Charles. After these two conditions had been fulfilled, peace could probably be negotiated.

Hue de Lannoy, chief nobleman from the Burgundian delegation, writes to his master in Burgundy that after having discharged his letters and spoken to King Henry VI in person, he and his party returned to London from the country and attended upon the Duke of Suffolk. They were admitted to his presence just as he and Duke Charles were rising from the dinner table. After their obeisances had been acknowledged, the ambassadors were pleased when Duke Charles walked toward them and took the hands of Hue de Lannoy.

"How is my cousin of Burgundy?" asked Duke Charles. "Where is he now?"

"He is very well," answered Hue de Lannoy. "He is pursuing the war in Champagne. He recommends himself very earnestly to you, Sire, and he has desired us to know personally of your good health."

"You may tell him that I am in very good health, but I am distressed because I am spending the best part of my life in prison."

"Sire," said De Lannoy, "by the pleasure of God, good may still come of it, and in a good way. . . . If by your good agency God should give you the grace to treat and be the mediator of a peace between these two kingdoms, and to make a general peace between the realms and the princes, you ought not to complain of the pains and dangers you have endured."

"Here is my good cousin of Suffolk," said Duke Charles, "who knows how toward the King of England and the lords of his council I have always presented myself for their use, and still do so. I am like the sword still encased in its scabbard; whosoever must use it must first draw it forth. Moreover, I have always said and still do say that I can do nothing of profit to either realm if I am not allowed to speak with certain of my friends in France, by which means alone I may be enabled to carry forth this task.

"It seems to me that if I could have words with certain especial friends of mine, I would derive great profit from them. For my belief is that certain powerful lords attached to the person of His Majesty, the King of France, those who cling to his party, would do my bidding and would be of sufficient weight to turn the balance toward a general peace.

"On my word," continued Duke Charles, "I so desire peace, and I should so desire to be the one who was cause and means of having achieved it and maintained it that I should gladly accept to die seven days after its signing! . . . I dare even say, here in your presence, cousin of Suffolk, that my cousins of Burgundy and Brittany can do more right now to bring about peace than any other prince alive."

The ambassadors do not comment on their conversation so far, but it is to be noted that Duke Charles openly referred to his cousin as Charles VII, King of France, although the Duke of Suffolk had only shortly before helped to crown Henry VI as King of France. In other words, Duke Charles was conveying more to the ambassadors about his own position than his mere sentences would seem to imply. They must also have noted that he somehow was informed of their secret negotiation concerning the Duke of Brittany.

"I know for certain," said De Lannoy, "that you, most dreaded Sire, were more desirous of peace than of anything else in the world, so as to obviate the great evils that every day brings, so as to raise up the poor people of France whom the war has utterly oppressed. I know that its accomplishment does not depend on you, Sire, but that you would bend your every effort toward it."

Then the Duke of Suffolk spoke to His Highness of Orléans. "Sire, I have always told you that His Highness of Burgundy is favorably disposed to peace."

"Of this I have no doubt," replied Duke Charles. "I know perfectly well that the evils which have fallen upon France were caused neither by him nor by me. In other days I once told you this, Sir Hue. Believe me that I am still of this same mind."

As he spoke, Duke Charles grasped Sir Hue's arm and squeezed it hard twice, showing that he could not say what he wanted to say, that he could not speak openly in the presence of Suffolk. Clearing his throat, he said: "I wish that the King of England would entrust the negotiations to me. He need have no fear about my person. I do not desire so much to be delivered as I desire to negotiate this peace." Again he squeezed the ambassador's arm and said, "I may even dare to say aloud that *I* have more facilities . . . than any prince alive."

"Come now, Sire," interrupted Suffolk, "you know that the king wills to employ your services, for he has just granted you another safe-conduct for several of your people to come instantly into England."

"You say truly, Cousin," replied Duke Charles. "I am dispatching my herald Cameo shortly."

As the Duke of Suffolk tried to dismiss the Burgundian ambassadors, Duke Charles followed them, again launching into urgent inquiries about Duke Philip's health. "Truly, he could not be quieted on the subject," wrote Sir Hue to Burgundy.

"How much I should like to see Duke Philip! How much I should like to speak with him for a few minutes," urged Duke Charles. Again he stressed how concerned he was for Duke Philip's health.

The ambassadors made their bows preparatory to withdrawing. "I beg you, Sir Hue, to come back and see me again."

"They will see you before they leave," interrupted the Duke of Suffolk.

"However," wrote Sir Hue to his master, 'we see from many different evidences and signs that the English will not let anyone contact the Duke of Orléans privately, and certainly not ourselves."

The legates were not able to see Duke Charles during the next few days. The greatest catastrophe that could occur to England would be the loss of the Burgundian alliance. It would be one thing to negotiate a peace between England and Burgundy on the one hand with King Charles VII, the Bastard of Orléans, and the Duke of Alençon hampered on the other hand by their concern for Duke Charles. Such protestations of friendship for Burgundy on the part of Duke Charles might or might not be innocent. He seemed to want to warn the ambassadors about Duke Philip's health. This could not sound well in the ears of the Burgundians, who knew that the English were trying to persuade Duke Philip to come to England and sit in Parliament with them. The Duke of Suffolk saw to it, therefore, that the Burgundians heard no further from Duke Charles—at least, not in his house.

Despite Suffolk's vigilance, Duke Charles managed to get in touch with Sir Hue two days later. The Duke of Suffolk's barber, a man named Cauvel, came to speak to Sir Hue at the prisoner's request.

"I am a Burgundian," said the barber, "born in Duke Philip's home city of Lille, so he can be sure that I would not misinform him for the world. I am also one of the guardians set to watch Duke Charles by my master of Suffolk. Now, Duke Charles has asked me to find ways of getting letters from him to His Highness of Burgundy. So will you tell Duke Philip that he will receive letters from Duke Charles and that they will be true and bona fide letters expressing his real intentions?"

"We shall tell our lord," assured Sir Hue, "and will you tell Duke Charles that our lord wishes him to be delivered and the peace negotiated."

Only on the morning of their departure were the legates permitted another brief interview with Duke Charles, and then only in the presence of the Duke of Suffolk. "Cousin of Suffolk, may I not write a letter to my cousin of Burgundy?" asked Duke Charles.

"You will be advised tonight," replied the duke. That night the ambassadors were handed letters by the barber Cauvel from the Duke of Suffolk, but Cauvel whispered to them that the French duke had not been allowed to write.

That made very little difference because it had been arranged for him to reach Duke Philip. What he wrote Burgundy was apparently of value. He may have said, for example: I know that you have been urgently requested to sit in the current session of Parliament. I know that you have been invited to visit England; if I were you, I would not accept. Accept rather my advice and the friendship of my cousin, King Charles VII, and of my friends of Alençon and Anjou, and of my brother of Orléans . . . and you will *live* longer!

The Duke of Burgundy had another grief against the English very soon. Without asking his permission, John Duke of Bedford remarried, taking as his wife the seventeen-year-old daughter of a Burgundian vassal—a beautiful, gracious, and "frisky" girl, says Monstrelet. Then, too, the war was going very badly for Burgundy, who was beginning to see the Bastard of Orléans, La Hire, and Xaintrailles making more and more frequent raids up into his own Duchy of Artois. The Bastard of Orléans and Xaintrailles even captured one of the English generals, the Earl of Arundel, in an apple orchard where they had ambushed him. The earl's leg had to be amputated, and he died within a few days.

For all these reasons Philip of Burgundy was only too happy to meet with the English and the French in order to discuss peace. Perhaps warned by Duke Charles, the Duke of Burgundy managed to obtain the consent of his English allies to hold the conference in his city of Arras rather than in the English-held port of Calais. Duke Charles was not allowed to attend the conference, but only to send his chief herald, or King-of-Arms Malo.

The first ambassadors to arrive in Arras during the summer of 1435 were members of an impressive delegation sent by the Pope. The Cardinals of Saint-Cross and Cyprus headed this party. The Cardinal of Saint-Cross was one of the most astute diplomats of the century, a writer who used the pen name of Aeneas Silvius, and a man of such ability that he later became Pope Pius II. He was therefore the ranking personage at the peace conference. The fact that he had arrived early boded no good for England or for Burgundy, unless the latter was prepared to accede to the wishes of the Pope, who had always deplored the division in France and who had worked unceasingly to unite Orléans and Burgundy. The Pope held another weapon over the heads of the delegates—the fact that Duke Charles of Orléans, so close still to the throne of France, was thirty-five years old, and unmarried. If he were to wed an English lady of high rank, such as the Countess Maud of Arundel, this would unite Orléans with England. The Cardinal of Saint-Cross had orders, on the contrary, to unite Orléans and Burgundy.

The second deputation to arrive in Arras was led by Duke Philip of Burgundy. Duke Philip was heavily guarded as he rode into town, quite surrounded, in fact, by a company of one hundred gentlemen and two hundred archers all in matching uniforms. Three days after the grand entrance of Duke Philip, or on July 31st, the French delegation from King Charles VII came riding in force, four to five hundred of them. This king was represented by his herald, the King-of-Arms Mountjoy.

Next came the Duke of Bourbon and Count Arthur of Richmond. Both were affectionately greeted by Duke Philip, who actually rode out of town to meet them. Both French warriors had married Burgundian princesses. The Archbishop of Rheims and the Lords La Fayette and Vendôme were also delegates. John of Alençon and the Bastard Jean of Orléans were conspicuous by their absence. If their liege lord was not invited, if he did not negotiate, neither would they!

On August 3rd the Duchess Isabella of Burgundy arrived, magnificently escorted into town on an open litter. Her father had sent his king-of-arms to represent Portugal at the conference. The duchess went immediately to pay her respects to the Cardinal of

Saint-Cross. This princess was to have the honor, unusual for a woman, of negotiating at Arras. Since her marriage she had actually proved herself capable of governing Burgundy while her husband was fighting in Champagne. She was the lady who wished to fulfill Joan's prophecy that Duke Charles would live to be delivered from his English prison.

It was not until the delegations from the Papacy, Burgundy, and France had arrived on the 19th of August that the English ambassadors rode into Arras. Their party of three hundred noblemen, churchmen, and diplomats was headed by the Duchess Isabella's tall and imposing uncle, Henry Beaufort, Cardinal of Winchester. The French legates did nothing to honor the English, who in turn noticed that the Burgundians and the French entertained each other frequently and exchanged fair compliments and rich gifts. Meanwhile, just to reinforce in Burgundy's mind the arguments of peace, all during the conference La Hire and Xaintrailles redoubled their raids into Burgundian territory. The news of their lightning attacks was brought daily to Duke Philip, who was often obliged to leave the Abbey of Saint-Vaast, where the meetings were held, in order to dispatch reinforcements and officers to his towns in Burgundy. The French were also besieging Saint-Denis, the northern gate to Paris.

The Cardinal of Winchester, who was accounted by the gossips the richest man in western Europe, remained only two weeks in Arras. By September 6th it was apparent to him that there was no peace possible since the English were prepared neither to forfeit King Henry's title to the kingdom of France nor to release Duke Charles. On September 6th, without bidding adieu or making any excuses, the English delegation withdrew. England would lose first her ally of Burgundy, and then the war! The great lords of England, including the Duke of Suffolk, returned home. The only friend they had left was the doubtful Duke of Orléans, who would probably prove a poor friend. It had become essential to see if he meant what he said, that he was able and willing to help them save something on the Continent.

Once the English were out of the way, the cardinals from Rome drew up the Treaty of Arras, consisting of thirty-one articles. Stipulations 1 to 10 dealt with conditions that King Charles VII swore to fulfill in reparation for the murder of John the Fearless on the Montereau Bridge. Articles 11 to 21 listed fiefs and taxes that the King of France guaranteed to Burgundy. Article 24 was the most essential one in the treaty, because it saved face for Burgundy personally by stating that Duke Philip would never have to do homage to King Charles during his lifetime. The other articles generally included promises made by France and guarantees to Burgundy and his vassals, that, if broken, would incur the pain of excommunication upon the French king. It was, however, not only a treaty of alliance but also one of mutual defense. In Article 25 King Charles promised to go to the aid of Burgundy against the English, but this aid was not particularly stressed. Burgundy was much larger than France.

The Treaty of Arras was followed by a private religious ceremony at which the Cardinals of Saint-Cross and Cyprus officiated. Empowered by the Pope, they released Burgundy from his feudal oath of friendship and alliance with England. This was indeed the worst possible news to England.

It is said that King Henry wept when he heard this news. It is also said that it killed John Duke of Bedford.

Ever since the death of his brothers Clarence and Henry V, Henry VI had attempted to rule France, prosecute the war, and keep peace in England between his uncle of Beaufort and his last brother, Gloucester. Duke John of Bedford died in France on September 14th. The Treaty of Arras was ratified on September 21st.

The Cardinals of Winchester and York had returned to rule England. In their party were also the Dukes of Suffolk and Somerset and Sir Adam Molins (more properly Molyneux), who was Keeper of the Privy Seal and Bishop of Chichester. Humphrey of Gloucester and the City of London were in the opposition.

The Duke of Gloucester now had every excuse to fly at Burgundy's throat. Sentiment ran high in England against the Burgundians, and rightly so. England had been betrayed in its turn, just as France had been so long betrayed by these dukes, father and son.

In France Richard de Beauchamp, Earl of Warwick, replaced the Duke of Bedford, or rather, did his best to replace him. In July of 1437 Warwick was created Lieutenant General of France and Normandy. That same year he also felt the approach of the end. His will, dated in August of that year, requested: "My body to be buried at the Abbey of Tewksbury . . . And my Image to be made all naked, and no thing on my head but myn hair cast backwardys." It was a strange request. The Earl of Warwick had very fine, light brown hair. He wore it parted in the middle and slightly curled at the ends, where it touched his shoulders. His hair was thin. As he sat for his portrait, he wore a string of large pearls about his head.

John Duke of Bedford was very suitably buried at Rouen. His death was a cruel loss not only to England but even to occupied France; for he had been a clement and almost enlightened ruler. His young bride, the "frisky" Burgundian lady, remarried soon after his death.

The new Monk of Saint-Denis who was to write the chronicle concerning the reign of King Charles VII, the Under-Chanter Jean Chartier, does not mention the passing of the Duke of Bedford. He does recount in some detail, however, the death and interment in September of 1435 of the French Queen Mother Isabeau. This lady had passed through the most extreme vicissitudes in her lifetime. As a girl she had come from Bavaria to wed the boy King Charles VI. She had lived through many pregnancies. She had seen two of her daughters crowned Queen of England, and all her sons die except the last one, whom she had repudiated. Despite her disavowal of him, she had seen this son become Charles VII. She had allied herself with Louis of Orléans, and at his death, with John the Fearless, and then with Henry V. She had nursed this English king during his last illness and survived to see her grandson crowned King of England and of France. Then, reduced by the English to poverty, she had realized that in losing the respect of her own family she had also lost the respect of the English. Her name had been reviled. Her loose morals were the scandal of Europe. In France she was known as *La Grande Gaure*—The Big Heathen. Had she been another kind of woman, historians would probably have pressed charges to the effect that she was also the mother of Joan of Arc.

Both Monstrelet and Jean Chartier, however, are distressed by the lack of respect shown to her in death. They are sorry that when she came to die all she had to bequeath was a small house near Saint-Denis and a few trappings that could be used in the church. Her body was conveyed by only four attendants, on the river in an open rowboat, "as if it had been that of the least housewife of Paris, which was a great shame and dishonor to every Englishman," adds Jean Chartier.

The Monks of Saint-Denis received her remains. They put on their richest robes, decorated with fleur-de-lis, to show their respect for a Queen of France. The grand prior of the monastery sang her funeral mass "because there was no prelate." "There was shown," concludes Chartier, "that the Golden Lilies had fallen very low and come to their decline." Jean Chartier had not counted on the oldest prince of the Golden Lilies, who was still in England.

On May 12, 1436, Duke Charles of Orléans was removed from Suffolk's custody to that of Sir Reginald Cobham. The change was indicative of the urgency of the situation in England. Lord Cobham was the father-in-law of Humphrey of Gloucester. Angry at the loss of "Dame Jake," Gloucester had married his mistress, Eleanor Cobham. At the death of the Duke of Bedford, Duke Humphrey was next in line to the throne of England. In his new prison at Wingfield, Duke Charles learned that his brother the Bastard Jean had stubbornly refused to ratify the Treaty of Arras because no mention had been made in it of his brother's forthcoming release. King Charles VII would not like to lose his best commander; he should then not forget the duke in England!

From England, however, Duke Charles appointed Jean Le Fuzelier from Blois as his chief treasurer. He requested permission to have the officer visit him in England. An even better indication that the war would soon be over, and the English obliged to withdraw from the Continent and release their royal prisoner, was the fact that Duke Charles ordered his most precious possessions, including his beloved books, returned to Blois Castle.

X   [*1436–1440*]   DUKE CHARLES SPENT AN anxious four years after he ordered his books returned to Blois Castle and Jean Le Fuzelier appointed as his chief treasurer. Would the English consent to ransom him, or would they not? On the one hand he cultivated the friendships of the Cardinals of Winchester and York, while on the other hand he addressed urgent notes and poems to Duke Philip of Burgundy and to his Duchess Isabella. His relationships with his brother of Orléans and his cousin Charles VII were the only ones he had no cause to distrust. Their determination to bring him home to France was unshakable and urgent. The kingdom of France needed the duke more than ever. His age and his experience in diplomacy, his flawless reputation, and his nearness to the throne combined to make him a symbol of authority that every noble in France was bound to respect and obey.

In 1436 the French rewarded the Kingdom of Scotland by receiving the Princess Marguerite as bride for the Dauphin Louis. Not long after her arrival in France, King James I was treacherously stabbed to death in his bedroom at Perth. Even his queen was wounded by the insurgent Scots lords. Therefore the Papal legate of Saint-Cross traveled into Scotland to make sure that King James's young son was upheld on the throne. Under the pen name of Aeneas Silvius, he wrote an interesting account of his perilous journey.

Very probably at this meeting, certainly not long afterward, Henry Beaufort was officially notified that the Pope had appointed Duke Charles of Orléans as his personal commissioner in England to treat a settlement in the war between England and France. It is no wonder that the cardinal invited Duke Charles to be his guest in his palace at Winchester. The duke would have admired the splendid reredos that the cardinal was having carved for Winchester Cathedral, would have seen the chapel where Henry Beaufort would lie after death, and would have been escorted down the Southampton Road to visit the Hospital of Holy Cross, so similar in its architecture to Blois Castle, which the cardinal had rebuilt and reendowed. The hospital would be a memorial to his name.

Duke Humphrey, after delaying unaccountably in England, finally led his army against Duke Philip of Burgundy. However, his adversary had already retired far into his domains. After years of angry threats and challenges, Duke Humphrey accomplished little more than the devastation of the area around Calais. Since he was the first-ranking nobleman in England and such an enemy of the cardinal, this new humiliation of Gloucester on the Continent made him only more irascible and unpredictable. Perhaps even more than he hated Winchester, Duke Humphrey hated Duke Charles. It must have been only the strength of his personal charm that saved the French duke during these most difficult years.

In France the war was going very well for King Charles VII, despite the excellent management of Warwick and York and the good soldiery of Lord Talbot. In 1437 La Hire almost captured

Rouen, the chief city of Normandy. King Charles took the town of Montereau, where John the Fearless had died, and made the Bastard Jean its captain. Then the one city that made it appear as if all France had been won back was finally seized and entered by the king in person. King Charles finally invested Paris, a capital so impoverished by war and sieges, so long occupied by Burgundians and by the English, so ravaged by famine and so extenuated that wolves ran in packs through its dark streets at night. Sixty to eighty citizens of Paris were killed and eaten by wolves before enough order was restored so that a bounty could be declared on these animals and they could be systematically driven out of the city.

King Charles reentered Paris, whose streets he had not seen since the night Tanneguy du Chastel saved his life by wrapping him in a blanket and rowing him across the Seine River. The dauphin accompanied his father. They were attended by Charles of Anjou, the two sons of Bernard VII of Armagnac, the Bastard Jean of Orléans, and La Hire. The latter had only recently been captured while playing tennis in the middle of a town he thought he held, and was released just in time for this great occasion.

The Provost Marshal of Paris welcomed the king. It is significant to note that the Parisian sergeants wore green and scarlet uniforms on that happy day—the colors of Duke Charles of Orléans. The king's men, wearing blue and crimson, carried a blue canopy richly embroidered with golden fleurs-de-lis over the king's head. To the strains of *Gloria in excelsis Deo* the king's party rode solemnly through the streets of Paris from Saint-Denis to Notre-Dame Cathedral, past pageants representing the dearest saints of France— Saint Michael, Saint Denis, Saint Louis, Saint Catherine, and Saint Geneviève, who had saved Paris from Attila the Hun.

Both the king and the dauphin were in complete armor except for their helms, which were borne behind them. The king's horse was covered with a canopy of blue velvet that fell to the ground. The soldiers and archers who escorted this magnificent parade of princes were led by the Bastard Jean representing the House of Orléans. He was also in full armor, golden with inlay work, and his horse was veiled in a gold-embroidered velvet caparison. A long gold scarf floated behind him. The streets were thronged with weeping people who cried, "Noël! Noël!" as they saw their "king and natural-born lord" returning in triumph to rule them.

After the ceremonial Mass in Notre-Dame, the sons of Count Bernard VII of Armagnac were allowed to disinter their father's body so that it could be borne home in dignity. The chroniclers do not mention the fact that with King Charles came his retinue of lawyers and administrators, headed by Duke Charles of Orléans's trusted magistrate, William Cousinot.

Duke Humphrey of Gloucester, wrong so often, despised so often for having cried "Wolf," would not now be heeded when he demanded angrily: "What if this Duke Charles teaches the King of France how to rule the kingdom? What will happen to us then?"

In England, Duke Charles worked night and day with his secretaries. There was no negotiation that did not bear the stamp of his hand, no ceremony that he had not planned and studied carefully before it transpired. He had received ambassadors from Armagnac just prior to the investing of Paris. His was the brain that had thought carefully to tie up the threads, to see that his father-in-law Count Bernard was properly inhumed. The Armagnac delegation had been honorably received in England and carefully checkmated by Duke Charles.

Their real intention was to contract a marriage between the Princess Marie of Armagnac and King Henry VI of England. How Duke Charles managed to head them off without hurting their feelings is a wonder. He had other plans for King Henry. Therefore he negotiated another wedding, marrying Marie of Armagnac to his own son-in-law, Duke John of Alençon.

During the four-year period from 1436 to 1440, the English saw the prisoner they had so carefully guarded for over twenty years become his real masterful self. Duke Charles was about to outlive them all. He had survived Henry V, Thomas of Clarence, John of Bedford, Richard of Warwick, Bernard of Armagnac, John of Burgundy, Charles VI, and Joan of Arc. He had passed from the twenties into the thirties, and from the thirties into the forties. The critical years from 1436 to 1440 found him at the very peak of his physical and intellectual powers. No person was so aware of this as Duke Charles himself. His life had begun again at the age of forty. He had earned "golden opinions from all manners of men," and he alone was guiltless of the death of Joan of Arc.

On every side of him those people who had played such important roles in the century continued to die while Duke Charles grew more powerful. In 1437 the Queen Mother of England, Joanna, died without ever seeing her beloved Arthur of Richmond again. On January 3rd Queen Catherine of England, aged thirty-six, died in Bermondsey Abbey outside London.

Since her secret marriage with the unbonneted Owen Tudor some years before, this poor princess in disgrace had been sorely persecuted by Humphrey of Gloucester. He had snatched away her two older sons, Edmund and Jasper. Her third son was to take holy orders. Her daughter died a few days after birth. No sooner was she dead than her handsome husband was clapped into Newgate Prison, a common jail, from which fortunately he promptly escaped to begin the second half of his life, a series of astonishing adventures.

The two older sons were committed to the care of a lady abbess, a relative of William de la Pole. Duke Charles must have been grateful to the protection thus given them by his friend of Suffolk. He must have had an eye on these distant relatives of his. The older boy would be the father of Henry VII, England's first Tudor king, and therefore a great-grandfather of the superb and magnificently literary Queen Elizabeth I. The second son, Jasper, would live to be created Duke of Bedford by his half-brother, Henry VI.

Queen Catherine's first son by Henry V—the unfortunate Henry VI, who was born at Windsor instead of at Monmouth—had not forgotten his young mother. On a New Year's Day he sent her a little locket of gold weighing thirteen ounces, with a crucifix set with pearls and the sapphires of Orléans. On her original tomb, for this unfortunate French princess was to be punished by lying unburied in Westminister Abbey for "over 250 years," Henry VI had carved in Latin that she had been "a maid and a widow, a perfect flower of modesty, a joy of this land, a brightness," and "the glory of mothers." Contrary to Gloucester's instructions, King Henry VI granted Owen Tudor an annuity from his own private purse.

Duke Charles, even granted that he did not yet hate Gloucester, must have watched that lord's treatment of his cousin Catherine with anger. Since the Duke of Orléans was in the London area, it is probable that he attended her funeral either at Saint Paul's or her first temporary interment at Westminster Abbey. It is certain that the whole story of her secret marriage, her subsequent persecution, and the rearing of her children under the wings of the Suffolk family drew Duke Charles closer to William de la Pole and set him more squarely against Gloucester.

Of all the documents extant from the fifteenth century, the last will and testament of the French Queen Catherine is one of the most pitiful. This poor mother, deprived of all her children one after the other, asks her son, the King of England, to be her executor:

"Right high and mighty prince and my full doubted lord, and entirely beloved son, in due humble wise, and with full hearty natural blessing, I commend me to your highness. To the which please to be certified that before the silent and fearful conclusion of this long grievous malady in the which I have been long and yet am troubled and vexed by the visitation of God (to whom be thanking and laud in all his gifts), I purpose by the grace of God and under your succour, protection and comfort (in whom only, among all other earthly, stands all my trust), to ordain and dispose of my testament both for my soul and my body.

"And I trust fully and am right sure that among all creatures earthly ye may best and will best tender and favour my will in ordaining for my soul and body, in seeing that my debts be paid and my several servants guerdoned, and in tender and favourable fulfilling of mine intent. Wherefore tenderly I beseech you by the reverence of God and upon my full hearty blessing that to my perpetual comfort and health of soul and body, of your abundant and special grace (in full remedy of all means that in any wise may *annéantise* or deface the effect of my last purpose and intent) grant, at my humble prayer and request, to be my executor; and to depute and assign such persons to be under you of your servants, or of mine, or of both, as it shall be like you to choose them, which I remit fully to your disposition and election.

"Beseeching you also at the reverence of our Lord God and the full and entire blessing of me your mother that, this done, ye tenderly and benignly grant my supplication and request contained particularly in the articles ensuing. And if tender audience and favorable assent shall be given by so benign and merciful a lord and son to such a mother being in so piteous point of so grievous a malady, I remit to your full, high, wise, and noble discretion and to the conscience of every creature that knoweth the laws of God and of nature that if the mother should have more favor than a stranger, I remit to the same; . . . my *soul shall pass as naked, as desolate,* and as willing to be scourged as the poorest soul God ever formed. . . ."

In life Catherine de Valois had been a beautiful woman—open-faced, with small features, high rounded forehead, blue eyes, and no eyebrows or eyelashes. In her portrait she holds her head on the side as if overburdened with the heavy wreathed turban she wears instead of a crown. She appears to have been a small woman with a full bosom.

The last person to kiss her on the lips was Samuel Pepys, who says in his Dairy that he saw her withered corpse in Westminster Abbey, disclosed naked from the waist upward. Immediately after her death, however, and as long as they lived, her second husband and his sons were to unite with their Catherine's first child, the King Henry who never forgave Humphrey of Gloucester for his cruel treatment of this queen during his minority.

In the April following Queen Catherine's death, Parliament was bestowing an unparalled confidence in her cousin, the French duke. He was suddenly allowed to leave England, to travel to the Continent to treat matters of peace to which he was so ardently devoted. He was empowered to take with him as many people as he liked and as much money—his own, of course. In May he was granted a safe-conduct for any and all ambassadors to come to him in England over a two-month period from May 10, 1437. In the same year Pope Eugene IV appointed Duke Charles conjointly with the Duke of Brittany as "impartial mediators" of peace.

. Meanwhile, the duke redoubled his efforts to be free, urging his brother Jean to help him in every way possible. His sense of immediacy comes through one of his letters written in 1437:

"As for our near departure into France a high finance is required, we hereby order to sell, mortgage, parcel our lands, baronies, cities, castles, forts, or otherwise deal for the goodness of peace, for the resource of a Christian people and to eschew the effusion of human blood, and also for the deliverance and return to freedom of our own person.

"All these things are preferred by us to all other goods, lands, and temporal kingdoms, *nor is there at all in this entire world a greater blessing than peace and liberty.*

"To obtain these two blessings we personally desire to spare no others. We hereby make known that we, desiring above all else the accomplishment and the perpetration of the above, in all honor and reverence to our lord, the king of France, for the good and reestablishment of the public welfare, considering the fruits and great goodnesses that peace can restore to all our people, and also to find a way in which we ourselves may be delivered from the captivity where we are, having taken counsel with due deliberation, now conclude and so ordain by these present letters as follows:

"Anything and all things belonging to us shall be sold and for-feited completely and forevermore to one or to several persons: our lands, our castles, our cities, our fortresses, our other revenues, our incomes—wherever they may be located . . . (we make exception only for our city and county and castle of Blois). . . . up to the sum of 42,000 écus in gold.

"We place our entire confidence in Jean, the Bastard of Orléans, who is Count of Vertus and Grand Chamberlain of France."

Jean of Orléans met his brother in France briefly in 1439. The two had not seen each other since before Agincourt Field, twenty-three years earlier, when Jean was only a child. Yet their love for each other and their mutual confidence had only grown. Each in his own way had served France long and fruitfully. The king and Jean were equally eager for Duke Charles's "deliverance." Besides the financial aspect of the ransoming, the two brothers also had to discuss the conditions to which England would be likely to consent before releasing their prisoner. Duke Charles probably had it well understood with his brother, and therefore with his king, that there was a wide gap between what he as negotiator of the peace would say and swear to fulfill, and what he would actually do and fulfill when the time came.

It was at Calais on July 21, 1439, that Duke Charles made the present to his brother that gave him the title by which he is generally known through the century: Count Dunois. In letters drawn up by himself and witnessed by five members of his council, Duke Charles says: "Because we desire the well-being, honor, and ad-vancement of our brother, because of the good love and brotherly affection we have for him, and because of the good and agreeable services he has rendered us in every way, services done day after day—and also because we wish our brother to be and to remain attached to us—we give him and his heirs the County and Vis-county of Châteaudun and Dunois."

Concurrent with this meeting between Duke Charles and his younger brother was the conference held outside Calais, which also treated the questions of ransom and the liberation of Duke Charles. This second meeting was held between the Cardinal of England and his suite on the one hand, and his niece, the Duchess of Bur-gundy, and her suite on the other hand. It is indeed a curious coin-cidence that two ladies named Isabelle should have played such an important role in the life of Duke Charles. The Duchess Isabella was still determined to complete the last prophecy of the Maid of Orléans.

Once back in England, Duke Charles drafted memo after memo, reasserting the terms of peace he would guarantee to procure for England. What he said was very similar to his previous proposals and equally misleading. He claimed that he would do homage to King Henry of England. Moreover, he asserted that various of his friends in France would so swear—the Counts of Armagnac, Foix, and Pardiac, the Duke of Alençon, the Archbishop of Rheims, and many more impressive personages as unlikely as himself to perform such an act of treachery. He even proposed to obtain the fealty of Italian noblemen if Henry VI was interested in their homage. He offered Orléans, Blois, Melun, and several duchies—most of which he did not own—to the English. He declared that he would be happy to exchange these estates in France for similar estates in England—implying that he expected to change nationalities. In one breath he assured England that he would try to get all of France for Henry VI. In the next he said that he would accept to return to France "free and without ransom."

It is not at all surprising that in June of 1440 Duke Humphrey of Gloucester denounced the Duke of Orléans as a traitor in a letter to Parliament. For once in his life Duke Humphrey showed an insight and a political acumen that made him a true brother of Henry V and Duke John of Bedford.

"Given the lack of wisdom and discretion and natural reason," wrote Duke Humphrey, "of my Lord's adversary (King Charles VII) as well as that of his oldest son, considering the subtlety and crafty disposition of the said Duke of Orléans, which is so well known to my said Lord's Council, they should never consent, counsel nor advise the deliverance of this Duke of Orléans.

"Not only this," continued Duke Humphrey. "It is also to be presumed that this Duke of Orléans, being so near to the throne of France, being of such great discretion as he is named to have, will by the advice of the great French lords and by the assent of the Three Estates there, be given the real governance of France and will become the Regent of that kingdom. . . . That he, knowing as well as he does, the disposition and state and condition of England at the present time, should labor to anything that would be worshipful and profitable to our King Henry VI,—that I cannot think!

"Suppose that this Duke of Orléans *were* to swear an oath of allegiance to King Henry VI. What would such an oath be worth? We know perfectly well that an oath taken while he was a prisoner would be of no value whatsoever!"

Duke Humphrey went on to say that such an oath would not be binding in any court of law. What is the matter with the council in England? Are they insane? Do they not know that Duke Charles has been secretly negotiating to suborn Englishmen right in England? Have they not heard that he has promised "my cousin of Huntington" the government of the Duchy of Guyenne, if my cousin will give him his vote? Can you consider this a moment? Are not the Counts of Armagnac, Foix, and Pardiac the old and proved allies of this Duke Charles? Does anyone in England seriously think that he would turn about and give *him* the governorship of Armagnac, Foix, and Pardiac?

This Duke of Orléans is no friend! On the contrary. He is one of my Lord's "most capital enemies." Just think of the trick he played on us at Calais with the Duke of Burgundy! Surely you are not considering letting this duke go free to join now with Philip of Burgundy! Do you not see what will happen? The two of them will join to drive the English from the Continent.

Duke Humphrey had still not finished. Reflect also how this duke has the love and the alliance of Rome! Who do you think would dare to be our ally against this duke, which amounts to saying, against His Holiness? "I doubt not but the most part of all Christendom," wrote Duke Humphrey scathingly.

Have you any idea of how beloved this Duke Charles is in France? *"His kin and his relations on the other side of the sea would give their very lives to save this Duke of Orléans,—and he them!* Since War is but Adventure, I cannot conceive of what adventure would befall us if ever we were to let him go. . . . All I can foresee is total Perdition!"

Duke Humphrey said he would also like to review the question of the ransom. Will this duke levy it from our lands of Normandy? There is not a lord in France who will not contribute money so that this duke can return. I ask you to think about the lives we lost in winning Normandy. I ask you to think about Henry V and the Duke of Clarence, my brothers, who gave their lives for these lands! If we release this "mischievous" duke, these lands will be "mischievously lost"! "I never in all my life had such cause to bewail!

"I protest, for my Excuse and Discharge, that I never was, am, nor never shall be Consenting, nor Agreeing to his Deliverance or Enlargement. I also ask to have this letter protesting such put in the records so that it can be read after I am dead and gone. . . .

June 2, 1440."

The treaty for the ransom and release of Duke Charles of Orléans, who had been a prisoner in England for nearly twenty-five years, was drafted in London, dated July 13, 1440, and ratified by the English Council, the French King Charles VII, the Dauphin Louis, the Duke of Burgundy, and many French noblemen. It was signed six times by Charles in the Latin form of his name:

Karolus Dux Aurelianensis

As stipulated by this "Convention of Westminster," Duke Charles was not required to swear fealty to King Henry VI of England, nor to recognize him as the King of France—"nor anything like it," says Rymer. Duke Charles refers in his part of the articles to Henry VI only as "the King of England." Furthermore, he did not cede any land in France to England, nor did he swear to cede any land. He did not pledge any hostages during the time he amassed his ransom payment—which was strictly in variance with the current policy of both nations. Nor did he even promise never to bear arms against England in the future.

All he swore to do was to pay 80,000 crowns to England before he left the country, and 120,000 crowns subsequently. It is a moot question whether he paid anything at all! The Cardinals of England and York had been wrapped about his little finger. Both had acted with zeal upon the occasion. The Privy Council, dazzled by the personality of this great nobleman, attentive to the fact that he had cited the Pope as guarantee of his word and his bond, bent over backward to make restitution for his long years of imprisonment and were flattered to be asked to believe in his honorable intentions.

The English were impressed by the alacrity and the amount of response Duke Charles had solicited from home. They were also impressed by the quality of the persons who went bond for this duke:

1) The Dauphin Louis of France: "Our very dear and very *famous* Uncle will pay within six months. We pledge to fulfill his debt ourselves and our heirs to the Crown of France 60,000 nobles
2) The Duke of Brittany
   Count Arthur of Richmond
   Count of Montfort   10,000   "

3) The Archbishop of Narbonne .... 3,000 "
4) The Lord de Mailles .... 2,000 "
5) The Duke of Alençon .... 10,000 "
6) Count Andreas de Laval .... 2,000 "
7) The Count of March
   The Count of Pardiac .... 5,000 "
8) The Archbishop of Rheims .... 5,000 "
9) Louis de Bourbon, Count of Vendôme .. 60,000 "
10) King Charles VII of France pledges his word and bond in guarantee of the *total sum* of this ransom.

By the first day of November, 1440, twenty-five years almost to a day since the terrible disaster at Agincourt, the final arrangements for the release of Duke Charles of Orléans had been accomplished. After the pages and pages of ratifying signatures came more pages of gorgeous, rolling Latin sentences from Duke Charles with his usual redundant "We have sworn and we do swear . . . We have promised and we do promise . . ." followed by his signatures carefully made in his firm, round handwriting.

Count Dunois had been granted a safe passage through English territories in France for himself and eighty knights-at-arms. Counselors, secretaries, and special servants from Blois were granted passports to travel into England. Three members of the Le Fuzelier family were among them. An escort of one hundred attendant knights was collected in England and another in France.

During his last days in England Duke Charles had his own private thoughts to settle, as well as matters of state. For twenty-five years he had been keeping a kind of diary of his private thoughts. More aware than anyone else that a long chapter of his life was drawing to a close, he finished the poem cycle he had begun years before.

In the fanciful, transforming but not less true allegory of the poet lies the key to the inner man. There could be no more transparent handwriting in the world than that of this prince. What he wrote is still perfectly clear to read—and perfectly unclear.

Let the reader judge for himself. The following are prose translations of what was originally French poetry and have for the sake of convenience been labeled ALLEGORY I and ALLEGORY II. Keep in mind that between them came a whole cycle of love poems dedicated to a lady, or to various ladies. It can only be imagined whether the duke is referring to the Princess Isabelle, to Bonnie of Armagnac, to the Countess of Arundel, to them all, or to English ladies with whom he appears to have carried on burning love affairs.

In 1440 Duke Charles had terminated a chapter in his literary production that corresponded to a chapter in his life. This is how he saw his own life up to 1440:

ALLEGORY I

In bygone days after Nature first brought me into this world, she put me in the governance of a Lady named Childhood, instructing this Lady not to let me suffer either Care or Melancholy, but to feed me and rear me tenderly. Childhood did her duty in all loyalty for which I owe her thanks. After this period Lady Nature sent me away in the care of Youth, into her house.

One morning of Saint Valentine's Day Youth awoke me early saying: "You have slumbered too long. Awake and dress yourself. I must take you to be presented at the court of a certain lord."

I answered, "Gracious Mistress, I obey you gladly, but I would like you to name the lord by name."

She said: "My child, since you so desire to know his name, I will tell you. He is the God of Love whom I have served and always shall, for I am one of his retinue. You will find in his company such pleasant people and such goods in abundance as you could not imagine."

"O Mistress," I said, "I beg you that I not see him for the present; for I have heard so many tell what sorrows Love has made them suffer. I know I could not endure such torments. I am too young for such great burdens. Let me rather remain in peace."

"No one will constrain you to love unless your heart wishes."

"Mistress, if you promise me that neither I nor my heart will be so obliged against our will, then I shall obey you, and pray God to convey me along the path of honor."

Later that day we walked a good distance together until we came to a manor house that was beautifully situated and pleasant to behold. There Youth told me: "This is the place where Love holds his court. How does it seem to you? Is it not lovely?"

"More than I ever saw."

Then Youth called to the porter at the lodge. "I have a stranger here with me. Let us enter. His name is Charles Duke of Orléans."

The porter opened wide the gate. "You are both welcome," he

told us. "Excuse me while I tell Venus and Cupid that you have come."

Very shortly the porter, whose name was Company, came back to us bringing with him Greetings and Pleasure who were in charge of the manor. When I saw them approaching us, I blushed and my heart skipped. Young people are always embarrassed in strange places.

Youth told me: "Do not be so shy. Be courteous both in deed and word."

"I greet you kindly," said my mistress, "and beg to present this child to you so that he may see the royal state and joyous cheer of the God of Love."

Greetings and Pleasure took me by the hand. "Our sovereign lord," said they, "begs you to draw near."

"I thank you for your welcome," I replied humbly, "and I shall go to meet him; for Youth has told me of his state and of his gracious presence."

Thus together we went to a garden where Love was singing and dancing with his courtiers. We fell to our knees and Youth addressed him: "High and most powerful Prince to whom each one is subject, I present to you this young son who is issued from the House of France, who bears upon his coat-of-arms the golden fleurs-de-lis.

Love answered: "He is welcome. Long days ago I knew his father and many others of his lineage who assumed my service—because of whose virtue I am happy to receive him. Come here, my son. What do you think? Did you ever feel the sting of my arrows? I think not, by your appearance. Come closer so that we may speak together."

With trembling heart I approached him. "Sire," I said, "I am a stranger in your court. Shame would fall upon your nobility were you to treat me cruelly."

"You shall never be constrained by me," said Love, "nor shall you ever go forth either until you are truly in love. . . . Beauty, come and assail him! . . . Let him neither sleep nor eat, neither night nor day . . . until he does me service and homage. Tame this wild bird as in past days you conquered Solomon the Wise and Samson the Strong. If you cannot overpower a child, then, Beauty, you will lose your fame."

Beauty came to me and sat down close beside me. "You cannot choose, Lover," she said softly. "You must yield to Love."

My eyes gazed upon Beauty! My eyes met hers and clung. When Beauty saw that I was looking straight into her eyes, she shot her arrow through my eyes and into my heart!

As soon as I knew what had happened, I cried aloud: "I hate my life and wish for death! I hate my eyes, for they have betrayed me! I hate my heart which is so foolishly lost! I hate this arrow which wounds my heart! I know it all now! Alas! My heart has been caught for the God of Love . . . by you, Beauty! Alas!"

Then I fell at the God's feet as pale as death, and as still as death. When he saw how white I was, he began to laugh.

"You need a Doctor, child," he cried. "I thought you were so strong that nothing could touch you, and look! You have already been wounded—and only by Beauty! Where is your spirit? You should be ashamed to have been overcome so easily by the very sight of Beauty that you fall fainting at my feet! If you cannot defend yourself better than that, you should surrender your whole life to Beauty. By choosing this lesser evil, you will be taking the better."

I was so racked with pain that I took no heed of his mocking words. When Youth saw that I had lost my senses to such an extent that I could not even speak, she interceded for me. "Sire, kindly grant him some respite."

Love answered, "Never! He shall have no respite until he has surrendered."

Then Beauty lifted my head and placed it on her lap. "With these hands I arrest you," she said. "Surrender to me, and you will be wise. Then you will do homage to Love."

"My Lady Beauty, I do so wish. I submit to you and to your will. My aching heart is wounded unto death, I feel. Have pity on my sadness—young, gentle, highborn Princess-beyond-compare!"

Then Beauty herself begged pardon for me. She promised Love that I would swear oaths of fidelity so that I could be admitted once for all to his good graces.

"First he will swear to serve you loyally," Beauty promised the God of Love. "He will love only one person truly and will never desire either to be cured of his love or to exchange it for another. He will keep Love's counsels in *absolute secrecy*. If he is granted any favors in love, he will never boast of them. From this day forward, he will attend to his person with care so as not to offend love. He will bear himself courteously and graciously. He swears henceforth to pursue honor and valiance to the best of his ability.

He will also show his generosity, for that is his first duty as a noble
lover. He will seek fellowship among people of honor who shun
villainy. Last of all, he promises to be a diligent scholar in Love's
school. He will learn the *arts of love* and all the gracious mannerisms
that keep it fresh and new; that is to say, he will learn music and
dancing, how to sing, how to write songs, and how to rhyme ballads
of love. He will also study all the other joyous pranks and past-
times so that he may fulfill the above-named Ten Commandments
of Love.

"True God of Love, I would have this boy swear now, if you
are pleased to summon him," concluded Beauty.

Then I was called. They had me place my hands upon a book
and swear that I would do my duty and to the best of my powers
adhere to the laws of love. Love next ordered Good Faith, his chief
secretary, to draw up my letter of retainer. This was done. Loyalty
sealed it with Love's signet and delivered it to me.

Thus Love put me in his bondage. For more surety, he kept my
heart as collateral. When I saw this, I protested that I surely could
not live in such a state, without my heart.

"My doctor, whose name is Hope, will keep you from death night
and day," Love answered, "until you shall have won the heart of a
lady who will gladly give hers for yours. Keep my commandments,
and I shall see that you are widely recommended as being worthy
of a lady's love.

Copy of the Letter of Retainer

The God Cupid and the Goddess Venus here salute you all and
make it known to you one and all that the Duke of Orléans, named
Charles, still very young at this time, is hereby retained in our
service.

And we here and now assign certain incomes to him, the fruits
of which he may enjoy as announced in these open letters, in the
hope that he will be loyal toward ourselves. We hereby also command the officers of our parliament to serve and abet him and
not to act contrary to his interests under pain of our sovereign displeasure and the forfeiture of their goods and their lives.

His oaths to serve us have been duly given and received in earnest
of which he has left his heart as security. In order that all fine
youths may see this example, we wish this duke to be richly rewarded and bountifully endowed with love.

Witness our seal here affixed in the presence of our vassals, counselors, and loyal servitors assembled at our express commands to do us service.

Given on this Day of Saint Valentine the Martyr, in the city of Gracious Desire, where we held our assembly.

By Cupid and Venus, Sovereigns.
Witnesses: Several Worldly Pleasures.

Allegory II

After the day which is made for labor follows the night ordained for repose. It chanced that one evening as I was heavy with sleep because of the torments I had borne all that day, I made myself ready for bed as soon as the sun had set enough to bring on twilight. No sooner had I lain myself down on my bed than I fell into a light sleep. And thus I dreamed: I seemed to see there in my chamber before me an old, old man whom I did not recognize although I felt queerly enough that somewhere I had seen him once before. I could not remember when nor where. I was annoyed not to be able to recall his name. Because I could not remember it, I could not address him.

For some time he gazed at me in silence before beginning to reason thus: "My friend, have you no recollection of me? I am Years, the messenger who once carried letters concerning you from Nature to Childhood. Thence you were remanded to Youth who governed you so long, so immoderately, and so unreasonably too. . . . I have come to warn you that Old Age, that relentless mother of grudges, is about to strike your person.

"Come what may," he said, "you cannot flee before her. A man cannot serve two masters, especially these two—Age and Love. Since Death has taken your lady, you should ask to be absolved from your vows to Love. As much as it befits young men to dally along a lover's lane, so much is it folly for the old to travel that road. Everyone then laughs! 'How amusing! This foolish old man wants to return to his childhood!' Only mockery is his lot.

"You may still leave Love's court," he said. "Say you do so from nonchalance. Then no man can afterward tell with a leer that you did it from impotence. They will only say you acted from displeasure alone—that you care not to love another since your peerless lady whose memory you wish ever to cherish is dead. . . . Petition Love to release you from your vows and to return your heart you left as guarantee. . . . Thus, if so released, you can still keep your honor and your reputation. . . .

"Whatever you decide in this matter, do not—under any consideration—put your trust in Fortune whose tactics are to flatter us all and to say that Everyman can safely hope to have better than he has. I know of no jade under the moon falser than she!

"I anticipate all too well what Fortune's objections will be. She will argue that once your heart is forever freed from Love's bondage, you will languish in a boredom worse than Love's martyrdom. . . . Then she will swear to make restitution for all the pain Love has falsely caused you to undergo. . . . Do not believe her! No man who puts his trust in Fortune but is sooner or later deceived by her."

I awoke with a start, trembling like a leaf on a tree. Alas! I thought, I never before had such a painful realization. It is true, that if Nature wishes to abandon me, I shall not know what to do. I shall not be able to keep my footing against Old Age. . . . Even had Years not come to remind me, I should have seen anyway that Old Age was intending to quarrel. . . . The news is bitter, even so. . . . It would be better, while awaiting the onset, to prepare myself by renouncing voluntarily all conquests. . . . It is time for my sore heart to rest. . . . I must keep my eyes closed and my ears deaf to Love's appeals. . . .

He who wishes to save himself from Love's surprise attacks must keep his eyes prisoners. If they escape, they will scream in the ears of his heart while it sleeps—so loudly that they will awaken it—shouting that they have just seen some peerless pleasure. . . .

I know all that calling by heart so well that for long years it has seemed to me that out of love there was no happiness at all, nor anything so worthy—as all the romances tell. But in those days what I did not know was love's grief. Now I see where I am. I have great cause never to forget it; I am out of Love's toils. My heart is still weary from its struggle. It will never again want to cross Love's threshold for better or for worse, whatever may befall.

Therefore, right away, before I even rest, I shall draft my petition so that it can be read at the forthcoming session of Love's court. I shall state my grievances and point out the little profit I have ever received from my amorous conquest. Thus, in the presence of all true lovers, shall I bid adieu to Love, and at the same time stop evil tongues as to my reasons. I shall take back my heart with my own hands. Then I shall leave to the young who are in the flower of their lives all prowess in Love and—my best wishes to them.

Petition to Cupid and to Venus

Charles, the Duke of Orléans, who was long one of your faithful vassals, begs you most humbly to deign peruse this present petition without refusing, but thinking that he has been constrained by doleful fortune to so write. Since Death has taken his Lady in the very first flower of her age, he will never take another princess, nor mistress; his heart agrees that this shall be so. And since when swearing fealty he left his heart as security, he now sues for its return, asking you to excuse him from ever being in love again.

And be so kind as to release him from his oath and also allow him to depart, and also return his heart. Furthermore, please instruct your chief notary under pain of your displeasure to draft letters of dismissal in such a way that none can censure him for his withdrawal from your service. And, if it please you, permit the above-named plaintiff to be lightened from care so that all his days he may be grateful to you, honor your name, and thank God for the grace he has been accorded.

At the next session of Love's parliament I presented my petition to Love, who replied: "I am grieved at the misfortunes which have befallen you; but from Love's dart there is, as you know, no recourse. Drive all melancholy thoughts from your head. Live henceforth like a man; let your conduct be guided by reason. Undertake a new conquest. I will second your desires so ardently that you will find a new lady ready to love you in all loyalty. I actually see no restitution other than this that can be done you."

"Alas! Sire, pardon me, if I tell you that through all my life I shall never take another lady for my love. Pleasure and gaiety have served foreclosure writs. Do not speak to me even of such an eventuality, I pray you. You are only testing my new resolution. What you propose stems from pure mockery; for why, indeed, should I invite more trouble at this point in my life? As you see, I am far from any such disposition. . . . I have acquitted myself honorably, as I was bound by your lordship to do. In the future I shall keep to myself. Therefore I ask that you grant my request, which is, in few words, to be in love no more . . . no matter what."

When Love understood that my decision was unshakable, he

replied: "I should have preferred to retain you longer in my service, but I see that you are unwilling. Reluctant as I am, I shall nevertheless grant your suit. . . . I cannot banish you, for you have manfully fulfilled your obligation. I can release you, and I will. My parliament will draw up your severance papers so that no person can ever malign you or question the terms of your discharge."

Some time later when his parliament had assembled in full session, Love granted the release which I had requested. Then as I knelt before him, Love drew my heart from a casket. It was wrapped in black silk. He gave it to me. I put it back in my chest to do with as I liked.

QUITTANCE

To whom it may concern, be it known that Charles, the Duke of Orléans, who was over the space of several years our loyal liege, is now acquitted of all obligations, oaths, and pledges toward us. Let it be known also as here certified that he has resigned voluntarily from our service, that he was not expelled by us for any default, forfeit, or vice whatsoever. True it is that too cruel Death wrongfully took his lady, his love, his friend, his only joy. Therefore the above-named wishes to be as faithful as the turtledove which keeps to himself when he has lost his mate. We have accepted his resignation in witness of which we affix our seal.

All Saints' Day. 1437.

As soon as I had received my quittance and my heart, I took my leave of Love, my eyes so blurred with tears that I could hardly see.

"Friend," said Love to me, "if there is anything in my power that can assuage your grief, do not hesitate to ask it."

I was so broken with sorrow that I could not speak a word, nor even half a word. Comfort took me by the hand and led me back to that castle where I had lived in my childhood. The name of this castle was Nonchalance. Pastime welcomed me at the porter's lodge. There in the halls of Nonchalance I will live out my years until Old Age bolts me in her bailey.

This Chapter of my life is finished, and the last pages of *Ballads, Songs, and Complaints* written, copied in my book, and blotted dry.

In 1415, after the battle of Agincourt field, Duke Charles had participated in the victory celebration of King Henry V in Westminster Abbey, and it was there that he participated in his last celebration in England twenty-five years later. The first ceremony was a thanksgiving Mass in honor of Henry V. The second was a thanksgiving Mass in honor of Duke Charles of Orléans.

The fact that such a ceremony was planned and performed reflects the prestige of the duke and the honor in which he was held throughout England. What the English noblemen had not required their captive to put in writing among the articles of his release they asked him to put into words before the altar of Westminster Abbey—knowing his true character, not as enemies weigh the strength of their adversary, but as friends feel respect for the word of an honorable man. This public ceremony was England's way of atoning for his long captivity.

The thanksgiving Mass sung at the release of Duke Charles was a command performance. The English nobles attended perforce in their splendid robes to make public reparation. Many of the prelates present were acknowledging a piety and a literary ability in Latin religious poetry equal, and in most cases superior, to their own. The Duke of Suffolk and his wife, Alice Chaucer, were honoring a poet whose works they had seen composed in their own home, works that would place this duke—and had already placed him—as a literary heir of Geoffrey Chaucer. Those great nobles of England who did not know Duke Charles well were ready to believe that, if he would not keep an oath he was forced to make in writing, he would keep one made voluntarily before the altar of God.

Therefore, on or about November 1, 1440, Duke Charles swore in the unfinished abbey at Westminster that he would work for a just and lasting peace between England and France and that he personally would never bear arms against England again. His friends the Cardinals of England and York were present. In the middle of this solemn ceremony there was a stir among the worshipers.

One English nobleman disrupted the Solemn Mass by leaving the church while the service was still in progress. In so doing, he not only offended the Duke of Orléans; he also insulted the King of England, the other peers of the realm, and the prelates.

An idea of how vital this ceremony was, what a store ordinary people in England set by it, how desperately England needed peace and longed for it, and how eager they were to believe in the French Duke can be seen from *The Paston Letters*.

Robert Repp writes to John Paston on November 1, 1440: "Duke of Orléans hath made his oath upon the sacrament, and urged it, never for to bear arms against England, in the presence of the King and all the Lords, *except my Lord of Gloucester*. And proving my said Lord of Gloucester never agreed to his deliverance, when the Mass began he took his leave. . . .

"God give grace that the said Lord of Orléans be true, for the same week shall he towards France. . . ."

Part Three

FRANCE

XI [*1440–1444*] WITH THE WHITE CLIFFS
of Dover behind and the white
cliffs of the Continent seen as a gray blur above the darker gray
waves of the Channel, Duke Charles embarked for home. Added
to the excitement of release, of doors unlocked, of words that could
be freely spoken, of future plans for peace between the kingdoms,
was the excitement of the sea voyage. The hawsers were cast off.
The sails flapped and grew taut in the wind. The ship advanced
cautiously through the small craft in the roadstead to meet the
first short swells of the Channel. Whitecaps soon hissed along the
vessel's hull and rapidly vanished astern on either side of the clear
green wake. Overhead the white gulls dipped and screamed as
Duke Charles filled his lungs with bracing sea air and strained his
eyes toward the Continent. As the hours went by, the eastern coastline became clearer. The one hundred attendants from England,
who would deliver their prisoner safe and sound on Burgundian
soil and obtain a release from him to that effect, sat in groups on
the deck or lolled along the rails. The ship made for the port of
Gravelines where the welcoming party had for hours been counting
the minutes.

Count Dunois, who had twenty personal attendants, stamped
about anxiously on the wharf at Gravelines. With him were Duke
Philip and the Duchess Isabella of Burgundy, the Archbishops of
Rheims, Narbonne, and Tours, the Lord of Dampierre, and scores
of French notables and French attorneys. The highest nobleman in
France, and the nearest to the throne after the dauphin, deserved to
be royally met. By the time the English vessel had entered the
outer harbor, had slackened speed, and was preparing to launch
her boat, a huge crowd had gathered along the pier. Townspeople,
priests, farmers, clerks, fishermen by the hundreds thronged the
water's edge. The English vessel slowly drew near, sounding as she
came. The crowds were silent. The great lords stood at attention,

heavily wrapped in furs and velvet cloaks against the sharp November air. They watched the tall ship drop anchor forward. A few minutes later her dory was launched. Then it was manned by two sailors. They could see a third man climbing slowly down her ladder into the boat. Even from the pier, from the beach, the throngs could see his crimson and green cloak, his crimson hood with the long scalloped scarf that was draped across his throat and over his left shoulder, and that blew out in the wind behind him. It was Duke Charles. It was Joan of Arc's beloved Duke of Orléans.

Cheers rose promptly from hundreds of throats at once, with one accord: "Noël! Noël! Long live the Duke of Orléans! Noël!" Tears streamed down Count Dunois's face as he fell to his knees on the pier, waiting to kiss his liege lord and brother's jeweled gauntlet. Duke Charles clambered up to the jetty. Duke Philip of Burgundy hesitated a second and then clasped his "dear cousin" in his arms. Was this the famous, the almost fabled duke? Duke Philip had hesitated.

The man before him was not what he had pictured. In his mind's eye he had seen the dashing youngster who everyone said had fought in Burgundy and at Agincourt. Before him was a commanding presence—a stalwart man with calm, level eyes; an *old* man with black hair streaked with gray! What a presence he had! What charm! Duke Charles advanced to make obeisance before the archbishops. They hardly understood his words of greeting— nor he theirs. It was with halting phrases and a clipped accent that Duke Charles addressed them, turning to present his attendants to the French lords, then addressing the French lords in English by mistake. He did not speak French half so easily as the English lords like Suffolk, who had fought on the Continent for so many years. The English chronicler Holinshed notes that thus returned to France Duke Charles of Orléans "speaking much better English than French."

The cheering crowds pressed closer and stood on tiptoes to catch a glimpse of this honored duke whom Joan of Arc had so wanted to bring home from England. Amid their hurrahs the chief lords passed into the silken pavilions where the final formalities would be accomplished. The English attendants sat at tables that had been provided. While the French lawyers and clerks took their seats, the final parchment treaty was unfolded for their perusal. All was in order. The document concerned Duke Charles on the one hand and King Henry VI of England on the other. The duke released King

Henry from any subsequent claim and reiterated his gratitude and his intentions to pursue a peace. If he lied, he hoped to be cast to the Devil and to eternal damnation. As a sign of his faithful and honorable intentions, he would underwrite his name with his own hand and seal. All that remained was to bid farewell to the English lords who had escorted him across the Channel, to ask them to convey news of his safe arrival to friends in England, and to thank them with words and gifts.

Duke Charles was weary. It was a strain to hear French. Unless he listened carefully, the words seemed an English that he did not grasp. After even those first conversations, his lips were stiff. He longed fleetingly for the peace and quiet of Pontefract, where year in and year out he had lived with his thoughts. He must not think of England. That man was dead. The new Duke Charles had just been born—he who would resume the role as chief prince of Europe's richest kingdom. All through the first evening in France, Duke Charles sat long hours with his brother Count Dunois. A decision of great moment, one that might affect the future of France, must be carefully discussed and then made irrevocably.

Clèves, is it? Clèves? Duke Charles raised his eyebrows and stared at the ceiling of the chamber where he, Dunois, and the advisors from Blois conversed late into the night. That was what the Duchess of Burgundy asked? And what about His Holiness in Rome? He not only approved. He so suggested.

When the counselors from Blois opened their books and started to read the results of their research, one raised finger from the Duke of Orléans was enough to silence them. The House of Clèves, mused Duke Charles. It is descended from one of the Nine Great Heroes of the world as they are represented on the Heroes Tapestries of my uncle of Berry. The three medieval heroes are Charlemagne, King Arthur, and the Crusading Godefroy de Bouillon. It is from this last hero that descends the House of Clèves.

Centuries ago, recalled Duke Charles for the counselors who struggled to follow his heavily accented French, there stood on the rocky banks of a northern river the heavy black castle of Schwanenburg. Its beetling ramparts and huge keep overlooked the green fields and barred access to the lower reaches of the great river. The lord of this castle was dead. Its mistress was his widow. She was young, lovely, gracious, and gentle born. Her hair fell in two long golden plaits from her small head to the tips of her tiny feet. As she walked along the dizzy walls of her black tower one day, she saw a strange sight in the river far below her.

Borne along by its current, proudly breasting its green waters, glided a magnificent and lordly white swan. In the sparkling sunlight over the sparkling waters she could see that around the swan's neck was a shining golden collar. Attached to the collar was a long golden chain of heavy links. Knotted to the chain's end was the curved beak of a ghostly ship.

The lady of the castle caught her breath. From the depths of the river she could hear the clear voices of the Rhinemaidens. Before her wondering eyes the swan pulled the silent ship close under her walls. Standing tall and motionless in the high prow of the dark vessel was a White Knight, all in white armor, white coat-of-arms, white winged helmet, jeweled sword, and long golden hair blowing in the light breeze of summer. When the swan had towed the ship up to her castle, the handsome knight came to life. Because he was noble and heroic, he married the lady of the Rhineland Tower. From such lofty lineage came Godefroy the Crusader and his descendants of Clèves. This was the noblest House of the Germanies.

Count Dunois listened silently to the story, his rough soldier's hands folded across his body, his bright eyes fixed upon his brother's calm, strong face. The counselors from Blois were charmed. Their days of research had been in vain. The master was home in his own country. The duke had only delved into his memory in order to recite the medieval romance for them. They would know better in the future. There would be no need for such statistics.

Wrapped in his story, Duke Charles had not even asked: How old is she? Is she beautiful? Is she cultured? Does she resemble the Duchess Isabelle? Is her skin fresh and rosy like that of the great English ladies? The duke was not even curious. He was not even very interested, except in his story. What was the child's name? Marguerite? Marie? No matter. It was of no earthly concern to His Highness of Orléans.

The important consideration was to satisfy Duke Philip of Burgundy. In the morning they would have one last look at the articles signed at Arras between King Charles VII and the Burgundian duke. The lord of Orléans would ratify them in the morning and so would his brother of Dunois. The prime consideration was to show Duke Philip every sign of friendship but still let him sense without having to be told that one's allegiance belonged first to the

King of France. It was also essential to present Duke Charles with a clear copy of the Ordinance of Orléans, which King Charles had passed the previous year. The idea sounded interesting. The king had created a standing army? That was a novelty, and one that boded no good for the English. He had also found a master artillery officer, a man named Jean Bureau? Very good. Then, blow the "proud" English first out of Normandy and next out of Guyenne!

Late into the night Duke Charles dictated to his secretaries details about England's internal politics, precious information about Gloucester's feud with the cardinal, suggestions for the choice of a French princess who would wed King Henry VI. Late in the night he dispatched messengers to Blois Castle. Let their anxiety at Blois be appeased. Let the bells toll from Saint-Cross Cathedral in Orléans. The duke had been released, had landed hale and hearty on home soil after an imprisonment of a quarter of a century. His hair was streaked with gray. He spoke much better English than French. But he had lived to come home. His every action had been predictable.

By daybreak the messengers were well on their way southward through Flanders. By that evening they had crossed the frontier of Burgundy and were spurring through the northernmost villages of France. Hardly a gaping farmer, hardly a portly burgher had ever seen Duke Charles of Orléans. All, however, had heard his name. Throughout France, as the news sped south toward Orléans and Touraine, tapers were reverently lighted in churches. France prayed tearfully. It was a memorable day. Happiest of all were the citizens of Orléans, who would now be able to show their lord how the English advanced here, up to the Tournelles. Then Joan said: "Save it for supper. I'll bring a God-damn along with me. . . ." and, "I came to save the poor people of Orléans."

Happiest of all were the people who gathered in buzzing knots around the protecting walls of Blois Castle. A great weight had just fallen from their shoulders. The good duke would care for them henceforth. Their worries were over.

What a life he had lived up to the age of forty-five! But he must know what they say: If a person's life is tragic during his early years, then he has already drained the cup of its sorrow. The second half of his life will be happy!

The Duchess Isabella, besides being an executive capable of administering territories the size of a kingdom, a diplomat astute enough to defeat Henry Beaufort of England at the conference table,

a very neglected wife and mother of a spoiled son, was also a senti-
mental woman. In her case the step from idea to execution was
easy. She had been touched by the life and death of Joan of Arc;
she therefore persuaded and negotiated until she had effected the
return of this poet-duke. The Duchess Isabella was at heart a match-
maker—and a clever one at that. Her personal reward was to select
from the maidens of her entourage one who fulfilled the qualifica-
tions of a duchess—one who was worthy of becoming even the
mother of a king.

Duke Charles of Orléans was invited to attend upon the Duchess
Isabella in her sumptuous apartments, in order to meet Marie, the
young daughter of the Duke of Clèves. The Burgundian princess
was introduced. Duke Charles saw a slender girl just entering adolescence. Marie of Clèves resembled her remote ancestor, the Swan
Knight from the Rhineland. She was of medium height, small-
boned, with delicate features, and had the bland and oval face of
a young Madonna whose innocent eyes have understood the an-
nunciation long before it has been made. This Princess of Clèves
wore her hair like a garment that falls loosely from a body. Her
hair was a pale golden veil that fell about her shoulders. Only a
thin circlet of gold kept it from her face. Her dress was that of a
grown woman, yet simple, with a silken inset across her flat chest.
She looked for all the world like a pretty blonde doll—expressionless
and fragile.

Whether or not Duke Charles really saw her as he made obeisance
before his future wife, he made no difficulties about accepting her
as his bride. If the German princess was the favorite of the Duchess
Isabella, if this marriage would please and honor Duke Philip of
Burgundy and Duke Adolf of Clèves, then there could be no objection on the part of the House of Orléans. King Charles VII acceded. There was no need to frighten the Burgundians by bringing
an English beauty to reign at Blois Castle. Incidental to this conclusion was the fact that Duke Philip had endowed his niece handsomely. He would not, however, expect any demonstration of affection from Duke Charles. No one expected him to love Marie
of Clèves. By the time she reached womanhood, her husband would
be in his fifties.

On the following day—there was no need for delays of any kind—
Duke Charles of Orléans wedded Marie of Clèves, niece of the Duke
of Burgundy, in a splendid ceremony at the church of Saint-Omer.
The little bride was as lovely as a white fairy in her diaphanous

wedding veil and mantle of golden hair. The French lords present were gratified, for their long-lost liege lord was a past master at the art of ceremony. Swathed in his scarlet robes he knelt, imposing and unflustered, by the side of the delicate blonde child. As the newlyweds returned down the aisle, the duke kept his dark eyes averted from his bride's face, but offered her the tips of his fingers with bent and deferential head so that all eyes were focused on the bride. She was a pretty creature who held her head up simply and who stole occasional looks at her bridegroom with candid eyes that were more knowing than he realized.

The Duchess Isabella had explained to Duke Charles that his bride knew how to read and how to write beautifully. She also told him that the Duchess Marie enjoyed poetry, that she longed to hear some of the poems from his private book, and that she had memorized the poems the duke had addressed the past few years to Duke Philip. The duchess herself was a patroness of literature. She had recently commissioned a book on protocol and court etiquette. She and the new Duchess of Orléans both solicited a poem from Duke Charles—a love poem, of course—addressed to the bride.

The wedding celebration lasted for ten days. They were happy ones for the guests, and days of reunion for Duke Charles. Most important to him, second in his heart after his brother, was the young knight whom the childless duke had always considered his son. John, Duke of Alençon, was to Duke Charles the only living memory of his daughter Joan, his dead daughter to whom he referred as "my only child." John of Alençon had distinguished himself during the long and seemingly hopeless years of the war. He had been preferred by Joan of Arc over all her attendants. He had been her "gentle John." It was with the deep tenderness of a father for a handsome and valorous son that Duke Charles greeted the Duke of Alençon, whose lands and castles were still held by the English. The Duke of Brittany, too, had journeyed up to the North for the wedding. In time Duke Charles would have to be told what had happened to their other companion-in-arms—the Lord Marshal Gilles de Rais.

As a climax to the celebration Duke Philip convened in extraordinary session the Knights of the Golden Fleece, his own private order of chivalry named in honor of Gideon's oracle. Duke Charles and the Dukes of Alençon and Brittany were inducted. Henceforth they would be sworn brothers to Philip of Burgundy. In return Duke Charles convened the Knights of the Golden Porcupine, into which he initiated Duke Philip. The Burgundian duke would henceforth wear Duke Charles's collar, and the Duke of Orléans and his friends would wear that of the pendant lamb.

During the secret sessions the foreign relations of France, Burgundy, and England, were discussed. Duke Charles, while he would never bear arms against the English, felt that they must be blasted from the Continent. He also told his friends of the honors England had bestowed upon him. Duke John of Alençon bitterly exclaimed against the King of France, who had not as yet helped him recover his duchy. He also pronounced many wild words, such as that in his opinion he would gain more by negotiating directly with England! Duke Charles sat silent. He was feeling his way. He sensed that there was trouble afoot.

All this time the duke was anxious to return into France, but he could not be the poor guest who allows his impatience to become obvious to his host. Duke Philip wanted to conduct his guest on a tour through Artois and Flanders. First he led Duke Charles in a triumphant entry into the thriving, if often rebellious, city of Bruges. The citizens were highly honored. Not only did the rich burgesses load down Duke Charles with precious gifts; many nobles were so charmed by the duke that they requested permission to serve him. Duke Philip acceded graciously. The same enthusiasm was manifested in Ghent and Tournay where the party delayed for several weeks in order to be honored and entertained. By the time Duke Charles and his duchess had arrived at the frontiers of France, they were followed by an army of three hundred knights. More than one astute observer noted—with some question as to why it was true—that Duke Charles was everywhere received as enthusiastically as if he were the actual King of France. There was, in fact, little enthusiasm abroad concerning King Charles VII.

After the Duke and Duchess of Orléans had satisfied their host's demands and bade farewell, they sent word to Paris asking the king to receive them. His answer showed that he knew of the frenzied rejoicings, the lavish presents, and the hundreds of new vassals who now accompanied Duke Charles. The king replied curtly that he would be happy to have his cousin's visit, if he came alone and unescorted into Paris. Duke Charles therefore did not go. Instead he kept south toward Orléans and Blois. The chroniclers thought that he was hurt by the king's assumption of his disloyalty.

In the winter months of 1440 the major vassals of France were generally disgruntled—Duke Philip of Burgundy more than the others. He had gained nothing from his prolonged English alliance, but he had lost a great deal. The French Court would never trust him again. The English reviled his name. Then, too, there was a particularly strong personal animosity between him and the king— an open hatred, known to all, that dated from the murder on the Montereau Bridge. The two men had never met face to face since that time. Duke Philip often boasted that if he ever met the King of France man to man, he would have only one word as his greeting: "Murderer!" The Burgundians resented the fact that this meager dauphin had remained true to his country and that he had won over the combined forces of England and Burgundy.

John Duke of Alençon was no longer the gallant knight he had been while Joan of Arc and of Orléans was still alive. The war and the ransom he had paid the English had ruined him. Count René of Anjou, supposedly the King of Sicily, had been recently released from a Burgundian prison. He also was ruined. He would do whatever Duke Charles of Orléans proposed, because twenty-five years before, the two had campaigned together against John the Fearless and because both were poets. Brittany was a sovereign duchy linked by marriage to Duke Charles. The Duke of Brittany was unhappy at the lack of generosity shown him by the French king, whose policy seemed to be to win the war at the expense of the great nobles.

To such men the return of Duke Charles meant that they had a leader who could, if the occasion seemed to merit it, replace King Charles VII on the throne—or help them crown the Dauphin Louis. No doubt they were pleased to learn of the king's snub, and even more pleased that Duke Charles had not submitted to it. If the nobles allied under Duke Charles—who could also bring Count Dunois and the Count of Armagnac into their rebellion—their chances of sharing more power would be great.

With such considerations running through his mind, Duke Charles rode home to Orléans. He was received by the bishop, a member of the Le Fuzelier family. The bells of Saint-Cross tolled while the duke and his beautiful duchess made their grand entry through the colonnaded streets of their capital, into the central square, and down the two short blocks to the cathedral. In this town prayers were still said regularly for Joan of Arc, for her banner had been blessed there.

Old men who remembered Duke Charles as a youngster came to kiss his hand, and young men who had been babies that October of Agincourt. The Duke of Orléans had time for them all. By the end of the week everyone in Orléans who wanted to speak to him had done so. They took him to see the house where Joan had lodged, showed him the razed suburbs, and spoke of their sufferings. They told him how the Lord Marshal Gilles de Rais had ruined himself by presenting a mystery play featuring Joan of Arc—a festival that lasted for days and that included free meals for all. The duke patiently heard their stories, granted them what he could in his straitened circumstances, and thanked them for their trust and their loyalty. Then he was free to go home.

It was with a beating heart and tears in his eyes that he rode down the white and dusty road from Orléans to Blois—past wheatfields bare of their crops, past the black and gnarled stumps of the vines, until he could see from his elevation on the plain that the ground under his horse's feet had begun to dip. He urged his mount to a canter. They were going downhill. In another minute he would see gray spires and the two towers of his castle. There below him, along the north bank of the Loire, snuggling between the ridge and the river, lay the town of Blois. The first members of their delegation had come out on foot to meet him.

First came priests carrying crosses. They were followed by the burgesses in their best robes shabby from long use, their faces red in the fresh November air. The women and children strewed the road with the last flowers from their gardens. The whole town was lined, weeping and cheering, both at the same time, all along the brow of the hill, down the curved streets and up to the Court of Honor. When the duke came to the wide paved entrance that led up to the castle portal, he dismounted. The people of Blois had followed him. They stood beneath the linden trees on either side of the ramp that formed the Courtyard of Honor. The duke stood looking up at the east wall of his palace.

Before he walked up the avenue, he stepped over to the trees on his left side. Beyond them was the parapet. In silence he leaned on the gray stones and looked down at the Loire. It was at low water, but still beautiful, still silver, still serene, still flowing silently toward Touraine and into distant Brittany. To his right the composite square towers of Saint-Laumer still rose to slender needle points of gray slate, their dozens of plane surfaces a cubist's dream. They shimmered and gleamed in the sunlight. The duke loosened his ermine collar. From where he stood on the ridge above the river, which centuries before the Counts of Châtillon had chosen for their seat, there was not a breath of air. All Blois, sheltered on the north by the high ridge of the central plain of Orléans, lay basking in the sun. Blois lay sheltered, facing south, parallel to the river, in the lee of the wind.

Then the duke walked up the ramp—wide enough for fifty knights abreast—and through the eastern and only gateway to Blois Castle. On his right, in the thickness of the wall, was the porter's lodge. He passed through the arch and into the courtyard. He saw his assembled vassals, his counselors, his attendants, and—against the walls of the rectangular courtyard—his scores of servants. He could not speak. He could only greet them with a raised hand.

During his long bitter years of imprisonment, when he often wished he were dead, the memories of Blois had sustained him more than all else. He would not have been a Frenchman if he had not cherished every stone, every tile, every pebble in the courtyard of his home. From that moment in the sunlit air, in a silence broken only by the cooing of pigeons and the occasional snort of a horse, the duke knew that the weary years had ended.

Still without speaking he set out on his first tour of inspection. For years in Pontefract, in Knaresborough, and in London he had played games with himself to while away the empty hours. How many stairs are there up to the Hall of the Three Estates? Carefully he turned toward the north side of the courtyard and climbed up to his great hall with its lofty wooden ceiling that looked for all the world like two ships' keels upended and upheld by the central row of fifteen pillars. It was a beautiful hall, sixty meters long by eighteen meters wide, with pillars seven meters in height from floor to vault and fourteen meters from the floor to the highest point in either vault.

Duke Charles had remembered that there were four types of bricks in the floor. In eagerness he looked down to verify his recollection. He had been correct. There were the plain apricot-colored bricks and the unglazed ones with the glazed design, four white fleurs-de-lis stemming from a central hollow circle. Then there were the pale turquoise glazed tiles, and lastly the ones with the white geometric design. The tiles were tipped so that they formed several lines of connected diamonds the whole length of the hall, the blue tiles on either side of the apricot ones—set in long zigzags, never meeting. The glaze on the blue tiles gave the floor its dull and then its shiny lines. The contrast of the soft density of the peachy tiles and the shiny blue of the glazed ones was still as striking. The war had passed over them without breaking a single one.

Nor was there a single slat missing in the thirteenth-century roof. The little painted boards were still nailed side by side all the way up the double vaults. Even the golden fleurs-de-lis traced on them were as bright and shiny as when he had last seen them. The ceiling was a brilliant sapphire overhead. The tapestries were in place along the walls. The carved mantelpiece in the north wall was also intact. So were the stairs and their landing leading up to the west wing of the palace. Tomorrow morning he would be coming down those stairs to preside at the meeting of his Three Estates.

The duke turned away with a smile and started back toward the door he had entered from the courtyard. As he passed the threshold, he looked up with a grin to see if the sculptured heads that had always amused him were as he remembered them. They were two heads of children that some long-dead artist had carefully cut from stone to suit himself. Both children were elf-like with pointed faces and clothing. Each one wore a blouse with full sleeves and wide cuffs, and long hose that met the smock at the trunk of the body. The one with the sly, roguish look on his face had been drinking milk from a gourd with two long spouts. He wore a pillbox hat flat on his skull. His hair was long, very curly, and very blond, as shown by traces of the original coats of paint. The imp wore soft felt boots with laces that folded them over and secured them at his ankles. He still looked down into the Assembly Hall, having just taken his lips from the jug's spout.

As the steps curved downward, Duke Charles looked up at another familiar face, that of a dwarf with outspread elbows, holding two huge balls in his hands. The duke smiled again to see the dwarf's long curly beard and moustache, his wrinkled forehead, his jester's cap, his flared cape that covered his arms, his lined gnome's face, and the square worn teeth that grinned down on the passersby. The artist had realistically captured the idiotic expression—so stupid that it was wise.

At the bottom of the stairs and under the tower were three more familiar figures. The first represented a pilgrim wearing a flowing, belted robe, a rufflike collar, and a hood. In his hands he held two feet of a wild boar with bristled spines along its dorsal column. The animal was draped over the man's shoulder. The pilgrim was a man of about thirty with a pleasant face, a moustache, and a long wavy beard.

The second figure portrayed a beggar in a short tunic with a purse for alms on his belt. He supported himself on crutches and leaned to the right. He was clean-shaven and his hair was neatly cut above his ears. His eyes were closed in obvious self-commiseration. His head was raised toward humanity as if he asked without hope of receiving. Near him was the God of the Winds, with puffed cheeks, jovial face, wide-open and merry eyes, his hair upswept like stylized leaves that had been wind-tossed. Above his thick and curled lower lip was a bulbous nose with flared nostrils and over his head a phallic symbol.

Once out in the courtyard, the duke could see the Gothic portals decorated with beautiful porcupines under each arch and surmounted by the Crown of Orléans with its sixteen sapphires around the base and its ten fleurs-de-lis wrought above them. From their vantage point at every cornice, dozens of open-mouthed gargoyles leaned out over the courtyard—thin, elongated, agonized.

Duke Charles strode happily back to the main portal just as his duchess entered in her open litter. She was smiling from the cheers her beauty had evoked. Her pretty golden hair was piled on her head now as a sign of her new dignity. It was partially covered with a white fur hood that was too becoming to be removed, although the day was warm in the lingering Saint Martin's summer. The Duchess Marie was enchanted with the south wing of the palace toward which her husband led her. The sunlight made the soft apricot-colored bricks of this two-story wing warm and welcoming. Along the inner wall was a colonnade under which she could pass without even wetting her feet on rainy days—if it ever rained in such a mild, soft countryside so different from Flanders, where it rained day in and day out, summer and winter alike.

The Duchess Marie burst into gales of girlish laughter as she looked up at the sculpture on the southern tower. In great excitement she proved to her erudite husband, who somehow looked less forbidding now that he was relaxed and smiling, that she, too, was learned. Although she had not traveled widely, she could nevertheless, with a little assistance, name all the rare animals that the olden-time sculptors had carved with such obvious resourcefulness.

There were a lion and a newborn lamb or the foetus of a lamb. There were a monkey wearing a wide belt and a marvelously real gorilla holding a horn. There was a writhing dragon with its head turned over its shoulder to belch fire at enemies behind it. There was a centaur with a beard and an odd hooded headdress. Up, down, and around were hundreds of beautifully carved fig leaves in set designs. Under the eaves was a little monkey holding its baby.

It will take years, thought the young duchess, to see all the marvels of Blois Castle. Her bright eyes swept over the palace and up to its second story. The sculptors who had worked on these figures had been very talented and had apparently been allowed a free rein for their fantasies. They had carved a winged cherub holding an open psalm book. Opposite this child was a defiant young woman in a long-sleeved, square-necked gown, a folded hood around her face. A chain of balls lay over her left shoulder and around her right hip. Then there was an idiot with his finger in his mouth. Not far from him was a beautiful woman with streaming hair who resembled a deserted Ariadne.

All in all, the new duchess was delighted with Blois Castle. Her apartments on the second floor of the south wing were warm and sunny. The oak floors gleamed and smelled of wax. The carpets were luxurious. The sheets and blankets on her bed were scented with sunshine and lavender. From her windows she could look out on the courtyard as she embroidered and planned her costumes for the festivals that would not fail to be held more and more frequently now that the war had reached a stalemate. At the end of the west wing was a blue chapel to which the lady had access along the colonnaded gallery. South of the chapel was a flower garden, an ancient stone fountain, and a parapet from which she could look directly down on Saint-Laumer's church and the Loire River. Very eager to become a part of her new life, the Duchess Marie adopted the colors of her dead mother-in-law, Valentine Visconti. She also asked her husband for a book of her own into which his poems could be copied, and for any poem he might care to write for her.

In his library at home, behind closed doors, alone with his most trusted advisers, Duke Charles asked for details of the political situation in France. He was particularly concerned by the king's lack of security and by the general precariousness of the kingdom. A principal source of trouble was the Dauphin Louis, who at the age of seventeen was disrespectful to his father, cruel to his wife—the Princess Marguerite of Scotland—and eager for power and glory at his father's expense. The year before, the dauphin had plotted with Bourbon, Brittany, and Trémoille—even with Count Dunois—to depose the king. This dauphin had a very sharp sense of politics. He often made lightning raids to the nobles—just to see what they were doing at home, he said.

That very year he had called upon the Lord Marshal Gilles de Rais, while the investigation which brought that great war hero to trial had already been instigated by the Bishop of Nantes. Duke

Charles shuddered at this reference. Gilles de Rais had died only a few days before the duke had left London for home. It was the most shocking story he had ever heard. Joan of Arc's foursome had been Dunois, Alençon, La Hire, and the millionaire Gilles de Rais. The latter had been at her side at Blois, at Orléans, and at the crowning of Charles VII in Rheims. He had been with her at the siege of Paris. As he had testified at his trial, he had relapsed into his old sins in 1431—the very year of Joan's death!

His sins were so terrible that the judges in the ecclesiastical court —churchmen who through years at the confessional might have thought they had heard the very worst of human degradation— ordered the secretaries to leave blank certain details in the marshal's testimony. A Carmelite named Jean Juvénal had shriven Gilles de Rais before he was remanded to the civil court where he subsequently stood trail for the murder of two hundred or more children between the ages of six and twelve. The judges in the civil court were so horrified that they interrupted the trial in order to have the crucifix covered with a black veil. Such a story made Duke Charles worry about John of Alençon, who, like Gilles de Rais, had been drinking heavily since Joan's death. How had the hanging and burning of this marshal affected Alençon?

The counselors also told Duke Charles about Prelati, an Italian chemist who had been involved with Gilles de Rais in his search for a method to turn mercury into gold. The Italian had not been executed because, although he had encouraged his master to sacrifice certain organs of living children to the powers of Black Magic, he had not murdered the children himself. Then the counselors lowered their voices. The duke should be wary of René of Anjou. It was he who had released Prelati from prison. King René was also a rabid alchemist who spent all the money he could scrape up to construct kilns and furnaces—and this despite the fact that alchemy had been forbidden by an edict passed under the reign of Charles VI! Although none of the people of Orléans had lost children, they were still very upset. They confused Gilles de Rais with Bluebeard. They were also confused because their Joan of Arc, whom Charles VII had raised to the nobility, had been burned as a witch. Then, too, there was the matter of the impostor who for years had been claiming to be Joan of Arc. Gilles de Rais had identified her positively as Joan. So had her brothers at Orléans.

The duke may very well have had an aching head when he considered the problems that faced him. All he could do, however, was to try to handle them one at a time. At the first meeting of his Three Estates, he complimented all present on their splendid effort during the terrible twenties and thanked them again for their devotion to him and his family. He said he regretted not being able to reward them as they deserved, particularly because he must still raise a large sum of money for the ransom of his brother, the pious John of Angoulême in England.

Duke Charles then made an announcement: "Being much happier to lodge men than to lodge wild animals, I should like to present every man in Blois with a new house at my expense." This gift was received with much applause. The duke ordained that his forest lands around Blois be thrown open to all his people so they could cut timber at their will. The first thing he had noted as he rode into town was the shabbiness of the houses. War had been hard on everyone. There was a fever of activity in that area for the next few months. At least one pointed-gabled, three-storied house—very gay with its carved balconies and half-timbers—was so well constructed that he could predict that it would still serve as a home in centuries to come.

In January of 1441 Duke Charles rode up to Paris to pay his respects to his cousin King Charles VII and to present his new duchess at court. Their visit was very successful. The king could not have been more gracious. The Duchess Marie was honored by His Majesty, who saw to it that her youth and beauty were sufficiently admired. King Charles VII, like Duke Philip of Burgundy, had a reputation for philandering. The duchess met Queen Marie, who had been Marie of Anjou. This lady had already been married for nineteen years. She was generally wearing mourning for one of her dead babies. In all she bore the king fourteen children, most of whom died soon after birth. The Duchess Marie also met the dauphin's wife, Marguerite of Scotland, a gay young person who longed to be pregnant but never was, and who meanwhile sang, danced, wrote poetry, and ate green apples to keep her figure.

After Duke Charles and his bride returned to Blois, the king set out for the siege of Pontoise, which he directed in person, since his vassals were awaiting the Duke of Orléans to direct some plot or another. The king struggled around Pontoise from June all through that summer, and in September finally captured it from the English, thanks to his artillery expert, Jean Bureau. The cannons had finally made a breach in the walls. The knell of the medieval fortress had sounded.

In December a solemn conclave of the leading vassals of the kingdom was held under the chairmanship of Duke Charles. Instead of sedition, however, the vassals drew up a set of grievances and then a list of suggestions as to how the kingdom should be administered. In this way the Dukes of Burgundy and Brittany released a good deal of hostility and proved to themselves, at least, their superior abilities. Duke Charles was asked to present these articles to the king. He agreed to do so. He could not have been in much of a hurry, however, for he did not present them to his cousin-sovereign until May of the following year!

At Eastertime of 1442 Duke Charles sent Count Dunois to the king in Pontoise to remind him that Angoulême was still ruled by England and by guerrillas. Count John would be returning from England soon. Could the king conquer the province and let Duke Charles entrust its administration to his vassal of Rambouillet? This plea was no sooner made than granted. Both Duke Charles and his brother were gratified.

In May the disgruntled vassals assembled at Limoges, where the king was holding his court, to hear Duke Charles present their case. Much to the astonishment of all, this hearing passed very smoothly. The king replied to each complaint and each suggestion as glibly as if he had prepared his answer in advance. This was all the more curious because he had hitherto been known as an uncertain, pusillanimous, and vacillating man. The king consented to allow English ambassadors to meet Duke Charles in Blois and in Tours for the purpose of drafting a peace. He assured his great vassals that they could draw their pensions of 14,000 francs per annum as soon as they behaved as they should. He added that he counted upon them to help him recover Normandy. He invited them to remain in Pontoise as his guests. He also made to Duke Charles a personal present of 80,000 francs, along with a written document elaborately stating to what extent he was in the debt of his cousin of Orléans. The king further added that the bond between himself and his cousin was one of pure love. Both men may have smiled to themselves. Let the Duke of Burgundy go down through the pages of history as having released Duke Charles from his prison, paid his ransom, and caused this duke to rebel against the House of Valois—if such lies gave him and his historians pleasure.

Following a festival at Limoges in celebration of Pentecost, the king undertook an extensive reorganization of his government, giving important functions to capable people. It really looked as if he would be able to rule France after all. In a continued burst of unusual energy, he led an army of eighty thousand troops into southern France, entering Toulouse on the 8th of June. Six months later he was still warring in the South. In December, La Hire, worn out from constant campaigns at his advanced age, died almost penniless. He had blithely squandered the riches the king had bestowed upon him.

While the king was in Armagnac, ambassadors from the Count of Armagnac were in London negotiating again with Humphrey of Gloucester. Count Jean IV, son of the murdered Bernard VII, was offering the Duke of Gloucester the South of France—Guyenne —in exchange for a marriage between King Henry VI and his daughter Eleanor. It was, of course, an excellent offer. By accepting their terms Duke Humphrey could save at least one part of the territories his father and his brothers had fought so long to win. Accepting this offer, however, meant that there could be no peace. Therefore, the Cardinals of England and York and the Duke of Suffolk, who was by this time the chief favorite at court, were opposed. The Duke of Gloucester, seconded by the Londoners, insisted. The next thing he knew, the ax had fallen. His wife had been arrested, charged with witchcraft, and imprisoned. The duke had been caught unprepared—too late to save her as Louis of France had saved the Duchess Valentine.

The pain and humiliation of the Duke of Gloucester were excessive. His wife was led through the public streets, reviled by the mobs, pelted with refuse, preached against at Saint Paul's, and then banished. Her illustrious husband, position and popularity notwithstanding, could do nothing for her. After her penance the Duchess Eleanor was dispatched to perpetual prison on the Isle of Man. She was never released. She died there in Peel Castle thirteen years later. During her imprisonment she also turned to poetry, composing verses to warn other women about the injustices of life. The Cardinals of England and York and the Duke of Suffolk thus sent the delegation home to Armagnac. They were waiting for Duke Charles to invite them to meet him in France.

Meanwhile, the war dragged on. In 1443 King Charles VII allowed his vicious son Louis to lead an army against the English at Dieppe. Count Dunois was sent along in an advisory capacity. The French forces were victorious. The dauphin's cruelty to the English prisoners was indicative of his nature; he had them hanged by the hundreds, even though they had surrendered. After this defeat the

Duke of Gloucester was heard one last time. He roused the council
in England so thoroughly that they dispatched the Duke of Somerset
to the Continent with one last army. England was almost ready to
halt the war. They were still hoping for instructions from Duke
Charles.

The Dauphin Louis was then ordered into Armagnac to reduce
Count Jean IV to submission. As a further token of his love for
Duke Charles and his brother, the king then bestowed upon Count
Dunois the County of Longueville, by which name his illustrious
descendants would be known down the centuries. The king had
more than one reason to be liberal that year, for in February he had
met "the sweet and simple dove" who was "whiter than a swan" and
"pinker than a flame"—the beautiful Agnès Sorel. This lady changed
the king's life, his character, and, some say, his whole being. The
king called her the Lady of Beauty because he had endowed her
with Beauty Castle near Vincennes. This seat had once been owned
by his unfortunate uncle, Louis of France.

Although Jean Chartier, the king's official chronicler, states em-
phatically that King Charles VII never laid a finger on Agnès Sorel
"from the throat down," that her pregnancies were her own concern and not his, it is generally believed that Agnès Sorel bore him
three children. Theirs is one of the best-known love affairs in
French history. Agnès Sorel was, indeed, an angelically beautiful
blonde.

In 1443 Duke Charles completed his arrangements. He moved
down the river to the superb city of Tours, between Blois and Nantes,
and there received the ambassadors from England. One of them was
his former host and now his friend, William de la Pole, Duke of
Suffolk. It was a pleasant reunion for both of them and an opportunity to speak English once more. Both dukes were poets. Both
had been imprisoned. Each had spent close to twenty-five years in
the other's country.

Along with the Duke of Suffolk came Dr. Adam Molins (or
Molyneux), who was the Keeper of the Privy Seal and the Bishop
of Chichester. There were also a Sir Robert Roos and three ranking
French nobles, including Louis de Bourbon, Duke of Vendôme. This
Diet of Tours was brilliantly successful and therefore a kind of
crowning point in the life of Duke Charles. He signed a truce of
eighteen months in the Hundred Years' War—a cessation of hostilities accompanied by a resumption of trade between the two king-

doms that was later extended for six years. The only person opposed was Duke Humphrey of Gloucester.

It must have been a double pleasure for Duke Charles—first, to have drafted what could become a permanent peace, and second, to entertain English lords at Blois Castle. Between the negotiations there were jousts and banquets where his young duchess, who was becoming a lovely woman, could preside. He must have been happy to have the English lords admire her. By this time the Duchess Marie had her own book in which some of her husband's poems had been copied. She was doing her best to please him. What she may have thought, if she knew it, of her husband's writing a poem to an English lady can only be imagined. The lady's name—Anne Molins —is artfully concealed in the verses.

Since the Duke of Suffolk had been so empowered, and even pardoned in advance by King Henry VI for any error of judgment he might commit during the negotiations, Duke Charles persuaded him to settle upon a bride for the King of England. The lady chosen, or rather the young girl, was Marguerite, daughter of René of Anjou. The lady was selected by Duke Charles with malice aforethought. It was common knowledge that despite the beatings administered to him in Rouen, Henry VI would never be able to rule England. It was therefore reasoned that he should have a wife who could replace him on the throne.

Marguerite of Anjou, niece to the Queen of France, was a likely candidate. She was handsome, headstrong, intelligent, and forceful. This time the French were not sending a child into England as they had in the case of the Princess Isabelle. Nor were they sending a victim like the Princess Catherine to Henry V. They were sending a dynamic young lady with orders beforehand to do what the Duke of Suffolk and the Cardinal Beaufort advised, and to finish with Humphrey of Gloucester once for all. Since Marguerite's father was an impoverished king without a country, Duke Charles could not promise any dowry. On the contrary, he would expect—and did receive—valuable territorial and financial concessions from Suffolk.

Duke Charles returned to Orléans and Blois very satisfied with himself. If he had hated England with all his heart—and perhaps he did—he could not have drafted a more pernicious agreement than that marriage contract. However, it is usually only possible to see historical forces at work after the fact. While the duke writhed at the knowledge that there were still English soldiers on French soil and while he exulted in his poems at French victories, it is probably not true that he maliciously intended both Dukes of Suffolk and Gloucester to die ignominious deaths by his machinations. Yet in retrospect, one can see that this was bound to happen not long after the Diet of Tours.

During that same summer Duke Charles ratified or reissued those articles of King Charles VII that had in 1429 elevated Joan of Arc and her brothers to the nobility under the name of Dulis. Such a new document, referred to by a subsequent King of France, and therefore unquestionably true, was probably necessary because Joan's family had all come to live in the Duchy of Orléans. As a matter of fact, they had moved there in 1440, the year Duke Charles returned from captivity. They were therefore his responsibility. The document cites Joan's brother, "Pierre d'Arc, formerly known by the family name *Dulis* . . . profession—soldier . . . having been advanced to the rank and title of knight by letters patent of the Duke of Orléans, given at Orléans, July 28, 1443." It further states that the duke "felt bound to so act to the brother of the Maid for the signal services rendered by this brother . . . with his said sister and after her death as much to the above-named lord and King Charles VII as to the said Duke of Orléans, since the fortunate deliverance which he had from his long prison, [was] under the auspices of the above-named Maid as it has appeared amply in several extracts of our Chamber of Accounts and other documents attached under the counter seal of these present letters. . . ." * Such a document is of prime importance, for the principal charge made against Duke Charles by French scholars over the past 130 years—or since his French poems were discovered in Paris—is that he never in any way recognized Joan of Arc's services to him or to France.

In 1444 the duke assumed again the role he had played since his return to France, that of a peacemaker. This time he interceded for Count Jean IV of Armagnac, the brother of his second wife, Bonnie. The fierce Dauphin Louis had treated this count badly. Having beguiled him into surrendering, the dauphin then arrested the count, his wife, his second son, and his two unmarried daughters. He threw them all into dungeons at Carcassonne. He then loaded the count with charges that he had coined money without permission, that he styled himself "Count by the grace of God," and conducted himself like a sovereign, that he had seized the king's bailiff sent to serve him

* *Chronicles of Monstrelet,* edited by Buchon, Vol. 34, Appendix.

with papers, that he had beaten his confessor when the latter had refused him absolution, and that he had tried to marry his daughter Eleanor to king Henry VI of England! Charles VI pardoned the count since Duke Charles asked it as a personal favor. The Dauphin Louis began to hate his "cousin" of Orléans.

While Duke Charles was frantically busy selling a county and collecting signatures from those friends who promised to underwrite his brother's ransom, he was not too busy to write poetry. His young wife was becoming prettier by the day—and, as a matter of fact, acting in a rather suspicious manner. From time to time her husband noted the swish of her hips and the huskiness of her voice. In the evenings she danced willingly with the young courtiers at Blois. She seemed to be tantalizing her somber and more than melancholy husband, who had foresworn love four years before.

She had not stopped teasing him to write her a poem. If he did so, in these years, he may have meant the following one for the frisky duchess:

Rondel CCCXLVI

"Soon as I know thou art entirely mine,
  And that thy heart loves mine with loyalty,
  Lady, I should play thee most treacherously
  If, without guile, I did not say me thine.

"Put me to trial. I shall not use design—
  Long as thou leav'st my honor be—
  Soon as I know thou art entirely mine
  And that thy heart loves mine with loyalty.

"And if thou sayst: 'How long wilt thou consign
  Thy heart to me in its entirety?'
  I'll answer thee, without sly subtlety:
  'I'll pledge my love forever unto thine
  Soon as I know thou art entirely mine.' "

The Duchess Marie, even if this poem was addressed to her, still could have had reasons to doubt her husband's sincerity. There is, after all, love and love. The duchess was at a tremendous disadvantage. She was not only trying to make her husband-poet take notice that she had become a woman. Since she had become a woman, his cursory attention would be far from sufficient. The poor duchess Marie had a rival—the worst kind of rival.

Duke Charles was obliged to act as chief magistrate in his duchy. He seems to have disliked this function; for in two cases, and also in one of his poems, he acted with a great leniency, belying a heart too soft for the office. In verifying his books, for example, he was sorry to learn that Jean Le Fuzelier, the trusted friend he had advanced to the nobility, had been embezzling funds over the years. Instead of prosecuting, the duke forgave the crime.

In 1444 his prosecuting attorney brought a case for verdict. In the abbatial Church of Saint-Laumer, just under the castle, the master had been pursuing a novice named Martineau. In order to evade his pursuer's hands the youth darted into the church. When his hiding place was discovered, he climbed up to one of the cross vaults in the roof. The vault cracked and then broke, tumbling the boy to the stone floor far below. Martineau was dead when they ran up to him. Instead of notifying the duke, which was mandatory in the case of a death, the monks buried Martineau and said nothing.

When the duke's attorney heard of it, he charged the monks with murder. Such a charge threw the case upon the Duke's jurisdiction. Duke Charles was shocked. He immediately revoked the monks' privileges. When they appealed the case, however, they were able to convince Duke Charles that Martineau had died accidentally. Therefore the duke reinstated them.

However, he imposed one penalty upon this church where once the Princess Isabelle had lain. He gave them as a duty that every year in August, on the day following the feast of Saint Mary the Egyptian, they should sing a Mass for the repose of "my wife Isabelle and myself."

The Duchess Marie had the worst kind of rival—a first love who has died but who is not dead.

XII [*1445–1450*]   THE YEARS 1444 AND
                    1445 were prodigal years in
the Kingdom of France. Such carefree festivities had not been seen
since the old days when King Charles VI and Louis of France were
gay young knights splashing madly on the crest of their father's brilliant reign. The Lady of Beauty set French women a difficult, an
impossible, standard of elegance and luxury. The young chronicler
Olivier de la Marche admits that he never saw such a beautiful
woman. Agnès Sorel had long flaxen curls, a winsome way, the eyes
of an angel, and the clothes of an Oriental princess. It was she who
recommended Jacques Cœur to the king. Jacques Cœur was a merchant prince who had turned France into a second Italy. He could
not rival the Florentine riches, or match the capital of Cosmo di'
Medici; but he, too, owned a palace, a fleet of ships, and trading
counters across the Mediterranean and into the Near East. When
Agnès Sorel tastefully enhanced her beauty with the satins and silks
of the Orient, there was not a lady in France who did not have an
aching heart. None was immune.

The Duchess Isabella of Burgundy was not immune. She had
gone down to France on a diplomatic mission as usual, for her husband could not meet the king. Although the Duchess Isabella gained
nothing during her visit, she conceded a great deal—even more or
less forgiving the debt to Burgundy of René of Anjou. She had to
watch King René's daughter fêted and entertained at court prior to
her marriage to the King of England. For the first time, the Duke of
Burgundy was making concessions. His father's sins and his own
were all beginning to fly home to roost. France and England both
despised him.

While King Charles VII intemperately recaptured his youth—a
flaming youth he had never experienced—in a round of sumptuous
celebrations where Agnès Sorel was the queen, the Duchess Isabella

and Queen Marie stole away for private talks. While the courtiers supped by candlelight, danced by moonlight, and took trips through the shady parks and along the rivers by daylight, the two great ladies sat sighing and commiserating with each other. It was scandalous of the king to conduct himself like an amorous adolescent swain. It was monstrous that Agnès Sorel was everywhere treated like the real queen. It was a wonder that someone didn't poison her! It was equally revolting to count how many illegitimate children Duke Philip boasted! Why did René of Anjou have to bring Agnès Sorel to the court in the first place? If his mother, the king's stepmother, were still alive, she would have put a stop to such immorality!

Duke Charles was present at most of this merrymaking, honored by all, esteemed by all, rewarded handsomely by the king, and deferred to by the English lords, who thanked him personally for the new truce and for having negotiated the wedding of King Henry VI. The Duchess Marie was also present, a little dizzy from such a round of gay parties, but very happy. She was chosen one of the two queens at a major tournament. Then her rank and her petulant beauty were in the limelight. Her husband celebrated the happy days of 1445:

Rondel CCCXLVII

"Supper or bath, or dinner or a boat;
  Was there ever such a merry company!
  One talks or sleeps, and one sings do-re-me
  While the rest of us write ballads by rote.

Let the old or new wine trickle down the throat;
  We're as happy as larks upon the lea!
  Supper or bath, or dinner or a boat;
  Was there ever such a merry company!

"What do I care for hounds or hunting coat?
  When it's said, the main thing seems to be
  To live life with the current the most carefree;
  If you want my advice, just try to stay afloat.
  Supper or bath, or dinner or a boat!"

That year Marguerite of Anjou was officially wed to the King of England. She left France to meet her new husband while her father and his old friend Duke Charles lolled about sipping wine and writing poems to each other and about each other "in that sainted and most happy season of peace and union." Olivier de la Marche says nothing happened at all worth writing about in his chronicle. He says they were "lazy" days with no news of war, and hardly a cloud on the horizon. King Charles VII had earned a rest. When the truce ended, either England would give back Normandy and Guyenne, or he would send Count Dunois and Jean Bureau to win them. Duke Charles should be highly praised, everyone said. England had promised—the Duke of Suffolk had promised—to return Le Mans to France in exchange for receiving the sixteen-year-old Marguerite, who brought as her dowry her loveliness and the Mediterranean islands of Majorca and Minorca. That is to say, she brought England the right to these islands—when the English armies could conquer them.

Unwilling to be outdone, and totally eclipsed by the brilliant French court, Duke Philip invited his friends and fellow brothers of the Golden Fleece to his castle in Ghent. His entertainment was much more lavish than that in France, one blaze of extravagant glory as the sun of Burgundy prepared to set. Charles VII had already warned this vassal: Do not style yourself Duke by "the grace of God"! Duke Philip had corrected his error.

First among the guests in Ghent was Duke Charles, who, says Olivier de la Marche, did not stand on formality as he could have done since he was the third personage in the realm. By this time the Duke of Orléans had collected the necessary signatures. In 1446 his brother John of Angoulême finally returned to France. His joy was now complete. John of Angoulême married a princess of the De Rohan family.

The puffy white clouds that had remained so peacefully on the horizon for three long years had been thunderheads, however. The storm struck England first when the Duke of Suffolk returned home jubilant over his successful negotiations. Humphrey of Gloucester, whose political life had ended when he rose from his knees in Westminster Abbey during the thanksgiving Mass in honor of Duke Charles, could not contain himself. Such a treaty was monstrous. It was treason. The Earl of Suffolk had been reduced to idiocy by Orléans. Suffolk was the "Ape Clog" in person. The inevitable happened. Humphrey Duke of Gloucester, last son of Henry IV, was arrested! At whose instigation? Perhaps at that of Henry Beaufort and the Bishop of Chichester. In February of 1447 the news of

Gloucester's death was announced. People said he had been murdered. He was Henry IV's last son. Henry IV had usurped the
throne of England!

Duke Charles had not recovered from this shock when six weeks
later Henry Beaufort died in his palace at Winchester. Down the
years Humphrey of Gloucester had charged this cardinal with many
faults, many errors of policy, and all the ills that had befallen England over the seventy or so years of this prelate's life. Henry Beaufort had released King James of Scotland when he should not have
done so. He had allowed Duke Charles to settle his quarrel with
Burgundy, which had been "a capital enmity like to have lasted forever." It was he who had permitted Orléans to receive safe-conducts
for his messengers from Blois Castle! It was also he who had arranged the transfer of the prince to London from Pontefract and
Knaresborough. Gloucester had not accused the cardinal of the political action that has made subsequent historians veer uncomfortably
away from his name—his condemnation of Joan of Arc. Nor did
Gloucester recognize the tireless activity of Beaufort through the
century, take into account his fidelity to the House of Lancaster, his
unceasing labors, his generosity with his wealth, his works of art in
Winchester Cathedral, or his endowment of Holy Cross Hospital
in that former capital.

Duke Charles was probably immensely relieved for Queen Marguerite when he heard the news of Gloucester's death. However,
Henry Beaufort, Cardinal of England, had been his obliging acquaintance for many years. Both men had believed in peace and had
championed peace. They had dined together in Wolvesey Palace,
Winchester. They had both discussed Jean Gerson with love and
understanding. This death was another bitter blow for England, and
a great loss for Suffolk as well as for King Henry VI. The power
behind the throne was gone. Henry Beaufort's heir was Edmund
Duke of Somerset, his brother. This nobleman was the Lieutenant
General of France for the English. Rumor had it that the Queen of
England was in love with him, and he with her. The queen's great
handicap may well have been her extraordinary beauty.

One of the saddest aspects of growing old is the losing of one's
dear friends. Duke Charles paused often to think of Henry Beaufort. It comforted him that he had seen the cardinal's chantry in
Winchester Cathedral, behind the splendid alabaster reredos that
Beaufort had commissioned for his beloved church. The chantry
where the cardinal would lie in death alone in the retro-choir had

already been completed and awaited only the body. The cardinal's likeness had also been carved and painted. It shows a very tall, heavy man with sandy hair and blue eyes. He is smooth-faced with a straight forehead, a small chin, full cheeks, flat jowls, and somewhat petulant lips. At his feet are the three lions of England and the three lilies of France. However wrong he was concerning Joan of Arc, the cardinal had been a true and honorable servant of England. History played a cruel trick on him after he clung to his life long enough to see the dangerous Gloucester in his tomb. With the cardinal dead, Suffolk was lost, King Henry VI was lost, and so was Queen Marguerite. In a certain sense so was Duke Charles. He had lost a real friend.

Cardinal Beaufort died in April. Duke Filippo Visconti of Milan, brother of Valentine Visconti, died on August 13th. Duke Charles of Orléans inherited overnight the Duchy of Milan, for his mother's marriage contract stipulated that when and if the last male heir of Gian Galeazzo Visconti died, the duchy would pass to the male heirs of Louis of France.

The period of the Italian Wars had begun. The duchy was not the property of Orléans until the duke had conquered it by force of arms. Duke Charles at the age of fifty-three was expected to don a warrior's armor and to set out for Italy at the head of an army. The era of tournaments and feastings was finished. The duke had not engaged in battle since Agincourt Field thirty-two years previous to that August. His life thus far had been full of surprises. He was now expected to conquer Milan. Therefore he would do his best. It must have been with some regret and many backward glances that he urged his young duchess to hasten, that he hastened himself, up to Burgundy to solicit an army. His brother's ransom had depleted his resources. The Duke of Visconti had died at a very wrong time, indeed.

He had also died very wrongly, purposefully spinning on the point of death a gigantic spider's web for such as would venture to approach his Duchy of Milan. In his will he had bequeathed his holdings to King Alfonso of Aragón. Then he had married his illegitimate daughter, Bianca Maria, to the illegitimate son of a common mercenary, Francesco Sforza, one of his captains. By rights his duchy reverted to the Emperor Frederick III. By right of his sister's marriage contract Gian Galeazzo had already willed it to the male heir of Louis I of Orléans. Still another contestant was the Duke of Savoy, greatly beloved in Milan, secretly championed by the Dauphin

Louis, who would champion anyone to further his own interests, especially if by so doing he could injure his father and the House of Orléans.

King Charles VII wrote to Savoy: "Our very dear and very beloved brother, the Duke of Orléans, presently Duke of Milan, through the death of his late Uncle who had just departed from this life, has purposely and duly notified us of the sure right he has to the above-named Duchy as he is next in line. . . ."

Meanwhile, Duke Charles, instead of dispatching Dunois into Italy on his errands as he had done since 1440, bestirred himself on his own behalf. Count Dunois had not appealed to the Italians south of the border; he was too cold, too logical, and too French. It was the unctuous Charles who was half Italian, and not Count Dunois. The people of Asti recalled with approval and affection the kind rule of Valentine Visconti whose son through her had the blood of the Visconti Snake. People in Italy knew of Duke Charles. A learned professor, a Dr. Antonio Astesano, had sent a literary composition to the duke, assuring him of their affection for Joan of Arc, Maid of Orléans.

Therefore, Duke Charles and his duchess trundled up the roads to Burgundy. The duchess was particularly excited. She had always longed to see Italy. She had been moved by the sad and willful death of her mother-in-law. She longed to see the land that had produced such a passionate princess and such a violent lady. Duke Philip, still the wealthiest man in Europe if one did not count the Florentine Cosmo di' Medici, could easily finance such an expedition. His credit would be good in Milan or in Venice. Duke Philip, as president of the Golden Fleece, could do no less than sanction Duke Charles. Duke Philip rose to the occasion. He met the request with grace by notifying the proper authorities in Italy that he stood behind Orléans. He authorized Duke Charles to levy an army in Burgundy.

The duke himself dispatched long, redundant letters south of the border to the effect that he was about to arrive at the head of an army. He also notified his representative and captain in Italy, Raymond du Presnay, to move forward in the conquest of Milan. The letters gave pause in Italy; they were most impressive.

The actual recruiting of the army in Burgundy was deputed to the Burgundian Count of Arguel, son of the Prince of Orange. This count had married a daughter of Charles's sister Marguerite. Therefore the winning of Milan could still be kept in the family. The sum of 6,000 francs, or 10,000 francs, was contributed by various Burgundian lords to this cause of Duke Charles's, which appeared legitimate to them. While the Count of Arguel was raising his army, Duke Charles himself, moving in state from one Burgundian city to another, seems to have been equally concerned with other subjects.

They could not leave for Italy immediately, in any event. The truce had lasted so long that swords and armor had rusted. The blacksmiths and armorers set to work. Forges and anvils knew a brief surge of activity. Duke Charles had time to wait. Meanwhile, he discussed literature with a new friend and protégé, the chronicler Olivier de la Marche. "And during this time," writes the historian, "I made the tour of Burgundy thanks to the Duke of Orléans, who gave me and showed me great signs of intimate favor; and this because he was an excellent rhetorician and because he delighted as much in his own writing as in the writing of others."

The duke felt sanguine about this expedition into Italy, especially since his right to the Duchy of Milan was clear and true. Had he not already forced Filippo Maria to return to him the Republic of Asti the previous year? In that city there was a *buon ricordo*—a good memory of his family. King Charles VII was on his side, and so was Duke Philip. Duke Charles also dispatched a herald into England to notify William de la Pole. Since Beaufort was dead, at least Suffolk would want to come to his assistance.

Olivier de la Marche does not specify how many Burgundians were recruited by Duke Charles and the Count of Arguel. He does say, however, that the citizens of Milan preferred the Duke of Savoy as contender to their duchy. He also notes that Francesco Sforza, the favorite captain of the late Visconti duke, was "valiant, subtle, wide, and abandoned." He was referring not to his political situation when he called him "abandoned," but rather to his character. Such a judgment from a medieval writer was to be expected. The old world of the Middle Ages would not understand the new age already in first flower south of the Alps, any more than the Renaissance could ever understand the Middle Ages. What happened to Duke Charles as he journeyed down to his mother's native land was illustrative of a great historical cleavage where a tradition and a way of life that had predominated for five hundred years was about to be discarded, condemned, and supplanted by a new one. Within one generation Olivier de la Marche would be answered by Niccolò Machiavelli.

The wily and hideously obese Duke Filippo Maria Visconti had died on August 13, 1446, surrounded by necromancers and astrologers, hoping gleefully that once he was removed from the world his demise would be followed by wars, murders, and vicious aftermaths. His nephew of Orléans must have spent September in Burgundy. Toward the end of that month, although no contingents had yet arrived either from King Charles VII (who still had to drive the English from Normandy and Guyenne) or from the Duke of Suffolk (who was so embarrassed at having promised the return of Maine to France that he did not even dare admit it in England), Duke Charles of Orléans, his Duchess Marie, his sister Marguerite and her children, and an unspecified number of hastily outfitted Burgundians started out across Burgundy and France toward Lyons on the Rhone.

In the fifteenth century the crossing of the Alps required a degree of physical daring and a state of health not common to a majority of poet-dukes in their fifties. Not that from Lyons their existence seems even credible. It was only after the second day's leisurely journey by horseback and litter that the party, jogging along a level plain already russet with the first frosts of autumn, saw clouds along the eastern horizon. They were beautiful towers of pink and ruby clouds lighted like a vertical wall by the setting sun. Even a second and a third view mistook them for clouds, so straight were they up to the arch of the sky. It was very difficult not to conceive of them as clouds. It was virtually inadmissible. Duke Charles stared at this wall of ice and pinnacles that were not clouds at all, but mountains. The Alps thrust their sheer granite peaks from the level plain to windswept, cloud-wreathed, ice-clad tiers that rose ridge upon ridge like the duke's "castles in Spain," unimaginable and forbidding. Beyond these icy ranges, beyond these vertiginous gorges, these battalions of crouching dragons, these vertical granite faces where the tiniest rolling pebble can set off an avalanche of boulders and crashing tons of rotten rocks and gigantic uprooted spruces, lay, Duke Charles had been told, the alluvial plain of the Po River.

The innkeepers along the route shook their heads wisely. The last herds came down from the foothills about the 1st of September. The roads were blocked and deep with snow by September 15th. One would be mad to venture out of Grenoble even into the Chartreuse after the twentieth of the month. The first big snowstorm of every year came on the same date. From Grenoble the travelers could see the three ranges of Alps on each side of the valley. In this city it was a mild and sunny Saint Martin's summer.

Without delaying any longer than necessary, they left Grenoble in the duchy of the dauphin and proceeded north along the banks of the Isère River to the city of Chambéry in Savoy. There they left the Isère and doubled south again along its tributary, the Arc, to the high mountain village of Saint-Jean-de-Maurienne. This was Julius Caesar's country, and before him, Hannibal's. From Saint-Jean they traveled to Modane and from there to Lanslebourg high in the Alpine peaks. The snow was deep, the air so clear they grew lightheaded. From Lanslebourg they could look up to the snowbound plateau of Mount Cenis at an altitude of 6,835 feet. They had arrived at the frontier of Italy and the only pass through the Alps except the northern one. Duke Charles refers to the Mount Cenis in a rondel that occurs in his Grenoble manuscript. This poem was not copied in his own private book, the book he made in England.*

Although Duke Charles did not make the passage of the Alps a subject for literature, another traveler who made the same crossing in 1769 has described it. The situation would have been the same, for the first road was not constructed until 1810. The Abbot Richard explains that no vehicle could proceed farther than Lanslebourg. In order to negotiate this last and most arduous passage across Mount Cenis and down its eastern slope into the Piedmont, all carts and wagons had to be dismantled piece by piece and loaded on pack animals. Each mule could carry three hundred pounds. The more precious possessions were packed in knapsacks and entrusted to mountaineers. Servants rode on mules. The lords were transported in wicker carrying chairs that were attached to a spruce shaft. It took six porters to carry the spruce pole from which the hard seat dangled. Perhaps more than six porters were required for Duke Charles and his noble escort, who must have been muffled to the ears, not in armor, but in furs.

The footpath from Lanslebourg to Mount Cenis was exceedingly steep and almost perpendicular, says Abbot Richard. On the summit of the mountain there extended a long plain deep in snow after the first of September. From all sides the higher Alpine peaks trailed their diaphanous wisps of cloud. The curved summit was dotted with mounds—shepherds' huts where in summer the inhabitants lodged their herds at night and where they made their Parmesan-type cheeses. The duke's party halted at the hostel on the summit where down the ages a café keeper and his wife kept a fire going on their hearth and supplied hot red wine in mugs for travelers. Duke Charles had probably never tasted a drink so welcome or so

---

* Edition of Champollion of Figeac, page 272.

delicious, with the gratuitous advantage of warming his stiff fingers along its sides as he sipped.

The duke's personal party had started across the plain while the porters and mountaineers were still strung like black uneven beads all the way down the western slopes in France. His guides pointed out the lake on the summit and its issuing stream, which was only one tiny part of the Po River's watershed. The descent down the Italian side was even more precipitous, like steep ladders down the massive cliff faces, with narrow clefts for footholds, zigzagging back and forth every few yards. They passed the superb cascade with its blue waters falling through ice fans and icicles. Directly below them lay the small Italian village of Suza, only two leagues from France. Once in Suza they were in Roman territory, as the crumbling arch of Augustus showed them. From Suza it was only two leagues along a pleasant valley into Turin. Duke Charles mused as his horse bore him comfortably along the road. How many Dukes of Orléans would pass that way after him? What would happen to his title after his death, since he had no heir of his own?

Duke Charles halted in Turin while his party caught up with him. Ambassadors from his county of Asti brought him their homage, their greetings, and a piece of very bad news. His lieutenant from Asti, Raymond du Presnay, in pursuance of his lord's instructions, had launched the conquest of Milan. He had been defeated on October 17th, and taken prisoner. The remnants of his forces had taken refuge in Asti, where they eagerly awaited the duke and his army. Four magical names pronounced by Duke Charles were enough to make northern Italy gape: King Charles VII, Burgundy, Suffolk, Brittany.

On October 29, 1447, just a few days after having, like Hannibal, passed the Alps, Duke Charles and his suite made their triumphal entry into the County of Asti, past its vineyards and mulberry trees, past its ancient encircling walls, past its fourteenth-century church dedicated to Saint John, its baptistery dedicated to Saint Peter, its collegiate church dedicated to Saint Secondo, its Tower of Saint Catherine, and its Trojan Tower with the huge clock. The notables of Asti, "robed and hooded all in white," bore a resplendent dais over the head of their duke. The lilies of France gleamed golden on his robes of state, shone splendidly over his crimson and green velvet robes of ceremony. A wave of enthusiasm swept through Italy. Here was a powerful and victorious French prince—and a son of Visconti—whose thousands of armed knights would soon follow him across the snow-clad mountains.

Their enthusiasm was short-lived. Duke Charles might dispatch his literate prose to the Venetians, might ask them for soldiers, might protest his might. Neither the Venetians nor the Milanese were naïve. They waited deferentially, most polite and urbane on the surface. No army appeared, either from France or from England, from Brittany, or from Burgundy. Duke Charles played his game month after month. To his surprise the Milanese turned out to be an ungrateful crew who refused to recognize his suzerainty. The allies of Florence and Venice temporized with one eye on Francesco Sforza. Finally, in May of 1448, the Venetians dispatched an ambassador to meet with Duke Charles in Asti. Rhetoric for rhetoric, ruse for ruse, the duke did his best to win soldiers from Venice. It was no use. They could see clearly enough that the French prince was impoverished. Even if Milan had been willing to recognize him, Francesco Sforza and his wife, Bianca Maria Visconti, would chase him out of Italy after one skirmish. This duke was no warrior. He had no army. He was not rich. And, worst of all, he was an idealist, a visionary, an old man openly dedicated to the arts of peace.

While he met nothing but contempt under an unctuous urbanity from courtiers in Italy, Duke Charles himself was a personal success among his own class, the intellectuals. Therefore, his visit to Italy had far-reaching consequences culturally. The duke opened his eyes and his ears. He was delighted with Italian furniture, jewelry, art, and literature. The scholars and poets he met were equally charmed by him. Most rewarding of all, he finally met Professor Antonio Astesano. This scholar had sent one of his compositions to Duke Charles in his English prison back in 1430, a work in praise of Joan of Arc. It was with a real delight that Duke Charles spent month after month with the Italian scholar, who told him how Greek was beginning to be taught again, how new translations were being made from authors whose masterpieces had been miscopied for centuries, how a new era of renaissance was opening for the Western world. The torch of learning, which medieval writers had seen as having passed from Greece to Rome to France, had just been snatched by Italy. They were in the pale dawn of a new era.

Professor Antonio Astesano was also kind enough to examine the poetry of Duke Charles—his French poetry; the duke had kept no copies of either his English or his Latin poems. The learned Italian thought highly of the work. The Venetian ambassadors could cool their heels, or grant an army or not grant an army. By the time a man is in his fifties, he knows what is important in life and what is illusion. Duke Charles of Orléans was by this time first a poet and second a prince. He asked Professor Astesano if he would not consent to join his court, return back across the Alps with him, and be his friend and companion for the rest of their lives. The Italian scholar consented. Thus Duke Charles continued a tradition begun before his time—for his grandfather had enticed Christina of Pisa to bring Italian culture into France—and which would continue long after him.

In the generation after Duke Charles, his failure to conquer Milan would be analyzed by that prince of analysts, Niccolò Machiavelli. It was, of all the contenders, Francesco Sforza who became the new Duke of Milan. "Francesco, by appropriate means and through great abilities, from citizen became Duke of Milan, and what he had attained after thousands of difficulties, he maintained with little trouble." Machiavelli illustrates more than the reason for Francesco Sforza's success. "The Milanese, on the death of Duke Filippo Visconti, hired Francesco Sforza against the Venetians, who, having overcome the enemy, allied himself with them against the Milanese." Duke Charles of Orléans, during his nine months in Italy, committed every error cited in Machiavelli's book. He let "his thoughts wander from the exercise of war." He neglected to choose being feared over being loved, as a result of which he was only scorned. He relied upon the power of others instead of upon his own power. He did not realize that "fortune is always a friend to the young" because they are more ardent lovers. As Machiavelli reasoned, a prince had to "be a fox to recognize traps and a lion to frighten wolves." This was a French prince who thought of himself as a mouse! "The desire to acquire possessions is a very natural thing," said Machiavelli. No one in Italy would have blamed Duke Charles for attempting to conquer Milan. Conquering princes were "always praised and never censured." Where Duke Charles merited only Italy's scorn was that he attempted and failed. In that he made "a mistake deserving great blame."

The ideas of Jean Gerson had met those of Renaissance Italy. On the political level there was total incomprehension. The Italians described Charles of Orléans as "naïve"—an adjective that, coupled with the intentionally insulting term "Gothic," has long characterized medieval letters and medieval art.

On August 10, 1448, Duke Charles passed the Alps again on his way back into France. The return journey was far less rigorous. On that crossing he could see the lake on Mount Cenis, the shepherds with their flocks, the mountain goats scrambling over the ledges, and the lavender *cols-chics* in bloom in the grass. He had by no means abandoned his inheritance in Italy. It was not his nature to give in so easily. The public man had recognized only that he could do nothing for the moment unless an army was forthcoming.

The private man's reaction to the whole situation is to be found in three of his poems. In Ballad CXXIII he says that everyone exerts himself to lie better than the next man. He says that he also would learn to lie if he did not see that many evils would be the result. "I might lie for pleasure, for amusement, as a pastime, or from exuberance . . . but not if I were trying to deceive falsely. False liars can traverse the mountains of Savoy, but they will not live to return," he says. "Let them sleep there, then; for they can do nothing without using deceit. Do they want me to war with them? Do they think that they can hold both ends of the earth's girdle . . . and the middle too? That's folly! They will fill themselves with profit and let the rest of the world go slam! I cry for peace! May God so grant it to us all! That is the real treasure which we should cherish. All good things stem only from peace which is not based upon treachery."

In Rondel CCXIX he writes that he longs only to return to Blois. "I have eaten enough big fishes and drunk enough wine from Grois; I want to go home to Blois. Henceforth at the court of the king I shall take no more thought for Grenoble or Milanese. I'll go home and confess my sins before Good Friday comes. I care for no more adventures."

In a third and most curious poem he tackles the subject of language in a most unusual way; for here is a multilingual poet and a consummate artist treating one of the most complicated linguistic and psychological problems of the world—the relationship of thought to language:

Rondel CCXI

"The sly translator of my thought
Speaks many tongues quite fluently;
One day he spoke a savagery
Which startled me, as well it ought.

"Then into French the message wrought
In language phrased explicitly;
The sly translator of my thought
Speaks many tongues quite fluently.

"But when my heart his meaning caught
He said: 'You misunderstood me.
I never said it purposely.'
In what strange country were you taught,
O sly translator of my thought?"

Once back in France, for the sake of the record, Duke Charles reiterated his claim to Milan. He continued to negotiate with his friends to the very last, until Milan hailed Francesco Sforza. In 1450, the year of the Jubilee in Rome, the young and victorious captain entered Milan. French lawyers and jurists filed the letters and Duke Charles's claim in their archives. When a more favorable day arrived, possibly under the dynamic leadership of some younger Duke of Orléans and some younger King of France, their rights would be reasserted. This would be the story of another century; for, as Machiavelli recorded, "Francesco Sforza, through being well armed, became, from private citizen, Duke of Milan; his sons, through wishing to avoid the fatigues and the hardships of war, from dukes became private citizens."

After having lost trace of Duke Charles for three years, Olivier de la Marche resumes his account of this deed in Italy. He says that the lord of Arguel and his Burgundian lords who had passed the Alps with Orléans returned home completely ruined. The duke was not even able to pay them for their services. There was no city of Milan conquered, and nothing but hardship for all involved. The duke remained at Lyons until he saw his last hope disappear and until his Burgundian friends were reduced to selling their armor, their saddles, and their harnesses in order to finance their return trip. Arguel even had to part with several of his estates and domains, which were bought up by his angry father, the Prince of Orange. Instead of settling them upon his oldest son again, the prince granted the estates to his other heirs. Thus disappeared the House of Arguel.

After attending a tournament at Châlons, the duke and duchess went up to Burgundy to justify themselves to Duke Philip, and then returned home. At this time Olivier de la Marche met Duke Charles's niece and nephew, the children of his sister Marguerite. This lady had married Richard of Brittany during the duke's captivity in England. Her children were both exceptional, says the chronicler—the niece of Arguel for her beauty, and the boy Francis, "handsome, virtuous and of great presence." This niece and nephew replaced the children Duke Charles did not have.

A principal reason for which King Charles VII could not have sent an army to aid his cousin of Orléans was that the war had begun again with England. Seizing upon a pretext, the fact that the city of Le Mans had not been returned to France as promised by Suffolk, King Charles gave Count Dunois and the Duke of Alençon the signal to advance, the former into Normandy and the latter to recover his domains. Lord Talbot and Edmund Beaufort, Duke of Somerset, were caught in Normandy without an army and without the support of Queen Marguerite. In a few months Count Dunois had reconquered Normandy, where the English garrison numbered their troops only by the dozens.

The great event was the seizure of Rouen by King Charles, Count Dunois, and various attendant lords and prelates. The Duke of Somerset and Lord Talbot had withdrawn into the city with probably not more than a thousand men. During the whole campaign the tone of the war had changed. The rules of chivalry again prevailed. King Charles and the English nobles met and settled the combat by gentleman's agreement. It would not be necessary to recapture the coastal cities of Normandy; Somerset would hand them over to France. The French king accepted a blanket ransom for Somerset, his wife, his children, his possessions, and the English garrison in Rouen who were then free to cross the Channel. Lord Talbot would remain as a hostage until the sum was forthcoming. It made a great difference to the French to realize that the King and Queen of England were both of French blood and that the Beauforts were old friends.

On December 10, 1449, King Charles VII made his official entry into Rouen, capital of Normandy, while Countess Dunois and Lord Talbot watched the procession. It was one of the proudest days of the king's life and even of all French history. First in the parade rode Count Dunois, who carried before him a golden sword set with rubies that was worth 20,000 écus. After him came the nobleman who had fought throughout the entire war, the Marshal de La Fayette. Then came William Cousinot, the Bailiff of Rouen, and the chronicler. After him rode the Chancellor of France, Jean Juvénal des Ursins. Just before the king rode the Gascon captain who had survived a thousand perils—Pothon de Xaintrailles, who then bore the proud title of Bailiff of Berry. Behind the king rode his brother-in-law, René of Anjou.

On February 15, 1450, King Charles VII ordered an official investigation into the trial of Joan of Arc. He said he wished to know about her trial and if she had been duly punished or if she had been unjustly done to death. This second trial was to last from May 2,

1452, to May 14, 1456. Because of the great numbers of witnesses summoned, and because of the various displacements incurred by the court so that they could hear testimony from the various regions of France where Joan had lived her short life, it was the greatest trial of the century. Not only was it fitting to inaugurate it in Rouen, where she had been tried, sentenced, and burned. It was only possible to inaugurate it there in 1450 or as soon as Rouen was reconquered. It was doubly fortunate that this retrial occurred after the deaths of those people who had condemned Joan, for otherwise they would have had to see their procedures and their findings thus thrown open to question.

The Cardinal of England was dead and so was Joan's judge, the Bishop of Beauvais. John Duke of Bedford and his Duchess Anne were dead. Richard de Beauchamp, Earl of Warwick, was dead. On the other hand, her constant companions—Count Dunois and John Duke of Alençon—were still alive. La Hire would never be able to testify, for he had died, nor would the infamous Lord Marshal Gilles de Rais be able to come to her defense. Of all the great lords who had been profoundly influenced by her life, one could not testify. He was King Charles VII. The second who would not testify because he knew nothing from first-hand observation was Charles of Orléans.

In February the Duke of Orléans, whatever he may have felt about the relapsed heretic whom the English had condemned to death, had such personal reasons for grief that it is no wonder this year caused him to withdraw voluntarily from public life. In February of 1450, while King Charles VII was ordering the investigation in Rouen, the Parliament in England was impeaching William de la Pole, Duke of Suffolk. The major cause of this disgrace was the truce that he and his friend of Orléans had enacted in Tours some years earlier.

At his trial William de la Pole testified that he had borne arms for thirty-four years, that he had been a Knight of the Garter for thirty years, that he had fought abroad in the wars without going home to England for seventeen years, and that he had spent the last fifteen years in England near the person of King Henry VI. He reminded his fellow peers that he had begged not to be sent to France to negotiate the truce, basing his objection on the grounds that he and Duke Charles of Orléans were close personal friends. The king had granted the Duke of Suffolk a pardon before the fact. Suffolk also reminded the court how he had been captured by Count Dunois, to whom he owed his life, and how he had paid 20,000

pounds from his own money as a ransom. He did not remind the
court of his mental anguish, how while he paced his prison cell in
Orléans, he was threatened. Someone had slipped into his hand
one of those little pieces of folded vellum, a prophecy telling what
would happen to a man who dared combat Joan of Arc!

The charges made against William de la Pole, as they appear in
the Rolls of Parliament for February 7, 1450, were many:

"First . . . the said Duke treacherously excited, counselled, provoked, and comforted the Earl of Dunois, Bastard of Orleans . . .
and Master William Cousinot, enemies. . . .

". . . at Westminster, . . . and divers other tymes and places . . .
for taking of money, and other excessive promises to him made by
Charles, Duke of Orliaunce, your enemy, counselled and steered of
hym selfe only, your highness to enlarge and deliver out of prison
the said Duke of Orliaunce . . . to th' entent that the said Charles,
calling hym selfe King of France, schuld recover, gete,—your said
realme of Fraunce, . . . by the wyle, subtill councill, might and ayde
of the said Duke of Orliaunce.

". . . on the first day of May [1439] at London . . . the same
Duke of Suffolk . . . traiterously councelled, comforted, stered and
provoked the said Duke of Orliaunce . . . to make and raise open
war ayenst you in France and Normandy."

On March 9th the Duke of Suffolk was brought from the Tower
of London to answer the two bills against him. On March 13th he
knelt before the king and denied all eight charges. He laid the
blame on Adam Molins, Bishop of Chichester, which was an intelligent and humane move because that bishop was dead. Then
Suffolk was ordered into exile for five years beginning the 1st of
May. On April 30th he therefore embarked at Ipswich for Flanders.

On that day he wrote a letter to his eight-year-old son, in which
he said:

"And to draw to you aid and to your comp(any good) and virtuous
men, and such as ben of good conversacion, and of truth, and be
them shall ye never be deseyved, ner repente you off . . . And I
wyll be to you as good lord and fader as my hert can thynke.

Wreten of myn hand,
The day of my departing from this land,
Your trewe and lovying fader,
SUFFOLK."

Two ships and a spinner or pinnace took the duke off the Suffolk coast to Dover. He dispatched the pinnace with letters to friends in Calais asking if he could land there. Before his eyes he saw his pinnace intercepted by large ships that were hovering near. Then one of the large ships drew alongside and ordered him to board her. The duke obeyed.

As he climbed aboard, the master of the vessel greeted him: "Welcome aboard, traitor."

Then the duke was asked if his two ships and the pinnace intended to defend him. At his negative reply he was informed that he could dispose of a day and a night during which to prepare himself for death. He was allowed a confessor.

On May 2nd William de la Pole, Duke of Suffolk, was made to descend into the ship's boat alongside where a block and an ax had been laid. An "Irish crew member" ordered the nobleman to lie down, stretch out, and prepare to die by the sword. A rusted weapon was used, so dull that six strokes were required to sever his head. The body was then stripped of his russet gown and velvet doublet. He was thrown on the sands at Dover, or his head was impaled on a pole, beside the body. Mock dirges were composed to commemorate his assassination. His crew was set free.

Such a death was an ignoble end for so brilliant a career. England was plunged into civil war. The House of York would oust the Lancastrian red rose, for so many defenders of the Crown had died. The list grew longer and longer. Duke Charles had been connected with the deaths of Joan of Arc, William de la Pole, and Adam Molins. He had been a friend of the Cardinal of England, and he had been a friend of the Duke of Suffolk, whom he had entertained at Blois Castle only a few years before. Some scholars believe that it was Suffolk and not Duke Charles who made the English versions of the latter's French poetry.

An English political poem reveals the hatred for William de la Pole. The poem laments the fact that the "Root is dead" (Bedford), the "Swan is gone" (Gloucester), the "Bear is bound" (Warwick), the "White Hart is put out of mind" (Arundel), and so is the "Velvet Hat that covered . . . from storme" (Cardinal Beaufort). In the same poem Suffolk is called the "Ape Clog." No one in England protested his murder. France was otherwise occupied in preparing to drive the English from Guyenne; then the war would be finally ended.

Duke Charles could have been referring to the death of his friend

when in Rondel CLXXIX he said that because "Plaisance" is dead
that particular May he is garbed in black. He says he is so dressed
out of duty and that the sight of his discomforted heart is pitiful
to see. The bad news came to him on a stormy day when it rained
so hard that the gates to the fields were shut . . . because "Plaisance"
was dead.

His distaste is apparent in a poem that follows shortly after the
one just described:

RONDEL CLXXXVII

"The world has seen enough of me
And I of it, I haste to say.
I know of nothing new today
That I would give a fig to see.

"My eyes survey life's misery,
Weep when grown men their grief display;
The world has seen enough of me
And I of it, I haste to say.

"A friend's sworn word is bought dearly;
Nobody sells for little pay
Because of which let me conveigh
My sharp complaint, and reasonably:
The world has seen enough of me.

XIII [*1450–1456*] TEN YEARS AFTER HIS RE-
turn to France, Duke Charles
could look about him and see visible evidence of great changes. The
country was well on its way to a unity and a prosperity that it had
not known for forty years, while England was plunged into civil
war and Burgundy's power was being curbed. King Charles VII
had a standing army, or *gendarmerie*. He and his generals by 1450
had reconquered Normandy. They held all of northern France except for such coastal cities as Calais, which they could not take
from England without commencing open war with Burgundy. The
King of France ruled with a new assurance. Historians could not
explain the change in the king. What had transformed this timorous
dauphin into a wise and capable ruler?

Some believed his metamorphosis was due to the confidence
Agnès Sorel had given him when she gave him her love. Others
believed it was due to the fact that he was so well "served" by the
financier Jacques Cœur, William Cousinot, Jean Juvénal, and others.
No one in France took any account of the Duke of Gloucester's
theory, that the change in the king was related to Duke Charles of
Orléans. In subsequent ages this king would be known as "The
Victorious."

The Burgundian chronicler Georges Chastellain, a brilliant writer
and a thoughtful man, tried to solve the mystery of King Charles
VII. Every subsequent historian has followed suit. In Chapter XLIII
of his History, Chastellain devotes space to a character analysis of
the French king. As to corpulence, says Chastellain, he was thin!
As to physical endowment, his foundation was feeble! His gait was
peculiar, without proportion. His complexion was wan, but fairly
attractive. His words were well phrased, elegantly put, and subtle,
although he was not an outstanding speaker. His demeanor was
graceful. He had, says Chastellain, three sovereign vices: changeable-

ness, diffidence, and—most annoying and most of all—envy of the third person.

After a very poor and even a wretched beginning, he made a glorious end to his reign. He corrected himself, "perhaps by the will of God," from several of his shortcomings. It seemed likely that his original errors had been due partially to the violence of his early associates, men such as Tanneguy du Chastel. When Chastellain makes this remark, one can see that he is wondering what effect the new counselors have had.

The industry of the French king, Chastellain adds, was really a marvel. His memory was excellent, quick, and sharp. He had a good knowledge of history. He told stories most entertainingly. He was a good Latinist. He was wise in council. He had managed to clear dangerous forest passages of bands of highwaymen. By 1450 the main roads in France were more or less safe for travel. His cities were peaceful and contented. The various ethnic groups within his realm were harmonious. King Charles was quick to honor those who did their duty and equally quick to punish deviation. For example, after the conquest of Normandy he raised Count Dunois immediately to the Lieutenant-Generalship of France.

Georges Chastellain further points out what was common knowledge among courtiers in France, but at the same time a well-guarded secret—that King Charles was an inveterate "corrupter of women." During the lifetime of his mother-in-law, Queen Yolande of Sicily, the king had been obliged to cover his sexual excesses under a cloak of stealth. After her death he had openly flaunted Agnès Sorel before his wife, before the burgesses of Paris, and before foreign visitors to his court. It was known that in order to keep her position Agnès Sorel was obliged to furnish the king with new conquests continually. During the fifties his appetites increased radically, but he was more careful not to let the outside world learn the real extent of his vice.

"He was no place sure, no place strong," remarks Chastellain in summary. "He always feared lest he perish under the sword because of the murder of John the Fearless. This fear caused him to regard Duke Philip of Burgundy with a venomous and heinous imagination!" He was justly called the Victorious, nevertheless. Before the coming of Joan at Orléans, his downfall had been imminent. In 1428 King Charles, then the dauphin, was considering an attempt to escape either into Spain or into Scotland. Twenty years later he had driven the English out of northwestern France and was preparing to dislodge them from Guyenne. He had curbed the power of his warring nobles—even that of Burgundy. He had not made the fatal error of sending an army into Italy while English troops were still on French soil. Another historian, François Eudes de Mézeray, remarked cogently that this king "could have been called the Fortunate if he had had another son and another father." Mézeray is assuming that King Charles VII was the son of the insane King Charles VI and not therefore another brother of Duke Charles of Orléans.

The king was very unfortunate indeed in his son and heir, Louis. This dauphin had been plotting against his father at least since 1439. No measures had succeeded in winning either his allegiance or his love, to say nothing of his elementary courtesy. Duke Charles had already felt his influence, for the dauphin had sided with Francesco Sforza against the Orléanist claim to Milan. At court he was a constant danger, for he hated both Agnès Sorel and the merchant prince Jacques Cœur. His nefarious plots were felt strongly in Burgundy, where the dauphin led Duke Philip's son and heir astray as much as possible, and this was not difficult. Duke Philip, growing old rapidly and in poor health, was already having trouble controlling his son, the future Charles the Rash. The dauphin loudly based part of his grievances on a chronic lack of funds. He borrowed money right and left. He was always in debt, despite his generous allowance, and always mindful of those who refused him cash. His chief passion in life was an unbridled desire for power. His second passion was hunting.

This dauphin was held largely responsible for the untimely death of his wife, the pretty Princess Marguerite of Scotland. He had shown her no affection and no admiration, although she was vivacious, learned, and very clever. He had allowed stories concerning her morals to be carried to the king. One was an unlikely story of her having been found in mixed company after dark in an unlighted room—or, as the princess tried to explain, in a room lighted by a large fireplace. Her slanderers claimed that she was never pregnant because she cinched her waistline too tightly. In a country where she was so unwelcome and so unloved, the girl was happy to die. "I say fie on life," she said as she expired.

The death of this gallant princess increased the dauphin's reputation for cruelty. Too many charming stories had been told about the pert and vivacious young girl during the peaceful years of the realm. Once she was said by the chroniclers to have come across the poet Alain Chartier asleep in an orchard. She bent down and kissed him on the lips. When her attendants expressed their shocked surprise, the princess replied that she wanted only to kiss the lips that had formed such lovely poems. It was a pretty story, quite typical of the picture the century had formed of this Marguerite. However, Alain Chartier had been dead for some years before this time. If she kissed a poet, it must have been either Duke Charles or his friend René of Anjou.

During the early forties the dauphin had been cordial to his "great uncle" of Orléans. On one occasion he sent him the present of a mule with a gracious note in his own handwriting to the effect that he would like his uncle to send him a greyhound. Under this pretense of cordiality, however, he hated Duke Charles. First of all, the duke had withdrawn the great nobles from the dauphin and attached them to the king. Second, the dauphin knew that his own conduct had often been a subject for discussion in the "great council" where the king spoke openly of his son's treachery and asked Duke Charles for advice. Then, too, the dauphin was aware that his dealings with Francesco Sforza were known and condemned. In order to be avenged while he waited impatiently to become King of France, Louis started stories concerning the Duchess Marie. Duke Charles had been married now for over ten years. His wife was a strikingly beautiful blonde in her twenties. There were no children. Therefore, Louis told ribald stories insinuating the duke's impotence and his wife's flirtations.

In 1450 the duke and his duchess rode up to Burgundy for a session of the Golden Fleece. They were not to meet Duke Philip again for some time. Shortly after their return to Blois a severe war broke out between the Duke of Burgundy and the citizens of Ghent. It lasted well over two years and was marked by wholesale massacres. In Orléans, on the contrary, there was not the slightest trouble. Duke Charles administered his duchy as easily as one would wind a clock. He dispensed justice, took trips on the river from Orléans to Blois, and spent happy hours studying, reading, and discussing literature with his professor from Asti. The Italian was busily translating Duke Charles's French poems into Latin.

News, both good and bad, reached them from the outside world. The French had won a great victory at Formigny, which completed the Normandy campaign. The duke ordered the bells to be rung throughout his duchy. Then he bade farewell to Count Dunois, who had to tear himself away from his building projects—for Count Dunois, like his father, was very much interested in architecture—

and ride off to war in southwestern France. Edmund Beaufort, Duke of Somerset, was ransomed and returned to England. Duke Charles knew Queen Marguerite could depend upon this last brother of the cardinal. Agnès Sorel had died on February 11, 1450, after an acute inflammation of the digestive tract. People in France said that she had been poisoned. King Charles VII was deeply grieved.

No one attempted to poison the Duchess Marie, however. Her life was smooth and tranquil. Not only did Duke Charles keep her near him and take her on his travels; he admitted her to his discussions of literature, and he taught her how to compose poetry. The day he copied one of her compositions in his own book must have been a very happy day for the young duchess.

It is not that trouble could not have started in the Duchy of Orléans, had Duke Charles been another sort of ruler. His subjects had suffered cruelly from the war and even more cruelly since the deliverance of Orléans. Their first suffering had been physical, and therefore easily forgotten. Their other and continued suffering was mental.

If Reginald of Chartres, King Charles VII, and others in France had tranquilly accepted the verdict handed down in Rouen on the girl Joan of Arc, the citizens of Orléans had not accepted it. They saw Joan's old mother year in and year out. They saw her brothers, whose nobility had recently been confirmed by the duke. They had delighted in the morality play given them by the Lord Marshal de Rais. Every year on May 8th, the anniversary of her deliverance of Orléans, they celebrated Joan of Arc with prayers and processions. Yet judges in Rouen had said that she was a heretic, that she had denied her voices, that she had confessed herself an impostor. The rest of France might believe this. In Orléans people somehow could not reconcile this story with what they had witnessed with their own eyes. Even in Poitiers folks pointed to a stone and said that she had stepped on it in order to mount that white horse of hers. If they asked Duke Charles, he could say only that one must abide by the court's decision.

Professor Antonio Astesano, of course, had not seen Joan of Arc. The poem he had written in her honor was a versification of a Latin letter sent to Duke Filippo Maria Visconti in Milan by a Perceval de Boulainvilliers from Orléans on July 21, 1429. Professor Astesano had written his poem in the first fire of his youth, as a boy of eighteen. Certain details reproduced in this poem from the letter were hard to reconcile with the court's alleged findings.

According to Boulainvilliers, Joan had said to her voices when they urged her to travel to the dauphin: "What am I to do and how shall I do it? *I* shall go? For I do not know the road, I am not acquainted with these people, they will not believe me, I shall be only a laughingstock among them and rightly so. What could be sillier than for a girl to say she will save France, and command armies, and win back victory from the enemy? What is more ridiculous than for a girl to wear men's clothing?"

Then the voices had answered: "The King of Heaven asks it and orders it, so that you are not to ask further how these things shall be done, since just as the will of God is done in Heaven, so will it be on earth."

Antonio Astesano also included those details about Joan that had struck the letter writer. She had a girl's pretty voice. Her facial expression was joyous. She adored the King of France. She was so hardy that she could keep on her armor for six days and six nights without once having to take it from her body. She burst into tears easily. By 1429 she had already told people in Orléans that the Duke of Orléans would be liberated.

There was one other detail in this letter and also in Astesano's poem. Joan had heard her voices for some years and seen her saints also. However, her vision of them became clearer suddenly from the day she learned that the Duke of Salisbury had actually set out from England for Orléans!

Since her trial and her death, both of which were known only from the official letter of King Henry VI, chance gossip, and various reports from witnesses at the trial, Professor Astesano had become more guarded in his admiration. During these years he said, "Joan of Arc, who we thought was sent from God." This could very well have been Duke Charles's attitude also, for he was not likely to have been willing to contradict a judgment of a court, particularly since he did not know what the findings of that court had been. The notes of the trial were still under seal at Rouen.

It is also probable during these years that Duke Charles, Count Dunois, John Duke of Alençon, the Duchess Marie, and the Italian professor discussed the rumors concerning Joan of Arc as well as the mysterious prophecies. They had certainly read Jean Gerson's treatise. In his poem Astesano also mentioned historical parallels— Lucretia, Penthesilea, and Camilla. Perhaps Duke Charles was aware that certain fertile imaginations were not content with accepting Joan of Arc as the simple country girl from the marshes of Lorraine.

Certain aspects of her story, even as she told it, were not credible to a rational mind. Since the court had said that she was not sent from God, then how was she sent? If the voices she heard were not those of saints, then whose voices were they?

Other answers were forthcoming, and perhaps Duke Charles heard them also. One theory was that Joan of Arc was a princess. This is the theory that Shakespeare later heard and used. Certain people claimed that Joan of Arc was a daughter of Louis of France and Queen Isabeau, that she had been secretly raised, or substituted for a dead child of the family in Domrémy. If Joan was a princess and secretly raised, then one could understand how she had learned to ride, wear armor, and use a lance and a sword. That would also explain how she knew about her sword hidden in the Church of Saint Catherine-de-Fierbois, near Orléans. It would explain how she recognized the dauphin and why she was so eager to save Orléans— to crown her brother as king, and to deliver Duke Charles from his English prison. It would explain her close relationship with her brother Dunois and with her niece's husband, John Duke of Alençon.

All this supposition would seem to indicate that it was as imperative for Duke Charles as for the king to scotch such rumors by requesting an investigation into her trial at Rouen. Since King Charles VII did not protest her capture and trial, or appeal to the Pope to stop the trial—if he wanted to stop it—it may have been Duke Charles who suggested this investigation to the king. The duke was living with Astesano at his court—a good reason for a continued interest in Joan of Arc. The Boulainvilliers family still remained at Orléans and Blois. Other faithful servants of the duke were the very ones who had seen Joan in Orléans—in particular, William Cousinot, the chronicler. Then, too, it may be assumed that the Duchess Marie encouraged her husband to clarify Joan's sentence. The Duchess Marie had been raised by Duchess Isabella of Burgundy, and this lady had worked very hard indeed to fulfill Joan's third prophecy or promise.

In the city and duchy of Orléans the interest in Joan of Arc was therefore as strong in 1450 as it had been twenty years earlier. The citizens were overjoyed when they had the visit in 1452 of William d'Estouteville, a legate from Pope Nicholas V. He arrived from Rome. In February he was at Tours and in June at Orléans. Both he and the Inquisitor Jean Bréhal had been appointed to make a preliminary investigation that would determine whether or not Joan's case merited reexamination and whether or not there appeared to have been a mistrial. Both prelates were eminent and learned. Duke Charles and his duchess received them with every honor. After several months of gathering testimony in France, the prelates returned to Rome. Such a thorough study required the opinions of a great many experts in civil and ecclesiastical law. The responsibility was enormous. It was necessary to make haste slowly, for the general public was still feeling the repercussions of Joan's career.

The great news of 1453 was the end of the Hundred Years' War. The chronicler Jacques du Clercq says that he had been so busy re-counting Duke Philip's war with the City of Ghent that he could not speak earlier of the conquest of Guyenne for fear of "interlacing" these two separate stories. King Charles VII had thought southern France conquered, when suddenly Queen Marguerite sent the aged "war dog" Talbot from England with an army to Bordeaux. After spending all winter in preparation, the king, Count Dunois, and the artillerymen went south in June. In July they besieged Chastillon, which Lord Talbot, mounted on a hackney because of his extreme age, hastened to defend. Lord Talbot was killed at Chastillon. He had commanded the English forces unarmed because he had sworn at Rouen, when the king accepted a ransom for him and allowed him to return home, that he would never bear arms against France again.

Later in July the king, this time assisted by John of Angoulême, besieged Cadillac and took it by storm. Then the French army tackled the large city of Bordeaux on the Gironde. This siege was marked by naval battles in the river between English ships and French ships that had come down from Brittany and other areas of northern France. Rather than pursue a long and murderous siege, the king decided to treat with the inhabitants and with the English. He agreed to accept the surrender and oaths of fealty of the leaders, to allow the English to depart in peace, and to exile only those among the French nobles who had previously gone to England to incite war against him. This agreement was ratified on October 19, 1453. On that day King Charles VII was able to say that all France then swore fealty to him, that there was not an English soldier in his domains from the Pyrenees to Flanders, with the sole exception of two small ports and Calais, to which he had no access.

Aside from this last treaty of October 19, 1453, there does not seem to have been any other ratification of peace between England and France. The Hundred Years' War had ended, however, whether so stipulated or not. France did not fear King Henry VI of England. In 1453 he became insane for the first time, recovering briefly the following year. Not long after this sad event there were ugly stories in England concerning Queen Marguerite, Edmund Beaufort (the Duke of Somerset who had surrendered at Rouen), and the birth of Prince Edward of Wales.

In Blois Castle Duke Charles, now fifty-seven years old, celebrated in a ballad the end of the war. He said: "Ah, how I now see the English confounded! Rejoice, frank kingdom of France! Now everyone understands that God hates the English since they have lost both courage and might—they who thought through overweening arrogance to conquer us and to hold us in bondage—they who falsely claimed that France was their right of inheritance! God has joined our side. He has laid low their pride and has returned Guyenne and Normandy to thee!

"Long years ago, O France, thou wert excluded from God's love like the wicked sinner Thaïs; in those days the English paraded with baubles, pomps, and tyranny like a sorcerer's sabbath.

"Have not the English often betrayed their own kings? Yes, indeed they have, as we all know. And even now the king of their country is in doubtful balance. Not an Englishman hesitates to speak ill of him. So do they show by such improper language that they would willingly outrage him. The question of who will be their king is a subject of debate among these people! Because of such a disgraceful state of affairs, what shall I say to thee, O France? . . . That God chastises them with his rod and that He has returned to thee both Guyenne and Normandy!

"O King of France, you have won this victory! Your actions have been as perfect as you are courageous and wise! I thank God, O France, for this great happiness. Fortune is now on good terms with us. See how she has joined with you to return Guyenne and Normandy!"

The duke does not devote a poem to the other great event of 1453, but the chroniclers devote several chapters to it. On May 29th Constantinople fell to the Turks, bringing to an end the Eastern Roman Empire and plunging Greece into slavery. In the annals of the Ottoman Empire it noted that as "the season of snow, of ice, of frost" drew to its close, "the sweet springtime followed it." The rose and the "amorous nightingale" and the "earth covered with its green carpet" awaited the legions of just Mohammed II whose faithful soon pitched their pavilions in the flowered meadows that were honored by the presence of "such true sons."

The chronicler Du Clercq, who had access to documents giving infinite details of the fall of Constantinople, tells how the emperor died and then had his head cut off, how his lady was carried off by the Turks to be a concubine, and how noble ladies and their daughters who had taken refuge in Saint Sofia were raped. Venetian galleys waited along the coast until noon and were thus able to save around four hundred Christians. An army from Venice arrived one day too late; the city had fallen. Other people were saved by galleys from Genoa. In Europe people said the Turkish sultan was more cruel than Nero, more ambitious than either Caesar or Alexander. Mohammed II had history read to him daily. He said that for a ruler like him it was only one step from Constantinople to Venice, and another to Rome, and another to Milan.

In February of 1454 Duke Philip swore a solemn oath that he would proceed to Constantinople under the banner of France, or alone with the banner of France, or in the company of other lords, and that he would do his utmost to drive the Turks from Europe. His son and his major vassals swore likewise, in written oaths to which they affixed their names. Duke Charles remained in Blois. He made neither an oath concerning Constantinople nor a poem. In 1453 his friend René of Anjou traveled into Italy to try to regain his inheritance of Naples, but Francesco Sforza and the Dauphin Louis foiled his efforts. King René returned as he had gone, by the coastal road. Duke Charles only sent his friend the Professor Astesano on a private embassy into Italy.

In 1454 Georges Chastellain noted the presence of Duke Charles and the Duchess Marie on a diplomatic voyage into Burgundy. The reason was the marriage of Duke Philip's only son and the daughter of the Duke of Bourbon. Since the latter duke was ill with gout at home, his lady went to meet Duke Philip along with the Duke and Duchess of Orléans. It was a very noisy and happy reunion, says Chastellain. For three days the negotiations for this marriage were deadlocked, however, because Duke Philip required that Chinon Castle be a part of the girl's dowry to his son, while her father wanted it settled on his son. The Duchess of Bourbon was beside herself with disappointment, caught as she was between the stubbornness of her husband and that of her brother of Burgundy. She tried tears and then "pitiful words," but nothing could move Duke

Philip, although he was fond of his sister. Finally Duke Charles and his duchess abandoned the attempt to arbitrate and went home. They could see that Duke Philip was more interested in talking about his forthcoming journey to Constantinople.

As late as 1455 Duke Philip was trying to persuade King Charles VII to allow him to take the oriflamme from Saint-Denis and use it as a rallying flag for the noblemen of western Europe. While the King of France was quite willing to assume the administration of Burgundy during the old duke's absence, he was not willing to allow any person other than himself to march forth with the sacred banner of France. Duke Philip never did leave for Constantinople.

In September Duke Charles and the Duchess Marie attended the wedding of their old friend René of Anjou to the Lady Joan de Laval. Theirs was a love match. The Lady Joan was as proud of her husband as if he had succeeded in winning his inheritance of Naples. She was as proud of King René as the Duchess Marie was of her husband, who also had failed to conquer the Duchy of Milan. The De Laval family were closely connected with the Alençon family and thus doubly dear to Duke Charles. Guy XIV de Laval had seen Joan of Arc and had written a famous letter about her to his mother. The old Duchess Anne de Laval was, in fact, a fine mother and a remarkable woman and warrior in her own way. She had fought a sharp and prolonged war with the Bishop of Rennes over a point of feudal priority in a church ceremony, and when she could not force the bishop to accede, she appealed to Pope Pius II. This prelate, the former Aeneas Silvius, was finally obliged to transfer the old lady to the jurisdiction of the Archbishop of Tours. The notorious Gilles de Rais was also a De Laval. All this family had therefore championed Joan of Arc.

King René after his marriage took his bride into Provence where they lived happily united by poetry, celebrating their loves in a new manner—or in an old one rediscovered—under the guise of a shepherd and his shepherdess. Duke Charles of Orléans was the most honored and most beloved guest at the wedding. Among his personal friends his wisdom, his chivalry, his noble character, and his poetry were all esteemed and appreciated. King René and his bride were really imitating Duke Charles and the Duchess Marie when they discovered in their turn that a mutual respect growing from a love for poetry unites a husband and a wife.

The one other traditional ally of Duke Charles was not present at the wedding of King René. This was the new Count of Armagnac,

Jean V, who acceded to the title in 1450. His sister Marie was the present Duchess of Alençon, a lady who had a wide reputation for saintliness like that of her relative Bonnie of Armagnac. No one invited Count Jean V of Armagnac to any wedding. No one, in fact—not even Duke Charles of Orleans—cared to be reminded of his ancient alliance. Count Jean IV, who had written a letter to Joan of Arc and received an answer from her, had been punished by the Dauphin Louis for his various crimes and offenses. Count Jean IV was an angel compared to his successor.

Count Jean V of Armagnac minted money without permission from the King of France. He also styled himself "Count by the grace of God." However, his personal life was the scandal of Europe. Count Jean was madly in love with his youngest sister, Isabelle, and she with him. They lived together as man and wife, and they had two children. Their union was all the more scandalous because Isabelle was a perfect beauty. The incest had been reported to the Pope, who ordered Count Jean to desist and do penance. The lovers therefore parted. No sooner had Count Jean received absolution, however, than the two returned to each other's arms. Not only that. Count Jean forced a local church to unite them in holy matrimony. He was forthwith excommunicated.

When King Charles sent an army into Armagnac to arrest this count, the two lovers defied the king's summons and fled into hiding in the mountains of Aragón. The king's troops, after great difficulties, hunted them down and brought the count back to Paris for trial. Even then Count Jean showed no signs of amending his ways. From prison in Paris, while awaiting trial, he still wrote letters to his sister Isabelle, which he addressed: "To my true companion forever." Their letters were, of course, intercepted. Jean V was condemnd to walk to Rome and beg his bread all along the road. There the Pope took pity on him, gave him absolution, a heavy penance, ordered him to reform, received his promise to that effect, and sent him home. His sister had retired to a convent—a tradition among the pious ladies of Armagnac.

When the Pope asked King Charles to reinstate Count Jean, the French king refused because he knew that the rebellious nobleman had taken Isabelle from her convent and that they were living to-gether again. Their tragic story did not end until 1473, when Jean V was executed before the eyes of his sister Isabelle, after which an abortion was performed on her and she was for the last time relegated to a convent.

Such a story scandalized France, and was told throughout Europe. Duke Charles and his duchess did their best to protect Jean V's sister, the Duchess of Alençon. This lady was having troubles of her own. Not only had Duke John of Alençon become a drunkard since the death of Joan of Arc; he had not forgiven King Charles VII —ostensibly for not having helped him pay his ransom or recover his domains from the English. He was so embittered against the king that he had begun to negotiate with the Duke of York in England—the enemy of the Lancastrian king and queen.

Almost everyone had his troubles in the 1450's: Duke Philip with Ghent and his undependable son; King Charles with the death or murder of Agnès Sorel, with the war, with his hateful dauphin, who kept trying to usurp the throne; Queen Marguerite with rebellious barons in England; Jean V with his loves in Armagnac; and also the Duke of Alençon. In Blois, however, they were long years with days too short for study, reading, and poetry. The House of Orléans was in good posture. Count Dunois had returned safely to his architecture. Count John of Angoulême lived happily with his wife. Duke Charles reigned in a new kind of court—a court of poetry.

The duke turned to poetry as if the days and years that remained as he neared the age of sixty would never be long enough to put into graceful words all his crowding thoughts, all he had learned in his busy life, all the beauty he still saw about him, even though the melancholy that had accompanied him since the murder of his father and the death of the Princess Isabelle was always near the surface. Everyone he loved came under the spell of his poetry and eventually caught the fever enough to write verses of his own. Thus the personal book of Duke Charles is a kind of family album in which he treasured poems from his friends. His love in many cases blinded him as to their poetic ability, which makes the selections all the more interesting. It would seem that the old duke wanted to turn every person he knew and loved into a poet. This was his great passion.

"When I find repose in my own lands," said Duke Charles, "I hardly know what countenance to assume; for Fortune loaded my back with work from my early childhood. How else can I express this to you? . . . I work through force of habit. Thus clothed in my thoughts I make castles in Spain or in France. I draw up ordinances for my domains beyond the mountains. Every day I settle a thousand or more problems, even when I find rest and quiet at home. . . . I have become as old and as gray as a cat. . . . People speak to me, and it goes in one ear and out the other."

Principal among the authors whose works he inscribed was his old friend King René. He and Duke Charles engaged in several literary contests, several battles of wits on themes such as: Which one of us has suffered more torments of love? Which one has been the more cruelly used by Fortune? Of all those who engaged in literary controversy with him, King René was the most clever and therefore the one Duke Charles enjoyed the most. In 1457 King René unwisely referred to a secret the duke had confided in him, to the effect that the Duke of Orléans had been in love with an English lady during his years of imprisonment. According to King René, Beauty—still unnamed—had been a real woman.

Duke Charles addressed a poem to his beloved John of Alençon, also. The answer he received was well-nigh nonsensical, but he copied it into his album nevertheless. In it there are poems from Olivier de la Marche, whom he had taken on the tour of Burgundy prior to the crossing of the Alps, and poems to and from "Georges," who is probably the chronicler Chastellain. Various young noblemen passing through Blois have their lovesick verses in the collection, and the duke's amused replies that give bantering advice to expend their energies more profitably and not to presume that he is a dupe to their pretended broken hearts. Then there are two poems from a Philip de Boulainvilliers, a young man who was the duke's favorite and whom he intended as his heir. This young man may have been a son to the Perceval who wrote the famous letter relating the coming of Joan of Arc. There are poems from Doctor Caillau, the duke's personal physician, whom he retained on an annual basis. Then, of course, there are the gently melancholy verses of the Duchess Marie. Duke Charles teases her kindly about her favorite novel. It seems that the lady adored the story of Troilus and Cressida.

The battle of wits that took place over the years at Blois Castle was not always on either an elevated or a melancholy theme. Duke Charles had his own earthy sense of humor. He enjoyed reprimanding the young swains who sighed amorously while all the time getting some local girl pregnant and being called upon publicly to come to her support. The duke made jokes about his lawyer, whom he called Master Stephen Nominative because his inclinations were copulative. Thus the poems indicate private jokes and are reminders of amusing adventures and anecdotes that the duke wanted to recall.

As the poet liberated himself more and more from cares of state, he was able to turn his thoughts about him more freely. Thus he chose subjects that had not been celebrated in French before, such as the sound of the street peddler crying his wares along the sidewalk under the windows of the study. The poet imagines that the wares may not be to the taste of the purchaser, that the goods are far from the treasures of Venice. Still, the role in life of the peddler is to walk up and down crying his wares for sale. Other poems are memorable for another aspect—the fact that they mark the first literary creations in modern French. They give the first feeling of French as that language finally crystallized. Technically speaking, the poems are superior to any lyrics that had ever been written in French thus far. This duke had created a poetic language that set his own works apart so clearly that they are unique and recognizable from among all French lyric poems. From Blois Castle the poet celebrated the changing seasons in rhythms that captured their especial beauty and harmony—the sweet savor of each new springtime, when the weather dropped his frosty cloak of snow and ice and slipped into an embroidered livery of shimmering jeweled tones; when every little bird sang in its own "jargon." The poet was often in a bantering mood, but never gay.

Perhaps under the influence of the Duchess Marie's cult of the Lady Valentine, he thought again of his mother and of that tragic device she had chosen in her grief. As he grew old he remembered his childhood, and rephrased his mother's words for himself:

Roundel CLII

"All I ask now: Leave me in peace!
  My thoughts are: Nothing is more mine.
  With this conclusion I resign;
Nonchalantly live out my lease.

"Let all demands upon me cease;
  Divers and sundry make no sign.
  All I ask now: Leave me in peace.
My thoughts are: Nothing is more mine.

"Fortune flying her golden fleece
  And piping sweet caught in her twine
  This bird she did to care consign,

Heart in her net without surcease.
All I ask now: Leave me in peace.

Blois Castle was a pool of serenity in the midst of a troubled world. Clad in his ideas, surrounded by his friends, loved by his family, the duke spent his declining years far from the alarms of war and such nice questions as whether or not Jacques Cœur had poisoned Agnès Sorel. Duke Philip was still trying to organize a crusade to Constantinople. The Dauphin Louis was still trying to usurp the throne, while his father tried to curb his ambitions and win his respect, if not his love. Queen Marguerite was about to be deposed in England along with her pitiful husband. The White Rose of York was in the ascendancy. Duke Charles's last personal friend in England, John Kempe, Cardinal of York, had died just in time to escape the Duke of Suffolk's fate or that of the Bishop of Chichester.

One half-hour of a Thursday midday at a place in England called St. Albans had decided the future of the Lancastrian dynasty. There the king and his lords had met the Duke of York with his. It had been three thousand against five thousand; "they joined battle anon, and it was done within a half-hour." The King lost Henry Beaufort's last brother, Edmund Duke of Somerset. After this battle the king and his lords went south to London, and in procession to Westminster. The Duke of York was made Constable of England, "and as for what rule we shall have yet, I wot not," say the Paston Letters.

Without knowing it, Duke Charles had put his finger on the basic trend that was distinguishing the march of history in England from that in France. He had wisely perceived that in England government was a subject for debate, of which he personally strongly disapproved. While at the end of the Hundred Years' War the power of the English king had been greatly reduced, the French king had, on the contrary, succeeded in gathering more and more absolute power at the expense of his nobles. King Charles VII and his dauphin were in agreement on one issue: the poweful feudal houses must be broken. The king must become the state. Duke Charles would have agreed. He believed in the divine right of kings. He therefore had no sympathy with England. He did not see that the English, in curbing their monarchy, were actually preserving it. King Charles VII had found reasons for complaint against the Houses of Burgundy and Armagnac; he would find neither rebellion nor sedition in Duke Charles or in his brothers.

Although the capture of Constantinople had slowed down work in Rome, in the fall of 1455 the rumor spread through Orléans and Blois that a decision had been reached concerning Joan of Arc. A flurry of excitement swept through the area. Surely the Pope had decided to reexamine her trial.

Joan's two brothers and her mother had requested that justice be done now that Rouen was in French hands at last. Finally the rumors were made official. Joan's living relatives were asked to travel to Paris. This summons set the whole town of Orléans agog. As Peter and John of Arc and their mother, Isabelle Romée—for the Maid of Orléans's mother was named Isabelle also—made their hasty preparations, the burgesses of Orléans likewise made theirs. Joan's family was to have two lawyers from the city to represent them. When the day arrived for their departure to Paris, they were not alone. A whole crowd of people from the city of Orléans also traveled up to Paris with them. This was too great a day for them to miss. Many were people who remembered Joan of Arc, people who had lived for seven months in a beleaguered city with the English just a few feet outside their walls. These people would have died if the dark-haired girl from Domrémy had not come to save them. They wanted to see her story all the way through.

Notre-Dame Cathedral, where Joan had never knelt in prayer, was the place chosen for this audience. Here Joan's family made the formal request that her trial be examined and that the Church to which Joan had appealed and to which her appeal had never been transmitted give them its decision. The Papal legates had completed their preliminary study.

The hearing in Notre-Dame Cathedral was open to the public on November 7, 1455. Joan's ailing mother was helped down the wide aisle. Her sons followed, there for all Paris to see. Then came the crowds from Orléans, weeping and sighing. The Church handed down its verdict. It appointed three judges and a court to study the case of Joan of Arc.

The crowds screamed so loudly that order could not be maintained. The vast cathedral hummed and echoed with their laments as the machinery of justice was officially set in motion. The power of the Church would now assemble to judge the judges whom the English had appointed to judge the French girl. There were to be three new chief magistrates. One was Jean Juvénal des Ursins, who was the Archbishop of Rheims. The second was the brother of the poet Alain Chartier, who was William Chartier, Bishop of Paris.

The third was Richard Olivier, the Norman Bishop of Coutances. The citizens from Orléans were asked to return home quietly. All those who wished to testify concerning Joan of Arc, either for or against her, would in due process be allowed to do so. The court understood that people might not be able to travel up to Paris again, that such a displacement might involve hardship or prevent them from appearing at all. Therefore, the court itself planned to travel throughout France in order to hear testimony on the spot. They could all return to Orléans. King Charles VII wanted to know the whole truth. So did Joan's family. So did England.

One month after this pitiful demonstration in Notre-Dame Cathedral the City of Rouen was summoned to turn its archives over to the court. The Norman notary who had kept the minutes of her trial was still alive. He was notified not only to give these records to the three prelates but also to prepare to testify as to their veracity. In good time all would become public knowledge.

In accordance with their instructions the judges journeyed the very next month into Lorraine, to the villages and towns where Joan had lived, where she had been born, raised, first heard her voices, and where she had first communicated with the king's officer who had arranged for her to travel to the dauphin. From January to February 11, 1456, her friends, the priests, her godmothers, her playmates—all those who had known Joan—came forward to testify. They all corroborated what she herself had said.

From February 22nd to March 16th the judges were in open sessions in Orléans, where Jean Juvénal presided. The star witness in Joan's story came forward, none other than Count Dunois in person. In a composed manner, logically, clearly, methodically, Count Dunois recited to the court how she had brought the convoy from Blois to Orléans, what she had said to him and he to her, how she had fought at the Tournelles and on the boulevard, how she had been wounded, how she had saved the city. Several times Count Dunois asserted positively: "I believe that Joan was sent from God." Then, carefully, and as if he had long resolved this in his own mind, Count Dunois enumerated his reasons.

Day after day in Orléans the judges heard witnesses telling them over and over again the same words and the same story. All manner of people testified. One was a dry-goods merchant who had supplied the material for her garments. Joan's modern historian, Mlle. Régine Pernoud, lists the name of thirty-five persons who volunteered information on the last day of the hearings at Orléans.

Mlle. Pernoud points out how a great many of them were women. William Cousinot had already noted in the fifteenth century how ardently the women of Orléans defended their city.

From April 2nd to May 14th the court was in session in Paris. There testified the second star witness, John, Duke of Alençon. Quickly and vivaciously, in words that down the centuries have kept their special flavor of admiration and fire, this grandson of the English Queen Joanna burst out in Joan's defense. His story was personal and intimate. At times he was so carried away with what he had kept pent up within himself for twenty-six years that he forgot to call her *Jeanne* (Joan) and instead referred to the Maid as *Jeannette*. This was the diminutive of her name, and her childhood name in Domrémy.

In words that tumbled from his lips, Joan's "gentle John" recalled how he had first met her after the deliverance of Orléans; how they had campaigned together along the Loire; how he had taken Jeannette to meet his wife, the former Joan of Orléans; how the Maid had saved his life; how he had often on a long campaign slept beside her under the stars, that he had noticed how beautiful her breasts were, and that he had never had any feeling of carnal desire for the girl. As far as he knew, she was a virtuous and a holy person. "I *know* that God was leading us at Jargeau," said Duke John. "She kept telling me not to be afraid."

It is a sad and an awesome feeling to know, as the historian does, that as the duke told his story of Joan of Arc to the court, as his brilliant mind re-created for them and a curious posterity his great adventure, he was himself a doomed man. Inside his own heart he must have been crying for punishment and not for retribution. It was too late to save Joan of Arc her anguish and her suffering. John of Alençon was partially responsible for her death, and undoubtedly no one will ever know why he or Count Dunois or the Lord Marshal Gilles de Rais or King Charles VII did not appeal to Rome. It is perfectly true that these men let Joan die. It is also true that because of her death England lost the war.

Why was not one of them present at Compiègne, where she was captured? The lord marshal did not long survive her. After her death he became an insane murderer who over and over again, with hundreds of children, tried to destroy purity and to sacrifice innocence. As the Duke of Alençon testified in May of 1456 in Paris, he too was not only telling his memories. Inside himself he was

asking to be punished; he was asking to be put to death dishonor-
ably.

It is unfortunately not possible to surmise the emotions of Duke
Charles of Orléans during these months of hearings. No witness
seems to lead to him in any way. His withdrawal is as discreet as
it is complete. No word of his incriminates either him or the king.
However, when he heard what else happened in Paris that May,
it must have been as if the walls of his private retreat had suddenly
all collapsed outward, leaving him and his naked heart exposed to
the cruelest grief.

On May 31st John, Duke of Alençon, was arrested in the name of
the king. The charge was high treason. The penalty was a dishonor-
able death and the extinction of his name.

When a man is born into this world, there is no guarantee that he
will not have to endure all the heartbreak to which mankind is
subject. Duke Charles of Orléans loved the Duke of Alençon more
than any person in the world. He had lived to be sixty-two years
of age only to see that man he always thought of as his own son
about to die a traitor's horrible and shameful death.

Joan's retrial resumed at Rouen on May 10, 1456, in sessions that
were to continue day after day until the end of that month. It was at
Rouen that those of Joan's interrogators who still lived were con-
fronted with their questions put so relentlessly to her years before
and with her answers. They could speak without fear of penalty or
reprisal, since they were protected by the king's amnesty. When con-
fronted with their own words and their own inhumanity, all they
could proffer was, "I don't recall."

In Rouen the two doctors who had treated Joan when she was ill
in her underground prison cell were summoned. One of them was
the Duchess Anne of Bedford's personal physician. They testified
that the English had wanted to keep her alive so that she could be
burned. The doctors were also embarrassed. Neither one recollected
anything. At Rouen were discovered the false translations of Joan's
words, the cruel treatment, her struggles at night to keep from
being raped, her pleas, her tears, and her intelligent answers, her
courage, and her resignation the morning of her death.

The testimony of Martin Ladvenu and Isambart de la Pierre was
heartbreaking. These two friars had accompanied her to the scaffold
and had remained so close to her that they were almost burned, too.
More than all the other witnesses, they were positive of her inno-

cence. She had never blamed the king. She had not incriminated him or anyone else in any way. She had not abjured her voices. She had repeatedly asked to be handed over to the Church. She had asked to have her appeal sent to Rome. She had begged to be remanded to an ecclesiastical prison.

In June of 1456 the Inquisitor Jean Bréhal, after having spent five entire years studying the masses of documents relative to the trial and the retrial, finished his summary, or *Recollectio*. In this work he noted among other irregularities the partiality of Joan's judges, the fact that her so-called abjuration was false, that Joan had been denied counsel, that she had been lodged in a civil prison, that her words had been distorted in the minutes, and that her sentencing had been not only irregular but plainly illegal.

As far as the fifteenth century was concerned, the last act in Joan's story took place in the Archbishop's Palace at Rouen on July 7, 1456. Jean Juvénal presided. Present on the bench with him were William Chartier, Richard Oliver, and Jean Bréhal. Summoned before the court was John of Arc with his two lawyers from Orléans. The Friar Martin Ladvenu was among the spectators in the front row. The room was packed with people from all walks of life.

Jean Juvénal des Ursins, whose father had been such a good friend of Louis of France, called the court to order. In an eloquent and concise speech he declared the trial of Joan of Arc null and void. He also declared Joan of Arc herself innocent of all charges that had been made against her.

The Inquisitor Jean Bréhal had finished his assignment. He passed through Orléans on July 21st, bound for Rome.

The grateful burgesses of Orléans entertained him at a banquet at their expense.

XIV [*1456–1460*]   THE NEWS THAT JOHN, Duke of Alençon, had been arrested by order of the king and that the charge was high treason caused great excitement and tremendous speculation throughout France and Burgundy. What crime had this duke committed? How were his actions treasonable? Duke Charles of Orléans could hardly believe his ears. He set about gathering information.

It seemed that on May 1, 1456, Duke John had sent a laborer named Pierre Fortin from his city of Domfront to Calais. Fortin carried a written message from his master to the King of England. The communication was tightly rolled into a tube and then concealed in a hollow stick. On May 5th when Fortin arrived in Rouen, he struck up a friendship with an unknown gentleman who, having in some way discovered that Fortin was a messenger, took him to the Archbishop of Narbonne in that city. The archbishop read the message and reported its contents to the king's officers. Then the message was replaced in the stick and the messenger sent on his was to Calais. On his return trip he stopped again at Rouen where his return message was intercepted, this time by William d'Estouteville. Because of his brilliant work in the retrial of Joan of Arc, this prelate had been appointed Archbishop of Rouen.

When Pierre Fortin arrived in Domfront again, he learned that his master was absent. He therefore journeyed to Paris, arriving there around May 30th, only to learn that the Duke of Alençon had been arrested.

The arrest had been made by Count Dunois, Alençon's old companion-in-arms. Count Dunois had been ordered to proceed to Paris on the king's business. It was alleged, so far as Duke Charles could learn, that the Duke of Alençon had retired there so that the English could land in France, march through his territories unimpeded, and proceed to the reconquest of Normandy.

Count Dunois entered the hôtel of Alençon in Paris. The duke was at home, he was told. The entrance to his hôtel was not guarded. Bowing low before Alençon, Count Dunois said, "Sire, it displeases me grievously to have to do this commission which the king has given me concerning your person; the order has been made for me to arrest you by placing my hand thus upon you and declaring you prisoner to the king."

When the Duke of Alençon saw this, says Chastellain, he was utterly dismayed. He did not resist arrest, however. He remarked only: "Cousin, I shall obey his Majesty willingly. . . . But what does he want of me?"

"Sire, I don't know," replied Count Jean of Dunois. "He didn't tell me about it, and I am doing only what he commanded me to do."

Then Count Dunois, who had come under heavy escort, requested the duke to mount quietly. He asked him not to give the alarm or to cause any scandal in the streets of Paris. The accompanying knights surrounded Alençon and rode out of the city as if they were leaving on a pleasure trip. The Duke of Alençon was imprisoned in a very sure place. When Golden Fleece, the King-at-Arms from Burgundy, hastened to the king, he received the same answer that Duke Charles of Orléans had already been given: this affair was too dangerous and too important. No pleas of friendship, no proof of brotherhood in any order of chivalry would prevail. The Duke of Alençon refused to answer any questions. He categorically refused to testify in private. He would therefore have to stand trial before the peers of the realm, at the king's pleasure.

Duke Charles and the Duchess Marie, meanwhile, extended their protection to the Duchess of Alençon, whose marriage Duke Charles had arranged so many years before from his prison in London. She and her young children came to Blois Castle. It was virtually impossible to get any more news concerning the prisoner. Something of tremendous import was behind this arrest. More was apparently at stake than just the arrest of a peer of France, although to seize such a personage was a gigantic step in itself. The Duke of Alençon and his heirs were among the potential claimants to the throne of France.

It became more and more clear during that summer from the actions of King Charles VII not only that he suspected treasonable dealings between Alençon and England but also that he felt sure

they were linked together in a plot to dethrone him. In that case
the man behind such an intrigue, and the one who would most
profit by it, would be the Dauphin Louis. This troublesome prince
had been banished to his own Alpine province some years before.
In April the dauphin had sent a letter to Duke Charles of Orléans
urging his "beloved uncle" to intercede for him, to support him
in his quarrel with his father. He had been peremptorily instructed
to address any further offers and complaints directly to his father's
headquarters. In August the king finally sent an army to Dauphiné.
He had decided to face his son and then take rigorous action ac-
cordingly. He therefore sent more than enough troops to bring
home the insurgent and rebellious dauphin.

The king's army was just a few hours too late. The Dauphin
Louis, pretending to have set out on a hunting trip with only six
of his friends, headed straight for Burgundian territory. He arrived
safely within the domains of Duke Philip on the 31st of August.
From that vantage point he challenged his father to come and get
him—if he could.

Two weeks later, when the Duke of Burgundy learned that he
had a royal bird within his nest, he so notified the king. Then he
begged the dauphin to make himself at home, to choose a castle
as his residence, and to accept from himself—as a future vassal—
a huge annual income. He politely credited the dauphin's story to
him: that he had come to Burgundy on a pilgrimage.

Meanwhile in France, the servants, the officers, and the secretaries
of the Duke of Alençon were being put to torture. The king's
suspicions must be proved. He believed that the Dauphin Louis,
Duke Philip of Burgundy, and the English were about to invade
France.

Georges Chastellain says that those were anxious days. Premonitions of disaster, of wars, and of the deaths of great princes were foretold. First of all, there was a bright light and a huge comet that trailed
a long tail of red flame across the heavens. It came from the direction
of Germany and was about as long as the diameter of the city of
Orléans. At about the same time another comet was seen that made
the whole city of Rome light up in red reflections. Then in Genoa it
rained blood. The tiles and paving blocks were stained with red
splotches. A young girl's kerchief was covered with red spots that
did not disappear no matter how hard she washed it. It was therefore
clear that very shortly high and noble leaders would die in their
blood.

While King Charles hunted for evidence and then summoned his relatives and chief vassals to convene, the rebellious dauphin was treated with all honor and deference in Burgundy. In a somewhat transparent attempt to appear the mediator, Duke Philip wrote to King Charles VII that the dauphin was really in a cruel state of depression and that he would not for all the world have wanted to incur his father's wrath, which he could not, in fact, understand. All the dauphin desired, Duke Philip claimed, was to have his father pardon his past offenses, reinstate him in Dauphiné, and so on. The king returned a very short reply to the effect that Duke Philip would do well to be on his guard for a change. "You are feeding a fox," said the king, "that will steal your hens."

The Dauphin Louis had not been in Burgundy very long before trouble did indeed break out there between Duke Philip and his son Charles. For some time the Duchess Isabella had been estranged and even separated from her husband. The chroniclers explain that the lady was devoured with jealousy. She had founded an order of nursing sisters in a forest, had built a hospital for them, and lived among them. In this refuge she welcomed the sick, the starving, and the wounded. The duchess herself, affirm the same chroniclers, actually washed their sores, bathed their dirty bodies, and fed and clothed all who came to her for assistance. Other stories had it that she was sulking because her son had not been allowed to marry an English lady like herself, from the House of Lancaster.

Not long after the dauphin went to hide in Burgundy, a quarrel broke out between Duke Philip and his son. The young man refused to obey his father in the question of an appointment. In this impasse the Duchess Isabella "showed herself a true woman," reports the Burgundian historian; for she took her son's part against the duke. Duke Philip was so incensed that he left home. He went storming out of his castle in the dead of night—it was the middle of February —leaped on his horse and galloped away, not caring where he rode. He kept riding aimlessly until he was completely lost in a dark wood, half-frozen from the cold, and very hungry. Georges Chastellain writes several pages to describe this terrifying adventure, which could have come straight from the pages of a medieval romance.

Duke Charles of Orléans watched the situation with anxiety. He had been given to understand that his "son," John of Alençon, had thus far haughtily refused to speak in his own defense, that he would deign to reply only in the assembly of the peers of the realm. King Charles would be really forced to convene a bed of justice, unless, of course, he invaded Burgundy and captured his son. If Alençon was involved in a plot with Burgundy and the Dauphin Louis, then he would be put to death summarily.

Early in 1457 the peers of France assembled to discuss measures. The king put the situation to them. He advocated immediate and open war with Burgundy!

King Charles VII was opposed by Duke Charles of Orléans. The duke told him flatly that he hated war, that he disapproved of war, and that he did not believe in war, except in a clear case of self-defense. He guaranteed the king that he would never for any reason less than aggression go to war against Duke Philip of Burgundy. He reminded the council that the Duchess Marie was a Burgundian princess, that he personally owed to Duke Philip the fact that he had re-established himself in his own domains. He also recalled for his fellow council members that he was a member of the Knights of the Golden Fleece and that Duke Philip was his personal friend.

The Duke of Orléans was seconded by the Duke of Bourbon, whose daughter had married Duke Philip's son after the failure of that first negotiation. They were joined by the Count of Nevers and also by other relatives of Duke Charles's sister Marguerite. Count Arthur of Richmond, who had become Duke of Brittany, was also of this mind. King Charles was therefore reduced to temporizing, for his peers apparently also disapproved of disinheriting the Dauphin Louis in favor of his young brother. Thanks to the good sense of Duke Charles and his friends, war was averted. The Duke of Alençon would have to remain in prison until the king had amassed enough evidence to try him. Duke Charles rode home to Blois Castle in the spring of 1457.

The coming of spring had always been a delight to him. It was his favorite season. Even though he was sixty-three years old, he still felt the surge of new life as he saw the meadows grow gay with spring flowers and the roses begin to bloom again on the castle walls at Blois. This was a special kind of spring for Duke Charles and the Duchess Marie.

By the first of May the official announcement was sent out to the King of France, into Italy, into Burgundy to Duke Philip, into Provence to King René, into Brittany to Duke Arthur, and into England to Queen Marguerite that the Duchess Marie of Orléans was pregnant. Duke Charles of Orléans expected to become a father during the month of December.

The chroniclers have not stated whether or not this was the first pregnancy of the Duchess Marie, the fragile blonde princess who was in her thirty-first year. Her pregnancy was a major event, however, not only because her husband was the most beloved prince in France but also because the Dauphin Louis still had no son. After the death of the Princess Marguerite of Scotland, the dauphin had defied his father and married a child, Charlotte of Savoy. Duke Philip of Burgundy arranged to have this princess travel to join the dauphin. Duke Philip realized how important it was for the dauphin to have an heir, particularly since he was already middle-aged. If the child of Duke Charles of Orléans was a son, this child would be third in line to the throne of France.

In June Duke Philip fell ill from a fever he contracted after becoming overheated in a tennis game. After three bouts he seemed better, when suddenly there occurred a severe relapse during which he lost consciousness and the use of his speech. The Duchess Isabella was summoned from her hospital. The members of his family rushed to the duke's bedside in Brussels. To everyone's surprise and joy, however, the aged duke recovered. The only person aggrieved, says Chastellain, was the King of France.

Later that same year King Charles VII fell ill from a suppurating sore on his leg. Despite all sorts of treatment, the sore would not heal. In their turns both Duke Philip and the Dauphin Louis congratulated each other and openly rejoiced. The dauphin moved his household by degrees closer and closer to the frontiers of France so that the minute he heard the good news that he had become the king, he could attend one short Mass and then triumphantly don the scarlet robes of royalty. More astronomers and scientists were summoned, for the dauphin, like his father, set great store by horoscopes and prognostications.

Contrary to the dauphin's high hopes, his father recovered. However, King Charles learned how his son had longed for his death and how he had spread rumors through the realm that the King of France could not last beyond March of the following year. The king was superstitious and therefore deeply affected. He became more and more somber. His son Louis had finally found the weak spot in his father's defenses. The king suffered from a phobia. His fear of death increased as each day brought him inevitably closer to death.

On the 17th of December, as the Duke of Alençon whiled away his second year in prison, Duke Charles and the Duchess Marie became the proud parents of a healthy baby girl who was born in Blois Castle. People in the city of Blois were hysterical with joy. Riders carried the proud news first to Orléans and then to all the nobility of France. The child's name was Marie of Orléans, and the world that heard of her birth from her father's poetry must have believed easily that she was not only beautiful but also precious, adorable, and just about as perfect as a baby girl could be.

With characteristic originality, Duke Charles wrote his daughter Marie a poem in baby talk. It was certainly the first poem in French to a child, and perhaps the only one for three hundred years, or until those of Victor Hugo to his grandchildren. Duke Charles seemed to be quite beside himself with admiration, with tenderness, and with awe. He says that when Marie had not been "bye-bye," you could tell it by looking at her angry red face under her bonnet. He says that it is really a pity when a baby girl wakes up too early in the morning and lies playing in her cradle instead of napping as she ought to do. A tiny girl prefers to lie on her soft cushions and be petted and fondled like a baby doll. But what a screeching when she hasn't had her nap! What a racket! Like every father, Duke Charles adored his daughter Marie. For him it must have been a very special gift indeed to hold his child, his second daughter, in his arms when he was already an old man.

While Blois Castle bustled and mustered its forces and all its skill to keep the baby alive during the critical first month, which had unfortunately fallen in the dead of winter, Duke Arthur of Brittany died in his castle at Nantes on the Loire River. He had kept the office of constable until his death, and he had notified King Charles VII that he would never sit in judgment on his former companion, John of Alençon. The reason he alleged was that he was not a peer of France; he was a Breton and a sovereign duke. Although Duke Arthur had been married three times, he had never had any children. Therefore the title passed to a younger brother, now deceased, and thence to his son, none other than the nephew of Duke Charles. This was his sister Marguerite's son Francis, whom Duke Charles had helped to educate as early as his trip into Italy.

Countess Marguerite escorted her son Francis into Brittany before Eastertime of 1458. He therefore inherited this duchy in 1457, for in the fifteenth century the year began at Easter instead of in January. Duke Charles must have been very relieved to see the troublesome Duchy of Brittany thus pass into the House of Orléans, as it were. He probably realized that his nephew, who had already incurred the dauphin's hatred by refusing to lend him money, would be more of a match for the dauphin than Duke Philip's son would ever be. As

Duke Charles and King Charles drew toward the close of their lives, the power would pass to these three men: the future Louis XI; Francis II of Brittany, who would be the last Duke of Brittany, and Charles the Rash, who would be the last Duke of Burgundy.

During that winter and into the spring and Easter season the roads in northern France were open and safe for travel. The northern counties of Brabant and Artois in Flanders witnessed several mass migrations of people, men, women, and children who all streamed through the towns and cities several thousands at a time. The chronicler Du Clercq saw these people and tried to find out who they were and where they were bound. The travelers came from Germany and from Brabant itself. They were all bound on a pilgrimage to the shrine of Saint Michael in Normandy, that marvelous rock in the bay off Avranches.

When the chronicler, as a conscientious historian, asked why they were going there, he was told by some that it was because a boy wanted to go. This child had seen his father drop dead before his eyes. It was Saint Michael who had defended the boy from his father's violent beatings. Other people answered that they were just going and they did not know why. They added that a feeling had just come over them. They could not rest either at night or by day. Their better judgment told them to go to the Mont-Saint-Michel at once.

By the month of May King Charles VII had finally decided that neither his son nor the Duke of Burgundy planned to invade France. He therefore sent word to the peers of the realm that they were to assemble in Montargis in June to sit in judgment upon a fellow peer.

The king's herald bore this summons to Duke Philip in Ghent, where he was recuperating in "the good air of his native city." The herald delivered his message in full audience before the lords of Burgundy. Duke Philip took offense immediately. By the stipulations made at Arras he had been dispensed of homage to King Charles VII of France! Duke Philip therefore found this summons not only peremptory, but highly insulting. He also knew that King Charles hated him, because he had sheltered and abetted the hostile dauphin, and even more since he had hoped and even prayed publicly for the death of the French king.

"Have you this message straight from the king's mouth?" asked Duke Philip.

"Yes, Sire, that is what he said to me."

"Let us see. . . . Did you *hear* him say that he summons *my* person?"

"Certainly, Sire. The king ordered it from his own mouth. . . . Pardon, Sire, for otherwise I should never have dared undertake it."

"Truly," drawled Duke Philip to his astonished courtiers, "it surprises me that the king has not let me know sooner or with greater forethought; for June is only three weeks away. . . . Well, since this is his pleasure, I shall try to hurry."

For three days the king's herald was wined and dined at Ghent by the Bishop of Toul, and then sent back to King Charles VII with remonstrances. He was followed shortly by Golden Fleece, who took with him three relays of mounted couriers so that news could be speeded back into Flanders every night along the journey into France.

In the meantime, Duke Philip had sent out word throughout his domains that an army was to be levied posthaste. Then the duke himself rode south of Lille, where he awaited the return of his King-at-Arms. Meanwhile, he dispatched his business and prepared to absent himself for this bed of justice. He planned to attend in great style and full regalia. His precautions were superfluous, however. King Charles VII had changed his mind even as he listened to Golden Fleece's message, carefully drafted at Ghent and succinctly delivered.

"Sire, my master Duke Philip of Burgundy, Dean of Peers and twice peer of France, is making all dispatch to meet you at Montargis. He is looking forward to the pleasure of seeing you for the first time, *face to face.*" At that phrase the King of France blanched. He had no doubt but that Duke Philip, if ever he were afforded the opportunity, would have in his eyes, if not on his lips, that one word the King so dreaded: Murderer!

The herald from Burgundy had not finished. "My master wishes you to instruct him on one point. He would certainly like to do you full honor. He therefore requests to know your good pleasure as to the retinue and train he is to bring with him. The Duke of Burgundy himself, from his own mouth, has instructed me to say that he will come with forty thousand men-at-arms, to do you service, and that he will never approach your presence with less!"

Perhaps King Charles had also heard the rest of Duke Philip's remarks to his own barons: "If the King of France thinks to constrain my person against my will, I will show him what he so much desires to see. For I shall not only lead to him forty thousand soldiers armed to the teeth and paid up to their beards for three months, or even for three years in advance, if need be, but never sign a mortgage or borrow a coin in order to do it either!"

Golden Fleece returned word that King Charles would be quite content if the Duke of Burgundy would send ambassadors only to Montargis. Let Burgundy himself be conspicuously absent from the bed of justice.

Duke Philip therefore sent two distinguished knights who were well known in France. They were instructed and dispatched along with the President of Luxembourg and Golden Fleece. Although they presented themselves duly at court, the king paid absolutely no attention to their presence. He also forbade them to approach his presence within a certain radius.

A month went by. June came and still the king gave no orders concerning his bed of justice. Duke Philip, meanwhile, met with English ambassadors at Calais, where the truce between England and Burgundy was prolonged, much to the satisfaction of the Duchess Isabella and her son. Both were strongly pro-English.

In order to find out what transpired at Calais, the king kept postponing his assembly in France. He sent agents and heralds disguised as merchants both by land and by sea. Some were intercepted by the Duke of Burgundy, imprisoned for a time, and then released. The king was still searching for traces of a greater conspiracy, for some link between Alençon and the dauphin.

This suspicion was relayed to Duke Philip in an unusual way. The four Burgundian ambassadors were summoned to an audience with the Bishop of Meaux, a prelate who had been born in the north at Amiens. This bishop notified the Burgundians that he possessed some information for Duke Philip and for the Dauphin Louis. He claimed that it would ease his mind and free his conscience if he could transmit it. He said that he no longer feared reprisals because he was ill and awaiting death momentarily.

When the President of Luxembourg waited upon him, the bishop declared in essence the following: "You noblemen from Burgundy who are to attend upon His Majesty, do not understand why this bed of justice is being held nor what it will treat. It is true that a short while ago I was present when they examined ten or twelve people of the Duke of Alençon to know if your master and the dauphin were a party to his treason. These people were approached diversely and from all sides both by fair measures and by ugly, and by every measure that could be used; never at all did they find in them any knowledge of such a relationship. Now you know on what footing you are here. I lie sick in my bed. Pray for my poor soul, for I shall never get any more use from this body of mine."

Two or three more months passed idly by while the king still did not think it possible to make a firm decision. Finally, however, he set the trial for the castle of Vendôme. The session was to convene on August 26th. So great was the crowd of lawyers, secretaries, jurists, and stenographers who traveled from Paris to Vendôme that all official business in the capital ceased. All courts were closed. All legal minds would be required at this great trial, either as consultants, recorders, or students.

The Duke of Alençon was transported to the town and across the drawbridge into the castle. The four Burgundian ambassadors were finally allowed to present themselves. The peers of the realm arrived with their escorts. The king made his grand entrance with his courtiers. Duke Charles of Orléans left his baby daughter and traveled the short distance from Blois up the river Loire. He attended not as a peer of the realm, but as a member of the royal family.

In the great hall of Vendôme Castle square wooden partitions about shoulder high had been erected so that the center of the room represented a room within a room. Thus the spectators could walk about three sides of the court while it was in session. Benches in tiers ran about the four sides of this square. Opposite the entrance to it was a high bench under a canopy where the king's throne had been placed. The benches were draped in heavy cloth. The room was carpeted and hung with draperies at the two corners to the right and to the left of the king.

The long and painful trial of the Duke of Alençon began. As Duke Charles sat on a high seat of honor with his hand before his face, the charges against this beloved son-in-law were read by the clerk of the court. The Duke of Alençon had plotted at Bordeaux with an Englishman who was to arrange a marriage between the duke's daughter and the brother of the Duke of York. The accused had communicated with an English herald named Huntington, who was urged to encourage his master to land in Normandy. The accused had volunteered in assistance of an English invasion "enough artillery to fight ten thousand men for a day." He had also mapped out a plan of attack whereby King Henry VI and the Duke of York would enter France through Normandy while the Duke of Buckingham landed in Calais in preparation for a drive southward through Picardy. The accused had further stated that he was the "best-beloved

Duke in all Normandy," where the country folk would rise up in support of him. He had dispatched a treasonable letter by a certain Pierre Fortin. This was only one of a series of communications—all treasonable.

During the reading of all these charges the Duke of Orléans had kept his hand in front of his face. When the clerk finished, he was able to raise his head. He looked down at the accused, who sat on a low stool like a common criminal. The Duke of Orléans smiled down at John of Alençon. He seemed to say, "Well, son, refute them." To his consternation, the court stenographer then stated that to all these charges the Duke of Alençon had already confessed!

There was a stir in the courtroom. Horrified faces stared at the Duke of Alençon.

With a wry smile on his face, the king then asked if anyone wished to say a word before sentence was passed.

After a few moments of silence, the Burgundian President of Luxembourg requested leave from the king to address the court. He asked that the King of France take pity on this duke for four reasons: because he was the King, because he was a near relative of the accused, because of the high fame of the accused's family, and because the Duke of Alençon was apparently simpleminded.

It was an exceedingly weak defense. The Burgundian President was most unskilled. In great embarrassment the Burgundian envoys withdrew from the courtroom. They would not remain to see a member knight of the Golden Fleece in such a hopeless posture.

The Burgundians were not only answered. They were totally routed by the king's answer as made by Joan of Arc's judge, the Bishop of Coutances. The learned prelate replied in rebuttal of such a defense that the king had every right and duty to ask for the death penalty. The reasons why he should so act had been advanced by the learned speaker from Burgundy. The Bishop of Coutances was unfortunately obliged to agree entirely with them also: the Duke of Alençon was, indeed, simpleminded.

By the time that the Bishop of Coutances had finished his summary for the king, there seemed no doubt at all but that the Duke of Alençon would be condemned to die. No one could save him now. The prosecution rested its case, leaving King Charles VII free to apply the law. What noble in France possessed either the temerity to challenge the king or sufficient skill in debate to answer the lord bishop's arguments? The courtroom was silent. The king was clearly justified in applying the law to its extremest letter. John, Duke of Alençon, would have to render to the throne more than his life. No one in the disheartened assembly would care to defend a traitor.

From his high seat, King Charles VII scanned the faces of the assembled peers of the realm. There was a thin smile on his lips. His nobles were seated in order of rank around the four sides of the great hall of Vendôme. The king sat looking down his long nose. It was not for nothing that he was called "The Victorious."

The trial of the Duke of Alençon had been an open-and-shut case. This duke was demonstrably guilty of *lèse-majesté,* proved in open court by treasonable documents addressed to the King of England in his own handwriting, attested to under oath by messengers and servants, and, what is more, corroborated by his own testimony.

Breathing heavily, the learned Bishop of Coutances folded his brief, returned to his high bench at the left of the king, and drew up his fur collar to protect his throat. It had been an excellent summation. The king continued to smile as his eyes moved about the crowded court. Alençon was a good beginning. His lands and castles would make a considerable addition to the Crown lands. What a pity he had not incriminated one of the two dangerously great nobles—either Duke Philip or the ruthless dauphin! Pleased by the wordless consternation in the courtroom, the king looked wryly down at the defendant. There before him on a common wooden stool, raised only a few inches above the floor, sat John the "gentle" Duke of Alençon, humbled before the court of his fellow peers, soon to be declared unfit for succession to the throne, soon to be handed over to the king's executioner.

There was obviously nothing more to be said. The king's sentence could be passed. It had been a long trial, from August well into November. The afternoon was very cold.

Suddenly there was a stir in the court. A voice said, "Monseigneur . . ."

King Charles came out of his thoughts with a start. He could hardly believe his ears. The room suddenly came to life as everyone searched for the voice that had addressed the king.

The great lay peers of the realm sat along the highest row of seats to the king's right. There was an empty place for the renegade Dauphin Louis, then the king's young son, and to his right the old Duke of Orléans. It was, indeed, the Duke of Orléans who was slowly making his way down the rows to the floor of the court. The voice had been his. He apparently intended to address the court. Gasps came from the spectators, who had stood day after day on the cold damp

stones of the great hall of Vendôme, outside the carpeted enclosure.
Word spread quickly among the crowd.

"Who will speak? Who is it?"

"It is the Duke of Orléans!"

"His Highness, Charles de Valois," announced the clerk of the
court, "Count of Asti, Count of Blois, Lord of Coucy, Duke of Orléans."

It was a name that everyone in the room knew very well, down to
the last university-bred clerk and advocate from the Paris Parliament,
even though they had never thought to hear his voice or to see him
from so close a range. How calm and dignified he was! So this was
the famous nephew of the beloved King Charles VI, the uncle of the
present king, and the father-in-law of Alençon by his dead daughter,
Madame Joan.

During the long weeks of the trial the Duke of Orléans had sat
hunched on his high seat of honor, bent and silent.

Slowly and with great dignity he took his stand before the king
and looked over the courtroom before beginning to speak. The
silence was intense. Surely he whom the king loved and trusted
above all men in his realm was not going to break a lifetime's devotion to the Crown! Surely he did not intend to defy the king. With
all eyes upon him, the Duke of Orléans gazed sadly for a second at
the handsome face of the defendant. Duke John smiled up at him
openly from his stool, as if to repeat words he had already proffered
the court: "Since I must die, as well soon as late. . . . Death to a
soldier . . ."

Every head in the courtroom was turned toward the duke. Surely
he would not attempt to defend a traitor! Not he, who was the soul
of honor! Not he, who was now responsible for a wife and an infant
daughter! Everyone knew his affection for Alençon, who during his
interrogation had said that he loved the Duke of Orléans more than
any man alive. The silence was fearful. No matter what the aged
duke said, it would be something just to have heard him—like hearing a voice from the dead, from a man who had in fact died twice
and been reborn from English dungeons, a prince of the royal house
who stood before them apparently beloved of God just as Joan of Arc
had said he was. No matter what he pleaded, it would be worth
telling one's children that one had actually heard his voice; for he
was a fabled man, reputed very learned, as princes could afford to be
in France before Henry V had made red the fields of Agincourt.

"Monseigneur . . ."

Curtly the king acknowledged the salutation. Even though he was cold and angry, he knew that he would be obliged to listen to whatever the duke wanted to say. Not that it would change his mind in any way. Alençon was clearly guilty of treason, and must die.

Duke Charles still stood silent before the court. He waited for the peers to stop whispering. He waited until the court stenographers had reopened their books and found clean sheets of vellum and dipped their pens into their inkwells. Still he waited until the crowds had found places along the railings and until they had settled down to listen. Then he began to speak:

"According to my opinion, in all matters of great import when a man feels called upon to give counsel to his king, there are three things to be considered: first, he who counsels; second, he to whom this counsel is offered; and third, the counsel itself and the manner in which it is given.

"On Point One, Saint Bernard has said: *'Multi multa sciunt et se ipsos nesciunt,'* which is to say, 'Many people know many things and do not know themselves.' When I, in fact, look upon myself and realize how I am beholden to counsel you loyally, for the good of your kingdom, knowing that I am neither wise nor learned, I find myself very embarrassed to speak after so many important and notable lords. I can at best bring only a small candle flame among such great lights of erudition and intellect as have burned brightly before you here. If therefore I utter any word that may have weight in this court, may God take all credit for it. Let me only beseech you to believe in my complete sincerity without noticing my lack of learning."

As the duke paused before commencing the second section of his oration, the five clerks of the court were able to lift their heads to examine the speaker. They had come down from Paris for this extraordinary trial. They could see that this Duke of Orléans was going to give the learned Bishop of Coutances a run for his money! They would not have missed it for the world!

Here in extraordinary session at Vendôme were assembled the twelve peers of France, or their ambassadors, two archbishops, eight bishops, four grand treasurers, two provost marshals, sixteen lay attorneys, six registrars for the king, and all the other most important personages and nobles of the land. It was not often that a King of

France convened a formal bed of justice. Versed as these legal experts were in court procedure, all had thought well of the Duke of Orléans's opening paragraph. He was, indeed, following the pattern of Cicero —an excellent *exordium*. From their low benches at their buffet, the clerks of the court held their pens poised, and prepared again to take dictation as the duke launched forth again:

"Second, I have said that account should be taken of the counselor. I speak to you in three manners: first as to my lord and master. I want it well understood by this august assembly here convened that as a dog lies at the feet of his master, so shall I remain always loyally at the feet of your obedience, ready to do in all that I should, my loyal duty. Second, I understand that it has pleased God to have me also born into the House of Valois, in how close a tie to you everyone present knows, by which link I am then by nature held to acquit my-self toward you. In the third place, I admit you as my sovereign.

"Now, when I think about what the word *sovereign* implies, I must conclude that it means something very great. For you, Mon-seigneur, are only a man like me, of flesh and bone, subject to dan-gers, perils, adversities, illnesses, and the tribulations of the world, all of which you suffered to a very high degree in your youth. Through these God showed you that he chastened well him whom well he loved, only to reward you with vast domains and honors in your mature years, for which let us give thanks to Him.

"Remember well that throughout the ages no King of France has ever held this realm so entirely in his hands as you do now."

At this point there was a stir in the court. The king stiffened with annoyance. He was no longer a child to be lessoned by the Duke of Orléans, nor was he any longer an insecure monarch. It had not oc-curred to him that the Duke of Orléans would make any trouble at this point. Surely he of all people did not object to the encroachments of the House of Valois.

The Duke of Alençon was also disappointed. He had lost interest from the words "tribulations . . . in your youth." He had been hop-ing to hear his "father" launch into a glowing account of King Charles's coronation at Rheims, or even into how Alençon and the Maid had campaigned along the Loire after the siege of Orléans had been lifted. Those were the good, old days when he and Jeannette had rode forth to boot the God-damns out of the kingdom.

"Now, when I note this word *sovereign* I conclude that it derives from *sovereign place* as in *King of Kings* and *lord of lords*. You are called 'Very Christian King,' which means you were put into this Kingdom of France as the Lieutenant of God and as his representative, by which all Frenchmen are bound to serve you and to counsel you loyally insomuch as they must give an account of their actions both to Him and to you, in all good conscience.

"As for my third point, the matter counseled and the manner in which it is offered, I know that it touches you personally as well as all the others here present. It is the most tragic event that ever I have had to enclose inside my heart. I am referring to the death of my lord and father, may God pardon him. When my lord and father died, I was a young child who knew not how to feel grief deeply . . . as I was to feel it and to know it during my imprisonment. Even then, even in prison, I could think how I had been captured while I was loyally performing a soldier's duty to his country. In which thought I know that God will condone me and will come now to my aid, as He most certainly will to all those in this Kingdom of France who did not fail me then, when I needed their help, and who will long after my death commend my soul to God in their prayers.

"Until this trial today I could not believe, no matter what stories men told me, I could never have believed until I heard it from the lips of the accused Duke of Alençon, to whom I am linked by lineage . . . linked also by my dead lord and father, who cared for the father of this accused, a man whom I found such a perfect knight and so kind a friend. . . . In the quarrel of my lord and father, the father of this accused abandoned all his lands and administrations and at his own expense outfitted me when I was an inexperienced boy and an orphan, provided me with a retinue of eight hundred knights and squires for my protection. For this reason, and also for the love I have always felt for this family, I contracted to this accused the hand and person of my only child. . . ."

The Duke of Orléans could continue no longer. Before the court he raised a hand to shield his eyes. All in the room were moved with him at the sight of his grief. Many had known and seen his gentle daughter both before and after her marriage to Alençon. They remembered that her father had never seen her as a girl, nor as an adult woman. They remembered the sad life of this princess, this

daughter of Duke Charles and the tragic Princess of France, Queen
Isabelle of England. They had heard of the excessive grief of the duke
at the sudden death of the Lady Isabelle. They knew how the little
Madame Joan had been raised during the darkest days of that war
which had lasted now for a hundred years, raised without a mother's
care, her father a prisoner somewhere in England. Madame Joan had
been happy as Alençon's duchess. Once her husband had taken that
other Joan, the Maid of Orléans to meet his wife. Both girls were
dead. People remembered what a blow the deaths of two Joans had
been for Alençon. Before the death of his duchess, no one had ever
seen him drunk; while since, he had often remained drunken and
weeping weeks on end.

"And how often have I told you, to all of you present, how this
accused Duke of Alençon has received my entire confidence and my
great love as no other man has done. However, he has repaid me ill
in wanting to make us lose Normandy to the English. In this deed he
would have caused me personally to suffer the loss of lands that bring
me annually ten thousand pounds. By this he could have caused the
destruction of the kingdom, of all of us Frenchmen, if ever we had
fallen into the hands of the English, the ancient enemies of France.

"And as I have sat here in this great hall these many days, turning
this thought over in my mind, in great sorrow of heart, there came
from my memory a story which I saw once in a book. I think it is
very apt and fitting. I shall not recite it to you from start to finish;
that would take too much time. What is more, I should not know
how to do so, for I saw it many years ago and could never remember
it all; but, in short, let me tell you as well as I can that part of the
story which treats the matter we have under judgment today."

On the first tier of benches, just above Charles of Orléans and between him and the king, sat Count Dunois, now the Grand Chamberlain of France. In his stubby fingers he grasped the staff of his office.
Despite the dignity of his position, the wiry, hard-bitten soldier
Count Dunois could not restrain the light in his eyes. For a second he
allowed himself to glance over the courtroom. Yes, indeed, the duke
had aroused their curiosity. All present leaned forward, their good
ears strained to hear this story from a book.

Not many of them so much as owned a book, for such a treasure
was worth the value of an estate. They had to listen carefully, for

Duke Charles spoke in the soft idiom of central France, slightly accented with English. Count Dunois was proud of his lord brother. The House of Valois-Orléans had a real chief. What a pity Duke Charles had not been present to defend the Maid of Orléans! What a shame he had never known her! She would have found in him the moral fiber that she always dreamed he possessed. Duke Charles would show these ignorant barons something of the culture for which his grandfather, Charles V, was famous; something of the charm and wit and grace of his mother, the Italian Valentine. Let them listen carefully to his story from a book!

"True it is that in this story it was written that God had two courts, one of Justice and one of Mercy. In our psalter we know that David, who was inspired of the Holy Ghost, put Mercy above Justice, saying, 'I shall always sing your *Mercy* and *Justice,* O God.'

"Now it so happened that a poor sinner and wrongdoer was brought into the court of Justice. Then there came to him a lawyer named Reason, who based his plea upon a verse from the psalter: 'Let all sinners and all people who forget God be led into Hell.'

"This writ is to my ears most horrible and greatly to be feared; for all of us, just as we are, are sinners and are even now forgetting the Lord our God, notwithstanding the remembrance He had bequeathed to us of Himself through the Holy Scriptures where He reminds us of all His good works not only in the creation but also that He redeemed us through the death of His son. For this has He often visited us with tribulations, sorrows, and diseases of this world in order thus to chastise us and make us remember Him. Therefore effacing ourselves before Him, trembling and weeping, we summon another lawyer whose name is Pity. Him the sinner besought to uphold his cause and plead for him—for otherwise he would be in great danger, even unto perdition.

"This second lawyer took his stand before the court and began by saying, 'Reason, you have condemned this man lightly and cast him into the common mold. To answer your charge I shall take a verse from the psalter even as you have chosen to do, and I shall reply, *Suavis Dominus universis et miseraciones ejus super omnia opera ejus,'* which is to say in French, 'Our Lord is sweet to all and His compassion is above all His works.' It does not say His compassion is above the good or the bad, above the wise or the foolish, nor above the mighty or the lowly, but above *all* His creatures!

"Now because you have so carelessly condemned this poor sinner, we shall appeal from the court of Justice to His court of Mercy, which is in front of God.

"And so our aforesaid lawyer named Pity drafted a plea to God, in which he wrote, *'Si iniquitates observaveris, Domine, Domine, quis sustinebit?'* Which is in French, 'Sire, if you look closely at our iniquities, Sire, who is there among us who will stand upright?'

"Afterward the said malefactor quotes to our Lord, speaking through his lawyer Pity, the verse of a hymn which begins, *Jhesu nostra redemptio*—Jesus Our Redeemer. In this hymn are the words also, *Ipse te cogat pietas ut mala nostra superes parcendo.* In other words, 'Pity so constrains you that you rise above our evil by pardoning us.' It does say *cogat.* It does not say, 'This pity *te inclinet'*— 'inclines you'; but, on the contrary, it says *'te cogat'*—'compels you!' How marvelous for us to think that even so is Our Lord—*even He— compelled!*

"Therefore, since pity can constrain our Lord in Heaven, will it have less power to constrain His Christian Majesty, King of France and of the French?"

It was a telling point. Holding his parchment before him, the old Duke of Orléans had raised his head and directed his question straight at his nephew, King Charles VII. The only sound in the courtroom was the scribbling of the clerks' pens as they hastened to complete their dictation. All eyes stared pensively at the king. Who indeed among them was guiltless? Had not the Duke of Orléans saved this king from a conspiracy back in 1440? Had not a majority of those present thus been saved from treason? And what of the absent?

Although the Duke of Alençon's testimony had not incriminated the Dauphin Louis, his seat at the king's right hand was likely to remain empty as long as King Charles VII should live.

"Moreover," continued Duke Charles of Orléans, "when this was said, Pity addressed to our Lady the following verses:

" 'Si pro peccato vetus Adam non cecidisset,
    mater pro nato non exaltata fuisset.

" 'If old Adam had not fallen for his sin,
    Our Mother would not have been raised on high for Her Son.

"But

" 'Quia peccatum proprium portare nequibat,
 Virgo parit natum per quem medicina redibat.

" 'Because he was not able to bear his own sin,
 The Virgin gave birth by whom our help returned.

" 'Ergo pro miseris interpellare teneris
 que mater Christi propter peccata fuisti.

" 'Therefore you ought to pray for the wretched
 Since you are the Mother of Christ because of their sins.'

"As soon as the blessed Lady of Paradise heard these words, she fell on her knees before her Son, because *omne judicium pater dedit filio*—the Father gave all power of judgment to the Son.

"And our Lady said, 'My Son, you know the first title of honor that was given me. It was when the angel Gabriel came to greet me saying, *"Ave gracia plena"*—"Hail, full of *grace."* And ever after, whenever one speaks of me, one calls me *"Maria, mater gracie, mater misericordie"* . . . "Mary, mother of grace . . . mother of mercy." May you, because of this, I beseech you, wish always to guard my honor, that of your Mother. May mercy and grace never be lost, by which would be lost my renown. And all you, Frenchmen, who hold me as your advocate and mistress, if you do not grant grace and mercy, which is my title—then call upon me not in your need and necessity, as you have done. Know through this how much I have always aided you. . . . For if through you I lose that which belongs to me, when you next call upon me as it will suit you to do, fail you I must, since you shall thus have failed me.'

"Then spoke our Lord: 'I am called *summum bonum*—highest good'—and thus Saint Ysidore speaks in his book: 'Since I am the sovereign good, I have by right all manner of perfect goodness in me.' Therefore do I wish to keep Mercy and Justice both—to whom I shall say as my final verdict that *nolo mortem peccatoris sed ut convertat* [*ur*] *et vivat*. I do not wish the death of the sinner but that he be converted and that he live!'

"When Reason heard this, for Reason was the name of the second lawyer, he said, 'Now take care of your words when you show favor to Mercy and trample Justice underfoot.'

"At which our Lord replied: 'You did not hear clearly what I said.

309

For, on the one hand to protect the power of Mercy, *Nolo mortem peccatoris*—I do not wish the sinner's death; but on the side of Justice my will is that the guilty one be corrected *and* that he be converted—*and* that he live! For which reason I desire you all to return to the court of Justice. There I wish you to take a scales. On the one side you will put all the crimes of this culprit—which are to be corrected; and on the other side you are to weigh his good deeds—for which he is to be rewarded.'

"You will find in this plea sent to the court by this present Duchess of Alençon along with her request that it be considered, how two of the ancestors of this duke here present before us in judgment today, died on the battlefield for the Kingdom of France. His grandfather died at Crécy, Sire, and his father at Azincourt. This same malefactor has himself shown the greatest love that any man can show, for it is written: 'Greater love hath no man but that he lay down his life for his friends,' and justice is to be rendered to one and all alike. . . . This is his share.

"Now, let us look at this Duke of Alençon to see if he did not imperil his soul—and his life, and whatever else he had—at the Battle of Verneuil. It was there on that field that the Duke of Alençon was taken prisoner for the good of our king and the kingdom.

"God entrusted to Saint Peter two keys, one *ligandi* and the other *solvendi*. The first key for locking, which is the execution of justice, that you, Monseigneur, have the power to enforce; indeed, you do enforce and entrust it every day to your officers—at whatever moment it may so you please. . . . But the other key, which is for unlocking or untying, remains in your hand until you exert your mercy. This key you must keep in the strongbox of your conscience.

"Now, since you are on the seat of our Lord, you ought to follow his practice. For, it is written: *Exemplum dedi vobis ut quemadmodum ego feci, ita vos faciatis*. I have set an example for you that whatsoever I have done, thus you may do likewise. *Et qua mensura mensi fueritis, remecietur vobis*. And with whatever measure you have meted out [justice], in like measure shall it be meted out to you.

"As to the form my counsel, of which I have spoken to you before, will take—I come in conclusion to advise five lines of conduct to you.

"The first is relative to the saving of his life in two ways: one of his body, and the other of his soul.

"I say again that you ought to follow the judgment of our Lord, which I have already cited above: to wit, *Nolo mortem peccatoris*. Similarly you should not desire his death; for, considering his works, we must conclude that his former good sense had failed him. It there-

fore follows that if he is put to death without having had the leisure
to reconsider and to correct his soul, he would be in that danger for
which you and I and all of us who counsel you would be—all of us
answerable to God when this case is reviewed before Him. This duke,
if condemned to death, might then very well say in his own defense:
'If I had received the necessary time, counsel and correction, I should
have been able to amend my faults, to the great good pleasure of
God, and also to make satisfaction to Him for my salvation. . . . But
those who kept me in prison, and who abridged my life, have this to
answer for!'

"We must think carefully to this point, for confessors tell us that
sins cannot be pardoned without due satisfaction having been rendered.

"Who is the one among us who could so clear himself if he were
condemned? . . . Let me go even further. Since it has been asserted
here that in view of the gravity of the crime of *lèse-majesté,* no punishment sufficiently great could be devised, I shall reply that according to my beliefs, if we wish to inflict upon this accused the entire
rigor of the laws, it will cause him more pain to make him undergo
at length suffering and displeasure *in this world* than to make him
die once for all. Such a death would only deliver him from the pains
and sorrows of the world.

"I have some understanding of this myself. During the time that
I lived, for twenty-five years of my life shut up in English prisons—
owing to the sorrows, the physical sufferings, and the dangers among
which I was lodged, I very many times wished that they had found
me *dead* upon that field of Azincourt where I was taken prisoner!
How often did I long to be put out of the misery I so long endured!
For the sorrows and humiliations I have seen in the course of a lifetime, I should for nothing in this world sanction his being put to
death.

"Secondly, since it concerns the safety of the realm, I counsel that
this defendant be guarded well and closely so that he may do no more
evil, even if he so desired—therefore that he be imprisoned in whatever place and manner this court shall decide.

"Thirdly, you as king should take into your hands all his strongholds, and his lands to dispose of them as it shall seem fit to you to do.

"Fourthly, you must provide for his wife and for his children, that
they may have the means to live according to their station. According
to the Scriptures: *munera super innocentem non accepit*—He did
not take goods from the innocent. Considering, Monseigneur, that
you have always shown your devotion to the Innocents, you can

surely not do them any greater good than that for the love of them, you take care of these poor innocent souls, these ones who can in no way provide for themselves. And you should arrange for their marriages and you should provide. Then, if you see that they govern their conducts well, and that they are cut out for fine lives, you should do such good acts for them that they may have cause to say: 'Our father, who brought us into this world, was the cause, by his misdeed of our undoing; but our good Christian king engendered us anew and is a father to us. He it is who raised us from the dead according to the miracles of God who quickens the dead. To this king, this Lieutenant of God, we are endebted more and more deeply; to him we are in fealty sworn to live and to die, loyally and utterly his. . . . So must we take pains, if God grant us grace, to make amends for the misdeeds of our father, insomuch as we can.'

"Fifthly, it seems to me that you must take recognition of his servitors whom you have not found to have been at fault, but on the contrary honorable and loyal. If they hold offices, they should continue in those functions. In this way those who have been seen worthy of high policy-making may serve by their example as a lesson for others to follow.

"This opinion which I have delivered before this so notable assembly, I now ask to have registered in the King's Archives, just as has been decreed for the preceding briefs. I wish now to acknowledge my words in all conscience and before Almighty God. I take full responsibility for what I have said here and before you, Monseigneur, in full duty toward this kingdom, and according to my honor and reputation in the world. Furthermore, I wish to invoke as witnesses all these present who have heard me speak. I shall recall my words to them upon the Day of Judgment before Our Lord, who will know with what purpose, intention, and courage these counsels of mine have been uttered.

"From this day forward, let them all be witnesses in all places whatsoever, when the time and the occasion shall present itself, that I, Charles Duke of Orléans, here do acquit myself as it seems to me that I was bound to do . . . according to my little knowledge and my great power."

Soon after the Duke of Orléans had finished his plea and climbed to his seat at the right of the king, the court was adjourned. Sentence would be read by the king's chancellor on the 23rd of November.

Across the completely silent courtroom the prisoner was led to his prison weeping to know that at the hour of his trial his faithful "father" had appeared for him. Now he knew the depth of a love that would risk possessions, honor, and the lives of those near and dear to him in a son's defense.

The President from Luxembourg had made a feeble attempt to intercede in favor of a fellow member of the Golden Fleece. Jean Juvénal des Ursins, long a supporter of the House of Orléans, had also spoken in the defense of Alençon. But Charles of Orléans, despite his age and his infirmities, had pleaded eloquently to save the life of the "gentle" duke whom Joan of Arc had also once saved from death.

Following the king the lay and the ecclesiastical peers of France filed from the great hall of Vendôme Castle, many of them sad at heart and some of them angry at their own cowardice. All marveled at the ingratitude of the king. As a young boy Alençon, not too many years after his father's heroic death at Agincourt, had rallied to this sallow dauphin. Alençon and Joan had escorted this dauphin to his coronation at Rheims. Joan and Alençon had crowned this Charles VII.

During the trial Alençon had been asked by the king: "As you were riding through the French town of Semblançay, did you say, 'Now here would be a good line for England's eastern frontier'? Are you a traitor?"

"Monseigneur, I am not a traitor, but perhaps I did make certain alliances with certain great lords to recover certain of my properties that I lost in the war."

The great hall of Vendôme Castle was silent and deserted. In the cold November evening its tapestries of blue and gold blew from the stone walls, making the embroidered white deer seem to prance in the dusk. On the tiers of benches the white carpets with the golden fleurs-de-lis glowed carelessly, as if the august peers of France had never been warmed by them that afternoon.

In their garrets the chroniclers sat hunched over their expensive parchments, transforming into elegant letters as fast as they could the deeds of that memorable day, each historian pleading the cause of his lord and master, engraving his exploits for a distant posterity. The trial speech of the Duke of Alençon, as made by Charles Duke of Orléans, was therefore entered into the Archives of France. Duke Charles kept no copy for himself, but the Duchess Marie had it copied into her private book.

Duke Charles of Orléans also passed from the hall of Vendôme.

As in every great occasion in his life, he had made a choice that his conscience dictated . . . and he had made it alone. More than he loathed the crime of treason, he loved the man who committed it. Therefore he had seen his way clearly. He had therefore acted without fear. In his secret heart he knew that King Charles VII would never dare put the Duke of Alençon to death.

XV [*1460–1465*] IN DEFERENCE TO THE Crown, the death sentence was passed upon the Duke of Alençon. He was transported to the gloomy castle of Loches, where he awaited execution on the day when it would please the king to give the order. Charles VII claimed that he would so ordain at his convenience. Duke Charles of Orléans knew that such a day would never dawn.

That a peer of the realm of France could so dishonor his name and could be so condemned was proof enough, it seemed, that the old order was, indeed, changing. When Duke Charles looked upon the world about him, he could not recognize it any more than he could identify with the new generation.

For the last year or so there had been a rage of witchcraft, in the North particularly. Eighty-five percent of those indicted were women who either under torture or of their own free will revealed horrible tales of black magic, of traffic with the devil, and of disgusting practices. The case of one girl from Arras so puzzled people everywhere that even Queen Marie of France from her seclusion at Amboise Castle asked to have a verbatim account of this Deniselle's testimony written and sent her. Most people, however, tended to be skeptical to the point of refusing to believe in witchcraft at all. The king tried to shrug off the whole matter. Finally he sent Joan of Arc's judges and the Inquisitor Jean Bréhal up to Arras with instructions to liberate such deluded persons from their prisons, to halt their trials, and to recommend that less attention be given where it was not due.

At the French Court the privileged could listen to the soothing and intricate counterpoint of John Van Ockeghen, the king's chapel-master, a musician capable of composing motets for thirty-six different voices. The rest of France had lost their hearts to the theater, to elaborate and impassioned mystery plays that lasted for days on the porches of the cathedrals, and to morality plays. From the middle of the century tastes had changed considerably. In Paris, as elsewhere, people thronged to the cemeteries to twist and gyrate in the frenzied *danse macabre* and to admire artists and actors who reproduced grinning skeletons in the act of carrying even the Pope himself away to "dusty death." Mortuary statues were now fashionable if depicted with gaping wounds, torn entrails, and red splotches of blood dripping from emaciated rib cages. Poems were composed to Death. Codifications of demonology were compiled. The new generation opposed its preferences to those of the old and reinforced them with its zest compounded with its natural hostility to authority from elders.

After his unexpected defense of Alençon, Duke Charles withdrew again from the political scene. Occasionally he still took a pleasure trip when one of his friends was married. Once he rode as far as Tours, a three days' journey from Blois. The workmen on the bridge into that city hailed his passage, which meant liberal gifts for them, although the duke was so impoverished that he wore a mended robe. Duke Charles enjoyed tossing golden coins into the stream and watching little boys dive for them. He tried to divorce his thoughts from the wayward Alençon, even while he continued to protect that duke's wife and children.

How severely he was touched by the misfortunes he had seen in the last few years can be seen from many of his poems, such as the following:

RONDEL CCVI

"Sell your sadness down the hill;
    As for me, I cannot care.
    Brimming full, more than my share
    I have drunk against my will.

"Never cross I more the sill
    Of my memories, this I swear.
    Sell your sadness down the hill;
    As for me, I cannot care.

"Let your tears fall as they will.
Persuade grief to lodge elsewhere.
All along life's thoroughfare
Black misfortune rides to kill.
Sell your sadness down the hill."

His own home was a place of great happiness. The birth of his daughter Marie had been followed by the birth of a second daughter, Joan (or Anne). Therefore Blois Castle was a busy and a noisy place. The duke destined his second daughter for a career in the Church. His plan for her was that she would become the superior general of a large abbey such as the one at Fontevrault then ruled by Marie de Bretagne. Fontevrault was a double monastery with several thousands of monks and sisters of the Benedictine order. Its beautiful buildings included a leprosarium and several other hospitals. It was there that Richard the Lion-Hearted was entombed and also his brother's wife. Because of her royal rank Duke Charles's daughter would be eligible for such an important executive post, if she showed academic ability.

The older daughter, Marie, was to become a great lady in worldly circles. On July 17, 1460, the duke presented her to his Duchy of Orléans. This was her début in the feudal high society that she must learn to grace with her presence. Marie of Orléans was two and a half years old when she participated in this ceremony symbolizing her legal right to the Duchy of Orléans. She had her father were the chief actors. The duke and his child traveled by boat from Blois to Orléans. Then they entered their capital at the head of a splendid and imposing train that paraded solemnly to Saint-Cross cathedral. There the young heiress prayed and was blessed. Duke Charles proudly held his small daughter on the pommel of his saddle as he walked his horse through the wide, white streets of the city.

Marie's entrance was also celebrated in a magnificent poem by a wandering poet who, although claiming to have been everywhere else during the years 1457–1461, must have been in Orléans not only when the duke and his daughter entered, but also thereabouts when Marie was born. The wanderer was known variously throughout the thirty or so years when there is any record of him. He was named either De Montcorbier or De Loges, but posterity has known him under the name he gave Duke Charles. The duke accepted the poem in honor of Marie, paid the poet, gave him permission to renew the acquaintance, and entered Marie's poem in his personal book with the author's name: François Villon.

There could hardly have been a more interesting confrontation than that of Duke Charles and François Villon, who could have had at most only a few similar tastes or points of common ground. Both were educated and both were great lyric poets. In 1461 Duke Charles was sixty-seven years old, and Villon was about thirty. The former represented the epitome of chivalry, breeding, social position, and importance. The latter, although a Bachelor from the University of Paris, had apparently never known drudgery or even work of any kind, and was wanted in Paris on two charges: armed robbery and murder. The older poet had spent his years among the great nobles of England and France while the latter was a criminal and a vagrant who celebrated the brothels and taverns of the Paris slums. The two were not only of different worlds. They were clearly also of different generations.

Duke Charles wrote a French so pure that its vocabulary has remained. François Villon saw the possibilities of slang and dialect. The tone of his poetry shows his cynicism, his disillusionment, his distress, his despair at his rebellious youth, his horror of death, and his brutal and outspoken condemnation of the age in which he lived. Yet François Villon wrote with a power and an urgency that Duke Charles had not imagined possible. It was a confrontation of two extremes.

In the *Grand Testament* of François Villon there are four poems referring to Duke Charles: one celebrating the birth of Marie, one celebrating her entrance into Orléans, one written to Duke Charles, and the fourth and most famous composed at Blois. This last poem is based upon a verse given by the duke: "I die of thirst right near the fountain." It is called the "Competition at Blois," for there are eleven variations in the duke's book upon this line, the most fascinating of which is the Villon poem. Villon refers to Duke Charles's book and in his other poems also seems to recall lines from the duke's trial speech, especially his quotations from Saint Bernard and the latter reference from *Ezekiel* to the sinner who should not die but be converted and live.

François Villon did not in his literary will bequeath anything to Duke Charles. If admiration there was, it seems to have been on the latter's part. No doubt the aging duke did not know he was patronizing a murderer. During the summer of 1461 Villon almost perished in a dungeon near Orléans, at Meung-sur-Loire. He was released in the fall but not through the efforts of the duke. Villon returned to Paris, where he stood trial for the robbery, the murder, and another armed attack in which he was an accomplice. He was sentenced to death and then mysteriously reprieved. His punishment was commuted to banishment from Paris for ten years. In January of 1463 he disappeared, and no sure trace has so far been found of him since that date.

The old duke must have been astonished by François Villon. That was an acquaintance who opened his eyes to the squalor of life in his century, to the reek of slums, to the bitterness of a poetic genius who had squandered his youth and been drawn into crime. Yet such a man had been blessed equally with the gift of poetry. The duke must have pondered the case of this young Parisian who had grown up in the streets of a large city. He must have wondered at Villon's horror of death . . . and not been surprised. Except that he acquired new and superb poems for his collection, Duke Charles must have thanked his own nature and the code that had guarded him from rebellion in youth and from excesses throughout his life.

Duke Charles became more pious every year. He also made a pilgrimage, to the celebrated church of Saint Catherine-de-Fierbois, where Joan of Arc had predicted that they would find her sword —and where it was found, old and rusted, just as she had said. Every Friday the duke did penance by admitting thirteen poor people to his hall, bathing their feet himself in memory of Jesus and the Apostles, and sharing his dinner with them. He, too, was impoverished, but during the last years of his life he did not despair like François Villon. Instead he laughed quietly at himself and even then found pleasures—fewer and fewer, more and more simple, but which still sufficed to bring a smile to his lips:

RONDEL CCCXLVIII

"In wintertime stir up my fire,
In summertime drink, drink;
More ponderous thoughts I do not think
When riding through my shire.

"No more nor gambler nor liar
At my sentence will even blink;
In wintertime stir up my fire,
In summertime drink, drink.

"Hot morsels answer my desire,
Console the coldest chink,

318

By autumn apples will be pink;
My wants are few; my heaven no higher.
In wintertime stir up my fire."

While François Villon wept and cried out from the depths of his
dungeon in Meung during the summer of 1462, the old order heaved
one of its last sighs. The war of nerves between King Charles VII
and his older son Louis had finally taken its toll of the father. Jean
Chartier, the official chronicler, writes that in July a certain captain
warned the king that he was about to be poisoned. He assumed
that his son was attempting to kill him. The king knew that Burgundian servants bought poisons in Italy, and Duke Charles has
attested to that fact in the poem where he said he might not have
lived to return across the Alps had he not yielded to his better
judgment.

Always neurotic on the theme of death, and always under the
spell of astronomers and quack scientists, King Charles therefore
refused to eat or drink for a period of seven or eight days. Then,
when his physicians remonstrated with him and pointed out that
he must take nourishment, the king finally agreed. When he tried
to retain food and liquids, however, he was unable to do so. The
chronicler explains that the passages had closed from disuse. King
Charles VII died on July 22nd at the age of fifty-eight in the thirty-
ninth year of his reign.

On July 30th the city of Paris was illumined in red light from a
comet. Jean Chartier mentions this as having signaled the passing of
the king, and adds a prayer that the city be protected from bursting
into flames.

Duke Charles of Orléans was the chief mourner at the funeral
service of his king. On August 5th at ten o'clock at night the body
was conveyed to Paris to the Church of Notre-Dame-des-Champs.
The bells of Notre-Dame de Paris began to toll their death rhythm
at seven o'clock the next morning. This cathedral was resplendent.
Its portals had been hung with blue curtains and decorated with
fleurs-de-lis. The body was draped with cloth of gold for this state
Mass sung at Notre-Dame.

As the funeral procession left the cathedral, the body was followed
immediately by the four chief mourners on horseback: Duke Charles,
his two brothers—Count Dunois and Count John of Angoulême—
and the Count of Eu. The chronicler Coucy was impressed by the
fact that in this ceremony the two brothers kept their half-brother

Dunois beside them and not behind them. In Notre-Dame the four mourners had occupied the first four seats on the right side of the choir in this order: the Duke of Orléans, the Count of Angoulême, the Count of Eu, and Count Dunois. Each one wore a long black cloak that fell to the ground, and a black hood.

All along the streets of Paris the heralds had been crying that day to the populace: "Pray for the soul of the very high, very powerful and very excellent Prince, King Charles VII of that name." This cry was repeated. Then they added: "Come to the great church of Notre-Dame de Paris to accompany the body all the way to Saint-Denis of France."

After the Mass in Notre-Dame, Duke Charles rose from his seat, advanced to the body, and bowed low before it "just as if the king were still alive." Then he asked the monks to sing a *De Profundis*. While this was being performed, the duke remained kneeling and in prayer before the altar. Then rising, he bowed low again in reverence to the king.

The long and solemn crossing of Paris and the trip to the northern suburb required the whole day. The funeral procession arrived at the portals of Saint-Denis only at eight o'clock that evening. The chief mourners wanted to carry the bier upon their shoulders into the church, but they could not lift it. A quarrel almost broke out between rival bearers. Therefore, Count Dunois stepped forward and said that since the Parisians had carried their king all across the city on their shoulders, the honor of bearing him these last few yards should go to them and not to the men at Saint-Denis.

The Church of Saint-Denis had rivaled Notre-Dame that day, so it was agreed that efforts at adorning this church were "as triumphant." The services began soon after 8:00 P.M. At the offertory the heralds approached Duke Charles and escorted him up to the body, where again he paid homage.

Then the duke led a small party of heralds, a few noblemen, and the Duchess Marie into a small adjoining chapel, where the body would be lowered into the floor of the church. The heralds held a curtain before the door during this last part of the burial rite, which lasted about a half-hour. No others besides the select few present were allowed to see the king's body entombed. Once the body had been lowered into the pit, Duke Charles knelt beside the open grave and recited aloud "the most devoutly that he could" the prayers for the dead.

While this ceremony was being performed with the three brothers standing shoulder to shoulder, united in their honoring of Charles VII, and equally united for the painful days ahead when the vindictive Louis would have become their liege lord and master, Louis himself and Duke Philip of Burgundy were merrily riding toward Rheims for the coronation. Duke Charles would not attend the coronation of Louis XI. He had a perfect excuse in that he was in deep mourning. Count Dunois would not attend either, for he was too brusque and not used to curbing his most expressive tongue. Count John of Angoulême would represent the House of Valois-Orléans at Rheims. Of the three brothers, he was the only one with whom Louis XI could not pick a quarrel for the simple reason that Count John was incapable of losing his temper. Nor would the new king presume to use foul language or open threats in his presence. Count John's reputation for holiness was so extensive that he was once considered for the Papacy.

Irrespective of their fear and hatred of the dauphin, a great many thinking people in France sincerely mourned the passing of King Charles VII. Those who grieved—Duke Charles, Count Dunois, and Jean Juvénal—realized that the new king planned to insult them, despoil them, and discard them. In thinking of the late sovereign, they would have noted an astonishing series of meritorious actions that he had taken. During the reign of Charles VII, between the years of 1432 and 1460, there had been founded and endowed eight new universities within the small kingdom of France, which must be something of a record: Caen (1432), Bordeaux (1441), Poitiers (1432), Angers (1432), Troyes (1436), Sainte-Barbe in Paris (1460). King Charles had also commissioned William d'Estouteville to draw up a reform of the University of Paris in 1452. The Dauphin Louis had founded the University of Valence in 1452, thinking to replace the University of Grenoble, at which he was angry. Duke Charles's nephew, Francis of Brittany, had founded a University at Nantes (1460) in order to keep step with his family.

On the 14th of August the new King of France, Louis XI, entered the city of Rheims. He was accompanied by the Duke of Burgundy and his son Charles, the Duke of Clèves, and most of the other nobles from Burgundy. All were spendidly outfitted at some trouble and at an expense that was in many cases beyond their means, in the hopes that the new king would keep in mind their devotion to him during the years of his feud with his father. The Burgundian noblemen stood out from all the others in one respect; they had recently shaved their heads out of love for their duke. During a recent and severe illness Duke Philip had been advised by his doctors to shave his head, and since this measure had ensured his recovery, the duke had requested his vassals to follow his emergency measure.

The coronation took place on the following day, with Louis XI garbed in azure velvet embroidered in golden lilies. It was one of the few times in his entire adult life that he looked presentable, for Louis was the shabbiest king that France had ever owned. Prior to the ceremony, Louis knelt before Duke Philip, whom he asked to dub him knight. The chronicler Du Clercq thought this a strange request, for he understood that the royal children were knighted at their baptism. After the coronation King Louis created a few knights, as was the custom, but he soon grew bored. He then asked Duke Philip to substitute for him. About two hundred knights in all were so dubbed.

Duke Philip knelt before the new king, suing him not to harbor any grudge against himself on the grounds that he or any other Burgundian could have desired or fomented the hostility between the king and France. He also requested King Louis to keep the officers of the Crown in their positions—which was granted, except for eight persons whom the new king had decided to despoil and disgrace.

Duke Philip was the first nobleman to swear homage to the new king—bringing him Burgundy, Flanders, Artois, Brabant, Luxemburg, Lothier, Limburg, Hainault, Holland, Zeeland, and Namur. Subsequently the other nobles present swore fealty likewise, including Count John of Angoulême. After these proceedings the king and all his vassals left Rheims, traveled to pray at Saint-Denis, and entered Paris around the last day of August. They were preceded by six horses with golden trappings that reached to the ground and with heavy bells on their backs. The sound of their tolling was deafening. These horses were followed by six others caparisoned in crimson velvet and loaded with silver bells, each one about as large as a man's head. Then came three sets of three more horses, again with silver bells. Then rode the family of Marguerite of Orléans with fourteen horses, each with a silver bell on its back. The various Burgundian nobles paraded with their own archers and horses, each one with his own colors, his own sable-decorated lances, and his satin banners. Seventy-six heralds came riding as a body, in closed formation. Fifty-four trumpeters followed, but only the king's personal corps made music.

King Louis rode a white horse "in token of his nobility"; he wore
a white robe without sable, a crimson satin doublet, and a small
hood. Four citizens of Paris bore a golden canopy over his head "just
like the tabernacle that is borne over the body of Jesus Christ."
Twenty or thirty feet behind the king rode Duke Philip, the pommel of his saddle loaded with a pouch of precious stones worth "a
million in gold or 200,000 florins." More than twelve thousand
knights in all paraded that day. Most of the nobility graced the occasion. They were anxious. They did not dare fail to appear. No one
could say as yet what the new king would decide about their offices
and their pensions. Some of the burgesses of Paris walked to meet
the monarch, "but," says Du Clercq, "the turnout was very small
considering the population of that city."

He remarks immediately after this observation that the Duke of
Orléans did not attend at all despite the fact that he was present
right in Paris that very day! Duke Charles sent his apologies, alleging two reasons for which he could not do honor to the king: his
extreme old age and his mourning for the late King Charles VII.
The second was a dangerous excuse, less an excuse than a reproach.
Duke Charles and his duchess watched the parade, however, from
a window. With them was the Duchess of Alençon and her oldest
son, a boy of fifteen.

The festivals and tournaments in honor of King Louis lasted well
into September. One entertainment was a joust between Duke
Philip's heir and five of his friends against all comers. The Duke of
Burgundy rode to this joust on a splendid war-horse with his niece,
the Duchess Marie of Orléans, behind him in the saddle. On the
pommel was a beautiful girl of fifteen whom the duchess had chosen
so that the maiden's charm would flatter the old duke by drawing
applause. He reciprocated by including his niece in the last celebration with which he regaled high society, a two-day festival at Saint-
Denis at which prayers were said for all the kings of France there
interred. Then those who had journeyed to Paris—and their fifty
thousand horses—started streaming homeward along the roads. It
had been a very dry summer.

King Louis pardoned both the Duke of Alençon and the Count of
Armagnac whom he reinstated in their titles and domains. The
liberation of the first lord was a great joy to Duke Charles, although
he was sorry to learn simultaneously that both Jean Juvénal and
Count Dunois had been deprived of their offices. The Duke of Bur-

gundy was heard to remark about the new king: "That man will not reign long in peace without having a marvelously great amount of trouble."

After the coronation ceremonies, while the king was Duke Charles's neighbor at Amboise Castle or at Tours, he could dress as he liked and otherwise satisfy his inclinations. King Louis preferred to wear clothes of rough material and an old worn toque on his head with no ornament on it other than a leaden image of the Virgin. He sported a short jerkin that showed off his knobby knees and spindly legs to great disadvantage and which the contemporaries thought was too short for decency. They were used to seeing the high barons in magnificent cassocks. The king liked privacy, stealth, intrigue, and gossip. He was an incessant talker himself.

Georges Chastellain records with obvious pleasure that when King Louis rode through Abbeville beside the resplendent Duke Philip, ordinary people in the streets who had never before actually seen the monarch marveled aloud: "Benedicite!! Is *that* a King of France? Is *that* the greatest king in the world? Why, *that* wouldn't fetch twenty francs—horse and trappings included!" Such a yarn is characteristic of both King Louis and the Norman French.

Of Duke Philip, the king said that he was so inclined toward sex that granted his advanced years this vice would one dark night lead him straight to the grave. While assuming a high degree of friendship with Charles the Rash of Burgundy, the king wrote of him that this was a proud animal not too far removed from a wild beast. In the case of Duke Charles the witticisms were more cruel. The king said that the Duke of Orléans was so senile that for every three or four intelligible words he uttered there were twice as many that made no sense at all.

The majority of the king's jokes concerning the Duke of Orléans, however, were focused upon the pregnancies of the Duchess Marie. The king repeatedly belabored the fact that, according to him, Duke Charles could not be the father of the children. He not only made such remarks aloud; he also put them in writing. It was fairly clear that in the coming struggle for supremacy between Francis II of Brittany, Charles the Rash of Burgundy, and King Louis XI, Duke Charles of Orléans had more than ample provocation for favoring his nephew and the Burgundian heir against the king.

Duke Charles entertained Charles the Rash at Blois Castle just before Christmas in 1461. The Duchess Marie was three months pregnant at the time. Therefore, King Louis was furiously jealous.

If the old Duke of Orléans fathered a son this time, the child would be sure to rule France one day.

In the early summer of 1462 Queen Marguerite of England returned home to France after having attempted for so many years to lead the Lancastrian party, or the Red Rose, against the White Rose of York. Since Charles VII had championed her party, Louis XI favored the House of York. The Duke of York had his son crowned as Edward IV. After Queen Marguerite had personally commanded eighteen thousand troops in pitched battle, she was reduced in 1462 to waiting upon King Louis, who had granted her asylum in France. She had left her husband and the Prince of Wales in Scotland. Although strongly urged, all the French king would grant the queen was a loan for a year with the understanding that upon failure to repay she would forfeit the town of Calais. During her difficulties and her heroic struggles in England, the two sons of Queen Catherine de Valois and their father Owen Tudor had remained faithful to King Henry VI. Owen Tudor was beheaded by the Yorkists in 1461.

Queen Marie of France, the widow of Charles VII, died at Amboise Castle in 1462. In June of that year her older son, the new king, was also obliged to remain at Amboise. Day after day he stormed and fretted under the hot summer sun of the Loire Valley without daring to absent himself from the castle. Messengers from Blois Castle arrived every few minutes. On the 27th of June the news he had been expecting was brought—news that so piqued him that he was stung into a fury of exasperation. The Duchess Marie of Orléans had been safely delivered of a son!

King Louis left Amboise immediately and traveled that night as far as Choisy. He had no intention of prolonging the ordeal any longer than was absolutely necessary. He would have no son to succeed him. His brother Charles would have no son to succeed him. Therefore the Duke of Orléans had fooled them all! At the age of sixty-eight he had become the father of a strapping, dark-haired son who had the same heavy frame as his father, and who would have the same level gaze, massive and jutting chin, and long nose.

Since the king was in such a hurry, the baptismal ceremonies were planned for early on the morning of June 28th. King Louis was on horseback by dawn. He and his party clattered through the portal of Blois Castle as if they had not a minute to spare. Duke Charles greeted them in person. No words from the king could spoil the beauty of the early morning. He was the father of a son. It was a thrilling day. Now he could feel confident that his duchess and his daughters would in a few years' time have another strong defender to replace him.

The baptismal ceremony was held with great pomp in the collegiate church of Blois Castle. Since this was in the diocese of Chartres, the bishop of that city officiated. He, too, had been waiting day after day for this birth. The godfathers were King Louis XI and the Count of Maine, and the godmothers the Queen of England and the Countess of Vendôme. Their rank was especially suitable. They were christening a future King of France, the future Louis XII, father of his country. It was only an accident that the infant's name was the same as that of the present king. Duke Charles had named his son in memory of his beloved father, Louis of France.

The church was packed to bursting, but everyone was very quiet in order to hear the ritual. In any case, it was not a large church. Therefore, the loud voice of King Louis XI was more than distinctly audible as he aimed an insult at the Duke of Orléans. "Godfather?" rasped the king. "I'm not the godfather of this baby. I'm his grand-godfather!"

Despite this interjection the baby was baptized. Immediately after the ceremony the king climbed up to the castle and burst in upon the Duchess Marie where she lay in her bed.

"God save you, lady my girl," he blurted out in greeting her. "Lady my girl, that child of yours, which was just born yesterday, pissed up my sleeve as I was holding it over the fonts. What is that the sign of? Isn't that a bad omen?"

Despite soothing words from the duchess, King Louis XI was so upset by this portentous occurrence that he said he must leave immediately. He hastily bade farewell, ordered his party to mount, and prepared to leave the bedchamber. As he turned to go, however, he caught his foot on the chamber carpet. He stumbled and almost fell. "That's two!" he cried as he bolted down the stairs. Although the duchess sent messengers after him to urge him to remain at least for dinner, King Louis had already galloped out of Blois Castle.

It is significant that although Duke Charles "loved the Duke of Alençon more than any man alive," he did not ask him to stand as godfather for his son Louis. Perhaps the duke guessed that John of Alençon had not been chastened by his years in prison, that he had only become more rebellious and more bent on his own destruction. This duke continued his treasonable schemes until he was again arrested and held for trial.

In asking Queen Marguerite to be godmother of the child Louis,

Duke Charles asserted his old loyalty to the Lancastrian party, to the memory of Suffolk and Beaufort. The queen departed that same year for England, taking with her a Norman nobleman with two thousand men and the promise of Francis II of Brittany that he would support her. The tide of fortune had changed for this unfortunate queen, however. Her fleet was separated by a storm in the Channel. Although she managed to rejoin King Henry VI and the Prince of Wales, they were soon defeated and separated again.

King Henry VI was taken prisoner and conveyed to the Tower of London. The Queen escaped with her son into a forest, where she was captured by thieves. While they quarreled over her jewels, she and the prince managed to escape into the woods. When she had come to the end of her strength, she met a highwayman, whom she commanded to take her son and thus save the prince's life. This highwayman helped Queen Marguerite find a barque on the coast. In this way she fled again across the North Sea to Burgundy. Duke Philip gave her a purse of money and sent her home to her father, King René of Anjou. This courageous queen persisted in her efforts to secure the throne of England for her husband and for her son during ten more years, until both of them were assassinated. At the age of forty-six she finally returned to France, where she died seven years later. Her last years were spent in poverty. Her famous beauty had vanished along with her loved ones.

Less than a year after the birth of his son, Duke Charles was stricken. In May of 1463, when he made a gift of money to his favorite church in Blois, the document shows that he was unable to sign the order with his usual round, firm hand. It is strange to know that illness had robbed him of the use of his hand, for he had been concerned with writing and with copying poems in his book more than with any other physical exercise.

In a poem that he translated into English, he had said many years before that honor and praise should abound to the person who first found the "ways of writing." He explained that writing had afforded him "great comfort" and also "a great tranquillity." He noted that when a writer is "wrapped and wound" in grief, the fact that he can send his works to his lady relieves him of his "sore feeling." The duke does not speak either of his professional knowledge of Latin grammar or of the years he spent polishing and perfecting what he wrote. He says only that he personally had found "the craft" of writing in his own heart.

Philosopher that he always was, the duke could not have been surprised by this illness, which was a warning from death itself. He had certainly walked down the main road of the century until in old age he had given his wife and his country a son to continue after him. The vicissitudes of life had not found him unprepared—not since that first tragedy in November of 1407, when as a young boy he had learned the horrible news of his father's murder. He had already noted in English how changeable a man's life was:

> "Methink I lead a life like to the moon:
> Now full, now wane, now round, now changèd thus."

His brother Count Dunois was also ill, afflicted with gout. Duke Philip of Burgundy and the Duchess Isabella—"not a lady to cross" —were both drawing to the close of their lives. Xaintrailles had passed away only recently. King Louis XI would survive until 1483.

Despite his illness, the Duke of Orléans did not relax his attention to business during these last years. On May 19 of 1464 he signed the marriage contract of his two-year-old son with Jeanne de France, the newborn daughter of King Louis. The king would later insist upon this marriage because his daughter was a cripple and also sterile. In this way King Louis assured that the son of Duke Charles would have no heir to the throne, which was the case, despite subsequent marriages to Anne of Brittany and Mary Tudor, the sister of King Henry VIII. After the death of Louis XII, the Crown would pass to the grandson of Count John of Angoulême, the dashing Francis I.

In 1464 King Louis XI had settled his disputes with Duke Philip sufficiently well to turn his attention toward Francis II of Brittany, nephew of Duke Charles. The Duke of Orléans had seen all through the century how important it was to conciliate Brittany. The Duchess Marie had been well schooled in this matter, so well, in fact, that her son Louis would divorce Jeanne de France in order to marry Anne, the daughter of this same Francis II, and thus bind Brittany again to the Crown of France.

In 1464 King Louis XI stealthily sent troops all along the frontiers of Brittany, thinking to capture Francis II or to defeat him. The Duke of Brittany was saved by the prudent advice of Tanneguy du Chastel, nephew to the provost who had once saved the life of the Dauphin Charles. Therefore, Duke Francis replied to King Louis that he was willing to submit to him, but that he would have to solicit first the consent of his Estates of Brittany. King Louis was thus beguiled into extending to the duke a stay of three months. He also recalled his troops meanwhile. Then Duke Francis secretly presented his case to the French nobles, who agreed with him that the king was a "low-hearted" tyrant who had long before determined to ruin the feudal houses of the kingdom. Duke Philip, now aged sixty-eight, drew closer to his son Charles; these two were not intimidated by the French king. Neither did they seem ready to start a war either of aggression or of mutual assistance with Duke Francis.

Therefore, King Louis confidently convoked the grandees of France to a general assembly in the City of Tours for December of 1464. His motive was to give some sort of legal coloring to his intention of crushing the Duke of Brittany.

The noblemen who attended included Duke Charles of Orléans, King René of Sicily, the Dukes of Berry, Bourbon, and Nemours, Count John of Angoulême, and the Counts of Eu, Maine, Nevers, Saint-Pol, and Penthièvre, and an imposing number of others. Both the Chancellor of France and the attorney general made long speeches listing the king's complaints against Duke Francis: he had refused to lend the king four thousand écus back in the days when he was the dauphin, he had sent him no military assistance, he had arrested a bishop who was superior in power to a duke and not subject to his jurisdiction, he had accused the king of offering Normandy and Guyenne to Edward IV of England, he had called King Edward "most honored Sire" and the King of France only *"the* King Louis," he had entertained relationships with Burgundy that were prejudicial to France, and his legate had told the Pope that Duke Francis would rather see English soldiers in Brittany than French ones, and so on, and so on.

After this long list of grievances, King Louis XI made a speech himself. This was not unusual, for he particularly admired the sound of his own voice. Various observers noted that it was almost impossible to slip a word in edgewise with him. His garrulity was uncontrolled and as much a sign of his envy and hostility as the treacherous and successful plots he fomented constantly. He drank heavily, also, and was tortured by a skin disease that no doubt aggravated his nervosity—or which his nervosity aggravated.

In a very long and rambling discourse King Louis XI retraced the pitiful story of his life. As his own biographer he saw in himself a most persecuted prince. He appealed for sympathy from the noblemen present by painting for them the forlorn image of his wandering youth when even his own father had hated him. He reminded them also how, upon assuming the crushing weight of the Crown, he had found France in the most appalling state of disorder, a confusion that he had labored long to correct. He urged them all to see how in December of 1464, by virtue of his unfailing efforts, the kingdom had recovered all its pristine glory. The king said he was, of course, not asking for any personal credit. He maintained that this fresh luster was due to the combined and harmonious efforts of the great princes. He knew that they stood behind him. Then he launched into anathema concerning Brittany. At the end of a hymn of self-praise, King Louis XI warmly urged the noblemen present to speak their minds freely—that is, to stand up and agree with him.

The first person to avail himself of this opportunity was King René of Sicily, the king's uncle and the old friend of Duke Charles. King René said that he spoke in the name of all present in expressing their common gratitude to the king for the manifold services that he had so unselfishly—nay, so tirelessly—rendered the kingdom. King René further stated that every man present would gladly lay down not only his personal possessions but also his very life if such actions would assist the king to bring Francis II of Brittany to his knees in open acknowledgment of his proper and salutary respect for the Crown of France.

The next person to avail himself of this privilege was Duke Charles of Orléans, who had celebrated his seventieth birthday the previous month. This time the aged Duke of Orléans was not permitted to finish his speech. He was rudely interrupted. He had launched into a warm and carefully documented justification of Duke Francis! He did not offer either his wealth or his life to King Louis. On the contrary, he could not see how the king's actions were any more justified than his allegations were true!

The nobles were aghast at the words of Duke Charles. All knew the cruelty of King Louis, who more than once had smilingly ordered that a certain vassal be brought into his presence and then made himself more explicit by explaining: "It is only his head that interests me. You can leave his body where it is." Fortunately for Duke Charles, he was not allowed to finish his defense. It was King Louis himself who interrupted.

A stream of foul invective poured from the king's lips. He insulted Duke Charles in the roundest terms, accused him of political incompetence, threw his age and his illness in his face, twitted him with senility, and again publicly sneered at his pretensions to having fathered any children at all. He called him stupid, talkative, inconsequential, and haughty—a man who, because of his ridiculous family feuds, had laid France open to civil war and invasion from which he, Louis, had rescued the state.

This humiliation was the last straw. His friends protected Duke Charles and his family from the king's vengeance by asserting loudly that Duke Charles of Orléans was indeed senile, that he had not clearly heard what had transpired, that he had misunderstood the situation completely and was therefore to be scorned and pitied rather than punished. The old duke was in fact seriously ill. His last act on earth was in a certain sense one of defiance.

The chroniclers would be forced to report—all those who were interested or who dared to report anything—that King Louis XI, by his vile language, had caused the death of the aged Duke of Orléans. The chronicler Du Clercq is a champion who explains that since 1440, when the duke returned to France, he "had traveled on a beautiful and virtuous road, had served God very well, and had never once done a single thing which a good prince should not do."

Two days later the Duke of Orléans had gained enough strength to be moved from the City of Tours. His thoughts were of going home, which to him had always meant Blois Castle. And from Tours, Blois Castle was three short stages away—three slow and painful days' journey for so sick a man. The first lap was the twelve miles eastward from Tours across the flat plain to the Castle of Amboise on the left bank of the Loire River. Then at Amboise he would have to cross the Loire and continue along its low banks and sandbars to Blois on the right bank.

The twelve miles from Tours to Amboise were long ones with frequent halts. The duke wished to stop again on the bridge as he left Tours so that the workmen could hail his passage and receive a few coins in their red and chilblained hands. It was January 4, 1465 but still 1464 to Duke Charles—the bleak season between Christmas and Lent. The poplar trees were bare of leaves. There were even thin patches of ice along the banks of the river. The world was in the ruthless grip of winter. It was bitter cold.

The duke lay jolted painfully in his litter thinking about the many long journeys he had taken in his lifetime. He remembered the frantic ride to Paris in 1407, with his youngster's heart beating tempestuously in his breast and his eyes bloodshot from fear and anger and the cold November wind. He recalled the first short canters into Blois Castle, where the Princess Isabelle waited with "her smiling mouth and laughing eyes gray—her breasts round, and long, small arms—her smooth hands, her straight sides . . . and her feet so light."

"What shall I further say . . . ? Farewell, Princess . . . your loss sore doth me grieve . . . And ever shall unto my ending day."

As the duke counted off the painful miles to Amboise Castle, he dozed fitfully between his memories. He recalled with a surge of warmth the pleasant journey to Gages Castle in Armagnac. How pleased they had been in the South to see him! How much they had enjoyed his poems—and he theirs—which was all that counted: the good he had done, the poems he had written, the friends he had tried to save, and the three little children who waited for his return at Blois Castle.

His greatest pleasure had come from books. There was no denying it. They could think him a failure at the Assembly in Tours. They could say, and rightly so, that he was a poor man who wore a mended robe. But his library at Blois Castle—those eighty priceless volumes he had so carefully acquired—were his fortune and also his life's work. They would form the nucleus of one of the world's greatest libraries, the Bibliothèque Nationale of Paris. Duke Charles's own beloved book and the Duchess Marie's book would be added to them —and disregarded for centuries, until the world learned one day with amazement that the Duke of Orléans named Charles had been primarily a poet and the author of ballads that others had claimed or that continued to reappear as "anonymous" five hundred years after his death.

Duke Charles remembered the bleak November when he first entered London, and then the graceful yellow towers of Pontefract as he first saw them that June day. He had not been a November poet. More than any other theme he had celebrated spring. Even in the darkest days of his imprisonment he had persistently sung of love and of the sweet, green ways of a springtime embroidered with satin petals.

He thought of that November in 1420, when his brother Philip of Vertus had died, and of the saddest November of them all, when Beauty's untimely death had dried up one source of his joy. During the long years of her widowhood the Duchess Marie would never know. She might ponder, but she would never know. Duke Charles smiled at the thought. She was protected from jealousy; she would never know if Beauty had been a real woman.

The twelve miles to Amboise Castle seemed endless. Again the thoughts of November crowded into his mind. He had left Dover on a November day . . . and in November had wedded his Duchess Marie, that frail blonde girl who had become a fierce defender of her husband and of her children—so fierce a lioness that she would not hesitate to champion her son Louis so loudly that the king would have to threaten to shut up her shrill highness in a Rhineland castle and remove her son from her custody.

The Duchess Marie would have her woman's revenge, anyway. No king could keep her from cramming her little son's head with stories of his father's power, his honor, his elegance, his learning, and his absolute and indisputable right to the Duchy of Milan. Having matured slowly behind her husband's broad, sure shoulders, the Duchess Marie would dare stand up for her rights after his death. The duke was certain of it. Then she could read his book, and all his poems, to her heart's content. Then she could pattern her demeanor all the more upon that of the glamorous Valentine Visconti, who had defiantly died from an unsatisfied thirst for vengeance.

The sound of his horse's hooves on the paving stones of Amboise woke the duke from his reverie. If there was one pleasure in the world second to arriving in Blois, it was that of arriving in Amboise Castle for the night. With his good left hand the duke opened the curtains of his litter.

They were passing along the narrow streets just behind the castle. He had not heard the crossing of the bridge. From the town they entered Amboise Castle by a keep that was a marvel of architecture, a constant delight to mind and eye. This tower consisted of a circular ramp constructed around a hollow cylinder. By following the ramp around and around inside the keep, the horses could carry their riders up to the courtyard of honor, the high rectangular platform level with the tower's roof. The first keep formed a corner of the castle. The opposite northern corner was made by a second keep called the Tour des Minimes, which gave access from the courtyard to the upper ramparts by means of a similar ramp that wound five times around its massive central cylinder. The roof of this second tower was also a marvel. It had been made of four concentric circles of stone. By lifting up the capstone one could look all the way down the cylinder. From this tower the gray spires of Tours were clearly visible across the Loire.

Duke Charles was happy to have arrived safely in Amboise. He heaved a sigh of relief as his horses brought him out on the castle platform, high above the town. His thoughtful hostess would have a good fire burning for him up on the third floor of the castle. Before retiring to his chambers, however, he would give thanks in the chapel.

The chapel in the courtyard of Amboise Castle was dedicated to Saint Hubert, the patron saint of hunters. It was perfectly designed and suited to the king's tastes. Duke Charles had never been a hunter of animals. Chess had been his favorite sport. His own youth had been spent in confinement, most of it solitary. However, he had been a traveler.

At the southeast corner of Amboise Castle stood this delicate chapel to Saint Hubert, with its cruciform structure and its dainty lacelike steeple rising gracefully into the blue sky. Its portal was carved profusely with deer's antlers and with miniature animals in their burrows—heads and tails sticking out, some gnawing on bones. Duke Charles said his prayers in the Chapel of Saint Hubert before entering the castle. He had finished one lap of his journey. There was s slow two-day ride from Amboise home to Blois. He was thankful for that.

After his devotions had been performed, he crossed the court and entered the main floor of the castle proper, which, like Blois Castle, stood on a ledge parallel to the Loire and high above it. This main floor was about twenty meters above the river. It consisted of guardrooms for the castle lieutenants and their men whose function was to supervise traffic on the Loire. The river was navigable up to the bridge at the foot of the Tour des Minimes.

On the second floor were the state chambers and banquet rooms with a wrought-iron railing that ran the entire length of the north façade and past its seven windows. The third story was devoted to chambers. Another balcony ran the entire length of these windows also, a balcony that was about level with the summit of the second tower, or about forty meters above the river level. It was a beautiful castle. The duke had always sought Beauty.

He was glad of the bright fire in his chamber. Wearily he allowed his valet to disrobe him and prepare him for bed. He would sleep deeply, for the next day's journey would be both painful and long. In his youth he would even then, despite the twilight, have jumped on his horse and been home before midnight.

The high bed looked warm and inviting. He watched his valet fill the bed warmer with embers and slip it between the sheets. The bed had proper curtains, thick enough to keep out any drafts. The duke allowed himself to be put to bed and tucked in warmly. He said goodnight to his valet and sent his compliments to his hostess. Everything had been lovely. The curtains were drawn. He fell asleep with a smile on his lips. He always smiled when he thought of home. He was only two days' journey from Blois.

This trip from Tours to Amboise on January 4, 1465, was his last voyage. It was the "ending day." For the first time in his life, Duke Charles was too weary to go home to Blois.

Rondel CCCCXXXV

"Give my regards to all your company
  Where new convened in quest of jollity;
  This my excuse, for home I have remained
  Instead of joining you: I am detained.
  Old Age has bolted me in her bailey.

"In bygone days under Youth's sovereignty
  They locked my door so long they lost the key;
  Though now I'm guarded much less vigilantly
  Yet, God above, perhaps you'll pardon me.
  Give my regards to all your company
  Where new convened in quest of jollity.

"I that knew Love's fierce passion intimately
  And cut a happy swath up in Paris
  Now bid adieu to days I shall not see,
  Loosen my cinch that was so tight constrained;
  The slackened reins of Age I have attained.
  Give my regards to all your company."

Sources

[PRIMARY]

MANUSCRIPTS IN THE NATIONAL LIBRARY, PARIS:
(*1*) fr. 25458, the autograph manuscript of Duke Charles.
(*2*) fr. 1104, beautiful manuscript containing the Trial Speech delivered at Vendôme.
(*3*) fr. 19139, contains sixty-nine poems of Duke Charles, plus poems by Alain Chartier.

ANTHOLOGIES, *Charles of Orléans* (IN FRENCH):
(*1*) Pierre Champion. Vols. I and II, Paris, 1923–1927.
(*2*) A. L. Champollion-Figeac. Paris, 1842.
(*3*) Jacques Charpier. Paris, 1958.
(*4*) J. Marie Guichard. Paris, 1842.
(*5*) Ch. d'Héricault. Vols. I and II, Paris, 1874.
(*6*) Henri Matisse. Original lithographs. Copy No. 522 in Special Collection, New York Public Library.
(*7*) Gilbert Ouy, *Canticum Amoris,* Società Editrice Internazionale, 1959.

ANTHOLOGIES, *Charles of Orleans* (IN ENGLISH):
(*1*) Robert Steele. Early English Text Society, No. 215 (1941) and No. 220 (1946).
(*2*) G. W. Taylor. Roxburghe Club, London, 1827.

AENEAS SILVIUS (POPE PIUS II), *Commentarii Rerum Memorabilium,* Frankfurt, 1614. (See also Smith College Studies in History.)
ANONYMOUS, *Chronique de la Traïson et Mort de Richart Deux Roy Dangleterre,"* ed. by Benjamin Williams, London, 1844.
——, *Le Débat des Hérauts d'Armes,* Société des Anciens Textes Français Vol. VIII.
——, *Mémoires concernant Arthus III, Duc de Bretagne,* pub. by D. Godefroy, 1622.
——, *Le Prisonnier Desconforté du Château de Loches,* pub. by Pierre Champion, Paris, 1909.
ASTESANO, ANTONIO, *La Vierge Guerrière,* trans. by De Latour. Orléans, 1874.
CAGNY, PERCEVAL DE, *Chroniques,* pub. by Moranvillé, Paris, 1902.
CHARTIER, ALAIN, *La Belle Dame sans Merci,* pub. Paris, 1945.
CHARTIER, JEAN, *Histoire de Charles VII,* pub. by Denis Godefroy, Paris, 1661.

Sources

CHASTELLAIN, GEORGES, *Chronique* (Vols. II, III), pub. by De Lettenhove, Brussels, 1864.

CHAUCER, GEOFFREY, "Works of," ed. by F. N. Robinson, Boston, 1957.

Choix des Poésies Originaires des Troubadours, Vol. II, ed. by M. Raynouard, Paris, 1817.

CLÉMENT, FRANÇOIS, Benedictine Monk, *L'Art de Vérifier les Dates,* Vols. I, II, III, Paris, 1783.

COMMINES, PHILIPPE DE, *Mémoires,* Book I, Paris, 1661.

COUCY, MATHIEU DE, *Histoire de Charles VII,* pub. by J. A. Buchon, Paris, 1838.

COUSINOT, WILLIAM, AND COUSINOT DE MONTREUIL, *Chronique de la Pucelle, Chronique de Cousinot, Geste des Nobles, Chronique Normande,* pub. by Vallet de Viriville, Paris, 1859.

DU CLERCQ, JACQUES, *Mémoires,* in the Petitot Collection (Series 1, Vol. 11), pub. by Petitot, Paris, 1826.

English and Scottish Popular Ballads, ed. by F. J. Child. New York, 1904.

FROISSART, JEAN, *Chroniques,* Vols. VII–XXV, pub. by De Lettenhove, Brussels, 1867–1877.

GERSON, JEAN, *Initiation à la Vie Mystique,* pub. Paris, 1943.

HOLINSHED, RAPHAEL, *Chronicles of England, Scotland and Ireland,* Vols. II and III, London, 1808.

Documents Relatifs à la chute de la maison d'Armagnac, pub. by Paul Durrieu, Paris, 1883.

Letters of Louis XI: Vol. I ed. by Étienne Charavay, Paris, 1883; Vol. II ed. by Joseph Vaesen, Paris, 1885.

LORRIS, GUILLAUME DE, *Le Roman de la Rose,* Edition of Clément Marot, pub. at Milan, 1954.

MACHIAVELLI, NICCOLÒ, *Il Principe* (trans.). ed. by De Montléon, Paris, 1816.

Mémoires de la Société des Sciences et Lettres du Loir-et-Cher, Blois, Vols. XIX, XXIX, XXX.

MARCHE, OLIVIER DE LA, *Chronique,* Parts I and II. pub. in the Petitot Series 1, Vols. IX and X.

The Paston Letters, Vol. I, ed. by James Gairdner, London, 1872.

PEPYS, SAMUEL, *Diary,* Vol. VIII, pub. London, 1896.

PISAN, CHRISTINE DE, *Œuvres Poétiques,* pub. by Maurice Roy. In the Société des Anciens Textes Français, Vols. I, II, III, Paris, 1886–1889.

Quelques Pièces Relatives à la Vie de Louis I d'Orléans et de Valentine Visconti, pub. by F. M. Graves, Paris, 1913.

QUILLER-COUCH, SIR ARTHUR, *Oxford Book of English Verse,* London, 1900.

Mémoires Relatifs à l'Histoire de France, Vol. II: Christine de Pisan, Jean Juvénal des Ursins, Journal d'un Bourgeois de Paris (anon.), Pierre de Fenin, Maréchal de Boucicault, pub. Paris, 1854.

MONSTRELET, ENGUERRAND DE, *Chroniques*, pub. by J. A. Buchon, Vols. XXVI–XL, Paris, 1826–1827.

Religieux de Saint-Denis, *Histoire de Charles VI*, Vols. I–VI (1), trans. and pub. by M. L. Bellaguet, Paris, 1840.

Rerum Britannicarum Medii Aevi Scriptores, Vols. 221, 221, Pt. I; 221, Pt. II, 32; ed. by Rev. Joseph Stevenson, London, 1857–1864.

RYMER, THOMAS, *Foedera, Conventiones, Literae, Acta Publica, Et Cetera*, Vols. IX, X, London, 1709.

THOMAS À KEMPIS, *Of the Imitation of Jesus Christ*, pub. London, 1954.

TITUS LIVIUS, *Vita Henrici Quinti*, ed. by Thos. Hearne, London, 1786.

Treasury of Middle English Verse, ed. by M. R. Adamson, London, 1930.

VILLON, FRANÇOIS, *Œuvres Complètes*, ed. by Jacob, Paris, 1854.

[S E C O N D A R Y]

ADAMS, HENRY, *Mont-Saint-Michel and Chartres*, Boston, 1933.

ALLEAU, RENÉ, *De la nature des Symboles*, Paris, 1958.

BARRÈS, MAURICE, *Autour de Jeanne d'Arc*, Paris, 1916.

BEAUFILS, CONSTANT, *Étude sur la poésie de Charles d'Orléans*, Paris, 1861.

BERGEVIN ET DUPRÉ, *Histoire de Blois*, Vol. I, Blois, 1846.

BOLITHO, HECTOR, *Romance of Windsor Castle*, London, 1946.

BOOTHROYD, B., *History of the Ancient Borough of Pontefract*, Pontefract, 1807.

BOUILLÉ, ANTOINE DE, *Le Maréchal de la Fayette*, Lyon, 1955.

BOURNON, FERNAND, *L'Hôtel Royal de Saint-Pol*, Paris, 1860.

Boutell's Heraldry (revised by C. W. Scott-Giles), London, 1950.

BROUGHAM, HENRY, LORD, *History of England and France Under the Lancastrians*, London, 1861.

BROWNE, JOHN, *Description of Representations and Arms on the Glass in the Windows of York*, York, 1859.

BURKE, SIR BERNARD, *Genealogical History of the Dormant, Abeyant, Forfeited and Extinct Peerages of the British Empire*, London, 1866.

BURNE, ALFRED H., *The Agincourt War*, Fair Lawn, N.J., 1956.

CABANÈS, DR. AUGUSTIN, *Moeurs Intimes du Passé*, Vol. III. Paris, 1908–1936.

CALMATTE, JOSEPH, *Les Dernières Étapes du Moyen Age Français*, Paris, 1944.

CHAMPION, PIERRE, *Charles d'Orléans*, Paris, 1908.

———, *Splendeurs et Misères de Paris*, Paris, 1934.

———, *La Dame de Beauté*, Paris, 1931.

———, *Histoire Poétique du XVᵉ Siècle*, Vols. I and II, Paris, 1923.

CHAMPOLLION-FIGEAC, A. L., *Notice historique et littéraire sur Charles Duc d'Orléans*, Paris, 1842.

———, *Louis et Charles, Ducs d'Orléans,* Paris, 1844.

CHATEAUBRIAND, VICOMTE FRANÇOIS AUGUSTE RENÉ DE, *Analyse Raisonnée de l'Histoire de France,* Paris, 1850.

COHEN, GUSTAVE, *La Grande Clarté du Moyen Age,* New York, 1943.

COLLAS, ÉMILE, *Valentine de Milan, Duchesse d'Orléans,* Paris, 1911.

The Complete Peerage, St. Catherine Press, London, 1953.

Dictionary of National Biography, Macmillan, London, 1898.

DODU, GASTON, *Les Valois,* Paris, 1934.

DUCLOS, M., *History of Lewis XI* (trans.), London, 1746.

FLEMMING, JESSIE H., *England Under the Lancastrians,* London, 1921.

FOX, GEORGE, *History of Pontefract,* Pontefract, 1827.

FRANCE, ANATOLE, *Œuvres Complètes Illustrées* (Vols. XV and XVI) (*Vie de Jeanne d'Arc*), Paris, 1929.

GAUJAL, BARON DE, *Étude historique sur le Rouergue,* Vols. I and II, Paris, 1858.

GORCE, M., *Roman de la Rose,* Paris, 1933.

HARGRAVE, E., *History of Knaresborough,* York, 1798.

HOFFMAN, EDWARD JOSEPH, *Alain Chartier,* New York, 1942.

HUME, DAVID, *History of England,* Vol. III, London, 1822.

JADART, H., *Jean de Gerson,* Rheims, 1881.

JULLEVILLE, PETIT DE, *Histoire de la Langue et de la Littérature Française: Moyen Age,* Vols. I and II, Paris, 1896.

KUKENHEIM AND ROUSSEL, *Guide de la Littérature du Moyen Age,* Leiden, 1957.

LACROIX, PAUL, *Vie Militaire et Religieuse du Moyen Age,* Paris, 1873.

LAVISSE, E., *Histoire de France,* Vol. IV, Parts I and II, Paris, 1902.

LEWIS, D. B. WYNDHAM, *The Soul of the Marshal Gilles de Raiz,* London, 1952.

LA MARCHE, A. LECOY DE, *Le Roi René,* Vol. I, Paris, 1873.

MARITAIN, J., *Étienne Gilson, Philosophe de la Chrétienté,* Paris, 1949.

MARS, DOM NOËL, *Histoire du Royal Monastère de Sainct-Lomer de Blois,* Blois, 1869.

MÉZERAY, F. DE, *Histoire de France,* Vol. II, Paris, 1685.

MICHELET, JULES, *Histoire de France,* Vols. IV and V, Paris, 1861.

MILNER, REV. JOSEPH, *History of Winchester,* Winchester, 1798.

MORALL, JOHN B., *Gerson and the Great Schism,* Manchester University Press, 1960.

MORGAN, LADY, *Italy,* Vol. I, London, 1821.

NOYES, ELLA, *Story of Milan,* London, 1926.

PARIS, GASTON, *François Villon,* Paris, 1901.

PERNOUD, MLLE. RÉGINE, *Lumière du Moyen Age,* Paris, 1944.

———, *Vie et Mort de Jeanne d'Arc,* Paris, 1953.

———, *Grandes Époques de l'Art en Occident,* Paris, 1954.

———, *La Poésie Médiévale Française,* Paris, 1947.

PRICHARD, T. J. LLEWELYN, *Heroines of Welsh History,* London, 1854.

REIFFENBERG, BARON, *Histoire de l'Ordre de la Toison d'Or*, Paris, 1834.

RICHARD, ABBÉ, *Description Historique et Critique de l'Italie*, Vol. I, Paris, 1769.

ROBINSON, A. MARY (MME. JAMES DARMESTETER), *The End of the Middle Ages*, London, 1889.

SAUSSAYE, L. DE LA, *Blois et ses Environs*, Blois, 1882.

SCOTT, SIR WALTER, *Tales of a Grandfather*, Vol. II, Boston, 1861.

SHAKESPEARE, WILLIAM (Oxford Standard Edition, ed. by W. J. Craig): *The Tragedy of King Richard II, The First Part of King Henry IV, The Second Part of King Henry IV, The Life of King Henry V, The First Part of King Henry VI, The Second Part of King Henry VI, The Third Part of King Henry VI.*

SICILIANO, ITALO, *François Villon et les Thèmes Poétiques du Moyen Age*, Paris, 1934.

SIMON, ABBÉ, *Histoire de Vendôme*, Vols. I, II, III, Vendôme, 1835.

SISMONDI, SISMONDE DE, *Histoire des Français*, Vols. XII and XIII, Paris, 1828.

STEVENSON, ROBERT LOUIS, *Familiar Studies of Men and Books*, London. 1892.

STRICKLAND, AGNES, *Lives of the Queens of England*, Vol. I, London, 1873.

THOMAS, ANTOINE, *Jean Gerson et l'Education des Dauphins de France*, Paris, 1930.

THUASNE, LOUIS, *Roman de la Rose*, Paris, 1929.

TIGHE, ROBERT RICHARD, *Annals of Windsor*, Vol. I, London, 1888.

URQUHART, WILLIAM POLLARD, *Life and Times of Francesco Sforza*, Vols. I and II, Edinburgh and London, 1852.

VALENTIN, F., *Les Ducs de Bourgogne*, Tours, 1857.

VIVENT, JACQUES, *La Guerre de Cent Ans*, Paris, 1954.

ZUMTHOR, PAUL, *Histoire littéraire de la France médiévale*, Paris, 1954.

———, *Merlin le prophète*, Lausanne, 1943.